W9-BCM-339

Social theory of modern societies:
Anthony Giddens and his critics

Social theory of modern societies:
Anthony Giddens and his critics

EDITED BY

DAVID HELD
The Open University

AND

JOHN B. THOMPSON
Jesus College, Cambridge

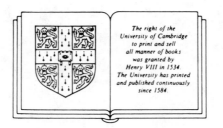

The right of the
University of Cambridge
to print and sell
all manner of books
was granted by
Henry VIII in 1534.
The University has printed
and published continuously
since 1584.

CAMBRIDGE UNIVERSITY PRESS

CAMBRIDGE

NEW YORK   PORT CHESTER

MELBOURNE   SYDNEY

Published by the Press Syndicate of the University of Cambridge
The Pitt Building, Trumpington Street, Cambridge CB2 1RP
40 West 20th Street, New York, NY 10011, USA
10 Stamford Road, Oakleigh, Melbourne 3166, Australia

© Cambridge University Press 1989

First published 1989

Printed in Great Britain by
Redwood Burn Limited, Trowbridge, Wiltshire

British Library cataloguing in publication data

Social theory of modern societies: Anthony
Giddens and his critics
1. Society. Theories
I. Held, David, *1951–*   II. Thompson,
John
301′.01

Library of Congress cataloguing in publication data

Social theory of modern societies: Anthony Giddens and his critics
/ edited by David Held and John Thompson.
p.   cm.
Bibliography.
ISBN 0 521 26197 X – ISBN 0 521 27855 4 (pbk.)
1. Sociology – Methodology.   2. Giddens, Anthony.   I. Held, David.
II. Thompson, John B.
HM24.S5444 1989
301′.01 – dc20   89–31431   CIP

ISBN 0 521 26197 X hard covers
ISBN 0 521 27855 4 paperback

Contents

Contributors

Zygmunt Bauman
is Professor of Sociology at the University of Leeds. He is the author of many books, including *Hermeneutics and Social Science* and *Legislators and Interpreters*.

Richard J. Bernstein
is Vera List Professor of Philosophy at the New School for Social Research, New York. His previous publications include *The Restructuring of Social and Political Theory* and *Beyond Objectivism and Relativism*.

Anthony Giddens
is Professor of Sociology at the University of Cambridge.

Derek Gregory
is Professor of Geography at the University of British Columbia. He is the author of *Ideology, Science and Human Geography* and *The Geographical Imagination*.

Nicky Gregson
is Research Associate at the Centre for Urban and Regional Development Studies, Newcastle University. She has published a variety of articles in economic history and human geography.

David Held
is Senior Lecturer in Social Science at the Open University. Among his recent publications are *Models of Democracy* and *Political Theory and the Modern State*.

Bob Jessop
is Senior Lecturer in Government at the University of Essex. His recent books include *The Capitalist State* and *Thatcherism: A Tale of Two Nations* (with Kevin Bonnett, Simon Bromley and Tom Ling).

Linda Murgatroyd
is a statistician at the Department of Employment, London. She has contributed several articles to a variety of journals and other publications.

Peter Saunders
is Professor of Sociology at the University of Sussex. He is the author of *Social Theory and the Urban Question* and (with John Dearlove) *Introduction to British Politics*, among other works.

Martin Shaw
is Lecturer in Sociology at the University of Hull. He edited *War, State and Society* and he is the author of *Socialism and Militarism*, among other works.

John B. Thompson
is Lecturer in Sociology at the University of Cambridge. His previous publications include *Critical Hermeneutics* and *Studies in the Theory of Ideology*.

Erik Olin Wright
is Professor of Sociology at the University of Wisconsin, Madison. He is the author of many books, including *Class, Crisis and the State* and *Classes*.

Abbreviations

Throughout the notes and references, the major works of Anthony Giddens are abbreviated as follows:

CMST   *Capitalism and Modern Social Theory: An Analysis of the Writings of Marx, Durkheim and Max Weber* (Cambridge: Cambridge University Press, 1971)

CSAS   *The Class Structure of the Advanced Societies* (London: Hutchinson; New York: Harper & Row, 1973; revised edition, 1981)

NRSM   *New Rules of Sociological Method: A Positive Critique of Interpretative Sociologies* (London: Hutchinson; New York: Basic Books, 1976)

SSPT   *Studies in Social and Political Theory* (London: Hutchinson; New York: Basic Books, 1977)

CPST   *Central Problems in Social Theory: Action, Structure and Contradiction in Social Analysis* (London: Macmillan; Berkeley: University of California Press, 1979)

CCHM   *A Contemporary Critique of Historical Materialism*, vol. 1, *Power, Property and the State* (London: Macmillan; Berkeley: University of California Press, 1981)

PCST   *Profiles and Critiques in Social Theory* (London: Macmillan; Berkeley: University of California Press, 1982)

CS   *The Constitution of Society: Outline of the Theory of Structuration* (Cambridge: Polity Press; Berkeley: University of California Press, 1984)

NSV   *The Nation-State and Violence*, vol. 2 of *A Contemporary Critique of Historical Materialism* (Cambridge: Polity Press; Berkeley: University of California Press, 1985)

STMS   *Social Theory and Modern Sociology* (Cambridge: Polity Press; Stanford: Stanford University Press, 1987)

Editors' introduction

DAVID HELD AND JOHN B. THOMPSON

We live in societies which are undergoing rapid social, political and economic change. Since the advent of industrial capitalism in eighteenth-century Europe, traditional forms of life have been swept away or transformed by a continuous process of industrial and political development. The transition from the pre-industrial societies of early modern Europe to the modern industrial order is a process that preoccupied many of the social and political theorists of the nineteenth and early twentieth centuries. Marx, Weber, Durkheim, Comte, Simmel, Tönnies: these and other thinkers have left us with an array of ideas, a diverse corpus of concepts and generalizations, of philosophical assumptions and methodological precepts, which continue to animate debates within the social sciences. Some of the contributions of these earlier thinkers undoubtedly remain relevant today, but in other respects their ideas have been eclipsed both by intellectual criticism and by the course of events. In social and political theory, as in other domains of the social sciences, there is a need for the ongoing renewal and imaginative reconstruction of concepts, assumptions and approaches, in order to take into account, analyse and understand the key characteristics and developmental trends of modern societies.

Among contemporary social theorists who are preoccupied with this activity of reconstruction and renewal, Anthony Giddens stands out as a figure of major significance. Since the early 1970s he has published nearly a dozen books which have had a profound impact on debates within social theory and the social sciences generally. His writings include not only a range of texts which have become the standard commentaries on classical and contemporary social theory, but also a series of substantial volumes which present a highly original social theory and offer a powerful analysis of modern societies. It is this ambitious and innovative project which is the focal point of the chapters that make up this volume. The chapters examine some of the central themes and claims of Giddens's work, subjecting them to sustained critical scrutiny. In a lengthy rejoinder, Giddens responds to the criticisms and elaborates his views. The volume thus represents the first systematic attempt to assess one of the most important bodies of work in contemporary social theory.

There are two main strands to Giddens's constructive social theory. One of them involves the attempt to think through and resolve certain problems of a

1

general theoretical kind. In some cases these problems have a lengthy history and have been discussed, in one form or another, since the beginnings of the social sciences in the eighteenth and nineteenth centuries. Giddens has reformulated them in a distinctive way and, in seeking to resolve them, he has developed an original and influential theoretical framework, the core of which is a cluster of conceptual innovations which he describes as the 'theory of structuration'. The second strand of Giddens's social theory involves the attempt to analyse the main developmental trends and institutional features of modern industrial societies. This aspect of Giddens's work draws heavily on the writings of Marx and Weber, but always in a critical way: Giddens is interested not only in the insights of these authors, but also, and perhaps more significantly, in what they failed to see. By critically appraising the work of Marx and Weber, among others, Giddens has tried to work out an account of the distinctive characteristics of 'modernity'.

Our aim in this Introduction is to provide a brief overview of Giddens's work and of some of the issues raised by his critics. We have refrained from detailed exposition of Giddens's views, not only because Giddens himself is an exceptionally lucid exponent of his own views,[1] but also because more detailed expositions can be found in each of the chapters in this volume. We shall begin by discussing Giddens's general theoretical approach, by means of which he has sought to resolve some traditional problems in social theory and to develop a coherent theoretical framework for the social sciences. In this context we shall review some of the critical arguments developed in the chapters by Bernstein, Bauman, Thompson, Gregory, Saunders and Gregson. In the second part of the Introduction we shall examine some of Giddens's more substantive contributions in which he has sought to analyse some of the structural features and developmental trends of modern societies. Here we shall consider the criticisms offered by Wright, Jessop, Shaw, Murgatroyd and Held.

I

One of the legacies of nineteenth-century social thought is that individuals working within the social sciences today are confronted with a number of deep and seemingly intractable problems of a general theoretical nature. Among these problems is the question of the relation between the social sciences and the natural sciences, a question which has elicited, and continues to elicit, strongly divergent views. On the one hand, there are those authors who take, explicitly or implicitly, the natural sciences as a methodological model for the social sciences: admired for their experimental basis and predictive success, the natural sciences are taken as the starting point for attempts to think about the character of social scientific knowledge and practice. This approach is evident not only in the work of recent philosophers of social science who are

[1] See especially his most recent volume of essays, *STMS*.

influenced by some form of positivism, but also in the writings of nineteenth-century social thinkers who shared the Enlightenment faith in progress through knowledge. On the other hand, many authors have argued that the social sciences, or 'human sciences', cannot be conceptualized in the same way as the sciences of nature. This argument has been developed in various ways and on differing grounds, from the early *Methodenstreit* in late-nineteenth-century Germany to the more recent and increasingly well-known writings of Winch, Schutz, Gadamer, Ricoeur and others.

Another problem which looms large in contemporary debates, and which overlaps partially with the question of the relation between the natural and social sciences, concerns the relation between the individual and society – or, to use more contemporary terms, the relation between 'action' and 'structure'. Here again, this problem has given rise to sharply contrasting positions. On the one hand, there are those authors who have argued that society, or social structure, is prior to the individual and serves to limit or constrain individual actions; and it is these structural features or constraints which form the proper object of analysis for the social sciences. This is a view which is widespread in the social scientific literature, from the methodological writings of Durkheim to the recent versions of structuralism (Lévi-Strauss) and structural Marxism (Althusser). On the other hand, this view has been contested or qualified by a range of thinkers who have argued that the social sciences must take account of the fact that the social world comprises, among other things, the meaningful actions, utterances and gestures of individual agents who have reasons and motives for what they do and who know, in some sense, what they are doing. This is an emphasis which is evident, for instance, in the work of Max Weber and in the writings of authors who have been influenced by the traditions of hermeneutics, phenomenology and ordinary language philosophy, among others. Each of these contrasting positions has its entrenched proponents in the contemporary theoretical landscape, which often seems like a battle-ground between objectivism and subjectivism, determinism and voluntarism, etc. But there are many people working in the social sciences today who think that the opposition has been overstated and that a more sophisticated account of the relevant conceptual and methodological issues would show that the social sciences can, and must, take account of both the meaningful actions of individual agents and the structural features of social contexts.

It is to the credit of Anthony Giddens that he has diagnosed these theoretical dilemmas with exceptional acuity and proposed an original and compelling way of moving beyond them. In a sequence of major works beginning with *New Rules of Sociological Method* and including *Central Problems in Social Theory* and *The Constitution of Society*, he has examined the major traditions of classical and contemporary social theory, identified their strengths and weaknesses, and drawn from them a range of lessons and ideas which inform his own constructive proposals. The centre-piece of these proposals is what he calls the 'theory of structuration'. This theory is an attempt to move beyond the apparent opposition between perspectives which emphasize structure and perspectives which emphasize action; it is an attempt to think through the ways in which actions and structure are interwoven in the ongoing activity of social life. Giddens's key conceptual innovation in this regard is to argue that we should cease to conceive of 'structure' as a kind of framework, like the girders of a building or the skeleton of a body, and that we should conceptualize it instead as the 'rules and resources' which are implemented in interaction. In interacting with one another, individuals draw on the rules and resources which comprise structure, in much the same way as an individual draws on the rules of grammar in uttering a well-formed speech act. Like the rules of grammar, structure is both 'enabling' and 'constraining': it enables us to act as well as delimiting the courses of possible action. By focusing on the generative character of rules and resources, we can see that structure is both constitutive of everyday action and, at the same time, reproduced by that action – a phenomenon that Giddens refers to as the 'duality of structure'.

From this perspective it can be argued that individuals know a great deal about the structural features of the social world of which they are part, just as the speakers of a language know the rules of that language, even if they cannot formulate them discursively. But the accounts that agents are able to give of their own action, and of the structural features of the social world more generally, are limited or 'bounded' in various ways, and it is part of the task of the social sciences to examine the aspects and processes of the social world which lie beyond the immediate grasp of the agents implicated in them. Here Giddens rejects the views of philosophers of social science such as Winch, who argue that there is no room in the social sciences for objectivistic concepts like 'cause'.[2] But Giddens agrees with Winch, and with authors in the traditions of hermeneutics and interpretative sociology, on one key point: that the social sciences stand in a unique and 'reflexive' relation to their subject matter. For the social sciences are not alone in seeking to analyse the social world and interpret action: these are activities which are also carried out routinely by the individuals who make up the social world. Unlike the natural sciences, the social sciences are characterized by a 'double hermeneutic'. The results of the social sciences are in principle available to the individuals who comprise the social world, and are also potentially critical of the beliefs, concepts and action frameworks of lay members.

The theory of structuration forms the linch-pin of what has become an elaborate and ramified theoretical system. Giddens has refined the concepts of action and structure and linked them to an ever-widening circle of related notions. At the same time, he has sought to employ these concepts in analysing a wide range of substantive issues. Giddens's theoretical approach and substantive analyses are increasingly becoming topics of debate in their own right. In this volume, the chapters by Bernstein, Bauman, Thompson, Gregory,

---

[2] See Peter Winch, *The Idea of Social Science and its Relation to Philosophy* (London: Routledge & Kegan Paul, 1958), and Giddens's critique of Winch in *NRSM*, pp. 44–51.

Saunders and Gregson address some of the key questions raised by Giddens's general approach. Richard Bernstein is concerned with the question of how, on Giddens's account, we are to understand the *critical* character of social theory and social science. Giddens maintains that the social sciences should be regarded as intrinsically critical disciplines, but how are we to understand the nature of such critique and the grounds for its justification? Bernstein carefully disentangles some of the relevant issues and argues forcefully that, on the key questions, Giddens is rather evasive: 'in tracking down what Giddens means by critique and critical theory', comments Bernstein, 'we discover not only ambiguity and vagueness, but conflicting and even contradictory claims'.[3] It is clear that Giddens's views on these issues, however elusive they may be, differ significantly from those of another major social theorist to whom Bernstein alludes – Jürgen Habermas. Over the last decade Habermas has been particularly concerned to examine the nature of social critique and to develop a framework for the justification or 'grounding' of normative judgements.[4] Habermas's proposals have proved to be highly controversial and have won few unqualified endorsements. But Bernstein is of the opinion that, whatever difficulties there may be in the details of Habermas's account, it has the merit of confronting directly a series of questions which cannot be avoided by authors who espouse, as Giddens appears to do, a strong version of the thesis of social theory as critique.

Responding constructively to Bernstein's charge, Giddens distinguishes between four levels of critique, all of which are implied, to some extent, by the conduct of social science. He describes these levels as intellectual critique, practical critique, ideological critique and moral critique; and he construes Bernstein's charge as pertaining primarily to the fourth level, that of moral critique. Giddens argues that the practising social scientist can legitimately make moral criticisms of states of affairs, and that such criticisms can be justified only by a form of argument which fuses together factual and evaluative claims. This position, which Giddens describes as 'contingent moral rationalism', differs significantly from the position developed by Habermas, for Giddens does not share Habermas's strong assumptions concerning the possibility of attaining consensus among participants of a debate. But Giddens's position also differs from that of social theorists and philosophers who are inclined to adopt some kind of relativistic or nihilistic approach – an inclination which is evident in the work of many contemporary French theorists, including Michel Foucault. For Giddens's view is that moral critique stands in need of rational justification, even if, in particular cases, such justification may not be altogether conclusive.

The chapters by Bauman and Thompson focus the debate more sharply on

[3] Richard J. Bernstein, 'Social Theory as Critique', Ch. 1 in this volume, p. 28.
[4] See especially Jürgen Habermas, 'What is Universal Pragmatics?', in his *Communication and the Evolution of Society*, translated by Thomas McCarthy (Cambridge: Polity Press, 1979), pp. 1–68; and Jürgen Habermas, *The Theory of Communicative Action*, vol. 1, *Reason and Rationalization of Society*, translated by Thomas McCarthy (Cambridge: Polity Press, 1984).

the theory of structuration as such. Zygmunt Bauman offers an elegant account of the theoretical background to Giddens's project. The theory of structuration, observes Bauman, has a dual purpose: to dethrone the concept of structure as an external determinant of action, and to deny the random character of human action. But in redefining the concept of structure in terms of rules and resources, Giddens merely reinstitutes, Bauman argues, an outer force which determines action without being determined by it, an outer force which seems more elusive and mysterious than ever. Giddens is guilty, in Bauman's view, of a kind of 'hypostasis' – that is, of turning a social pattern or distribution into some sort of process or thing. In its most elementary sense, 'structure' refers to the fact that some actions or events are more likely to occur than others. The problem arises when social theorists then try to *explain* the non-randomness of social life by postulating a structure, or a process of structuration, which underlies it. Structure and structuration are 'metaphysical props', as Bauman puts it, to account for the uneven distribution of probabilities in social life. Moreover, Giddens's emphasis on the actor, whose actions are said to be structured by rules and resources, is questionable as a focal point for social theory and sociological analysis. In seeking to recover the actor as a knowledgeable agent, Giddens has perhaps gone too far and has lost sight of the network of interdependencies in which actors are always and already enmeshed. Bauman suggests that Giddens's approach might best be replaced by something similar to Elias's 'figurational sociology', since the latter salvages the elementary idea of structure as regularity and focuses primarily on networks of interaction and interdependency.

John Thompson concentrates on Giddens's proposal to reconceptualize structure in terms of rules and resources, examining the development of this proposal in Giddens's writings and assessing its cogency and coherence. Like Bauman, Thompson casts doubt on the suitability of this proposal as a means of approaching issues concerned with the structural features of social life. It is by no means clear, for instance, how the proposal could illuminate, or indeed be connected to, the analysis of differential practices or opportunities, such as differential access to institutions of higher education. Moreover, the key term in Giddens's proposed reconceptualization – the notion of rule – is itself rather vague. There are many different kinds of rules which operate in social life, including traffic rules, bureaucratic rules, rules of thumb, rules of etiquette, rules of grammar, rules of football and so on. In describing such rules, are we describing the 'structure' of social life, as Giddens maintains, or are we diverting our attention away from a range of structural features that cannot be adequately analysed in terms of rules? In his recent writings Giddens has introduced more abstract levels of structural analysis and speaks of 'structural principles', 'structural sets', etc.; but what remains unclear, Thompson argues, is just how these more abstract levels of analysis can be reconciled with Giddens's proposal to conceive of structure in terms of rules and resources. Are structural principles some sort of rules, or has Giddens implicitly put aside his original conception? The main source of these problems, Thompson suggests, is that Giddens initially worked out his general conception of structure by reflecting on the nature of language and its relation to speech. Although Giddens never uses the linguistic example in an unqualified way, it is nevertheless clear that his proposed reconceptualization of structure owes a great deal to what philosophers such as Wittgenstein and Austin, as well as some authors writing within the tradition of structural linguistics (Saussure, Benveniste, Derrida), have had to say about the nature and function of language.

In reply to Bauman and Thompson, Giddens defends his approach and argues that their reservations can be met without altering the basic elements of his account. He offers several examples of rules and rule-following behaviour, and he tries to show how his conceptual framework can be connected to some of the more traditional problems of sociological analysis, such as differential access to educational institutions. Particularly important in this regard is the distinction which Giddens has drawn, and which he reiterates here, between 'structure' and 'system': whereas the former term refers to rules and resources, the latter refers to the patterning of social relationships across time and space. Many of the objections and counter-examples offered by Bauman and Thompson appear to Giddens to have more to do with what he would call systems and system reproduction than with what he regards as the proper domain of structure. As regards his use of the linguistic analogy, Giddens is, as he puts it, 'unrepentant'. In drawing on the linguistic example, his main concern, he explains, has always been to highlight the 'recursive character' of social life – that is, the fact that structure is reproduced in and through the succession of situated practices which are organized by it. He would not wish to push the comparison beyond this point. Whether, in drawing on this example, Giddens has succeeded in formulating a conception of structure which is coherent, illuminating and compelling is the issue that is at stake in this debate.

One of the most interesting and fruitful aspects of Giddens's theory of structuration is the way in which he has conjoined it with the analysis of time and space. Giddens has perhaps done more than anyone to show that an account of time and space is essential to social theory, and that such an account can provide a tool for analysing some of the most important features of social life. Rather than thinking of time and space as abstract categories or as frameworks within which action takes place, they can be more illuminatingly thought of, Giddens suggests, in terms of 'presence' and 'absence' – terms which he borrows from Heidegger. Every interaction involves different forms of presence and absence. A face-to-face interaction typically takes place in a definite setting and endures for a definite period; the other person is 'present' both spatially and temporally. But social systems can become 'extended' in space and time, in such a way that the other is no longer immediately present. This time–space distancing (or 'distanciation', as Giddens generally calls it) has been facilitated by the development of new forms of transport and communication. The significance of the invention of the telegraph, to take one example, was that it separated the process of communication from the physical transportation of messages, thereby enabling individuals to communicate quickly at a distance, without sharing a common physical locale. Giddens draws on the work of 'time–space geographers', such as Hägerstrand, in order to analyse in further detail the spatial and temporal characteristics of social systems. He shows how transformations in these characteristics are connected more generally with the generation of power and with the growing capacity of nation-states to store information about their populations, and thereby to monitor and control their activities.

Geographers, in turn, have taken up Giddens's work and engaged with it in a critical and creative fashion. In this volume the chapters by Gregory and Saunders exemplify this critical engagement. Derek Gregory provides a systematic and insightful account of the ways in which time–space relations are integrated into the theory of structuration. Writing from the viewpoint of human geography, Gregory compares Giddens's work with that of authors such as David Harvey, Manuel Castells and Henri Lefebvre, authors who are perhaps better known among geographers than they are within social theory. Viewed from this perspective, Giddens's work falls short, Gregory argues, on two counts: first, Giddens's conception of space in terms of presence and absence does not take account of what Harvey, Lefebvre and others call the 'production of space', including both the production of material spatial structures and the production of representations of space. Second, Giddens's account of time–space distanciation places too much emphasis on power and domination, and thereby downplays the significance of the symbolic and normative aspects of space and spatial representation, such as those involved in the codification of space through the production and reading of maps.

The issues raised by Gregory overlap to some extent with the criticisms developed by Peter Saunders, who assesses Giddens's work from the perspective of urban sociology. Saunders highlights the significance of time–space relations in Giddens's account of the development and distinctive characteristics of modern societies. As social systems are increasingly 'stretched' across time and space, the link between social activity and spatial location becomes ever more tenuous, and space itself becomes commodified and constructed – the 'created environment' of urban space in which most people in modern societies live out most of their lives. At the same time, the traditions and routines which provided individuals with a sense of 'ontological security' – that is, with a sense of confidence or trust that the world is as it appears to be – are transformed, and to some extent undermined, by the rapidly changing character of modern societies. Saunders expresses some scepticism about this thesis of the fragile character of ontological security in the modern world. Life in modern societies is also routinized, even if the routines are different and the environment through which we move is more created than natural. 'Why', Saunders pointedly asks, 'should people feel a deep sense of desperation, fatalism, meaninglessness or whatever when they go to work every morning on the same train, but not when in the past they walked to the fields every morning along the same footpath?'[5] Saunders finds no good reason to suppose that a natural environment is supportive of ontological security while a created one disturbs it, and he detects a certain nostalgic romanticism in Giddens's suggestion that in pre-modern societies human beings lived in a symbiotic relation with the natural world.

In response to these and other criticisms by Gregory and Saunders, Giddens clarifies his approach to the study of time and space and elaborates his account of ontological security in the modern world. While ontological security is based on certain general psychological needs, its relation to everyday routines can be shown, Giddens argues, to differ systematically between non-modern and modern societies. In non-modern societies the kinship systems and the locality served as grounding for the maintenance of routines, but in modern societies this is no longer the case. In the latter, new trust mechanisms are employed as a means of securing confidence in transactions between individuals dispersed in time and space. These mechanisms include abstract tokens such as money, as well as 'expert systems' which secure confidence by invoking professional expertise. But the ontological security established by such mechanisms is, Giddens suggests, of a rather tenuous nature, and has to be 'actively regrounded' by constantly building and renewing personal ties with others. The insecurity we experience is exacerbated by the existence of risks and dangers which derive, not so much from natural hazards like floods or droughts, but rather from the socially created environment and from the failure of the very mechanisms through which our confidence is supposed to be secured. These are some of the issues that Giddens plans to explore in his new book, *The Consequences of Modernity*.[6]

Although the theory of structuration, and Giddens's related work on time and space, have generated considerable theoretical debate, they have received a more cautious response from social scientists engaged in empirical research. For there are many who feel that Giddens's work, however interesting it may be on a general theoretical level, is too abstract and formal to be of much use in carrying out empirical research projects. This sentiment, which is evident in several of the contributions to this volume, is forcefully articulated by Nicky Gregson. She points out that Giddens has often stressed the importance of developing links between social theory and empirical research, but, until recently, Giddens has said relatively little on just how such links are to be developed. This virtual silence was broken with the publication of *The Constitution of Society*, a lengthy chapter of which was devoted to the question of the relation between structuration theory and empirical research.[7] Gregson examines in some detail the arguments and examples deployed in this chapter. She maintains that, despite Giddens's claims to the contrary, his discussion in *The*

[5] Peter Saunders, 'Space, Urbanism and the Created Environment', Ch. 10 in this volume, p. 225.
[6] Anthony Giddens, *The Consequences of Modernity* (Cambridge: Polity Press, 1990).
[7] See *CS*, Ch. 6.

Constitution of Society does little to demonstrate the relevance or usefulness of structuration theory for empirical research. Structuration theory is best seen, she argues, as a 'second order theory', concerned primarily with conceptualizing the general constituents of society (structure, agency, time, space, etc.), and as such is quite different from 'first order theory' which is more directly concerned with analysing and explaining the specific events or contingencies of particular periods or places.

Giddens does not accept Gregson's conclusion that structuration theory is of little value for empirical research and tries to show, in response to her chapter, that empirical research can be directly informed by the structurationist approach. Focusing on the example of marital relationships, he considers how structuration theory could sensitize the researcher to certain aspects of this phenomenon, such as the ways in which marital relationships are maintained through day-to-day and periodic activities. Here, as in other domains of social life, 'structure' is embedded in practice, that is, in the countless and seemingly trivial activities which make up everyday life. These localized forms of practice can be linked to broader aspects of social systems by examining the ways in which considerations of a more general kind, such as gender divisions and labour markets, enter into the situated practices of particular agents. By considering an example like this, we can see, Giddens argues, that structuration theory directs our attention to certain aspects of the social world and helps us to analyse particular phenomena in certain ways – it serves as a kind of 'operational principle of research'. It also reminds us that the results of such research may have an impact on the very phenomena under investigation, by being incorporated, via the double hermeneutic, in the self-understanding of the individuals who make up the social world. But structuration theory can also be seen to have empirical relevance in a rather different way: it can be developed in relation to a broad range of substantive issues which have been of central concern to Giddens, from the analysis of class relations and the state to the reconstruction of the institutional aspects of modern societies.

II

Many of the writings of the major social and political thinkers of the nineteenth and early twentieth centuries were concerned with trying to understand the nature and distinctiveness of the new industrial order which was emerging in Europe and rapidly spreading to other parts of the world. This new social order seemed to be intrinsically dynamic and self-propelling; the traditional ways of life characteristic of medieval and early modern Europe were being progressively undermined, as individuals were swept off the land and drawn into the new factories and communities of the expanding urban centres. The emergent social order gave rise, in turn, to new problems, as well as to new opportunities for progress and social change. The writings of Marx, Weber, Durkheim, Simmel and others could be seen, to some extent, as attempts to come to terms with the rapid and revolutionary changes which were being ushered in by the development of industrial capitalism, and as attempts to diagnose the shortcomings of, and the prospects for, social and political life in the modern world.

The attempt to analyse the broad contours of modern societies is a task which Giddens has taken up and pursued in several major works, from his early writings on Marx, Weber and Durkheim (*Capitalism and Modern Social Theory*) and on the theory of class (*The Class Structure of the Advanced Societies*) to his more recent work on historical materialism, war and the state (*A Contemporary Critique of Historical Materialism* and *The Nation-State and Violence*). Through a critical appraisal of classical and contemporary social theory and a perceptive analysis of developmental trends, Giddens has formulated a distinctive account of the nature of modern societies – or, as he puts it, of 'modernity'. According to Giddens, there are four main institutional aspects of modernity: capitalism (the production of commodities for markets), industrialism (the transformation of nature through productive techniques), surveillance (the control of information and monitoring of activities by states and other organizations), and military power (the concentration of the means of violence in the hands of the state). These four institutional aspects of modernity are irreducible to one another, and they provide a framework for understanding some of the distinctive tensions and inherent developmental tendencies of modern societies.[8]

A great deal of Giddens's discussion of classical social theory is focused on the writings of Marx. There can be no doubt that Marx's work is of great significance in understanding the nature of modern societies. His powerful analysis of the mechanisms of capitalist production and exchange, and his critical deciphering of the forms of class domination and exploitation, retain their relevance today. But Giddens argues that, however important Marx's contributions may be, there are massive lacunae in Marx's thought and in Marxism more generally, lacunae which prevent Marxism from merely being 'patched up', 'corrected' or 'brought up to date'. These lacunae include the absence of a satisfactory account of power, particularly military power and the use of violence by individuals, collectivities and states; an inadequate basis for analysing nation-states and nationalism; and a failure to consider systematically exploitative relations between the sexes and between racial and ethnic groups. Moreover, most forms of Marxism depend on an evolutionary account of social change, an account which Giddens regards as untenable.

Erik Olin Wright's chapter in this volume, while sympathetic to some aspects of Giddens's critique, seeks to defend the value and usefulness of the Marxist approach. Among the many issues Wright confronts is the charge that historical materialism is guilty of a crude 'class reductionism'. Wright agrees that Giddens is correct to emphasize that there are a number of different forms of domination and exploitation that have to be understood in any satisfactory account of social life and social change (including class, gender, ethnicity and

[8] See especially *NSV*, Ch., 11.

the power of nation-states), but he argues that not all of these have equal
analytical and explanatory weight. Wright acknowledges that it is 'difficult to
argue systematically for the structural unity of economic and political relations'.[9] It is tempting to accept 'causal pluralism'. Nonetheless, he says, this
temptation ought to be resisted, for class does have primacy over other social
forces. Wright unpacks a number of different conceptions of the primacy of
class and argues, ultimately, that the dynamics centered on property relations
impose fundamental limits on the overall process of social change. From this
and related considerations, it is possible, Wright contends, to recast the
evolutionary elements of historical materialism and to elaborate them into a
strong argument about the nature and direction of societal development – an
argument, he suggests, which is closer to Giddens's own approach than
Giddens himself appears to appreciate.

In response, Giddens asserts that, if anything, his previous writings owed
too much to Marx. Far from conceding that earlier criticisms might be
misplaced, he argues generally that they did not go far enough. He elaborates
his critique of Marxist theory by developing the view that the capitalist
economic order is but one of several structuring dimensions of modern societies. Moreover, the capitalist order never was an 'all-enveloping totality'
within which all aspects of social life could be located. Some mechanisms of
institutional ordering and some types of social relationship pre-existed the
advent of modern capitalism – for example, gender inequality and ethnic
discrimination. Exploring the implications of these issues, Giddens concludes
that class analysis is simply too limiting. The thesis of the primacy of class, and
the evolutionary account of social change, must be abandoned once and for all.

The debate about the significance and value of Marx's contribution carries
over into the analysis of the state and the nature of political power. Central to
nineteenth-century liberal and liberal democratic traditions was the idea that
the state can claim to represent the community or public interest, in contrast to
individuals' private aims and concerns. But, according to Marx and his
followers, the opposition between interests that are public and general and
those which are private and particular is, to a large extent, illusory. The state
defends the 'public' or the 'community' as if: classes do not exist; the relationship between classes was not exploitative; classes do not have fundamental
differences of interest; these differences of interest do not define economic and
political life. Marx challenged fundamentally the idea that the state is an
independent structure or set of institutions above society, that is, a 'public
power' acting for 'the public'. On the contrary, the state is deeply embedded,
in the Marxist view, in socio-economic relations and linked to particular
interests.

One of the issues that emerges in this context is how the relative balance
between economic and political power is to be analysed. Giddens approaches

---

9 Erik Olin Wright, 'Models of Historical Trajectory: An Assessment of Giddens's Critique of
   Marxism', Ch. 4 in this volume, p. 99.

these issues by emphasizing that, while the state in capitalist society 'is a state in a class society', the dominant economic class 'does not rule'.[10] The state is dependent upon the activities of capitalist employers for its revenues and, hence, operates in the context of various capitalist imperatives. However, while the state must sustain the process of accumulation and the incentives for the private appropriation of resources, it is not merely a defender of capitalist economic relations. For it can in some part be seen, when viewed historically and comparatively, as a force able to shape the nature of interests and public policy. Contra Marxism, Giddens insists that one must recognize the *sui generis* powers of the modern state. He argues that the state can only be properly understood as a 'nation-state' which exists in a complex set of relations with other nation-states.

In Ch. 5, 'Capitalism, Nation-States and Surveillance', Bob Jessop examines Giddens's contribution to understanding the state and develops a number of criticisms. In the first instance, Jessop argues that there is a 'politicist' bias in Giddens's work, for it neglects the state's own economic resources and its functions as an economic force. The state is able to accrue considerable economic power and therefore cannot simply be characterized – as Giddens sometimes does – as dependent on, or subordinated to, the logic or imperatives of the market. Moreover, Giddens does not adequately establish how and to what extent the state is enmeshed in modern capitalism. Giddens's position wavers between seeing the state as a 'capitalist state' and as a 'power system' in and of itself. In short, 'the relative primacies of class versus non-class conflicts and of economic versus political power in Giddens's analysis of capitalist nation-states remain uncertain'.[11] Furthermore, Jessop argues that Giddens's analysis of the state far too often remains abstract. Accordingly, it neglects many features of the modern state – for instance, the welfare dimensions of the state – and it neglects the many differences that exist between modern capitalist states.

Giddens replies to these criticisms by explaining that one can legitimately describe modern states as capitalist states if one grasps that what makes a state a 'capitalist state' is that the wealth through which government institutions are funded is generated to a large extent by economic activity organized around market criteria. Thus, capitalist states are dependent upon business leaders for a good deal of their revenue, and recognition of this is in fact part of the outlook of most government officials. However, Giddens also emphasizes that this does not mean that the autonomy or independence of the state is undermined. On the contrary, he tries to unpack the idea of 'state autonomy' in relation not only to the space political authorities manage to create with respect to economic power, but also with respect to powers accrued through surveillance and the direction of information, territorial prerogatives, and the control of the means of violence.

[10] *CCHM*, p. 211.
[11] Bob Jessop, 'Capitalism, Nation-States and Surveillance', Ch. 5 in this volume, p. 122.

The question of the control of the means of violence by the state is at the heart of a set of themes explored in Giddens's most recent writings. Throughout the nineteenth and twentieth centuries most of the leading perspectives on societal change assumed that the origins of social transformation are to be found in processes internal to society. Change is presumed to occur via mechanisms 'built in', as it were, to the very structure of a given society, and governing its development. Among the many factors downplayed by these perspectives is the history of war. Many nineteenth-century thinkers conceived of war as a purely exogenous force – that is, as an 'external' event which impinges on and threatens social life. The interrelations between the state, society and warfare were barely explored. Twentieth-century social thinkers have continued this record of neglect. As Martin Shaw puts it in his chapter, there has been a 'virtual absence of the problem of war in the mainstream traditions of social thought'.[12] It is an extraordinary lacuna. Socio-economic issues have largely predominated over political and military concerns in classical and contemporary social theory.

Anthony Giddens has been one of several writers who have tried recently to make good this neglect. Giddens's contribution is particularly distinctive because it seeks to integrate the issues of war and violence into a general theory of state and power. At the centre of Giddens's approach is an examination of the way the means of violence became concentrated in the hands of the state during the formation of modern capitalist societies. He argues that the struggle for freedom of contract, along with the pursuit of related demands by the bourgeois classes, involved the 'extrusion' or expulsion of violent sanctions from the newly expanding labour market during the early phases of modern capitalism. However, the eradication of the immediate threat of violence from day-to-day life went hand-in-hand with the growth of surveillance as a form of political control. In Giddens's view, the growth of state surveillance – the capacity of the state to store information and manage subject populations – corresponds with the reduction of violence within societies ('pacification') and, in particular, with the reduction of violent class conflict. The growth of state power is, thereby, connected to the growth of a 'new technology of subjection'. Accordingly, the state becomes the 'purveyor of violence' in both domestic and foreign affairs.

In his contribution, Martin Shaw comments critically on several aspects of these ideas. First, Shaw casts doubt on whether one can claim that organized class violence has been undermined by the growth of state power. In Shaw's view, organized class violence has been commonplace (through fascism and communism, for example) even in the twentieth century. Class struggle certainly continues and remains an endemic feature of contemporary Western capitalist societies. Therefore, 'pacification' seems a somewhat premature conclusion. Second, Shaw contends that Giddens does not really explore the meaning of violence as war. Giddens fails to relate the international, military,

[12] Martin Shaw, 'War and the Nation-State in Social Theory', Ch. 6 in this volume, p. 129.

political-ideological and socio-economic processes involved in the making of war. Military power 'tends to be presented as a resource of states; it is not clear that Giddens has quite come to terms, theoretically at least, with the destructive logic of actual war'.[13]

Giddens responds to these remarks by addressing Clausewitz's thesis, highlighted by Shaw, that 'war is the continuation of policy by other means'. Giddens argues that to the extent that this observation is true, it applies only to 'early modern warfare', to the period prior to the mechanization of weapons, mass conscription and the development of the industrialized war economies. Thereafter, the era of 'total war' changed the meaning of both diplomacy and warfare: war can no longer be considered as an extension of diplomacy, for diplomacy must now be thought of as central to the prevention of war. The next major war, after all, will in all probability leave the 'victors' with little, if anything, to celebrate. As warfare between the two superpowers has become more unlikely, a variety of other forms of violent confrontation between them have emerged, and Giddens attempts to examine these in relation to a global consideration of the balance of power.

Just as it is striking that a great deal of classical and contemporary social theory neglected the study of warfare, it is also striking that the issue of gender has not been at the centre of social and political theory. It is noteworthy, for example, that Marx wrote virtually nothing about the possible intersections between class exploitation and the exploitation of women. Although Engels did attempt such a task in *The Origin of the Family, Private Property and the State*, it is generally agreed today that there is little in Engels's account that can be defended. It is unquestionably the case that most social theory in the nineteenth and twentieth centuries assumed that the main unit of analysis was the male individual or men organized in various collectivities. Not only has most class analysis been centered upon males, but so too has the bulk of social theory. Referring to this tradition of analysis as the 'malestream', Linda Murgatroyd shows, in her chapter in this volume, how Anthony Giddens's own theoretical and empirical work has contributed to it. She argues that Giddens has failed to deal seriously 'with either the gender dimension of social relations or any of the areas of social activity in which women typically participate more'.[14] The consequences of this for Giddens's work are considerable. At the very least, it results in a 'lop-sided picture' of society and a 'blinkered' theoretical analysis, for it ignores, among other things, the fact that most families are not engaged in production as a unit but as individual wage-earners or employers; the fact that a significant proportion of household units are made up of single adults, or one-parent families, or families where the adult male is unemployed or retired; and the fact that the contribution of women's work inside the household as domestic labour, and outside the

[13] Ibid., p. 27.
[14] Linda Murgatroyd, 'Only Half the Story: Some Blinkering Effects of "Malestream" Sociology', Ch. 7 in this volume, p. 148.

household as paid wage labour, is far more important than class theory has
heretofore recognized. It is simply not justifiable to write as though the
activities and attitudes of women are just a pale reflection of those of the males
in their families, or of little relevance. The relation between the sexes is
conditioned by the division of labour in the family and by a variety of
connections between the internal division of labour and the broader political
and economic system. No adequate account of social relations either inside or
outside the domestic sphere can be complete without a systematic examination of both these domains.

Giddens accepts the force of Murgatroyd's observation that he has not
accorded questions of gender the attention they 'undeniably deserve'. He goes
on to ask, however, how exactly gender should be analysed, and in what
precise ways the difference that is gender 'makes a difference' to the analysis of
social life. Raising doubts about Murgatroyd's own approach to the analysis of
gender, Giddens explores the contribution of psychoanalysis to the understanding of gender differences, and the roots of these differences in unconscious feelings and images. Linking psychoanalytic insights with a sociological
perspective offers the most promising way, in Giddens's view, of understanding how gender is constructed and reconstructed in everyday life. He illustrates this thesis with a brief examination of the tendency of gender and
power relations to converge across the public and private spheres. Understanding these issues, he affirms, is one of the most important tasks on the
agenda of contemporary social and political theory.

Asymmetries of power – whether these be based on class, gender, race,
ethnicity, or other sources – have fundamental consequences for the opportunities people have to establish themselves 'in their capacity of being citizens'
(Arendt). These consequences are explored in Held's contribution, which
takes up the theme of citizenship and its relationship to wider social and
economic structures. The *locus classicus* on citizenship in social and political
theory is Marshall's study, 'Citizenship and Social Class'.[15] According to
Marshall, the concept and reality of citizenship are among the great driving
forces of the modern era. Marshall's thesis is that the successful development
of citizenship rights has contained or 'abated' the excesses of class inequality
stemming from the capitalist market system. In other words, the expansion of
citizenship has remoulded the class system. Giddens takes issue with aspects of
Marshall's analysis on a number of grounds and, in so doing, tries to provide
an alternative account of the substantive problems, conflict areas and
struggles of democracy. Giddens argues that the origins of democracy have to
be understood in relation to the expansion of state power from the late
sixteenth century which led to the progressive reliance of the state on new
relations with its subjects – relations based on consent rather than force.
Developing this idea, Giddens seeks to show how the development of citizen-

---

[15] T. H. Marshall, 'Citizenship and Social Class', in Marshall, *Class, Citizenship and Social
Development* (Westport, Conn.: Greenwood Press, 1973).

ship was a more fragile and contested affair than Marshall recognized. In Giddens's judgement, Marshall seriously underestimated the way citizenship rights have been achieved largely only in and through social struggle. Furthermore, Marshall underestimated the extent to which the balance of power was tipped to the least powerful in democracies only during times of war, particularly during and immediately after the two World Wars.

David Held finds much in Giddens's position which is compelling. However, he argues that the value of Giddens's analysis is weakened considerably by a number of difficulties. Problems in Giddens's account derive, in the first instance, from Giddens's acceptance of too much of Marshall's initial terms of reference, and from lack of precision concerning the notion of rights. In addition, Held argues that there are categories of rights which neither Giddens nor Marshall examines – categories which are linked to a variety of domains where, broadly speaking, social movements which are not class-based have sought to reform power centres according to their own interests and objectives. An important example of such rights are 'reproductive rights' at the centre of the women's movement. Moreover, Giddens's account – like Marshall's – suffers from too strict a focus on the citizen's relation to the nation-state. Citizenship is formed and moulded at the intersection of complex patterns of national and international relations and processes which neither Giddens nor Marshall has properly grasped. Held stresses how the idea of citizenship and the theory of democracy have to be rethought in relation to substantial changes in political, social and economic life which derive from, among other things, the dynamics of the world economy, the rapid growth of transnational links and major changes to the nature of international law – a project scarcely begun today.

Giddens accepts, in response, that his previous work on citizenship overstressed the importance of class conflict in the development of citizenship rights, despite his own criticism of Marshall on this very matter. He accepts that citizenship cannot be studied as though it were simply a matter of how far it serves to alleviate class inequalities. He points to areas of his work, however, where he has already attempted to move beyond this narrow framework. Building on these texts Giddens explores the question of the relationship between citizenship rights and the sovereign character of the nation-state, elaborating a tension between the universal values embedded in the constitutional rights proclaimed by modern states – such as the declaration of human rights built into the American constitution – and the enshrinement of such rights within the institutions of the nation-state. He points to a tension which exists between rights as 'citizenship rights' and rights as 'human rights'. Using this formulation he suggests that one of the most pressing questions of our times is: how can citizenship rights be effectively translated into human rights, which intrinsically they are? In other words, how can human rights be nourished and protected as genuinely universal rights – rights which transcend the claims and boundaries of the nation-state? Giddens stresses there is no easy answer to this question, although it will become ever more pressing, he believes, as a result of the acceleration of processes of globalization.

The critical essays in this volume, together with Giddens's lengthy reply, raise and pursue many of the issues which are central in contemporary social and political theory. For over a decade Giddens has been at the forefront of debates in the social sciences and it is hoped that this volume, in offering an appraisal of his contribution, will help to clarify some of the most important questions and problems faced by all those engaged in the project of understanding and explaining social life and the dilemmas of the modern world.

1

Social theory as critique

RICHARD J. BERNSTEIN

Structuration theory is intrinsically incomplete if not linked to a conception of
social science as critical theory.
The Constitution of Society, p. 287

The extensive *oeuvre* of Anthony Giddens is already a remarkable achievement.
There are few contemporary social theorists and sociologists whose thinking
exhibits comparable scope, diversity and subtlety. Giddens is in the process of
attempting nothing less than a rethinking of the modern sociological tradition.
He has written incisively and provocatively about Marx, Weber, Durkheim,
Parsons and Habermas. He has grappled with every major sociological movement, including the varieties of structuralism, functionalism, systems theory,
ethnomethodology, phenomenological sociology and symbolic interactionism.
He has a keen sense of the relevance of contemporary philosophic currents for
social thought ranging over Anglo-American, German and French philosophy. He has expanded the domain of sociological thinking by showing the
importance of themes as diverse as Heidegger's reflections on temporality and
the significance of time–space studies in human geography. He is always
seeking to explore the dialectical interplay between theory and empirical
research, and has confronted thorny questions – neglected by many other
social theorists – such as the distinctive character and role of nationalism and
the nation-state in contemporary societies. And he has done all this with rare
hermeneutical skill. Giddens combines a flair for judicious sympathetic
exposition with an uncanny ability to locate and specify problems, strengths
and weaknesses in the positions and thinkers he examines. The most important and impressive feature of his work is not his intellectual virtuosity, but the
systematic impulse that is evident even in his earliest writings, and which has
become more focused and dominant in his recent books. Giddens is engaged in
the ambitious project of developing a comprehensive textured social theory
adequate for our time which at once incorporates the insights of the major
social thinkers, which rejects what is inadequate and mistaken, and which can
guide and illuminate empirical sociological research. It is this systematic
project that I want to explore – a project that centres on what Giddens
calls 'The Theory of Structuration', a theoretical approach that reconstructs
the duality of structure and human agency. I want to probe the relevance of
the theory of structuration for understanding the *critical* functions of social
theory.

Given the diversity and richness of Giddens's writings and his own constant emphasis on the importance of time–space context, the initial problem is to gain a proper orientation. Let me begin to situate his project by comparing and contrasting his recent book, *The Constitution of Society* (1984) with Robert Merton's classic, *Social Theory and Social Structure* (1949).

Merton's work served as a manifesto and statement of the sociological consensus for a generation of sociologists. One way to discern the change (progress?) in social theory during the past thirty-five years is to examine the differences between these two texts. There is not a major thesis advanced by Merton that Giddens does not directly challenge and/or seriously qualify. We can begin to understand what Giddens is 'up to' by examining what he combats – and why he so strongly opposes it. Merton began his famous chapter 'Manifest and Latent Functions' with a bold claim:

> Functional analysis is at once the most promising and possibly the least codified of contemporary approaches to problems of sociological interpretation ... The accomplishments of functional analysis are sufficient to suggest that its large promise will ultimately be fulfilled, just as its current deficiencies testify to the need for periodically overhauling the past the better to build for the future.[1]

Giddens, although he concedes that functional analysis has 'strongly emphasized the significance of unintended consequences of action', tells us in an unqualified manner that 'conceptually its influence has been largely pernicious' (p. xxxi).[2] Giddens's sustained and multifaced attacks on functionalism (in all its varieties) are only the tip of the iceberg of his disagreements with Merton (and with those sociologists who share Merton's sociological orientation).[3] Merton begins his book by reflecting on the nature of sociology as a discipline, the logical character of sociological theory and explanation, and the relation of theory to empirical research. Giddens challenges every major claim made by Merton.

Merton compares the development of sociology with other natural sciences such as physics, chemistry and biology. He tells us that it is more 'realistic' and 'psychologically more rewarding' to compare the accomplishments and potential of twentieth-century sociology with seventeenth-century medicine rather than with twentieth-century physics. 'Perhaps sociology is not yet ready for its Einstein because it has not yet found its Newton' (p. 7). Merton never seriously questions the appropriateness of the analogy between sociology as a scientific discipline and the other natural sciences. He even suggests that sociology may achieve results comparable to twentieth-century physics when it has benefited from the 'billions of man-hours of sustained, disciplined, and

---

[1] Robert K. Merton, *Social Theory and Social Structure* (Glencoe, Illinois: Free Press, 1949), p. 21. All page references to Merton refer to this book.
[2] Unless otherwise noted, all page references to Giddens refer to *CS*.
[3] Giddens criticizes functionalism in several of his recent books. In addition to his remarks on functional analysis in *CS*, see 'Functionalism: après la lutte', in *SSPT*.

cumulative research' (p. 7) which were required for the achievements of contemporary physics. But for Giddens the very analogy between sociology and the natural sciences is misconceived. He hits hard at the popular thesis that sociology is a young or 'immature' natural science. Sociology is not and never can be the *type* of natural science of human beings which Merton presupposes to be its goal and rationale. (This does *not* mean that sociology cannot be scientific.) Merton sharply distinguishes the 'history of theory and the systematics of theory'. Superficially Giddens himself might accept such a distinction, but he strongly opposes the way in which Merton makes his distinction. For Merton the history of social theory consists of 'who said what by way of speculation or hypothesis' and includes 'the false starts, the archaic doctrines and the fruitless errors of the past'. 'The systematics of theory' presumably consists of 'the highly selective accumulation of those small parts of earlier theory which has thus far survived the tests of empirical research' (p. 5). For Giddens, this facile distinction between the history and systematics of theory is misleading. It is indicative of how much Merton (and other naturalistically inclined social scientists) have uncritically accepted a now discredited logical empiricist conception of natural science. This is further illustrated by what is perhaps best known in Merton's manifesto, his defence of 'theories of the middle range'. Merton was advocating a *via media* between theories which are 'all-embracing and grandiose' and 'minor working hypotheses', but his notion of theory is essentially a deductive-nomological conception of theory. He distinguishes two types of sociological generalization: empirical generalization, 'an isolated proposition summarizing observed uniformities of relationships between two or more variables'; and 'scientific laws'. 'The second type of sociological generalization, the so-called "scientific law", differs from the foregoing inasmuch as it is a statement of invariance *derivable* from a theory' (p. 92). Giddens brings a whole battery of arguments against this very understanding of theory. This is the concept of theory which was privileged by logical empiricists. But the post-empiricist philosophy of science has shown that it 'has turned out to be of quite limited application even within the natural sciences' (p. xviii). If this is the way in which theory is conceived, then 'anyone who would seek to apply it to social science must recognize that (as yet) there is no theory at all' (p. xviii). Giddens hits harder. The very seductiveness of the deductive-nomological conception of theory and scientific law is based on a misguided assumption: 'the idea that the "theory" in social theory must consist essentially of generalizations if it is to have explanatory content' (p. xviii). But this is a fiction. 'Most "why?" questions do not need a generalization to answer them, nor do the answers logically imply that there must be some generalization lurking around which could be invoked to back up the answer' (p. xix). Giddens goes even further in his attempt to demolish and deconstruct the very understanding of theory, explanation and generalization that Merton advocates, and which has been (and continues to be) accepted in weaker versions by many social scientists. Merton not only mystifies the conception of social theory, but obscures the character and role of empirical generalizations in sociology. Giddens tells us that 'uncovering of generalizations is not the be-all and end-all of social theory' (p. xix). Furthermore, empirical generalizations do not consist solely of propositions 'summarizing observed uniformities of relationships between two or more variables'. There are also generalizations (which have major importance in Giddens's theory of structuration) which 'hold because actors themselves know them – in some guise – and apply them in the enactment of what they do. The social scientific observer does not in fact have to "discover" these generalizations, although that observer may give a new discursive form to them' (p. xix).

Furthermore, the claims that Merton makes about theory, law, explanation and empirical generalization obfuscate what he wants to clarify – the relation between sociological theory and empirical research. His conceptual apparatus leads us to think that the primary role of empirical research is to 'discover' those empirical generalizations that confirm or disconfirm sociological laws derivable from theories. But this conception of the role of empirical research is far too limiting. It slights the empirical contributions of the type of ethnographic research which is not at all concerned with summarizing observed uniformities of relationships between two or more variables, but with providing 'thick descriptions' of the forms of life of social agents.

One could continue in this vein showing in detail how doggedly Giddens deconstructs the edifice of sociological theory as presented by Merton (and which was widely shared by sociologists). Functionalism is not the only sociological orientation attacked by Giddens. He is equally relentless in his criticism of structuralism, objectivism, subjectivism, naturalism and evolutionism. Giddens uses a variety of guerrilla tactics in attacking all these 'isms'. Even his prose becomes more barbed and terse when he 'goes after' the spectres that still haunt social theory. There are few who can rival Giddens as a penetrating critic of the dogmas, misleading metaphors (e.g., the variety of biological and systemic metaphors) and unquestioned presuppositions that pervade sociological thinking. But Giddens is not merely a 'critical critic', or a 'negative critic'. What informs his detailed analyses and gives them so much punch is the way in which he uses them to elaborate an alternative substantive sociological approach to understanding, explaining and criticizing contemporary society.

Let me illustrate this by returning to the question of functionalism. I have already indicated that Giddens does think that functional analysis has made a positive contribution in emphasizing the importance of 'unintended consequences' of social action. His point is that we can appropriate this positive emphasis without any appeal to functional concepts. What precisely is wrong with functionalism? Although Giddens raises many different types of objections to functionalism, his central objection is that a functional explanation 'does *not* really explain anything. We can bring this out by contrasting the types of account' (p. 294).

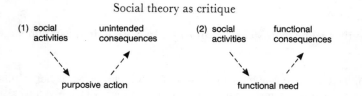

(1) social activities → unintended consequences → purposive action

(2) social activities → functional consequences → functional need

Interpretation (2) is the type of account favoured by functionalists. But 'interpretation (2) is not an explanation because it does not supply a mechanism linking the positing of a functional need and the consequences that are presumed to ensue for the wider social system in which the activities to be explained are involved' (p. 295).

Consider Merton's 'functional interpretation' of the Hopi rain ceremonial. The manifest function of the ceremony is to bring about rain, but the latent function is to reinforce 'a unitary value system' required to sustain such a small society. This *may be* the unintended consequence of the social practice of the rain ceremony, but we can state this without any appeal to functional concepts. (This is the point of interpretation (1).) We only mystify this situation by suggesting that these consequences occur 'because' of a 'functional need'. So pseudo-functional explanations not only fail to supply a mechanism linking a 'functional need' to unintended consequences, but the very concept of a 'functional need' is a fiction (a fiction which in part gains plausibility because of the misleading appropriation of biological metaphors about the 'needs' of social systems).

Giddens digs deeper. The crucial concept of 'unintended consequences' itself presupposes a viable concept of human agency. This is what Giddens seeks to elaborate. We cannot legitimately speak of unintended consequences unless we clarify the criteria for distinguishing intentional from unintentional action. Giddens knows that systematically clarifying the nature of human agency demands explicating a series of interrelated concepts such as power, motives and reasons. (Here we can follow Giddens's creative appropriation and *reconstruction* of the Anglo-American philosophic analysis of agency and action.) Furthermore human social agency cannot be adequately grasped unless we conceptually understand how agency itself is reflexively and recursively implicated in social structures. In short, thinking through what is right and wrong about functionalism, probing and critically assessing what functional interpretations presuppose, brings us to the very heart of the theory of structuration – the theory intended to illuminate the duality and dialectical interplay of agency and structure.[4]

[4] My focus on Giddens's critique of functionalism, and how it both supports and is informed by structuration theory, is intended to illustrate what is characteristic of his critical approach. Giddens is not merely concerned with 'scoring' negative points against the doctrines he opposes, but with showing us how *thinking through* the insights and inadequacies of those doctrines contributes to the articulation and support of structuration theory. I suggest this is the most illuminating way of interpreting his critiques of evolutionism, objectivism, subjectivism and naturalism. In this respect, Giddens's approach reflects a point which has been forcefully made in the post-empiricist philosophy of science, i.e., we can judge the adequacy of a theory – such as structuration theory – by its ability to explain what is valid and invalid in rival theories.

What then is the theory of structuration? In a preliminary statement, Giddens tells us:

> *Structure*, as recursively organized sets of *rules* and *resources*, is out of time and space, save in its instantiations and coordination as memory traces, and is marked by an 'absence of the subject'. The *social systems* in which structure is recursively implicated, on the contrary, comprise the situated activities of *human agents*, reproduced across *time and space*. Analysing the *structuration* of social systems means studying the modes in which such systems, grounded in the *knowledgeable* activities of situated actors who draw upon rules and resources in the diversity of action *contexts*, are produced and reproduced in interaction. Crucial to the idea of *structuration* is the theorem of the *duality of structure* . . . The constitution of *agents* and *structures* are not two independently given sets of phenomena, a dualism, but represent a duality. According to the notion of the duality of structure, the *structural properties* of social systems are both medium and outcome of the practices they recursively organize. Structure is not 'external' to individuals . . . Structure is not to be equated with constraint but is always both constraining and enabling.   (p. 25 (my italics))

On first reading, the above summary statement is extremely dense. *The Constitution of Society*, as well as much of Giddens's recent writings, can be seen as an explication, elaboration and explanation of what this means and entails. (For brief explanations of the italicized expressions in the above passage see his Glossary, pp. 373–7, in *The Constitution of Society*.) The concrete details of Giddens's theory of structuration are so rich and complex that in this context, one can hope only to convey its leading themes, to articulate the central vision that informs the theory. For while the theory provokes numerous questions and is still very much in the process of being developed, one can already discern its contours. The theory is powerful and attractive because it expresses a deep understanding of what we are as reflexive knowledgeable human agents who are always conditioned by and are constantly reproducing social structures.

We can bring forth this central vision from a variety of perspectives. One way of gaining a purchase on the theory is to view it against two extreme poles that have characterized a great deal of twentieth-century sociology. There are social thinkers who have primarily focused their attention on structures, social constraints and systemic features of society, and who have claimed that this is the proper domain of sociological analysis. These impersonal structures must be discovered and explained if we are to understand how human beings function in society. Frequently, from this point of view, the task of the sociologist is taken to be the discovery of those forces, laws, tendencies and 'structural constraints' which are always working 'behind the backs' of social agents. There are even those who argue that the social actor *dissolves* into a series of structures or is to be located as a mere 'place holder' within a dynamic impersonal system. When such a structuralist orientation is pressed to its extreme, it elicits a backlash. There arises a deep suspicion about any talk of impersonal structures. From this opposite extreme, all such talk is understood to be a reification or hypostatization of what is always fluid and changing – what is always in the process of being negotiated and renegotiated. Whether advocates of this extreme think of themselves as 'methodological individualists' or ethnomethodologists focusing on the face-to-face interactions of individuals, they have little sympathy with anything resembling reified structures. When these opposing poles are pressed to their extremes we are confronted with a stark either/or. *Either* we are left with a dance of impersonal structures, *or* with an interplay of nominalistic actors.

Of course, the situation is not nearly as simple and as blatant as this. Advocates who are attracted to one of these poles – the poles of structure and agency – claim to be able to accommodate the 'insights' of their opponents. Giddens shows that most of these 'compromises' do not work. They do not work because we cannot simply amend a deficient approach by adding a few concessionary corollaries. If we are to escape this unstable opposition then a reconstruction of the concepts of structure *and* agency is required. We must analyse social structure so that we can clearly discern how it *requires* agency, and analyse human agency in such a manner that we grasp how all social action *involves* social structure. For social structure is always both *constraining* and *enabling*. It at once limits and determines 'the capability of the individual to "make a difference" to a pre-existing state of affairs or course of events' (p. 14). This is the primary force of Giddens's claim that 'the constitution of agents and structures are not two independently given sets of phenomena, but represent a duality' (p. 25). Each is dependent upon and implicates the other.

Another perspective for grasping what is central to the theory of structuration is to view it (as Giddens does) as a commentary and elaboration of Marx's famous claim that 'Men [let us immediately say human beings] make history, but not in circumstances of their own choosing.' After citing this passage, Giddens remarks: 'Well, so they do. But what a diversity of complex problems of social analysis this apparently innocuous pronouncement turns out to disclose!' (p. xxi). It is precisely these 'complex problems' that the theory of structuration is meant to illuminate and to solve.

I think the clearest way to gain an understanding of the central thrust of the theory of structuration is to focus on the concept of 'practical consciousness'. Giddens tells us that 'the significance of practical consciousness is a leading theme of [*The Constitution of Society*]' (p. xxiii), and it is a leading theme of the theory of structuration. Giddens summarizes (in his Glossary) what he means by 'practical consciousness'.

> What actors know (believe) about social conditions, including especially conditions of their action, but cannot express discursively; no bar of repression, however, protects practical consciousness, as in the case with the unconscious.
>
> (p. 375)

Practical consciousness must be distinguished from discursive consciousness on the one hand and the unconscious on the other hand. When Giddens speaks about the knowledgeability of activities by social actors, he is referring primarily to their practical knowledgeability (know-how). Human agents practically know a great deal about what they are doing, about their society, about the rules of the games in which they find themselves (and even how to get around these rules). Social agents are always reflexively monitoring their action. We are not 'cultural dopes', nor are we agents who are self-transparently aware of what we are doing. We are always in the process of making history in circumstances which are not of our choosing, and we are not (and cannot be) fully aware of what we are doing and making.

William James once commented that 'any author is easy if you catch the centre of his vision', and he went on to suggest that in order to appreciate the technical details of an author's system, one needed to catch the centre of his vision. Perhaps James was a bit sanguine, but his remarks are relevant for understanding Giddens. If one is to grasp the technical details of Giddens's reflections on time–space studies for social analysis, the significance of the duality of presence/absence, regionalization, ontological security, etc., then we must see how such discussions are informed by, contribute to and texture his central vision of the duality of structure and agent.

I have stated that the vision which is at the centre of the theory of structuration is powerful and attractive without fully warranting this claim. I do think Giddens is on target when he focuses on the 'flip-flopping' character of so much contemporary sociological analysis. Indeed I think we find this same unstable swinging back and forth not only in the entire range of the social disciplines but in all cultural disciplines – including political theory and philosophy. In all these disciplines there has been an unstable oscillation between a nominalistic obsession with isolated individual agents and a fascination with dissolving agents into sign systems, structures and *epistemes*. Think, for example, of the typical ways in which 'the philosophy of action' is approached by Anglo-American analytic philosophers who model their analyses on isolated intentional agents, and contrast this with the French fascination with *différence*, the play of structures and the 'decentering of the subject'. Both tendencies can be found in Nietzsche – which may be one of the reasons why he is so much in vogue. But after all the fashionable talk of deconstruction, the deepest intellectual need of our time is for reconstruction. This is what Giddens is tenaciously attempting to accomplish. His project of reconstruction is not only theoretically important, but has enormous practical significance. For without falling into the despair of thinking that there is a 'logic of history' which is always working behind our backs with inexorable necessity or falling into a simplistic voluntaristic illusion that we can be complete masters of our fate, Giddens enables us to understand both the limits of and opportunities for shaping our destinies. For these reasons, what he has already accomplished has significance that goes far beyond the domain of sociology.

There is, of course, plenty that is open for serious criticism in Giddens. His intellectual vices are the other side of his virtues. In his desire to be comprehensive, he frequently writes as if he has a well-thought-out opinion on virtually every topic or theme which has been addressed by any social thinker. Consequently, there is unevenness in his analyses. (For example, his detailed examination of the nature and varieties of types of social constraint is subtle, discriminating and illuminating, while his claims about the unconscious and its role in social explanation tend to be superficial.) One sometimes feels that Giddens is not always in control of the material he is discussing. Where one expects detailed explication and justification, too often there is repetition and 'eloquent' variation. Temperamentally, Giddens is foxlike in his approach to issues, although his systematic ambitions require him to be like the hedgehog. Given the sheer variety of topics, themes and thinkers he treats, one can understand why he tells us 'This was not a particularly easy book to write and proved in some part refractory to the normal ordering of chapters' (p. xxxv). Giddens is guilty of a 'sin' common among other sociologists who think in a grand manner. For whenever he confronts a difficult problem, he is tempted to introduce a plethora of distinctions and schemas. (Giddens is critical of Parsons and Habermas for engaging in this practice, but he is guilty of it himself.) Many of these distinctions are illuminating, but one frequently has the uneasy feeling that much more needs to be said about the *criteria* of their applicability. Giddens is self-reflective about the interplay of theory and empirical research. While he rejects the narrow idea that the sole or main function of empirical research is to confirm or disconfirm 'laws' derivable from theoretical postulates, and the naive inductionist view that we can build theories by generalizing empirical observations, he does argue that theory can 'sensitize' us to empirical research.

> The concepts of structuration theory, as with any competing theoretical perspective, should for many research purposes be regarded as sensitizing devices, nothing more. That is to say, they may be useful for thinking about research problems and the interpretation of research results. But to suppose that being theoretically informed – which it is the business of everyone working in the social sciences to be in some degree – means always operating with a welter of abstract concepts is as mischievous a doctrine as one which suggests that we can get along very well without using such concepts at all. (pp. 326–7)

The final chapter of *The Constitution of Society*, 'Structuration, Empirical Research and Social Critique', is a *tour de force* in which Giddens shows how structuration theory can serve as a sensitizing critical device for evaluating and showing the theoretical significance of widely different types of empirical research. Nevertheless, given the elaborateness (and what sometimes seems to be the over-elaborateness) of the multiple concepts and distinctions of structuration theory, one sometimes suspects that Giddens himself is guilty of the mischievous practice of 'operating with a welter of abstract concepts'.

The flaws mentioned above are to be expected in a theoretical perspective

that is as elaborate and comprehensive as structuration theory. Many of these
difficulties can be resolved by subjecting structuration theory to the rigorous
criticism that it deserves. Giddens, who continually refines his concepts and
distinctions, has demonstrated his ability to respond creatively to criticisms.
(See for example his refinement of the senses and varieties of 'constraint' in
chapter 4 of *The Constitution of Society*.) But I want to concentrate on one area
where many of these problems come into sharp focus, and where there is
evidence of serious confusion and conflicting tendencies. It concerns Giddens's reflections on social science as critique – 'structuration theory is intrinsically incomplete if not linked to a conception of social science as critical
theory' (p. 287). Yet in tracking down what Giddens means by critique and
critical theory, we discover not only ambiguity and vagueness, but conflicting
and even contradictory claims. In fairness to Giddens, it should be noted that
he has frankly admitted that he has not 'really worked out in any detail' how he
is going to tackle the relevant issues.[5] My concern is not primarily with what he
has left unsaid, but with what he does say.

To locate the specific problematic issues, two preliminary sets of remarks
are necessary. The first concerns how Giddens understands 'theory' when he
speaks of social, sociological or critical theory. The second deals with what he
considers to be a mistaken or inadequate conception of critical theory. For
Giddens is clearer about what he is 'against' than what he is 'for'.

(1)   As a benchmark, let me return to Merton's conception of scientific theory
– a conception which owes a great deal to the analysis of scientific theory by the
logical empiricists. One 'virtue' of this conception of theory is its relative
clarity about what does and does not constitute a 'legitimate' scientific theory.
For Merton, theory consists of those concepts, distinctions, postulates and
theorems that form a deductive system. Theories are used to explain empirical
phenomena because 'scientific laws' can be *derived* from theories; and these
laws in turn can be confirmed or disconfirmed by empirical generalizations.
Theory is *not* to be understood as '*consisting of general orientations toward data,
suggesting types of variables which need somehow to be taken into account* . . . ' Theory
consists of '*clear, verifiable statements of relationships between specified variables*' (p. 9:
italics in the original). Theory is not to be confused with methodology, or with
a miscellaneous 'analysis of sociological concepts' such as status, role, *Gemein-
schaft*, social interaction, *anomie*, etc. Nor does theory consist of '*post factum*
sociological interpretations' (p. 90) which can account for almost any data.
Theory, 'properly speaking', is formulated on the model of hypothetical-
deductive explanation.[6]

Giddens, drawing upon the critiques of this conception of theory by post-

[5] For Giddens's reflections on critical theory and the critical function of social science, see his
interview 'Historical Materialism Today: An Interview with Anthony Giddens', in *Theory,
Culture & Society*, 1 (1982), 63–77.

[6] See my critical discussion of Merton's conception of social theory in *The Restructuring of Social and
Political Theory* (Oxford: Basil Blackwell, 1976), pp. 7–18.

empiricist philosophers of science, rejects it as too narrow, limiting and distortive. Ironically, much of what Merton tells us does not belong to theory *proper* is (when stripped of its negative connotations) included in Giddens's notion of theory. For Giddens, theory or a theoretical orientation is much more open-textured than Merton or the logical empiricists suggest. Giddens makes a rough heuristic distinction between 'sociological theory' and 'social theory'.

> I use the term 'social theory' to encompass issues that I hold to be the concern of all the social sciences. These issues are to do with the nature of human action and the acting self; with how interaction should be conceptualized and its relation to institutions; and with grasping the practical connotations of social analysis. I understand 'sociology', by contrast, to be not a generic discipline to do with the study of human societies as a whole, but that branch of social science which focuses particularly upon the 'advanced' or modern societies. Such a disciplinary characterization implies an intellectual division of labour, nothing more. While there are theorems and concepts which belong distinctively to the industrialized world, there is no way in which something called 'sociological theory' can be clearly distinguished from the more general concepts and concerns of social theory.

> 'Social theory' is not a term which has any precision, but it is a very useful one for all that. As I represent it, 'social theory' involves the analysis of issues which spill over into philosophy, but it is not primarily a philosophical endeavor ... Social theory has the task of providing conceptions of the nature of human social activity and of the human agent which can be placed in the service of empirical work. The main concern of social theory is the same as that of the social sciences in general: the illumination of concrete processes of social life.   (pp. xvi–xvii)

I have cited the above passage at such length not only because it conveys the flavour of Giddens's understanding of social and sociological theory, but also because it shows how sharply he departs from more 'precise', 'limiting', 'restrictive' logical empiricist conceptions of theory. We can see how far Giddens is from logical empiricists (and an earlier generation of methodologically self-conscious social scientists) who were obsessed with the problem of sharply demarcating scientific theory from what is taken to be non-scientific or pseudo-scientific speculation. But this more open-textured conception of theory harbours its own problems. It is so open that one has difficulty discerning what does and does not belong to a theoretical orientation.

(2)   Giddens clearly wants to distance himself from the specific conception of 'critical theory' employed by the Frankfurt School, and especially as it is used by Jürgen Habermas. He categorically rejects 'the programme of grounding critical theory because I want to set up the idea of two houses, neither of which is a safe house, the factual and the moral critical house that you move between'.[7] He tells us 'I use the term critical theory, but I don't really have in

_____

[7] See 'Historical Materialism Today', 74.

mind anything that has connections with Frankfurt writings from which the term obviously springs.'[8] But informing us about what he is 'against' and why he opposes it does not yet clarify what he is advocating.

> I want to follow the strategy of, so to speak, firing critical salvos into reality and attempting to focus them around those issues that I mentioned before: the distinctiveness of the modern world, the implications of that by contrast to the traditional world, what this leaves in the way of obvious formulae for political theory and then how one can, as it were, spin a web around them. I don't really think that I'd support any programme of trying to ground critical theory, but nor will I support the opposite, that is the idea of a purely immanent critique or ungroundable form of critique. I would probably work more from within a sociological conception which would seem to me to suggest that some things are clearly noxious and other things are clearly desirable and that it isn't necessary to ground them in order to proclaim this to be so.[9]

But however attractive one may find this pluralistic and foxlike understanding of critique, one can still have the uneasy feeling that Giddens is not facing, but rather, dodging, some tough issues. Let me pursue this in detail.

Sometimes in speaking of the critical function of social science, Giddens appeals to what may be labelled the 'minimalist' conception of critique. Any theoretical orientation, no matter how open it is, which has *some* determinate content will rule out some other theoretical orientations. In this minimal sense, every theory has a critical import. If, for example, we accept structuration theory as valid, then we must reject functionalism or structuralism. But not only is this minimalist sense of critique reversible (if functionalism is valid, then we would reject structuration theory); it is a characteristic of theory in every discipline. So this minimalist conception, although quite important when assessing *specific* competing theories, does not carry us very far in grasping what if anything is distinctive about critical social science.

Sometimes Giddens confuses the issue of the *practical* consequences of social science on the social world with its *critical* impact. This is evident in his appeal to the example of Machiavelli's discourse on the state and sovereignty – an example he uses in *The Constitution of Society* (pp. 350–4) and in other writings. His basic point is that the very concepts of state and sovereignty forged by Machiavelli became constitutive of the social reality that individuals confronted. Human beings began to think and act in a 'new' social reality. This example is intended to illustrate the 'massive practical impact on the social world' of social thinking. Now although I agree with much of what Giddens says about Machiavelli and the ways in which his discourse was appropriated and embodied in social reality, I *fail* to see how this is sufficient to clarify the critical function of social science and theory. Giddens does show that social science is not merely epiphenomenal, that it can and does have practical influences, even a massive impact on our everyday lives. But did we need Giddens to tell us this? Consider the many ways in which classical and

---

[8] Ibid., 77.   [9] Ibid., 72.

neo-classical economics have deeply influenced the ways in which we think, talk and act. 'Cost–benefit' analysis not only seeps down into our everyday language but has influenced the ways in which people think about their careers or even their sex lives. Or think of the many ways in which psychological jargon has infected and affected contemporary bourgeois life, especially in affluent societies – a theme that Philip Reiff, Christopher Lasch and Alasdair MacIntyre emphasize in their sociological analyses of contemporary life. Here are instances where social science (economics and psychology) has had 'a massive practical impact on the social world', but this scarcely shows that 'social science is necessarily connected to critical theory, in some sense of the term'. To show this, to really confront the question of the critical function of social science, one must clarify precisely what is (or ought to be) the relation of social science to critical judgements – whether these be the critical judgements of social theorists and investigators or the participants in a social interaction. One can agree with Giddens that 'furthering the critical character of social science means fostering a developed conceptual awareness of the practical connotations of its own discourse' (p. 353), but such 'a developed conceptual awareness' requires something 'more' if it is to be genuinely critical. It requires some standards or criteria for making critical discriminations about these 'practical connotations'.

Giddens himself distinguishes a 'technological' critical function which is characteristic of the application of the theories and findings of the natural sciences from the critical function of the social sciences. He tells us that

> the social sciences, unlike natural sciences, are inevitably involved in a 'subject–subject relation' with what they are about. The theories and findings of the natural sciences are separate from the universe of objects and events which they concern. This ensures that the relation between scientific knowledge and the object world remains a 'technological' one, in which the accumulated knowledge is applied to an independently constituted set of phenomena. But in the social sciences the situation is different. As Charles Taylor puts it: 'While natural science theory also transforms practice, the practice it transforms is not what the theory is about ... We think of it as an "application" of the theory.' In the social sciences, 'the practice is the object of the theory. Theory in this domain transforms its own object.'   (p. 348)

The above claim is a variation on a theme that has been persistent in Giddens's work – the 'double hermeneutic' of social science and theory. (See his Glossary, p. 374, for a succinct characterization of 'double hermeneutic'.) But even if we accept some form of Giddens's 'double hermeneutic' thesis, this still leaves open crucial questions about the critical function of social science and social theory. First, as Giddens knows and has shown, a 'technological' attitude or approach is not unique to the application of the findings and theories of the natural sciences. This is precisely the attitude that many policy social scientists adopt in using the findings of the social sciences. The fact that the 'application' of such findings may transform the objects they concern (i.e., human beings) does not in any way call into question the possibility or success of such technological application of social scientific findings. We can use the techniques of behavioural modification to eliminate undesirable behavioural symptoms or to brainwash human beings. The critical question still remains open: to what ends or purposes are we to use our 'scientific knowledge'? Secondly, even if we do justice to Giddens's point that, in many cases, the participants – the subjects studied – can and do appropriate what the social investigator discovers, this still leaves open important questions about the critical use of social scientific knowledge.

Giddens extensively analyses Paul Willis's study (*Learning to Labour*) of working-class children in a school located in a poor area of Birmingham. He thinks of this as an exemplary piece of research that is theoretically suggestive when approached from the point of view of structuration theory. But despite Giddens's own illuminating discussion of this research, he leaves us with a crucial ambiguity concerning the critical function of social science. To the extent that Willis enables us to understand 'the lads' in this school situation, and even how much they practically know about how authority works and how they can react to it, this information can be used in radically different ways. It can be used by the 'authorities' to increase their 'efficiency' and 'effectiveness' in the schools. Or it may be used by 'the lads' or those sympathetic with them to unmask and call into question the legitimacy of these authorities. We can still ask who will use this knowledge, and for what ends. In short, I do not think Giddens himself has provided us with a sufficiently determinate grasp of the critical function of social theory to distinguish it from what he opposes, i.e., the 'technological' application of social knowledge. This even becomes clear in his analysis of social 'contradictions'. Giddens wants to defend the applicability of the concept of contradiction for social analysis. There are real social structural contradictions (which are not to be confused with social conflicts). The concepts of contradiction and conflict need to be carefully distinguished. Structural contradiction is the 'disjunction of structural principles of system organization', while conflict is 'struggle between actors or collectivities expressed as definite social practices' (p. 198). Contradictions may (but also may not) breed conflict. But it is hard to see what is the difference that makes a difference between this concept of contradiction and what functionalists labelled 'systemic dysfunctions'. Once again the critical question is left open. Even if we grant the 'legitimacy' of Giddens's concept of a structural contradiction, our approach may be one of seeking to diffuse conflict, finding some way to ameliorate or eliminate the pernicious effects of such a contradiction (without significantly modifying a 'social system', *or* seeking to foster the type of conflict where actors become 'aware of their interests [and] are able and motivated to act on them . . . ' (p. 199). (Needless to say, these are not the only two alternatives.)

Let me conclude by posing the problem in the strongest possible way that I think Giddens has dodged. Giddens may well find all the talk of grounding critical theory intellectually abhorrent and unnecessary. But he must at least squarely face the issue that such a project is intended to confront. What, if anything, is the basis for our critical judgements and proposals? How are we to warrant these critical judgements? (And who is or ought to be this 'we'?) We do not have to endorse some 'bad' form of foundationalism to appreciate the legitimacy of these questions. Otherwise 'firing critical salvos into reality' will be like shooting in the dark. Giddens is clearly uncomfortable with the either/or posed by Weber versus Habermas where we 'must' *either* acknowledge that the norms to which we appeal in making critical social judgements cannot be rationally justified *or* acknowledge that they are based on rational 'foundations'. This either/or has defined the conceptual space for reflecting on the character of social science as a critical discipline in the twentieth century. If there is a way of escaping this either/or, Giddens has (not yet) shown it. Giddens fails to realize how much of what he says is compatible with the 'technological' attitude that he opposes. For he leaves open the question *who* is to use social knowledge and to what ends. I do not think that Giddens gets any closer to answering these questions when he emphasizes the practical consciousness and knowledgeability of social agents and the double hermeneutic of social science.

The issues I have been raising about the meaning, role and warranted basis for critical social science are central for Giddens's *own* understanding of structuration theory. Until and unless he clarifies and squarely faces these issues, there is a serious danger that structuration theory will turn into the very opposite of what Giddens intends, and that it will be haunted by the dilemmas and *aporias* that face any social theory that avoids confronting its critical function.

2
Hermeneutics and modern social theory

ZYGMUNT BAUMAN

In contemporary social theory Anthony Giddens occupies a place all of his own. The very volume of his contribution is difficult to match; less usual still is the range and centrality of topics which, with varying degrees of comprehensiveness, he has addressed. Particularly rare is the ambitious intent of Giddens's theorizing; it has been aimed, right from the start a decade or so ago, at nothing less than a critical reassessment of theoretical lore, leading to the articulation of a new theoretical canon for sociology to come. The non-partisan nature of Giddens's partisanship is unique; and the declared purpose of his effort is to integrate, not to divide, and thus to offer notoriously fissiparous sociological theory the unity it never enjoyed before. Giddens's theory has been to date, and promises to remain, a wide and hospitable river which admits and absorbs pure waters carried by each and every mountain spring as well as drawing on ample subterranean currents. For all these reasons, his theoretical work is a radical departure from purposes and practices of sociological theorizing well-nigh universal in recent years. To a considerable number of present-day sociologists, this work is unprecedented in their collective memory: no wonder it attracts widespread attention and gives rise to great expectations. It also invites close scrutiny.

The really close scrutiny Giddens's work deserves is beyond my ability. Giddens's power of synthesis has few equals, but its products are scattered over a large number of writings which themselves demand a synthesizing effort; many a formulation represents a stage in the development of an as yet incomplete theory, and has been (or is likely to be) superseded at some later stage. A full assessment of the new theory is not possible without its final, positive presentation, which – given the spiral fashion in which Giddens's ideas develop – is not likely to be made soon. Hence the following comments cannot claim more finality than their subject. Insofar as most of Giddens's published work to date bears a clear mark of 'progress reports', my own remarks can only be, at most, 'reports on progress reports'. Even so, they are unlikely to be equal to the task of an analysis as wide-ranging and erudite as Giddens's unique project would require; and this is because of my own shortcomings.

In his own words, Giddens's purpose is the elaboration of a hermeneutically informed social theory. This involves, on the substantive level, the development of the idea of 'structuration', meant to replace *both* the concept of 'structure' as bequeathed by the natural-scientific tradition in sociology and the idea of 'free agent' lingering in social science as a constant reminder of its utilitarian origin. On the level of methodology, a hermeneutically informed social theory would require, above all, a 'double hermeneutics', taking note of the essential identity of the linguistic medium from which both the social reality and its sociological account are woven.

The sought-for hermeneutically informed social theory – so Giddens has repeatedly asserted – will constitute a decisive departure from the 'orthodox consensus' (comprising the acceptance of the alleged 'natural-scientific' model, functionalism and the theory of industrial society), and will simultaneously put paid to the theoretical disarray which followed its demise.

Since (to paraphrase Borges' adage) each theory creates its own predecessors, the advent of hermeneutically informed social theory as, it is hoped, the new consensus of social science would require a thorough rewriting of sociological history, structured as it was before by the self-awareness of the 'orthodox consensus'. In particular, one would need to revise the belief in the centrality of the 'problem of order' as well as to explode the myth of the conservative provenance of sociology.

This summary comes nowhere near doing justice to the richness and complexity of Giddens's manifold concerns. But it does pinpoint, as far as I can see, the main articulations of the project. These are, after all, the recurrent themes to which he returns with each successive loop of the spiral. What follows is my discussion of these themes. I hope, therefore, that however incommensurate with Giddens's project, this discussion will relate to its strategically paramount topics.

'Hermeneutically informed social theory' in historical perspective

There is little doubt that Giddens's project lies at the very heart of contemporary sociological discourse. It draws its urgency from the most poignant afflictions of present-day sociology and sets about meeting its strongest-felt needs. The dissipation of a secure world in which sociology had been safely anchored led to a panic-stricken search for a substitute haven. Disenchanted with manifestly insolvent systems, sociology has embarked on a reconnaissance of heretofore poorly charted territories in the hope of discovering new guarantors of security. Most sociologists travelled to places which seemed promising in this respect precisely because the bluff of systemic control over them has been resoundingly called, to the actors, their motives, their meanings. Collective amnesia combined with the Columbus complex (both well documented, in relation to a similar episode, by Pitirim Sorokin) set the pendulum of shifting sociological concerns in full swing and helped it to reach fast the point where kinetic energy is reduced to zero and the only movement possible is a swing backward. It is against this historically specific background

that Giddens's project acquires its particular significance. It promises to sift
out valuable finds from the recent expedition and mark the tracks which
proved blind; but it promises as well to salvage precious elements of the old
tradition only too hastily abandoned and condemned in the universal stam-
pede towards new-found fad idols. Recognizing that no more mileage is left in
the direction sociology took in recent years, Giddens's project – like all
attempts at synthesis – promises to stop the pendulum, just about to start its
backward swing, before it reaches the other extreme from which sociology
tried to escape just a couple of decades ago.

But there is no doubt either that Giddens's project lies at the very heart of
sociology as a 'discursive formation' – this supra-temporal, lasting and self-
reproducing set of 'sites of authority', 'surfaces of delineation', and the problems generated in the co-operation of the two which underlies the mystery of
continuity achieved through epistemological breaks, and of reciprocal mean-
ingfulness between logically contradictory propositions. Indeed, it was the
incessant effort to solve the puzzle of purposeful action of knowledgeable
actors producing 'unintended consequences', or of the evident incapacity of
'free actors' to exercise their freedom in the course of end-orientated action, or
of the stubborn tendency of the multitude of individual actions to sediment
into a reality independent of these actions and in its turn making the action
dependent on itself which, for all intents and purposes, constituted the history
of sociology. Marx's blunt statement about people who make history but not
under conditions of their choice drew the 'surface' along which all important
problems of sociology have been 'delineated'; or only those problems constituted a part of the discursive formation of sociology which had been delineated
along this surface. Giddens's project, by its very centrality, is another, but
certainly not the first, attempt to prevent this surface from generating mutually incongruent or incompatible solutions. If one more try is needed, it is
not because no one made the attempt before, but because the history of
sociology thus far has been a graveyard of failed attempts to overcome theoretically the practical contradiction of the human condition: the contradiction
between people making history (society, system, structure etc.) and history
(society, system, structure etc.) making people. The theories trying to overcome the contradiction are too many to mention. Suffice it to remember Marx
(consider his famous 'Freedom, Equality, Bentham' paradox in *Capital*),
Durkheim, Weber, Simmel, Mead and Thomas. And, indeed, Parsons. Or
Elias.

It is useful to remind ourselves that the project which took Talcott Parsons
half a century to develop (if not to complete for universal satisfaction) had
been triggered off by his concern with very much the same dilemma that lends
urgency to Giddens's work. Parsons embarked on *The Structure of Social Action*,
the thousand-page-long manifesto of his own version of a 'hermeneutically
informed social theory', because he was appalled by the inability of utili-
tarianism (positivism as applied to the study of humans – Parsons's then vision

of the 'orthodox consensus') to square the circle of the human condition. Parsons articulated the latter as the dilemma between voluntariness and the evident non-randomness of human action. Positivistic thought – Parsons complained – 'is caught in the "utilitarian dilemma"'. That is, either the active agency of the actor in the choice of ends is an independent factor in action, and the end element must be random; or the objectionable implication of the randomness of ends is denied, but then their independence disappears and they are assimilated to the conditions of the situation, that is to elements analyzable in terms of nonsubjective categories, principally heredity and environment ... '[1] Parsons perceived that in so far as the natural-scientific model is forced by the 'orthodox consensus' of positivism upon the study of social reality, the only way of accounting for the empirical regularity (non-randomness) of actors' behaviour is the assumption of some sort of 'determinism' – be it biological, social–environmental or structural (in the last case, the postulate of the essential rationality of action may be used as a linchpin).

It is against this vicious circle of the positivist handling of the 'voluntariness – nonrandomness' dilemma that Parsons rebelled. 'As opposed to all types of positivistic theory the basic tenet of the voluntaristic is that neither positively nor negatively does the methodological scheme of scientifically valid knowledge exhaust the significant subjective elements of action.'[2] To Parsons, actors must be conceived of as knowledgeable – as his witty example of potato-baking in the highlands of Peru was meant to demonstrate. Actors are knowledgeable much in the same sense as the one discussed later by Schutz in reference to Carneades' ideas of *periodeusis*: 'scanning' the context of their action, actors know how to discern the 'situational conditions' which must be respected and the resources which can be employed with a reasonable chance of success. This is, in Parsons's as much as in Schutz's view, all the knowledge the actor needs to act in a way amenable to the description in terms of ends and means, i.e., to act meaningfully. Though different words had been used, Parsons would recognize immediately his own strategic design in Giddens's assumptions of 'capability' or 'practical consciousness' of the actor.

Parsons would also rediscover his own original hopes in Giddens's determination that 'neither subject (human agent) nor object ("society", or social institutions) should be regarded as having primacy. *Each is constituted in and through recurrent practices.*' It was, after all, Parsons at the start of his half-century-long journey who promised, 'in transcending the positivist–idealist dilemma, to show a way of transcending also the old individualism–social organism or, as it is often called, social nominalism–realism dilemma which has plagued social theory to little purpose for so long'.[3]

Whatever Parsons did, he never assigned to the question of 'primacy' any

---

[1] Talcott Parsons, *The Structure of Social Action* (Free Press, 1949), p. 64.
[2] Ibid., p.81.   [3] Ibid., p. 74.

socio-theoretical importance. In his theoretical scheme, both 'society' and 'individual' had the status of analytical projections from the only empirically accessible unit of knowledge – social action. Both were, to use Husserlian terms, 'transcendental conditions' of action, *noema* constituted in the process of *noesis* originating from the idea of social action; the question of primacy was therefore invalidated a priori by the very epistemological status of both concepts. In Parsons's own words, 'the action frame of reference may be said to have what many, following Husserl, have called a "phenomenological" status. It involves no concrete data that can be "thought away", that are subject to change. It is not a phenomenon in the empirical sense. It is the indispensable logical framework in which we describe and think about the phenomena of action'.[4] 'Personality and social system are very intimately interrelated, but they are neither identical with one another nor explicable by one another'.[5] Anyone who wrote that social system should be seen as the 'stabilised and reinforced ... cumulative and balanced resultant of many selections of many individuals'[6] would not disown Giddens's assertion that '(s)ocial systems are constituted as regularised practices, reproduced across time and space', or his definition of structure as 'recursively organised rules and resources'. Anyone who wrote that 'means are ... the aspects of properties of things which actors by virtue of their knowledge of them and their control are able to alter as desired '[7] would not take issue with Giddens's proposition that '(r)esources are the media whereby power is employed in the routine course of social action; but they are at the same time structural elements of social systems, reconstituted in social interaction'.

The similarity of concerns and purposes is indeed striking; this does not imply, however, that the two resulting projects are identical. Parsons's was, first and foremost, a phenomenological investigation into the essence of social action and the logical process through which this essence apodictically generates some other *noema*, like 'personality' or 'society'. It was perhaps Parsons's undoing that time and again, probably to placate the American reader and to make his own offer more palatable, he departed in his declarations from his true beliefs and interests: one can easily cull from Parsons's writings an impressive number of allusions to the 'empirical' status of described relations, blatantly at odds with the much more seriously advanced claim to their phenomenological (necessary, apodictic, *sine qua non*) modality (with the incongruence between the two modes occasionally patched up by a smug prognosis of the impending convergence of societies, as they are, with the phenomenologically construed models). His weakness made him vulnerable. It invited the vulgarizers, and the critics of vulgarizers' products, to interpret, say, 'systemic prerequisites' as 'imperative demands of the system', instead of as 'conditions of thinkability of the system', as intended. This, in turn, spelled

---

[4] Ibid., p. 733.   [5] Talcott Parsons, *Social System* (Free Press, 1951), p. 7.
[6] Ibid., p. 25.   [7] Talcott Parsons, *The Structure of Social Action*, p. 732.

the doom of Parsons's authority once the right of the system to make demands, and the wisdom of meeting such demands, came to be questioned.

Though Giddens's presentation of basic concepts and their relations is fraught with phenomenological insights, the project as a whole is clearly not another 'search for essences'. This is a self-confessedly empirically orientated project, which locates the links between actors and societies in the actors' practices, rather than in the indispensable features of social action which could be dug up through a process akin to phenomenological reduction. Giddens's discussion of such practices takes the form of empirical description. At least up to the present stage in the development of a 'hermeneutically informed social theory' Giddens's attention seems to have been focused on the task of working out a sociological vocabulary appropriate to such a description of human practice as would be able to accommodate both the 'doing' and the 'suffering' aspects of the human condition.

In the latter respect, Giddens's project bears remarkable affinity with another recent attempt to accomplish a similar task – the 'figurational sociology' of Norbert Elias.

As far as I can judge, the central category in Elias's sociology – 'figuration' – is given a meaning similar, in a number of respects, to the central category of Giddens's project – that of 'structuration'. Both categories are meant to grasp the processual link between the actor and the society; such links as (in Elias's words) render 'the individual' and 'society' 'two different but inseparable levels of the human world'.[8] Elias defines figuration as the 'changing pattern created by the players as a whole – not only by their intellects but by their whole selves, the totality of their dealings in their relationships with each other'.[9] As there is no absolute concentration of power in the hands of any one of the players (compare Giddens's 'dialectic of control') – 'the course of the game is not in the power of any one player'.[10] Hence the appearance of the independence enjoyed by the game in relation to the players' moves. Previous moves of the players sediment, so to speak, into conditions of their later moves, which are thereby 'limited' or 'constrained'. 'Only the progressive interweaving of moves during the game process, and its results – the figuration of the game prior to the twelfth move – can be of service in explaining the twelfth move'.[11]

To account for the apparent autonomy of the game in relation to the players, Elias, like Giddens, employs the concept of 'unintended consequences'. He seems, however, to attach more than epiphenomenal significance to the reality hidden behind the concept. Elias castigates 'so-called action theories' for not being able to step beyond taking into account 'that intentional interactions have unintended consequences'. What in Elias's view action theory, taking the

---

[8] Norbert Elias, *What is Sociology?* (Hutchinson, 1978), p. 129.   [9] Ibid., p. 130.
[10] Ibid., p. 96.
[11] Richard Kilminster, *Praxis and Method* (Routledge & Kegan Paul, 1979), p. 97.

motivated actor as its primary datum, is incapable of grasping is 'a circumstance which is central to sociological theory and practice, namely that unintentional human interdependencies lie at the root of every intentional
interaction'; 'the unplanned course of the game repeatedly influences the
moves of each individual player'; 'people's interdependence as players exerts
constraint over each of the individuals bonded together in this way; the
constraint stems from the particular nature of their relatedness and interdependence as players'.[12]

For Elias, therefore, the autonomy of the game is not a mere illusion. The
experience of the autonomy is real, and its reality derives from the network of
interdependencies already set and fixed the moment any single game has
started. This is a subtle but vital shift in emphasis. It brings back into the sight
of social theory the fact that no social action can be conceived as taking place in
a void or starting from scratch (much as Heidegger's dismissal of theorizing
about Being which is not already 'Being with others'). For a figuration to exist,
there must be already given a set of dependencies between the actors; indeed,
this set is exactly what makes a collection of actors a 'figuration', a social
entity. Once again we find an impressive similarity with Giddens's project:
Giddens devotes much attention to 'unacknowledged conditions' of action
which in the course of interaction are modified by the 'unintended consequences' of otherwise knowledgeable behaviour. Structurally (from the point
of view of the place occupied within the processual model of structuration),
'unacknowledged conditions' are equivalent to Elias's 'interdependencies'.
Substantively, however, there is a significant difference between the two.

Having opted for the concept of 'unacknowledged' conditions, Giddens has
committed himself to the criterion of knowledge (more exactly: awareness) as
a major tool in the typology of the sources of conduct. What, in Giddens's view,
distinguishes his own 'hermeneutically informed theory' from the radical
Wittgensteinianism of Winch is the inclusion in the description of action of the
'unconscious' alongside the 'conscious' sources of behaviour. Giddens insists
that there are some conditions of action of which the actors are not aware.
Hence, what sets these conditions apart and underpins their special status is
the actors' lack of knowledge. Elias, on the other hand, emphasizes the fact
that some of the conditions of action are irretrievably beyond the actors'
control. This lack of control is not merely a function of ignorance, as acquisition of knowledge would not alter the 'supra-individual' status of such
conditions.

'Interdependencies' capture, therefore, a somewhat different aspect of
human action from 'unacknowledged conditions'. They take cognizance of the
fact that actors enter the field of interaction already tied to the other participants not merely through the use of socially shared resources (for instance, use
of words, which 'involves the speakers in the long-term history of the
language'), but through the circumstance that any action one actor or a group

12 Norbert Elias, *What is Sociology?*, pp. 94–6.

of actors may undertake is bound to influence the initiation, the course and the outcome of actions of all other actors or groups belonging to the same 'figuration'. What one actor or group of actors do, makes a difference to what other actors or a group of actors may do and achieve; and the volume and direction of this difference is in no way related to the degree of awareness of any of the actors of the genuine nature of their interdependence. Knowledge has indeed considerable bearing on what the actors do; but not on what they may do nor what the outcome of their doing might be. Thus the appearance of two hunting tribes on a ground with game too scarce to meet the feeding requirements of both, or the appearance of one hundred applicants for one available university lectureship, renders the figurations in which the tribes or the applicants are inadvertently cast a 'zero-sum' game, making the failure of some the condition of the success of others, co-operation between participants pragmatically non-viable, and mutual antagonism the rational way of adaptation. None of the participants, however knowledgeable, can change this 'figurational logic'; this, in Elias's view, is the substance of the 'autonomy' of figuration in relation to psychological capabilities of actors – a circumstance which supplies sociology with its subject-matter.

There is one more feature of 'interdependency', as distinct from 'unacknowledged sources of action', which is worth mentioning. The concept of interdependence (better still, 'network of dependencies') couples the idea of the preconditions of action from the start to the recognition of the differentiation of actors and their capabilities in virtue of their involvement in the figuration. If 'knowledgeability' is a quality which may, in principle, be evenly distributed between the partners of the interaction, the idea of 'dependency network' lifts into prominence the potential asymmetry of the location within figuration. If interdependency constrains the actors, it constrains different actors in different ways. Not just the information about universal circumstances of 'human actors' as such, but a lot of quite specific information about peculiar limitations of action and its prospective outcomes in the case of prisoners and prison guards, parents and children, generals and privates, 'established' and 'outsiders' etc. can be read from the scrutiny of the figuration itself before hermeneutics is applied to the deeds of its actors. This is what, presumably, Elias understood by his precept that 'actions and ideas cannot be explained and understood if they are considered on their own; they need to be understood and explained within the framework' of figuration.[13]

Elias's and Giddens's projects are two reactions to the disaffection with Parsons's attempt to solve the central dilemma of sociology (and particularly against the 'era of hypostasis' into which Parsons's domination of the sociological scene degenerated). The two projects have much in common; they also share much with the theory they set out to overcome (most obviously, its original hopes). They also, however, differ from each other in some important respects. I think that the essential difference between the two projects can (not

13 Ibid., p. 96.

without risk) be summarized in the following way: Giddens wants to solve the central sociological dilemma with a theory which incorporates *both* the voluntary and knowledgeable agent and the system (even if defined aetiologically, as 'reproduced'). Elias wants to accomplish the same task with a theory which makes *both* redundant. Giddens's strategy puts him dangerously close to Parsons; much effort will be needed to prevent the 'hermeneutically informed theory' from taking at some point the turn which confounded Parsons's hopes. Elias's strategy, though proposed almost a century ago by Simmel, has not yet been put to a conclusive test.

On 'structuration'

Along with 'double hermeneutics', 'structuration' is the key concept in Giddens's 'hermeneutically informed social theory'.

Introducing the idea of structuration, Giddens legitimizes his venture by the twin needs of avoiding the traps of an 'objectivist' social theory ('in which human agency appears only as the determined outcome of social causes') and staving off the threat of 'sliding into subjectivism' – the fate which the initial over-eager reactions to the collapse of Parsons's dominion were not careful enough to escape. But the nub of the matter – the very reason why one should bother with coining concepts like 'structuration' – is, for Giddens, the need to 'recover the subject' as a 'reasoning, acting being'.

The goal which is to be served by the new concept is twofold: on the one hand, to dethrone the concept of 'structure' as an external, pre-existing determinant of action; on the other, to deny the random or entirely self-propelled character of actors' behaviour. I have observed before that this dual purpose, but for the updated vocabulary, is a restatement of the dual concern which triggered Parsons's work in *The Structure of Social Action*.

In the end Giddens has not disposed of the concept of 'structure' altogether. He has retained it, however, in a subsidiary, 'meta-structuration', role. The concept of structure has been shifted from the realm of objects to the realm of rules. Since human actions have a 'structurating' character, and not just that of a Brownian movement, one can – starting from recognition of their regularity – identify 'structures' 'as sets or matrices of rule-resource properties governing transformations'. And thus once again structure 'governs' action, though this time in the algebraic rather than mechanical sense. Whatever the sense, the redefined structure remains as before outside the realm of action. 'Structuration' refers to the agents' mediation between 'unacknowledged conditions' and 'unintended consequences' of action, which in their turn become, as one would guess, conditions for the further activity of the agents. But it does not refer, as far as I can see, to questioning, negotiating or transforming the rules of mediation themselves, i.e., the 'structures' in their new formulations. The change of definition notwithstanding, structures are still exempt from the 'structuring' potency of human agents. The substitution of the plural 'structures' for Lévi-Strauss's universal 'structure' adds to the mystery, rather than solving it, as we now feel ignorant not just about the aetiology of structure, but also about the mechanism responsible for its differentiation, influence between structures, diffusion, etc. On the other hand, a case can be made that having redefined 'structure' as he did, Giddens uses the term 'structure' very much as Parsons used 'culture', to denote the set of rules/resources which normatively govern social action. One could surmise that were Giddens, in a later stage of his project, to confront the task of spelling out and classifying the rules structures are the sets of, he would in all likelihood end up with a description similar in principle to the famous Parsons typology of cultural norms (cognitive, cathectic, evaluative etc.).

Once again the need to account for the non-randomness of action has led to the postulation of an outer force (be it substantive or normative) which circumscribes the action without being circumscribed by it. To say, with Giddens, that 'social systems are not structures; they have structures or, more accurately, exhibit structural properties', shifts the initial worry into a different place, but in no way dispels it. And Giddens needs some sort of an outer force; having, not unlike Parsons, selected motivated action as the nub of the sought-for social theory, he must postulate an outer force lest he should slide into 'random voluntarism' of a utilitarian kind.

In its most elementary, school-independent essence, the idea of structure conveys the recognition of the fact that in a certain set of events probabilities are not distributed at random: in other words, that some events, given sufficiently long time and a large volume of cases, are more likely to take place than their alternatives. Well before it is given sophisticated theoretical articulation (more often than not suffused with aetiological hypotheses) the term 'structure' is used far and wide to encapsulate such elementary observation as 'a black girl from New Cross is much less likely to become a City manager than a white Etonian applying to Oxford', 'the odds are that, among a thousand people of fifty years old, fewer weddings will occur next year than among a thousand people of twenty years old', 'workers in a car plant are more likely to go on strike after announcement of a pay freeze than on hearing of the radical increase in unemployment figures'. At this level, 'structure' simply denotes the commonsensically evident feature of social reality: not everything may (normally) happen, and some events are more likely to happen than some others.

The difficulty starts when social theorists, ostensibly pursuing the task of 'defining', 'clarifying', or otherwise making the concept precise, attempt in fact to substitute the 'how' question for the 'what' question; when, in other words, they try to explain how the structure comes into being and how 'it' 'operates'. Then, and only then, the danger appears. The name of the danger is hypostasis.

In daily speech, hypostasis is common. We find it normally helpful, often indispensable, seldom confusing. We say 'the river flows', 'the rain falls', 'wind is blowing'. Hypostasis in such figures of speech remains harmless, since we don't ask 'What is the river by itself, independently of its manifestation in flowing?', 'What does the wind do when it does not blow?', or 'What is the rain like when it does not fall?' We do not seriously suppose, therefore, that the river is an object which flows in the same way as the rifle fires, or that wind is an 'outer force' whose activity consists in blowing. We do not suppose all these things, and yet we find the quasi-hypostasizing forms of expression convenient. Presumably, we feel the need of 'condensing' the verb, which refers to an activity, into a noun, because we wish to report the steadiness, regularity, resilience of the activity in question: 'the flowing' is constantly along the same trajectory; the air or the waterdrops move steadily in one direction, and not the many others. As long as this is what we do, the logical error of hypostasis does not materialize and does not confound the clarity of our thinking. It is not at all difficult, in daily speech, to limit the uses of a noun in order to prevent the suggestion that the noun represents something more than steady movement from being taken seriously.

The less our speech is subject to the constraints of daily life ('constraints' means here the virtual elimination of occasions for semantic self-reflection), the more distant its referent from direct experience, the more suffused the content of speech with mediating and secondary interpretations, the easier it is for the quasi-hypostasizing habits of speech to produce, through recursive practices of theory, the logical errors of hypostasis. The concepts of 'system', 'society', 'culture' – and, indeed, structure – supply radical examples of such a situation.

Without the intervention of theoretical reflection, a phrase like 'structure constrains' conveys merely a simple observation that the probability of people doing something differs depending on who the people in question are. It hardly occurs to the non-theoretical speaker that somewhere a 'thing' waiting to be dubbed 'structure' can be found which actually confines people's movement (remember the arduous efforts of Durkheim to convince his readers, against all their thinking habits, that moral norms could and should be treated as things; and consider the experience of our annual ritual of selling the idea to our first-year students).

The substantive form in which the idea of 'structure' is expressed does not necessarily entail commitment to determinism; nor does it imply the denial of the processual or reproductive character of social differentiation. Both the commitment and the denial are 'value-added' to the idea of structure at the stage of explanation and theoretical modelling. By itself, 'structure' connotes merely the regularity with which the allocation of social positions and actions tends to reproduce itself over time. This elementary meaning of 'structure' was cleansed from theoretical distortions and brought into relief again when Giddens proposed to encapsulate it in the concept of structuration.

But Giddens did more than this. Having removed from the concept of structure its elementary content, for which a new term has been devised, he left the old concept to denote only the theoretical shell: the very thing which caused our disaffection with the idea of structure as used or abused in theoretical practice. I am afraid that – contrary to Giddens's intentions – so 'purified' a concept of structure will be yet more, rather than less, exposed to the dangers of becoming the 'metaphysical prop' of the new, 'hermeneutically orientated' social theory. Even more than before it may offer itself as the needed 'determinant' to all those who would wish to ask and to answer the question *why* people act as they do, and stubbornly so. Moreover, after being separated from the mechanism and the process of structuration, 'structure' appears more than ever to be a name for an 'outer force', a prerequisite no action can do without and no action can affect.

I do not believe, therefore, that the noxious duality of action and its external determinants has been truly overcome by the conceptualization Giddens proposes. If anything, it has been restated and rearticulated; in a sense, even reinforced – through transforming an internal confusion inside the concept of structure into an overt opposition of two separate concepts.

In his attempt to reconceptualize sociological inquiry Norbert Elias was moved, much as was Anthony Giddens, by the theoretical abuse of the concept of structure, which, as Elias felt, had been perverted beyond repair. The coining of 'figuration' was, in a way, an attempt to flee from the hopelessly distorted uses of a discredited term in order to recover its pristine and still valid content. What Elias supposed, however, was that in order to do so it is not enough to substitute new, freshly defined terms for the old ones, too entangled with improper interpretations to be salvaged. In order to restore the elementary intuition encapsulated in the idea of structure as the regularity of social interaction, it is necessary as well to dispose of 'social action' (almost by definition, but certainly by application, meaning 'individual action') as the centre-piece of social theory. Once social action is retained as the 'basic unit' of the sociological model, as the 'thing to be explained', the rest follows relentlessly. After all, no one has successfully challenged the accuracy of Parsons's contention that the opposition between personality, culture and society, as well as the opposition between 'the actor' and 'the system', is irremovably contained in the essence of 'social action'. Indeed, phenomenological analysis can show them to be apodictically necessary. It seems that Elias concluded that to continue to build a social theory out from and around the concept of social action and to hope that one can still escape the 'mistakes' of one's predecessors is futile. Hence not only the recovery of the original idea of structure (with its *Aufhebung* of the oppositions between continuity and change, action and system, voluntarism and determination), not only the encapsulation of this idea of the 'structured' character of social interaction in a new term, unburdened by improper uses, but also the substitution of this idea for social action as the axis of sociological theorizing.

The result is a 'figurational sociology' rather than a corrected version of 'social action theory'. Apparently, Elias did not believe that the latter could be rectified, as social action itself is a false beginning for social theory. One can say that Elias's 'figuration' differs from 'social action' much as Heidegger's 'Dasein' differed from Husserl's 'transcendental subjectivity', thereby avoiding the hopeless task of generating an 'inter-subjective world'. The social reality from which Elias starts his theorizing is *ursprünglich* one of interdependencies, and hence provides for regular differentiality of actions and their consequences. The message contained in this choice is that one cannot conceive of social reality amenable to theorizing other than already 'structured'. The idea of a social actor ready to act but needing norms and resources to do so is as preposterous as the idea of the system needing some 'functional prerequisites' to remain one. Unlike 'action' or 'system', 'figuration' is a phenomenologically self-sustained and self-explanatory entity, and as such does not have needs or prerequisites. It is, therefore, immune to hypostasis.

In promoting the idea of structuration, Giddens intended to achieve, for the understanding of social action, the same emancipatory act Spinoza had accomplished regarding our treatment of nature, when he proclaimed *Natura* to be both *naturans* and *naturata*. What has been left in the shadow, however, is the circumstance that the two aspects of 'structuration' – 'structuring' and 'being structured' – are, as far as the actors are concerned, distributed unevenly. Some are in a position to 'structure' more than to 'be structured'; some others, on the contrary, are more likely to 'be structured' than to 'structure'. This crucially important aspect of social reality has been well incorporated and assigned a paramount role in the concept of 'figuration'. It cannot be well assimilated in the idea of social action once the latter is considered on a level of generality similar to the notorious 'man as such', 'man as species being', etc. Hence, contrary to the original intention, a social theory which starts from the idea of action confronting the task of structuration, rather than from the recognition of an-already-structured-world, will inevitably generate the need for some 'metaphysical prop' to account for the empirically evident uneven distribution of probabilities.

On 'double hermeneutics'

Following Winch, Giddens introduces the idea of 'double hermeneutics' in the context of the relationship between the vernacular of lay members of society and the technical language artificially created and employed by the scientists. The context, and the worries it tends to spawn, are peculiar to the social sciences, since the objects of natural scientists do not have an equivalent to ordinary language, and hence the artificial language of science is the only language for scientists to interpret and to understand.

Double hermeneutics, therefore, has been legitimized in terms of the issues entailed in the inter-linguistic communication, or the mutual translatability, of the two languages. Since both are languages, the task of translation

appears to be a matter-of-fact one. As in all similar cases, we need diction-
aries, rules of correspondence, some knowledge of idioms etc. However,
this does not by itself support the idea of double hermeneutics. The need for
double hermeneutics is, one would suspect, only apparently rooted in the mere
need for translation. Something more is involved. It seems that the concerns of
double hermeneutics derive not so much from the ordinary worries of translation as from the attempt to justify an exceptional intention to attain rules of
translation which, by their nature, are applicable only one way. Or, put more
generally, they derive from the conflict over authority to declare the correct-
ness of the translation.

Giddens's formulations do not render this truth apparent. The controversy
which double hermeneutics is hoped to solve has been presented as one
over who is to understand what, rather than over who has the authority to
declare the propriety of the translation. Giddens disagrees with Schutz's
precept that social-scientific concepts, to be adequate, must 'be understood by
the actors themselves in terms of their own concepts'. In his rejoinder, Giddens
takes the view that it is not the condition of adequacy for social-scientific
concepts that the actors whose conduct is being described should be 'able to
grasp' them. This, however, does not meet Schutz's point in full. Or, rather,
Giddens's rejoinder implies a somewhat limited interpretation of Schutz's
precept. The problem, as Giddens seems to articulate it, is one of knowledge or
ignorance of a language; if a contest of rights is involved, it is only a conflict
over the social scientist's right to employ a technical language which has not
been mastered by the objects of social scientific study. Moreover, it is not clear
from Giddens's argument what useful purpose could be served by the objects
of study mastering this language in due course – since the adequacy of social
scientific hermeneutics depends, according to Giddens, solely 'upon the social
scientific observer accurately understanding the concepts whereby the actors'
conduct is orientated'. But this response glosses over another, more trouble-
some, postulate potentially contained in Schutz's principle, and related to an
issue Giddens does not confront: who is to judge the 'accuracy' of understanding?

Two different issues reside side by side in Schutz's postulate. One is the
issue of the social scientist's right to develop and employ his own language,
and hence express his observations and their interpretations in a vocabulary
different from the one which is used by the objects of these observations to
account for and to interpret their actions. Another is the issue of the authority
of the social scientist to impute (in whatever language) to the actors motives
and orientations which they would not recognize as their own. The first is the
issue of linguistic form. The second is of the contents which one language or
another expresses in mutually translatable forms. Giddens takes a stand on the
first issue. But he glosses over the second. Moreover, he presents his views in a
way which is open to the following interpretation: he implies that recognition

of the social scientist's right contested in the first issue (something easily granted) grants by proxy the authority contested in the second (something demanding much more complex argument, once faced point-blank).

The second issue in its turn is a blend of two distinct problems, largely autonomous and calling for a separate argument. The first problem is one of the necessity, desirability or just relevance of the consensus between social scientists and their objects. Is the negotiation of findings an integral part of their verification? Is the process of truth-finding contained wholly in the social scientist's study? Does the social scientist have the final (and the only relevant) say in deciding the adequacy of his description? The second problem is the old question of the meaning of hermeneutics as turned upon social life: what is to be understood? In terms of what should the social scientist interpret the conduct of his objects? Consequently, what, if anything, is to be negotiated with the objects in the course of the verification of his findings?

As we are only too well aware, the second problem has a history as long as sociology itself. For many a decade it was discussed in terms of the opposition between 'explaining' and 'understanding'. Weber and his disciples set about transcending this opposition by assimilating the task of explaining to that of understanding and proving that understanding *is* the scientific way of explaining social phenomena. It was Weber who coined the phrase 'explanatory understanding', which was intended to wed once and for all the task of explanation in social science to that of the study and reproduction of the motives of actors. This, however, if taken literally, came dangerously close to the assigning to the actors themselves of the supreme and final authority over the description of their actions, and to the undermining of the authority of the social scientist. The danger has been staved off from the start by the stratagem of 'unconscious motives' (much like '5 pm on the Sun', as Wittgenstein would jibe). The threatened position of the social scientist had been reinforced by the assertion that '(i)n the great majority of cases actual action goes on in a state of inarticulate half-consciousness or actual unconsciousness of its subjective meaning'.[14] Hence the motive (of the actor's action) could be defined as 'a complex of subjective meaning which seems to the actor himself *or* [my italics] to the observer an adequate ground for the conduct in question'.[15] Ostensibly, such a definition puts the actor and his observer on an equal footing: your explanation is as good as mine. Lest this should land social analysis in the plight of perpetual inconclusiveness, the equality is immediately qualified: 'it is the task of a sociologist' 'to describe and analyse' the motives even though they have not 'actually been concretely part of the conscious "intention" of the actor'.[16] With one master stroke, two worries are disposed of: the threat to the social scientist's authority to adjudicate in the question of 'true understanding', and the threat to his scientific status contained in the idea of understanding as a congenial experience of somebody else's thoughts and feelings. The

[14] Max Weber, *Theory of Social and Economic Organization* (Free Press, 1964).
[15] Ibid., pp. 98–9.   [16] Ibid., p. 97.

price, however, for this remarkable achievement was the opening up of the haunting issue of imputation, and hence again, on a new level, of the old problem of the role of the actor in negotiating the truth about his actions. The only way out of the new quandary was to accept a quasi-psychoanalytical theory of human behaviour. Weber did it, to an extent, intuitively. Habermas merely spelled it out and thereby exposed to a theoretical critique what was the practice of post-Weberian sociology. Critique notwithstanding, the practice seems unavoidable as long as imputation is seen as the method of understanding sociology; compare Giddens's 'unconscious sources of conduct'. Giving up the psychoanalytical theory would mean the vesting of ultimate control over truth with the objects, rather than the subjects, of sociological inquiry – precisely the effect which rendered Thomas ('definition of the situation'), Znaniecki ('humanistic coefficient') or Winch unacceptable as foundations of social science.

The whole question of the legitimacy and validity of imputation becomes a problem in so far as the understanding sociology is able to attain is interpreted as the reconstruction (or construction) of actors' motives and orientations. Normally, the practice of imputation is made immune to questioning by the expedient of redefining the motives and orientations in question as constructs of the social scientist's analytical operations, only hypothetically related to the actual springs of the described action. Such motives and orientations are grounded solely in the analyst's theory and methodology, and hence their recognition by the actors is irrelevant to the success of the enterprise. The trouble is that such 'motives' are truly like '5 pm on the Sun'. A verbal shell, emptied of its original meaning, has been retained, probably in order to reassure the analyst that his is still a 'subjectively orientated' sociology. What is now an illusion rests solely on ostensible verbal associations – as the original intention to fathom the experience of social actors has been, for all practical intents and purposes, abandoned.

This quandary goes back ultimately to the 'original sin' of selecting social action as the basic unit of sociological analysis. To understand action one must, indeed, refer to motives, true or construed, and all the problems listed above follow on immediately. Perhaps social action is a wrong site on which to build sociology as a valid endeavour? We know already the obtrusive structural faults of such a building, and there is a large enough experience to suggest that these faults have something to do with the quality of the site, and that no skills of a successive builder are likely to prevent them from recurring.

I would like to suggest, again, that 'figuration' may well prove to be an alternative, and reliable, site. The proper domain for the social scientist to understand is the network of dependencies in which actors are entangled and which set the parameters of whatever the actors may do and whatever they are likely to do. Here the social scientist is truly on his own. The complex network of intercrossing dependencies are not and cannot be seen from the standpoint of individual actor's experience. The actor is unlikely to explore them unaided.

But the actor needs such exploration; its findings would not just offer him an 'improved version' of what he is supposed to know, or be able to know, already, but would genuinely broaden his understanding (who knows? perhaps even mastery) of his plight. Having studied the figuration of which the actor is a part, the social scientist can tell the actor not just of what was knowable but unknown, but of what was, under the circumstances, beyond his control whether known or not.

The first of our two problems (is the negotiation of findings an integral part of their verification?) appears in this case in a new light. Caveats of the sort 'the adequacy of the description does not depend on actors' recognition' suddenly become redundant, as there is no reason to suppose otherwise. The authority of the social scientist is not in question and need not be defended by arbitrary postulates or overstretched analogies. As far as the description goes, it is the task of the social scientist, and the social scientist alone, to test and to verify the structure and the mechanism of figuration.

No negotiation of truth, then? No, as long as the work stops at the description. Inevitably, however, once the social scientist succeeds in demonstrating the self-sufficiency of figuration, the fact that it needs no ground but its own presence, the possibility arises that the figuration in question may be different from what it is. What is then opened up is the realm of the possible, the territory explored by critical sociology. Its propositions are of different epistemological modality. They relate to the truth not through the process of verification, but through the practice of authentication. It is in such a practice that the dialogue between the social scientist and his objects becomes an integral part of the truth-establishing effort. But the propositions which are subject to such negotiation and which may prove their truth only through it are not concerned with the shape of the figuration as it has been or is, but with the degree of its solidity, and hence with the possibility of the reshuffling of the present probabilities of social action.[17]

'Hermeneutically informed social theory' in sociological perspective

The state of a dialogue with its object – society – is, for sociology, a paramount methodological issue. But it is also its mode of existence as a discursive formation.

I think that a most distinctive feature of sociology as a continuous 'surface drawing' and 'problem-delineating' activity is that it is a discursive formation 'sans frontières'. Giddens's promotion of 'double hermeneutics' is, after all, a call for more self-awareness rather than a postulate to reform sociology's engagement with its object. There would be little point in advising, say, a biochemist to embark on a double-hermeneutical exercise. Addressed to a sociologist, the precept means, in its core, just 'know thyself'.

The discursive formation called sociology has no clearly defined or neatly

[17] Cf. Kilminster, pp. 268–9; also Bauman, pp. 103ff.

drawn frontiers for the simple reason that the phenomenal field which constitutes the object of sociological interpretation is not under sociologists' control.
The events the sociologist takes as his task to interpret are, on the whole,
available to general observation and hence open to many interpreters; also
such interpreters are not mutually bound by a joint authority structure or
subject to a joint normative code which legitimizes the 'sites' from which one
can speak with authority. There is, therefore, no a priori ground for the
superiority of a sociological over a 'lay' interpretation. One of the consequences of this unusual situation of sociology is the equally unusual attention
paid by sociologists to the 'scientificity' of their methods; methods, after all,
must carry in sociology the burden easily borne elsewhere by monopoly of
control. This is not, however, a topic which we either can or need develop in
the present context. Much more relevant to the issue at hand is another
consequence of the openness of sociology as, so to speak, an incomplete
(understructured?) discursive formation: sociologists' endemic lack of control
over the subject-matter of their own discipline.

It is not the sociologists who set the agenda for their discussion. Since the
object of their interpretation is already saturated with 'lay' meanings (indeed,
it is, in the end, an arrangement of lay meanings), sociologists' freedom of
interpretation is severely limited from the start. Sociologists are to provide a
meaningful interpretation of what is already meaningful; and their interpretation must be recognizable as such – that is, remain mutually 'translatable'
with the lay interpretations. What is more, sociologists are not allowed, in the
long run at least, the right to decide unilaterally the rules of translatability. If
some usurp such a right, they do it at their own peril. Sooner or later they are
relegated to a position of marginality, proclaimed an 'orthodox consensus',
and eventually replaced by a new set of interpretations more in tune with the
changing self-awareness of the lay world.

Since its inception, the products of sociological hermeneutics bore unmistakable marks of the lay interpretations fed into the social reality they were
meant to interpret. The products differed from each other (as different various
brands of toothpaste aimed to tackle the problem defined as 'tooth decay'),
yet, for every stage in the history of sociology, there was little doubt as to what
had to be interpreted. The themes of sociological inquiry were, and still are,
and probably forever will be, determined by the way in which those in power to
do so define the meaning of social reality.

The themes which occupied the minds of the 'founding fathers' of sociology
were dictated by the self-consciousness of the nineteenth century. Let us name
some of them.

First, the direction in which the world will develop had been settled and, in
principle, is no longer a matter of accident or conjecture. This direction is, by
and large, towards a society in which the labour processes are subject to the
criterion of ever-growing efficiency and hence based on detailed division of
tasks and increased expertise in performing them.

Second, parallel and related to the above, there will be growing synchronization between the needs arising from the efficient management of society as a whole and the springs of individual action. With the general progress towards rationality, the actors will increasingly tend to prefer efficient and effective behaviour over conduct induced by inadequate knowledge or misinformation.

Third, both developments will set the stage for the growing congruence between the modality of social reality (on both the societal and the individual level) and that of science. As it becomes more and more an application of reason to the management of social affairs, social action will need scientific expertise; and science, uniquely equipped as it is to test and measure the relation between means and ends, causes and effects, will find social reality ever more 'transparent' and demystified.

These three beliefs combined into a vision of a solid, trustworthy world, which – to recall the confident opinion of Marx – will not put on the agenda problems before it is capable of solving them. Included in this vision was a society which more and more will become an object of intelligent management. Even if the term itself was not in general use, the idea of 'social engineering' was an uncontested source of legitimacy of social scientific work. Projected upon the shared world-vision, the idea seemed to guarantee the congruence of rational social science with the historical process leading towards an increasingly rational society populated by increasingly rational actors. Social science itself seemed an advance party of things to come.

None of these beliefs is particularly popular today. Their fall from favour is only partly due to changes in intellectual fashion. There are other, more serious reasons. Some of them have been captured in their manifestations, if not in their roots, by writers as diverse as Sennett, Carroll or Lasch: the advent of the 'me age', withdrawal from the public arena, the obsession with intimacy, absorption in the cultivation of self coupled with growing anxiety about its identity; the arcane depths of the self, rather than the public stage, seem now the true locus of human reality. Other reasons have been put forward by Habermas and Offe: the demise of the achievement principle (the major device linking individual and social rationality), or, more generally, legitimation crisis. Some others still are related to the shifting balance of world power, erosion of the superiority of the West, and ever more evident diversification of developmental tendencies. Finally, there is a growing disenchantment with the pastoral benignity of the state, with the old utopia of caring society turning into a dystopia of ubiquitously oppressive state, as the individual feels more and more watched, tested, assessed, recorded, drilled and bossed by forces he does not control and only vaguely understands. In addition, the message of the new but all-penetrating visual media helped to dissolve the imagery of the public and supra-individual in the familiar experience of the personal and subjective.

If the world of the founding fathers – both in its structure of real powers and its intellectual articulations – rested on the superiority-cum-confidence of the West, our world is fast approaching a new 'base-superstructure' congruence as the crumbling superiority of a particular civilization comes to be reflected in the melting of its self-confidence. To recall the musings of the adolescent Marx, once again – like moths – we seek the light of the domestic lamp when it is dark outside. As the hope and desire of the perfect blend of social rationality and individual happiness fade away, we seek in the self the bulwark against encroaching disharmony. We hope again that many domestic lamps will somehow brighten up the frightening blackness on the other side of the window.

It is in this new world that social sciences must redefine their role. The growing realization that the role tacitly (and comfortably) assumed in the past was no longer viable, and the resulting urge to find a new social-scientific *raison d'être*, will probably be seen by future historians as the major cause of the recent orgy of sociological self-flagellation and proliferation of eschatological formulae. In the past, the right of sociology to speak with authority was woven into a solid world with conclusive history and unambiguous future. Such a right was the prerogative of sociologists as legislators or expert commentators on legislators' activity. But this would not do in this world of ours, which can boast neither a conclusive past nor a clear future; above all, this world does not seem solid any more, as the awesome hierarchy of superiority has been edged away by the multitude of conflicting authorities in an increasingly polycentric setting. In such a world, the tasks of communication seem much more topical and imperative than those of the management; and the role of interpreters much more realistic and urgently needed than that of the legislators.

Hence the growing popularity of the many hermeneutically inspired varieties of 'interpretive sociology' (well represented by instances so different in other respects as ethnomethodology or Geertz's 'dense description'), and the surging interest in *Verstehen*. The respect previously vested in the 'system' is now being increasingly reallocated to the actor. It is the actors who, it is hoped, provide the few solid rocks in the sea of drifting totalities; it is on these rocks that many sociologists today want to build their second church.

The recent crisis of sociology was, first and foremost, a crisis of the authority of sociology (this was not really visible from the vantage-point of a country where such an authority had never been truly established). The legitimation of sociology's right to speak with authority in and to the changing world occupied most of the theorists' time and effort. No wonder that most theorists did not bother with the major revision of the substance of social theory, confining themselves to a successive swing of the pendulum within the traditional frame of sociological discourse. A truly radical shift took place only in the quoted source of authority: here hermeneutics has replaced natural laws.

Concern with the right to speak with authority is an artefact of academic life. It arises from the need to justify the place of sociology among better-established academic disciplines. Hence the remarkable amount of time which new academic areas of study of somewhat uncertain provenance (i.e., such areas as have not evidently 'hived off' from the old nest) dedicate to the issue of the 'scientificity' of their methods (i.e., the reasons why their activities should be recognized by the disciplines with an uncontested status as belonging to the same kind). Hence also why the question of reliability and validity of sociological work took pride of place in the thinking and writing of Professors Durkheim or Weber. The question took, after all, much less room in the writings of Marx or Simmel – this was later seen by their more academically situated readers as a regrettable case of methodological negligence.

Giddens is much less guilty than most of this 'trade-unionist bias' of current social theorizing. He is, unlike many other theorists, engaged in profound analysis of modern society and the reassessment of its history in the light of tendencies revealed to date. This other aspect of Giddens's work I value most highly and consider to be among the most seminal developments in contemporary sociology; but it is not the topic of this chapter. Here, I am concerned with Giddens as a theorist, the role in which his impact in British and international sociology is, thus far at least, most strongly felt. And as a theorist, Giddens does not deviate, or does not deviate visibly enough, from the current tendency. The message Giddens's theoretical writings convey is that in sociology theory is, first and foremost, the theory of the 'scientificity of sociology'; and that the royal road out of the present crisis leads through devising and adoption of right methods which can establish the credentials of sociological activity relevant to the role it now seeks; what we need, in other words, is a set of 'new rules of sociological method'.

Again, however, rules of method are an internal affair of sociology, part of its power rhetoric and of a pep talk turned upon itself; above all, this rhetoric is a manifestation of a crisis of confidence caused by uncertainty regarding the substance of the sociological project. 'Rules of method' tell us little about the subject-matter of sociology; moreover, in no way do they contain a guarantee that sociology would have something valid and relevant to say on this subject. A theory by which the relevance of sociology in the contemporary world will stand or fall needs to be a theory of contemporary society, and not a contemporary theory of sociology.

The topic of theorizing in general, and in particular the way in which priorities are distributed within the theory project, reflects the diagnosis of the roots of the present weakness of sociological practice. I wish to propose that these roots do not lie in the obsolete 'natural scientific' ambitions, outdated structural-functionalism, hypostasizing of structure or neglect of hermeneutics. I wish to propose that these roots lie instead in sociology's failure to come to grips with what is truly novel in the society of today, and its persistent tendency to bar the understanding of contemporary phenomena by attempting to contain them in a straightjacket of traditional and increasingly ill-fitting concepts.

If our sociology is still 'nineteenth-centuryish', this is not because of belief in an outmoded model of science or the ignorance of more recent philosophical ideas. It is, rather, because the conceptual system of sociology still very much in operation and hardly ever seriously questioned had been designed to cope with the past century's experiences and anticipations. 'Society' understood mostly as tantamount to the nation-state; direction of change guided by 'historical class'; labour–capital conflict conterminous with the problem of division of social surplus; class division as synonymous with social inequality; work as the central locus of social integration and control; politics as the institutionalized manifestation of interests of preformed social subjects; power as property which can be variously shared; power as an extension of economic struggle by political means: these are just a few examples of the past wisdoms of which the present-day sociology remains a staunchest guardian. Anyone who wishes to contribute to the understanding of late-twentieth-century society would need to examine first how wise it is to preserve such wisdom.

To put it bluntly, the academic setting of modern sociology induces an effort to update the methods of investigating increasingly outdated issues. We do make progress in the philosophical sophistication of our methods of interpretation. With all this refinement, however, we still have little to say about the crucial experience of our time. Here, most sociological statements are barely distinguishable from 'informed public opinion'. Like the rest of us, the main body of sociology reproduces collective historical memory, to the shape of which contemporary sociology's ancestors crucially contributed, but which contemporary sociology seems no more able to revise. Like the generals, sociology tends to fight the victorious battles of the past over and over.

This is why I think that to claim the right to speak with authority sociology would have to update its theory of society, rather than its idea of social action. Let us concentrate on this central task.

3
The theory of structuration

JOHN B. THOMPSON

The problem of the relation between the individual and society, or between action and social structure, lies at the heart of social theory and the philosophy of social science. In the writings of most major theorists, from Marx, Weber and Durkheim to a variety of contemporary authors, this problem is raised and allegedly resolved in one way or another. Such resolutions generally amount to the accentuation of one term at the expense of the other: either social structure is taken as the principal object of analysis and the agent is effectively eclipsed, as in the Marxism of Althusser, or individuals are regarded as the only constituents of the social world and their actions and reactions, their reasons, motives and beliefs, are the sole ingredients of social explanation. In both cases the problem is not so much resolved as dissolved, that is, disposed of beneath a philosophical and methodological platform that is already located in one of the camps. Few questions in social theory remain as refractory to cogent analysis as the question of how, and in precisely what ways, the action of individual agents is related to the structural features of the societies of which they are part.

In recent years several authors have confronted directly the problem of the relation between action and social structure and have attempted to deal with it in a constructive and systematic way.[1] Essential to these attempts is the shift from a static to a dynamic perspective, from a theory of structure to a *theory of structuration*. What must be grasped is not how structure determines action or how a combination of actions make up structure, but rather how action is *structured* in everyday contexts and how the structured features of action are, by the very performance of an action, thereby *reproduced*. The theory of structuration is thus inseparable from an account of social reproduction, that is, from an account of the ways in which societies, or specific forms of social organization, are reproduced by the activities of individuals pursuing their everyday lives. The theory of structuration is also linked, in a fundamental way, to other aspects of social analysis. For an adequate characterization of the relation between action and social structure would provide a framework within which other concerns, such as the analysis of power and ideology, could be recast.

My aim in this chapter is to examine some of the claims and the prospects of

[1] In addition to the writings of Anthony Giddens (cited in n. 3), see Pierre Bourdieu, *Outline of a Theory of Practice*, tr. Richard Nice (Cambridge: Cambridge University Press, 1977) and *Le Sens pratique* (Paris: Minuit, 1980); and Roy Bhaskar, *The Possibility of Naturalism: A Philosophical Critique of the Contemporary Human Sciences* (Brighton, Sussex: Harvester, 1979).

the theory of structuration.[2] I shall do so by focusing on the contribution of its leading exponent, Anthony Giddens. In a series of publications stretching over the better part of a decade,[3] Giddens has elaborated a highly original formulation of the theory of structuration, a formulation which is far more sophisticated in its detail and far more suggestive in its application than any of the other versions currently found in the literature. The first section of this chapter will present a brief overview of the basic elements of Giddens's account. In order to offer a rigorous assessment of this account, however, it is necessary to retrace a particular development in Giddens's work. For while the conception of structure originally presented in *New Rules of Sociological Method* is preserved *in principle* in his most recent writings, this conception is supplemented *in practice* by a much more ramified account of the structural features of societies. I shall thus begin my critical assessment by focusing on the original formulation and arguing that it is deficient in certain key respects. I shall then introduce the more ramified account and try to show that it is only partly successful in overcoming the deficiencies of the original formulation. In the final section I shall focus on Giddens's analysis of action, suggesting that this analysis fails to do justice to the role of structural constraint. Amid these critical remarks I shall point to some of the ways in which the theory of structuration should, I believe, be developed and refined. For it is my view that, while the details of Giddens's account may be wanting, his overall aims are perfectly sound: the dualism of action and structure must give way to the systematic study of processes of structuration and social reproduction.

Outline of the theory

Let me begin by outlining the central themes of Giddens's account. This account is formulated with a view towards building upon the strengths, while avoiding the weaknesses, of certain theoretical orientations in the social sciences. Functionalism has rightly emphasized the institutional features of the social world and has focused attention on the ways in which the unintended consequences of action serve to maintain existing social relations. Structuralism and 'post-structuralist' approaches have developed novel conceptions of structure, of structuring processes and of the subject, conceptions which have been applied with particular efficacy to the analysis of texts and cultural objects. But what functionalism and structuralism lack, in spite of much discussion of the 'action frame of reference' and the 'theory of the subject', is an adequate account of action and agency. The latter have been principal con-

[2] This chapter develops remarks initially made in my *Critical Hermeneutics: A Study in the Thought of Paul Ricoeur and Jürgen Habermas* (Cambridge: Cambridge University Press, 1981), pp. 143–9 and 173–8; and in my review essay, 'Rethinking History: For and Against Marx', *Philosophy of the Social Sciences*, 14 (1984), 543–51. I am grateful to Michelle Stanworth for her helpful comments on an earlier draft of this chapter.

[3] The publications of Anthony Giddens most relevant to this essay are as follows: *NRSM*; *SSPT*; *CPST*; *CCHM*; and *CS*.

cerns of 'analytical philosophy' during the last two decades, as well as of the 'interpretative sociologies' influenced by Husserl, Wittgenstein and others. In various ways these philosophers and sociologists have portrayed individuals as competent agents who know a great deal about the social world, who act purposively and reflectively and who can, if asked, provide reasons for what they have done. But where functionalism and structuralism are strong, analytical philosophy and interpretative sociology are weak, for they largely neglect problems of institutional and structural analysis.

Giddens seeks to move beyond these various orientations by rethinking the notions of, and the relations between, action and structure. Rather than seeing action and structure as the counter-acting elements of a dualism, we should regard them as the complementary terms of a duality, the 'duality of structure'. 'By the *duality of structure*', writes Giddens, 'I mean that social structures are both constituted *by* human agency, and yet at the same time are the very *medium* of this constitution.'[4] Every act of production is at the same time an act of reproduction: the structures that render an action possible are, in the performance of that action, reproduced. Even action which disrupts the social order, breaking conventions or challenging established hierarchies, is mediated by structural features which are reconstituted by the action, albeit in a modified form. This intimate connection between production and reproduction is what Giddens calls the 'recursive character' of social life. His theory of structuration is a sustained attempt to tease out the threads that are woven into this apparently unproblematic fact.

Action, according to Giddens, should be conceived as a continuous flow of interventions in the world which are initiated by autonomous agents. Action must be distinguished from 'acts', which are discrete segments of action that are cut out of the continuous flow by explicit processes of categorization and description. Not all action is 'purposeful', in the sense of being guided by clear purposes which the agent has in mind; but much action is 'purposive', in the sense that it is *monitored* by actors who continually survey what they are doing, how others react to what they are doing, and the circumstances in which they are doing it. An important aspect of this reflexive monitoring of action is the ability of agents to explain, both to themselves and to others, why they act as they do by giving reasons for their action. Individuals are, Giddens repeatedly emphasizes, *knowledgeable agents* who are capable of accounting for their action: they are neither 'cultural dopes' nor mere 'supports' of social relations, but are skilful actors who know a great deal about the world in which they act. If the 'rationalization of action' refers to the reasons which agents offer to explain their action, the 'motivation of action' refers to the motives or wants which prompt it. Unconscious motivation is a crucial feature of human conduct and Giddens takes on board, primarily through a critical appraisal of the so-called 'ego-psychology' of Erikson and Sullivan, a cluster of psychoanalytic concepts. However, in place of the psychoanalytic triad of ego, super-ego and id,

[4] *NRSM*, p. 121.

Giddens adheres to distinctions between the unconscious, practical consciousness and discursive consciousness. While the latter two are separated from the
unconscious by the barrier of repression, the boundary between practical
consciousness and discursive consciousness is a vague and fluctuating one.
Much of what actors know about the world is part of their 'practical consciousness', in the sense that it is known without being articulated as such; but that
such knowledge *could* be rendered explicit and incorporated into 'discursive
consciousness' is a vital consideration which has important consequences for
the status of social scientific research.

These various aspects of action and agency are part of what Giddens calls
the 'stratification model of action'. The model could be represented as shown
in figure 1.[5]

Figure 1

This model brings out the limitations of any attempt to analyse action by
focusing on the individual agent. For the accounts which agents are able to
give of their actions are 'bounded', both by unintended consequences of action
and by unacknowledged conditions of action (including unconscious sources
of motivation). The significance of the unintended consequences of action is
stressed by Merton, who introduces the concept of 'latent function' in order to
show that practices may serve to maintain institutions and organizations,
regardless of whether this outcome is intended by the agents concerned.
Giddens firmly rejects any suggestion that such a demonstration would *explain*
the existence of the practice: 'there is *nothing*', he asserts, 'which can count as
"functionalist explanation"'.[6] But he wishes to preserve the insight that action
may have unintended consequences which become the unacknowledged conditions of further action. There are two principal ways, on Giddens's account,
in which this feedback process can occur. Unintended consequences can
become unacknowledged conditions by being incorporated in 'homeostatic
causal loops', such as the so-called 'poverty cycle' of material deprivation
→poor schooling→low-level employment→material deprivation. Unintended consequences can also become unacknowledged conditions in so far as
the unintended consequence of action is the reproduction of the *structure* which
renders further action possible. To clarify the latter process we must take up
Giddens's discussion of the concept of structure.

In the sociological literature 'structure' is often conceived in a quasi-

[5] Adapted from *CPST*, p. 56.   [6] *CCHM*, p. 17.

mechanical, quasi-visual way, like the girders of a building, the skeleton of a
body or the 'patterning' of social relationships. Giddens does not dismiss this
connotation altogether; as we shall see, he preserves elements of it in his notion
of 'social system'. To the concept of structure, however, he ascribes a different
sense. Here I shall focus on the sense ascribed in *New Rules of Sociological
Method*, reserving for later a consideration of certain modifications which are
presented in subsequent works. In *New Rules of Sociological Method* Giddens
approaches the concept of structure through a comparison of language and
speech – 'not because society is like a language', he hastens to add, 'but on the
contrary because language as a practical activity is so central to social life that
in *some* basic respects it can be treated as exemplifying social processes in
general'.[7] Thus, whereas speech is spatially and temporally situated, presupposing a subject as well as another to whom it is addressed, language is 'virtual
and outside of time' and is 'subject-less', in the sense that it is neither the
product of any one subject nor is it oriented towards any other. Giddens
employs this comparison to draw a similar distinction between *interaction* and
structure in social analysis. Whereas interaction is constituted in and through
the activities of agents, structure has a 'virtual existence': it consists of 'rules
and resources' which are implemented in interaction, which thereby structure
interaction and which are, in that very process, reproduced. As Giddens
explains, 'by the term "structure" I do not refer, as is conventional in functionalism, to the descriptive analysis of the relations of interaction which "compose" organizations or collectivities, but to systems of generative rules and
resources'.[8]

Giddens analyses the rules and resources which comprise structure in terms
of three dimensions or 'modalities'. These modalities are the lines of mediation
between interaction and structure, as figure 2 indicates.[9]

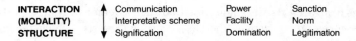

INTERACTION	Communication	Power	Sanction
(MODALITY)	Interpretative scheme	Facility	Norm
STRUCTURE	Signification	Domination	Legitimation

Figure 2

In the communication of meaning in interaction, agents draw upon interpretative schemes which, at the level of structure, can be analysed as 'semantic
rules'. When agents apply sanctions in interaction they draw upon norms
which, at the level of structure, can be analysed (in part)[10] as 'moral rules'. The
use of power in interaction involves the application of facilities which enable

[7] *NRSM*, p. 127.   [8] Ibid., p. 127.
[9] Ibid., p. 122; modified in accordance with the diagram in *CPST*, p. 82.
[10] In *NRSM* Giddens writes: 'the moral constitution of interaction involves the application of
    norms which draw from a legitimate order ... Structures of ... legitimation [can be analysed]
    as systems of *moral rules*' (pp. 122–4). In subsequent writings the notion of moral rule is
    subsumed under the more general category of 'normative sanction' (see *CPST*, pp. 270–1, n.
    63).

agents to secure specific outcomes; at the structural level, these facilities can be analysed as 'resources' which comprise structures of domination. Giddens emphasizes that the distinction between these three modalities is more analytical than it is substantive. 'In any concrete situation of interaction, members of society draw upon these [rules and resources] as modalities of production and reproduction, although as an integrated set rather than three discrete components.'[11] Thus the communication of meaning cannot be sharply separated from the use of power or the application of sanctions. These different modalities are woven together in social practices, so that even the most mundane action or interaction expresses overlapping aspects of the structural whole.

The rules and resources which comprise structure may be regarded as 'properties of social systems'. Social systems are regularized patterns of interaction involving individuals and groups; they are not structures in themselves, but rather they 'have' structures, in the sense that they are *structured by* rules and resources. Structures do not 'exist' in time and space except as moments in the constitution of social systems. When the regularized practices structured by rules and resources are 'deeply layered' in time and space, stretching through many decades and over large or fixed domains, Giddens speaks of 'institutions'. Institutions are clusterings of the practices that constitute social systems; they can be classified according to the modality which is most central in their structuration. In *Central Problems in Social Theory* Giddens offers the following classification:[12]

S–D–L	Symbolic orders/modes of discourse
D(auth.)–S–L	Political institutions
D(alloc.)–S–L	Economic institutions
L–D–S	Law/modes of sanction

The letters on the left refer to those aspects of structure which were distinguished above (S = signification, D = domination, L = legitimation); the first letter in each sequence indicates which aspect is primary in the structuration of the institutions. When we study legal institutions, for example, we focus primarily on the aspect of legitimation, although signification and domination are also involved. The differentiation between political institutions and economic institutions is based on an important distinction between two types of resources. 'Authorization' refers to capabilities which generate command over *persons*, while 'allocation' refers to capabilities which generate control over *objects*. This distinction gives Giddens a critical purchase on certain forms of social theory, especially on those forms of Marxism which tend to associate domination with the ownership or control of property and which give insufficient attention to problems of authority.

In his recent writings Giddens has been increasingly concerned to examine the ways in which the concepts of time and space enter into the theory of

---

[11] *NRSM*, p. 124.   [12] From *CPST*, p. 107.

structuration. Social systems are not only structured by rules and resources, but are also situated within time and space; hence 'social theory *must acknowledge, as it has not done previously, time–space intersections as essentially involved in all social existence*'.[13] Time and space should not be thought of, Giddens argues, as boundaries to social analysis or as frameworks within which social life takes place. It is much more fruitful to think of time and space in the Heideggerian terms of 'presence' and 'absence' – or, more precisely, in terms of 'presencing' or 'being present'. Every interaction mixes together presence and absence in complicated ways. In face-to-face interaction the other is present both in space and in time. The interaction takes place in a definite setting or 'locale' and endures for a definite period; actors typically employ the spatial and temporal features of the interaction as a means of organizing their exchange. With the extension of social systems in space and time, however, the other may cease to be immediately present. Such time–space distancing (or 'distanciation', as Giddens calls it) was greatly facilitated by the development of writing, which renders possible communication with the past as well as with physically absent individuals. In more recent years, technological advances in transport and the media have rapidly transformed the time–space constitution of social systems, as 'time geographers' such as Hägerstrand have pointed out. With great imagination Giddens analyses the ways in which these transformations are connected with the *generation of power*. The development of writing, for example, greatly increased the capacity of societies to store information about their populations, and thereby to monitor and control their activities. If the power of nation-states and the threat of totalitarian political control are pervasive features of the modern world, their origins cannot be understood without examining the transformations in time–space relations which have rendered possible such terrifying power and control.

Structure as 'rules and resources'

I want to begin my critical assessment of Giddens's account by returning to his conception of structure. Few concepts in the social sciences are more basic and essential, and yet more ambiguous and contested, than that of structure. It is to Giddens's credit that he tries to give this concept a clear sense and to integrate it within a systematic conceptual framework. In so doing he also gives the concept of structure a *novel* sense, one which diverges considerably from the ways in which this concept is commonly used in the literature of the social sciences. While I do not wish to dispute the importance of conceptual innovation, it is my view that Giddens's proposal to conceive of structure in terms of rules and resources is of questionable value, for it is a proposal which generates more confusion than it dispels and which tends to obscure some important issues. I shall try to substantiate this view by focusing first on the loose and abstract character of Giddens's conception. This character derives

[13] Ibid., p. 54.

both from the ambiguities of the term 'rule' and from the very generality of Giddens's proposal, a generality which is apparent in his attempt to formulate a *general* notion of structure and in his tendency to neglect the *specific* features of *social* structure.

'Structure' is a vague and ambiguous term; the trouble with 'rule', as Austin might say, is that it does not stand us in much better stead.[14] We use the expression 'rule' in a great variety of ways. We speak of moral rules, traffic rules, bureaucratic rules, rules of grammar, rules of etiquette, rules of football. We say of someone who regularly does something at a certain time that, 'as a rule', this is what he or she does. Workers who resist employers by sticking to the letter of their contracts are said to be 'working to rule'. Giddens is fully aware of the diversity of senses encapsulated in the expression 'rule'. His way of narrowing down these senses and of attempting to give 'rule' a more rigorous application is to draw critically upon Wittgenstein's analysis of rule-following behaviour. To know the rules of a game is to know how to play it; to know a mathematical rule for the calculation of a series of numbers is to know how to continue the series, that is, 'how to go on'. To know a rule is not necessarily to be able to formulate it. As competent social actors we know countless rules which we would have difficulty stating in an explicit way: they form part, in Giddens's terms, of our practical consciousness. However, Giddens rightly warns against the tendency of Wittgenstein and Wittgensteinians to privilege the example of the rules of a game, such as chess. For these rules, Giddens remarks, are seldom *contested* in a chronic way. The rules which comprise structure are embroiled in struggles, are subject to rival interpretations and are continually transformed in their very application. Rules, in other words, cannot be conceptualized in isolation from the resources which facilitate the exercise of power.

These cautionary remarks are certainly in order, but they still do not give us a clear idea of exactly what, on Giddens's account, are the rules which comprise *social* structure. In *New Rules of Sociological Method* Giddens suggests, as I indicated earlier, that structures of signification can be analysed as 'semantic rules' and structures of legitimation can be analysed as 'moral rules'. Elsewhere he modifies this account, placing less emphasis on two kinds of rules and stressing instead that all rules have two 'aspects': they relate both to the constitution of meaning and to the sanctioning of conduct. But what, we may justly ask, would be an example of such a rule? Would 'That's a "butterfly"', said to a child on its first excursion into the countryside, or 'Hold your toothbrush horizontally', uttered by a dentist to a patient whose dental hygiene was poor, be examples of the sort of rule that someone interested in social structure should be studying? In fact, until the recent publication of *The*

---

[14] Alluding to philosophers who have urged us to stop talking about *meaning* and to study instead how expressions are *used* in everyday life, Austin complains that '"use" is a hopelessly ambiguous or wide word, just as is the word "meaning", which it has become customary to deride. But "use", its supplanter, is not in much better case' (J. L. Austin, *How to do Things with Words*, ed. J. O. Urmson and Marina Sbisà (Oxford: Oxford University Press, 1976), p. 100).

Constitution of Society, Giddens has said virtually nothing about these matters. In *The Constitution of Society* he considers various candidates for the kind of rule which is most relevant to social structure – or, as he prefers to say, which is most relevant to the analysis of 'social life'. He puts aside the sense of 'rule' which pertains to games like chess ('the rule defining checkmate is . . .'); the sense of 'rule' which is roughly equivalent to habit or routine ('as a rule I get up every day at 6 o'clock'); the sense of 'rule' that is exemplified by regulations like 'all workers must clock in at 8.0 a.m.'. Giddens suggests that the sense of 'rule' most relevant to the analysis of social life is that expressed by formulae such as $a_n = n^2 + n - 1$. 'It is in the nature of formulae', he submits, 'that we can best discover what is the most analytically effective sense of "rule" in social theory.'[15] Analytically effective or not, this suggestion does little to clarify the precise character of the rules which could be said, on Giddens's account, to comprise social structure. Is he suggesting, most implausibly, that semantic rules and moral rules should be seen as quasi-mathematical formulae, as if ' "butterfly" $=$ moth^2 + colour $-$ cloth'? Or does he wish to maintain that such formulae convey the sense of rules *other than* the semantic rules and moral rules in terms of which structures of signification and legitimation can apparently be analysed, and if so, *which* rules are these others? If Giddens expects readers to accept his proposal to conceive of structure in terms of rules and resources, then the onus is on him to provide clear and consistent examples of what would count as a relevant 'rule'.

So far I have been concerned to highlight the looseness of Giddens's conception of structure; I now want to offer some arguments against the view that it is useful and satisfactory to identify social structure with rules (and resources). In offering these arguments I shall focus on the study of rules, presuming, in the absence of a more precise account of 'rule' by Giddens himself, an intuitive understanding of this notion. I shall seek to establish the following point: while rules of various kinds are important features of social life, the study of rules (and resources) is not identical to, but rather distinct from and on a different level from, the analysis of social structure. There are four arguments which seem to me to substantiate this point.[16] The first argument bears upon the vagueness of the term 'rule' and Giddens's failure so far to render this term more precise. This failure is not mere oversight, for Giddens cannot clarify the sense of 'rule' and the kinds of rules which are relevant to social structure without presupposing a *criterion of importance*, and this criterion can never be derived from attending to rules alone. Thus, on the one hand, Giddens wants to regard rules as generalizable procedures implemented in every kind of social practice – shorthand summaries, as it were, of what actors know about their world and about how to act within it, about teaching and typing, speaking and shopping, voting, cooking and cracking jokes. On the other hand, Giddens is well aware that *some* rules, or some kinds or aspects of rules, are much more

---

[15] *CS*, p. 20.   [16] See my *Critical Hermeneutics*, p. 144.

important than others for the analysis of, for example, the social structure of capitalist societies. But what justifies this implicit criterion of importance, if not an analysis of social structure which is separate from the study of those rules that are singled out in its name?

The second and third arguments give force to the first criticism by calling attention to what may be called *structural differentiation*. Consider first the case of a cluster of 'semantic rules', such as those governing the application of an adjective like 'bloody' or a noun like 'the Left' in contemporary Britain. To study these rules is to study part of the *semantic* structure of English. However, to study these rules is not *in itself* to analyse part of the *social* structure of Britain. The study of semantic rules may indeed be relevant to the analysis of social structure; and one way in which that relevance may be shown is by demonstrating that the rules are *differentiated* according to class, sex, region and so on. But to study their differentiation presupposes some framework, some structural points of reference which are not themselves *rules*, with regard to which these semantic rules are differentiated. Consider next the case of institutions, such as schools or universities, in which certain individuals, or certain groups and classes of individuals, have restricted opportunities for entry and participation. It seems evident that such restrictions cannot be adequately conceptualized in terms of 'moral rules' or 'sanctions', since such restrictions may operate independently of the rights and obligations of the agents concerned. It also seems inadequate to conceive of such restrictions as unintended consequences of action, like the homeostatic causal loops involved in the poverty cycle. For the issue is not so much whether the restrictions are intended or unintended consequences which may become the conditions of further action. Rather, what is at issue is the fact that the restrictions on opportunities operate *differentially*, affecting unevenly various groups of individuals whose categorization depends on certain assumptions about social structure; and it is this differential operation or effect which cannot be grasped by the analysis of rules alone.

If Giddens's conception tends to blur the question of differentiation, it also provides no way of grasping the features which a multiplicity of 'rules' may have in common. It provides no way, that is, of formulating the idea of *structural identity*: this is the fourth argument against his view. The importance of this idea can be demonstrated by considering two enterprises in different sectors of the British economy, such as the UK plants of the Ford Motor Company and the various establishments of the Macmillan Press. Each of these enterprises is a complex institution possessing vast resources of machinery, stock and capital. Each is an institution which is organized and operated with the aid of specific and detailed rules which stipulate how work is to be done, how decisions are to be made, how personnel are to be hired and dismissed, and so on. But beyond the particular rules and resources which characterize each of these institutions, there are certain features which Ford and Macmillan have in common, namely the features which define them as *capitalistic* enterprises.

These features are not additional 'rules' which are 'drawn upon' by actors within these institutions, in the manner that a supervisor might 'draw upon' a rule in the contract in order to fire a worker who failed to turn up. The common features are of a different order altogether; they are better conceptualized, I believe, as a series of elements and their interrelations which together *limit* the kinds of rules which are possible and which thereby *delimit* the scope for institutional variation.[17] Whatever the merits of this alternative conception, these four arguments against Giddens's view will, it is hoped, demonstrate that the proposal to conceive of structure in terms of rules (and resources) is deficient, for it presupposes but fails to address some of the most important concerns of structural analysis.

Levels of structural analysis

I now want to return to Giddens's texts and to follow a line of thought which has become increasingly prominent in his recent work. Giddens would now accept, I think, that the account of structure presented in *New Rules of Sociological Method* is unsatisfactory in certain respects. It may be partially in response to considerations such as those adduced above that he has endeavoured to distinguish more clearly between different *levels of abstraction* in the analysis of the structural features of social systems. In *A Contemporary Critique of Historical Materialism* these levels are portrayed as in figure 3.[18]

LEVEL OF ABSTRACTION   ↑   Structural principles
                                        Structural sets (structures)
                                        Elements/axes of structuration

Figure 3

The study of 'structural principles' is the most abstract level of analysis. To study such principles is to examine the major alignments, the modes of articulation and differentiation, of the institutions which constitute a society. In Giddens's words, 'structural principles are principles of organisation implicated in those practices most "deeply" (in time) and "pervasively" (in space) sedimented in a society'.[19] The identification of structural principles provides the basis for Giddens's threefold classification of types of society. In 'tribal societies', including hunting-gathering bands and settled agricultural communities, the dominant structural principle 'operates along an axis', as Giddens says, between kinship and tradition; time–space distanciation is low, kinship networks are the *locus* of interaction and links with the past are

---

[17] This proposal is developed in my *Critical Hermeneutics*, pp. 145ff.; and in part III of my chapter, 'Theories of Ideology and Methods of Discourse Analysis: Towards a Framework for the Analysis of Ideology', in *Studies in the Theory of Ideology* (Cambridge: Polity Press, 1984).
[18] From *CCHM*, p. 54.   [19] Ibid., pp. 54–5.

maintained only through the actualization of tradition. The dominant structural principle of 'class-divided societies' (city-states, ancient empires and feudal societies) operates along an axis relating urban areas to rural hinterlands. The city – centered on temples and surrounded by walls – emerges as a special kind of 'storage container' for the generation of political and military power. In contrast to class-divided societies, the class societies of modern capitalism are organized along an axis relating state institutions and economic institutions. The rapid expansion of an economy based on the capital/wage labour relation creates the conditions for the accumulation of political power in the hands of the nation-state. At the same time, the predominance of the city–countryside relation is destroyed by the incessant commodification of time and space, which produces the 'created environment' wherein most people live out their daily lives.

At a less abstract level of analysis the structural features of social systems can be studied as 'structural sets'. By 'structural sets' Giddens means 'sets of rules and resources, specified in terms of "clusterings" of transformation/mediation relations'.[20] It is at this level of analysis, argues Giddens, that we can understand Marx's account of the key structural relations involved in the capitalist system of production. Consider the relations involved in the following 'structural set':

private property : money : capital : labour contract : profit

The development of capitalism is characterized by the universalization of the commodity form. The condition of this universalization is the formation of a *money economy* in which money, as the medium of pure exchange value, enables private property to be converted into capital and allows labour power to be constituted as a commodity, to be bought and sold on the market like any other. Capital and wage labour can thus enter into a definite kind of relation, governed by the labour contract, in which labour power is exchanged for wages and in which profit is produced via the extraction of surplus value. By studying the various relations of convertibility between private property, money, capital and so on – a study which could be extended, Giddens suggests, to industrial authority, educational advantage and occupational position – one can identify some of the principal structural features of the institutions created by capitalism.

The most concrete level of analysis is concerned with 'elements' or 'axes' of structuration. This level is the most concrete because it bears most directly upon the relations of co-presence established between agents in social interaction. Giddens offers the example of the division of labour within the capitalist enterprise. The division of labour is one source of what Giddens calls, in *The Class Structure of the Advanced Societies*, 'proximate structuration':[21] it links the broader characteristics of capitalism with the more immediate organization of

---

[20] Ibid., p. 55.   [21] See *CSAS*, pp. 107–8.

the industrial enterprise. In the early development of manufacturing industry, two forms of the division of labour prevailed. On the one hand, capitalists assembled workers with different craft skills and co-ordinated their activities into the production of a particular product; on the other hand, workers with the same skills were brought together and each worker was required to produce the same product. In both cases the productive process was broken down into detailed tasks, resulting, as Marx put it, in 'a productive mechanism whose parts are human beings'.[22] The division of labour is vital to the organization of the capitalist enterprise, not only because it enhances the productivity and profitability of the enterprise, but also because it creates conditions for the direct surveillance of the work-force and for the consolidation of labour discipline. Technological developments are closely connected with the division of labour, profoundly altering both the nature of the tasks and the boundaries between them. These boundaries in turn have a significant effect on the formation and fragmentation of class consciousness in contemporary capitalist societies.

This attempt to distinguish several levels of structural analysis represents, I believe, a substantial improvement on the rather blurred account of structuration presented in *New Rules of Sociological Method*. Nevertheless, it seems to me that these distinctions raise serious difficulties for certain aspects of Giddens's approach. In discussing these difficulties I shall, for the most part, put aside the question of content, that is, the empirical and historical adequacy of Giddens's analyses. I shall focus instead on questions of form or conceptual consistency. The first difficulty concerns the implications of these distinctions for the conception of structure as rules and resources. Even in his most recent writings Giddens continues to adhere to this conception. Thus, in *The Constitution of Society*, he writes: 'I treat structure, in its most elemental meaning at least, as referring to ... rules (and resources).'[23] But to adhere to this conception of structure, while at the same time acknowledging the need for the study of 'structural principles', 'structural sets' and 'axes of structuration', is simply a recipe for conceptual confusion. A structural principle, such as that which 'operates along an axis' relating urban areas to rural hinterlands, is not a 'rule' in any ordinary sense: it is neither a semantic rule nor a moral rule nor a 'formula' which expresses what actors know in knowing how to go on in social life. To insist that a structural principle *must* be some such rule, or must be capable of being analysed in terms of rules, is to force on to the material a mode of conceptualization which is not appropriate to it, and which stems less from a reflection upon the structural features of social life than from an implicit ontology of structure. Similarly it seems unhelpful and misleading to interpret Marx's account of the structural relations involved in the capitalist system of

---

[22] Karl Marx, *Capital: A Critical Analysis of Capitalist Production*, vol. 1, tr. Samuel Moore and Edward Aveling (London: Lawrence & Wishart, 1970), p. 320. For Giddens's discussion of Marx's account, see *CS*, pp. 189–90.

[23] *CS*, p. 17.

production in terms of 'sets of rules and resources'. The constitution of labour power as a commodity, the determination of its value as the labour time socially necessary for its production, its exchange on the market under conditions which guarantee that it exchanges at its value and yet simultaneously produces surplus value and profit: these features of the capitalist system cannot be treated as so many 'rules' that workers follow when they turn up at the factory gates, as if every worker who accepted a job had an implicit (albeit partial) knowledge of Marx's *Capital*.[24] The account offered by Marx would be better seen, I think, as an attempt to identify and explicate the differing kinds of conditions which render possible the processes of capitalist production and exchange. These conditions range from the circumstances which facilitate the formation of a 'free' labour force to the elements, the relations and the principles involved in the constitution of value and the generation of profit. I see no merit whatsoever in attempting to force these varied conditions into the conceptual mould of structure *qua* rules and resources. Moreover, I find it difficult to reconcile any such attempt with Marx's claim to be uncovering the essence of capitalist relations which is concealed beneath their phenomenal form, a form in terms of which the nature and value of commodities is *mis*understood by the very individuals involved in their production.[25] Giddens's account tends to equate social structure with practical knowledge and hence to elide the distinction between an analysis of the structural conditions of a certain kind of society, on the one hand, and a mere summary of what actors already know in knowing 'how to go on' in that society, on the other.[26] I believe that it is important to preserve this distinction, both for the purposes of social analysis and for the tasks of social science as *critique*. I believe, moreover, that this distinction can be preserved without succumbing to the 'derogation of the lay actor' which Giddens so rightly warns against.

The second difficulty I wish to raise concerns the consequences of Giddens's

[24] I do not wish to deny that people know a great deal about the conditions under which they work. In a remarkable study, illuminatingly discussed by Giddens in *CS* (pp. 289–304), Willis argues that certain aspects of the behaviour of working-class youths can be interpreted as 'cultural penetrations' of the structural conditions of capitalist production; their evasion of authority in the work-place, for example, can be interpreted as a penetration of the fact that labour power is a variable resource in capitalist society (see Paul E. Willis, *Learning to Labour: How Working Class Kids get Working Class Jobs* (Westmead, Farnborough, Hants.: Saxon House, 1977)). But Willis also argues that these penetrations are *partial*, that they bear on only certain aspects of the capitalist system and that even then they are 'repressed, disorganized and prevented from reaching their full potential or a political articulation by deep, basic and disorienting divisions' (p. 145). The interpretation of penetrations as *partial* presupposes an analysis of the structure of capitalist production which is independent of the *limited* knowledge possessed by the youths.

[25] See especially Marx's discussion of the 'fetishism of commodities' in *Capital*, vol. 1, pp. 76–87; see also his analysis of the 'mystified form' in which profit is understood by capitalists and economists in *Capital*, vol. 3, pp. 25–40.

[26] Bourdieu criticizes, rightly in my view, the tendency to project on to the object (or subject) of investigation the very models that one constructs in order to understand (or explain) it. This tendency is exacerbated by the notion of rule, which facilitates the 'sliding from the model of reality to the reality of the model' (Pierre Bourdieu, *Le Sens pratique*, p. 67).

distinctions for the problem of social reproduction. Part of the attraction of conceiving of structure in terms of rules and resources is that it offers a simple and readily graspable picture of how individuals, in pursuing their everyday activities, reproduce social structure. For in pursuing their activities individuals 'draw upon' rules and resources which are thereby reproduced, just as in speaking English one 'draws upon' and reproduces the rules of English grammar. This picture lies at the heart of Giddens's account; it is the constant point of reference in his many discussions of the duality of structure and the recursive character of social life. But the picture is deceptively simple. It presupposes that all structural features of social systems can be conceived in terms of rules and resources, where by 'rules' we understand something similar to the rules of English grammar. I have argued that this presupposition cannot be sustained. I have also argued that Giddens's own distinctions between different levels of structural analysis cannot be easily reconciled with this presupposition. These arguments call into question, in turn, the adequacy of Giddens's account of reproduction. And indeed it makes no sense, I would say, to suppose that 'structural principles' are reproduced by being 'drawn upon' by individuals in social interaction.[27] Hence what may have appeared to be the main attraction of Giddens's approach is in fact one of its principal shortcomings: the problem of reproduction is at best only partially resolved. In order to deal more adequately with this issue, I believe that one must distinguish more sharply than Giddens does between the reproduction of institutions and the reproduction of social structure. Institutions are characterized by rules, regulations and conventions of various sorts, by differing kinds and quantities of resources and by hierarchical relations of power between the occupants of institutional positions. When agents act in accordance with these rules and regulations or exercise the power which is institutionally endowed upon them, they may be said to reproduce the institutions. If, in so doing, the institutions continue to satisfy certain structural conditions, both in the sense of conditions which delimit the scope for *institutional variation* and conditions which underlie the operation of *structural differentiation*, then the agents may be said to reproduce social structure. Thus individuals who, in their everyday productive activities, reproduce the institutions of the Ford Motor Company may also be said to reproduce the conditions in virtue of which those institutions are capitalistic. But it is not difficult to imagine circumstances in which individuals may effectively transform those institutions *without* transforming their structural conditions. Every act of production and reproduction may also be a potential act of transformation, as Giddens rightly insists; but the extent to which an action transforms an institution does *not* coincide with the extent to which social structure is thereby transformed.

---

[27] Giddens appears to acknowledge this point in his somewhat cryptic discussion of 'circuits of reproduction' in *CS*, pp. 190–2; for 'structural principles' are here situated *outside* of the 'duality of structure' which connects 'structural properties' to the 'reflexive monitoring of action'.

As a third and final point, I want to forestall a possible objection to the criticisms made above. Surely I have overlooked, it may be said, Giddens's many references to the role of 'methodological bracketing'. According to Giddens, one may adopt one of two approaches to the study of the structural features of social systems. On the one hand, one can conduct an *institutional analysis* in which structural features are treated as chronically reproduced properties of social systems; on the other hand, one can pursue an *analysis of strategic conduct*, focusing on the ways in which actors draw upon structural features in the course of social interaction. Giddens stresses that this methodological distinction is merely a difference of emphasis: 'there is not a clear-cut line that can be drawn between these, and each – crucially – has to be in principle rounded out by a concentration upon the duality of structure'.[28] However, this is a distinction which must be treated with great care. For it can serve all too easily as a methodological blanket to cover over what are, I believe, deep conceptual difficulties in Giddens's account. Thus it will not suffice to object to my criticisms by saying that the analysis of structural principles, structural sets and so on is *not supposed* to show how such features are invoked and thereby reproduced by agents in social interaction, since it places interactional analysis in methodological brackets. This will not suffice because the problem is not a methodological but a conceptual one: a structural principle governing the alignment of institutions does not become a rule drawn upon in interaction by the mere removal of methodological brackets. I do not think that Giddens would wish to claim the contrary; but so far he has refused to acknowledge, as I think he must, that the recognition of different levels of structural analysis places intolerable strain on his original conception of structure.

Action, structure and constraint

To this point I have concentrated on the structural side of Giddens's attempt to overcome the dualism of action and structure. I now want to turn my attention briefly to his analysis of action and its relation to structure and constraint. Action may be conceptualized, Giddens suggests, in terms of a stratification model that takes account of the reflexive monitoring of action which agents routinely carry out, as well as the rationalization and motivation of action (including unconscious sources of motivation). Essential to the stratification model is the idea that, while much day-to-day life occurs as a continuous flow of intentional action, many acts have unintended consequences which may become the unacknowledged conditions of further acts. It is primarily in this way, according to Giddens, that action is linked to structure. For in pursuing some course of action the agent draws upon the rules and resources which comprise structure, thereby reproducing unintentionally the

---

[28] *CS*, p. 288.

structural conditions of further acts. '*Structure thus is not to be conceptualized as a barrier to action, but as essentially involved in its production*':[29] structure is *enabling* as well as constraining and is implicated in even the most radical processes of social change.

There are many aspects of Giddens's stratification model which I find attractive. He offers a framework for the analysis of action which makes room for the insights of many authors – from Heidegger and Schutz to Garfinkel, Goffman and Freud – without neglecting the dimension of institutions and social structure. Nevertheless, I believe that there are certain problems with this approach. Some of these problems can be raised by asking whether, in stressing the *enabling* character of structure, Giddens does justice to the role of *structural constraint*.[30] Let me begin to examine this question by returning to *New Rules of Sociological Method*, where the rules constitutive of structure are characterized as semantic rules and moral rules. In what senses do these rules operate as constraints on possible courses of action? Semantic rules are constraining in the sense that they oblige a speaker, who wishes to be understood by another, to adopt certain linguistic and grammatical forms; a speaker who uttered an expression like 'purple politicians spell in their sleep' would simply not be understood by a competent speaker of English. Moral rules are constraining in the sense that they are associated with sanctions which may be 'internal', relying upon the moral commitment of the agent or upon fear or guilt, or 'external', relying upon the offer of rewards or the threat of force. These are important kinds of constraint, and their significance in social life is not to be underestimated. It seems evident, however, that they are not the only kinds of constraint which are relevant to social analysis. When a school-leaver is faced with the choice of joining a youth training scheme or signing on the dole, the constraints which operate are not simply those of comprehensibility or sanctioning. For it is the *range of alternatives* which is restricted, and these restrictions do not stem from semantic and moral rules but from the structural conditions for the persistence (and decline) of productive institutions.

Giddens is aware of the importance of structural constraint and would no doubt accept that his earlier remarks on this theme are in need of elaboration. In *The Constitution of Society* he takes up the theme and seeks to show that his account can fully accommodate the role of constraint. There is no difficulty in showing, to begin with, that the theory of structuration is compatible with the recognition of limits imposed by the physical environment. Similarly it presents no problem to acknowledge that institutions, conceived of as regularized

---

[29] *CPST*, p. 70.

[30] For other discussions of Giddens's treatment of structural constraint, see Tommy Carlstein, 'The Sociology of Structuration in Time and Space: A Time-geographic Assessment of Giddens's Theory', *Svensk Geografisk Årsbok*, 57 (1981); Margaret S. Archer, 'Morphogenesis Versus Structuration: On Combining Structure and Action', *British Journal of Sociology*, 33 (1982), 455–83; and H. F. Dickie-Clark, 'Anthony Giddens's Theory of Structuration', *Canadian Journal of Political and Social Theory*, 8 (1984), 92–110.

practices which are 'deeply layered' in time and space, both pre-exist and post-date the lives of the individuals who reproduce them, and thus may be resistant to manipulation or change by any particular agent. But what of structural constraint, that is, of constraint which derives neither from physical conditions nor from specific institutions but from social structure? 'As with the constraining qualities of sanctions', proposes Giddens, 'it is best described *as placing limits upon the feasible range of options open to an actor in a given circumstance or type of circumstance.*'[31] Consider the limits imposed by the 'contractual relations of modern industry'. For individuals who have been rendered propertyless and deprived of their means of subsistence, there is only one alternative: namely, to sell their labour power to those who own the means of production. To say that there is only one alternative is to say that there is only one 'feasible option' – one option, that is, that actors having certain patterns of motivation (in this case, the wish to survive) will regard as reasonable to pursue. While a worker may have a choice between several job possibilities, in the end these options reduce to one, for ultimately the worker has no choice but to accept a job, whichever one it may be.

This elaboration of Giddens's views concurs with some of the modifications discussed in the previous section and is, once again, to be welcomed. Nevertheless, it seems to me that this elaboration raises two major problems for Giddens's account. In the first place, what Giddens now describes as 'structural constraint' cannot be readily reconciled with his proposal to conceive of structure in terms of rules and resources. The constraints which reduce the options of propertyless individuals to one – and increasingly today to the 'option' of unemployment – are imposed in part by the conditions of capitalist production and exchange; and I have already argued that it is unhelpful and misleading to try to force these conditions into the conceptual mould of structure *qua* rules and resources. The second problem concerns the relation between structural constraint and agency. A central theme of Giddens's account is that the concept of agency implies that a person 'could have done otherwise': 'an agent who has no options whatsoever', he insists, 'is no longer an agent'.[32] In his discussion of structural constraint, however, Giddens acknowledges the possibility that such constraint may reduce the options of an individual to one. It is not difficult to see that an individual who has one option has no options, for there are no other courses of action which the individual could have pursued and hence it seems senseless to say that he or she 'could have done otherwise'. Structure and agency no longer appear to be the complementary terms of a duality but the antagonistic poles of a dualism, such that structural constraint may so limit the options of the individual that agency is effectively dissolved.

Giddens's response to this evident problem is to emphasize the distinction

---

[31] *CS*, pp. 176–7.   [32] *CCHM*, p. 63.

between 'option' and 'feasible option'. An individual who has only one option is not an agent, for there is no sense in which that individual 'could have done otherwise'. But an individual who has only one *feasible* option is an agent, for the option is limited to one only in the sense that, *given* the individual's wants and desires, there is only one option that the individual would regard as reasonable to pursue. This response does not resolve the problem, however; it merely *bypasses* the problem by reaffirming a concept of agency which is, for all *practical* purposes, irrelevant. There is simply no imaginable circumstance in which an individual could not have done otherwise if, by 'the individual', we understand some pure and rarefied self, abstracted from every want and desire and always able to choose.[33] Giddens admits this much; even a prisoner who is gagged and bound and placed in solitary confinement remains an agent, 'as hunger strikes, or "the ultimate refusal" – suicide – indicate'.[34] Giddens manages to preserve the complementarity between structure and agency only by *defining* agency in such a way that any individual in any situation could not *not* be an agent.

A more direct confrontation with these issues would require, I believe, a more satisfactory conception of structure and structural constraint as well as a more systematic analysis of the wants and desires that are relevant to individual action and choice. All options are 'feasible options' in the sense that they are conditional upon the wants and desires of the agents whose options they are: a possible course of action would not be an option for an agent if it had no relevance to anything that the agent wanted. But options vary greatly in their range, their nature and in the character of the wants and desires upon which they depend. One of the key tasks of social analysis is to explore this space of possibilities, both in terms of the differential distribution of options according to class, age, sex and so on, but also in terms of the kinds of wants and desires, the interests and needs, which are themselves differentially possessed.[35] The differential distribution of options and needs implies that certain individuals or groups of individuals have greater scope for action and choice than other individuals or groups of individuals: freedom, one could say, is enjoyed by different people in differing degrees. To explore the space between the differential distribution of options, on the one hand, and the wants and needs of different kinds and of different categories of individuals, on the other, is to examine the degrees of freedom and constraint which are entailed by social structure. Such an analysis would show that, while structure and agency are not antinomies, nevertheless they are not as complementary and mutually supporting as Giddens would like us to believe.

[33] As Lukes observes, 'the way in which we answer the question "Could the agent have acted otherwise?" depends crucially on how the agent is conceptualized' (Steven Lukes, *Essays in Social Theory* (London: Macmillan, 1977), p. 25).

[34] *CCHM*, p. 63.

[35] Bourdieu's suggestive concept of *habitus* represents one attempt to explore the role of durable and differentially distributed wants and needs. See especially his *Outline of a Theory of Practice*, ch. 2.

Let me conclude this essay by summarizing my main criticisms of Giddens's work. I began by sketching the central themes of his account and by showing how, in *New Rules of Sociological Method*, the concept of structure is approached through a comparison of language and speech. While Giddens carefully qualifies this approach, nevertheless it is the source, I believe, of many of the difficulties in his account. For it is through a reflection on language and its relation to speech that he initially formulates a general conception of structure as rules and resources. I have argued that the proposal to conceive of structure in this way is unsatisfactory for several reasons: (1) the notion of rule is terribly vague and Giddens fails to provide a clear and consistent explication; and (2) the study of rules (and resources) does not address directly some of the key concerns in the analysis of social structure, such as the analysis of structural differentiation and the study of structural identity. We do not need a general conception of structure of which social structure, or the 'structures most relevant to the analysis of social life', would be a specific instance; we need a careful explication of what is involved in social structure and in the various forms of structural analysis in social inquiry. In his recent writings Giddens responds in more detail to the latter demand and distinguishes more clearly between different levels of structural analysis. While these distinctions are helpful, I believe that they place intolerable strain on the conception of structure *qua* rules and resources, a conception to which Giddens continues, somewhat tenaciously, to adhere. Moreover, these distinctions merely highlight the shortcomings of Giddens's approach to the problem of reproduction, an approach which is based on the over-simplified picture of an actor 'drawing upon' a rule. Finally, turning my attention briefly to the analysis of action, I tried to show that Giddens's emphasis on the enabling character of structure has led him to underplay the role of structural constraint. A more adequate treatment of the latter would have to acknowledge, I think, that action and social structure are neither contradictory nor complementary terms, but rather two poles which stand in a relation of tension with one another. For while social structure is reproduced and transformed by action, it is also the case that the range of options available to individuals and groups of individuals are differentially distributed and structurally circumscribed.

In developing my criticisms I have focused primarily on the conception of structure *qua* rules and resources and on the relation between action and structural constraint. For the sake of conciseness I have not examined the many interesting and important contributions which Giddens has made to the analysis of power, the theory of ideology and the conceptualization of time and space, let alone his more substantive work on class structure and the state. I have put aside these contributions partly because I accept Giddens's view that the relation between action and structure is in a certain sense primary, for it is in terms of this relation that the analysis of power, the theory of ideology and the conceptualization of time and space must be cast. It is my opinion that

Giddens has done more than any other contemporary thinker to advance our understanding of the complex ways in which action and structure intersect in the routine activities of everyday life. If my criticisms of Giddens's account are sound, then they will merely contribute to a task which he above all has set for social theory.

4

Models of historical trajectory: an assessment of Giddens's critique of Marxism[1]

ERIK OLIN WRIGHT

Critiques of historical materialism tend to be one of two types: either they are hostile attacks by anti-Marxists intent on demonstrating the falsity, perniciousness or theoretical irrelevance of Marxism, or they are reconstructive critiques from within the Marxist tradition attempting to overcome theoretical weaknesses in order to advance the Marxist project. In these terms, Anthony Giddens's two books, *A Contemporary Critique of Historical Materialism* and *The Nation-State and Violence*, are rare works: appreciative critiques by a non-Marxist of the Marxist tradition in social theory. While finding a great deal that is wrong with basic assumptions and general propositions in Marxism, Giddens also argues that 'Marx's analysis of the mechanisms of capitalist production . . . remains the necessary core of any attempt to come to terms with the massive transformations that have swept the world since the eighteenth century' (*CCHM*, p. 1). Indeed, there are certain specific discussions in the books – such as the use of the labour theory of value and the analysis of the capitalist labour process – in which Giddens's position is closer than many contemporary Marxists to orthodox Marxism. The books are thus not a wholesale rejection of Marxism, but rather an attempt at a genuine 'critique' in the best sense of the word – a deciphering of the underlying limitations of a social theory in order to appropriate in an alternative framework what is valuable in it. While, as I shall attempt to show, I think many of Giddens's specific arguments against historical materialism are unsatisfactory, the books are a serious engagement with Marxism and deserve a serious reading by both Marxists and non-Marxists.

An overview of Giddens's argument

The critiques elaborated in these books are rooted in Giddens's general theory of social agency and action, or what he terms the theory of 'social structuration'. In this chapter, however, I will not attempt a general assessment and

[1] This chapter is a revision of 'Giddens' Critique of Marxism', *New Left Review*, 138 (March–April 1983), 11–35.

Table 1. *Summary of Giddens's critique of historical materialism*

	Central Marxist concept	Giddens's critique	Giddens's alternative
1 Logic of interconnection of social whole	Functional totality	Functionalism	Contingently reproduced social system
2 Typology of social forms	Mode of production	Class and economic reductionism	Level of space–time distanciation
3 Logic of transformation	Dialectic of forces and relations of production	Evolutionism	Episodic transitions

summary of this broader framework. Instead I will focus on one core theme which is particularly prominent in the first of the two books: the critique of the Marxist account of the forms and development of societies and the elaboration of some of the essential elements of an alternative macro-structural 'theory of history'.

The heart of Giddens's argument revolves around three interconnected problems: (1) The methodological principles for analysing the interconnectedness of different aspects of society within a social whole or 'totality'; (2) the strategy for elaborating classification typologies of forms of societies; and (3) the theory of the movement or transition of societies from one form to another within such a typology. Giddens criticizes what he considers to be the Marxist treatment of each of these issues: functionalism in the Marxist analyses of the social totality; economic or class reductionism in the typologies of societies rooted in the concept of mode of production; and evolutionism in the theory of the transformation of social forms. In place of these central errors, Giddens offers the rudiments of his general theory of social structuration: instead of functionalism, social totalities are analysed as contingently reproduced social systems; instead of class and economic reductionism, forms of society are differentiated on the basis of a multi-dimensional concept of 'space–time distanciation'; and instead of evolutionism, transformations of social forms are understood in terms of what Giddens calls 'episodic transitions'. These critiques and alternatives are summarized in Table 1.

Functionalism and the social totality

Giddens correctly observes that much Marxist work can be characterized as covertly functionalist. He criticizes such functional explanations on a variety of familiar grounds: functionalist explanations rest on a false division between statics and dynamics; they tend to turn human actors into mere bearers of social relations, lacking any knowledge or intentionality; and, most importantly in Giddens's view, they falsely impute 'needs' to social systems. Giddens illustrates this critique in a brief discussion of Marx's theory of the reserve army of labour:

> Marx's analysis can be interpreted, and often has been so interpreted, in a functionalist vein. Capitalism has its own 'needs', which the system functions to fulfill. Since capitalism needs a 'reserve army', one comes into being. The proposition is sometimes stated in reverse. Since the operation of capitalism leads to the formation of a reserve army, this must be because it needs one. But neither version explains anything about why a reserve army of unemployed workers exists. Not even the most deeply sedimented institutional features of societies come about, persist, or disappear, because those societies need them to do so. They come about *historically*, as a result of concrete conditions that have in every case to be analysed; the same holds for their persistence or their dissolution.   (*CCHM*, p. 18)

The only way in which Giddens feels functional arguments can be legitimately employed in social science is when such arguments are treated in a strictly *counterfactual* manner: 'we can quite legitimately pose conjectural questions such as "What would have to be the case for social system x to come about, persist or be transformed?"' (*CCHM*, p. 19). But stating such conditions of existence does not constitute an explanation of anything; it merely points the direction towards what needs explaining.

Giddens is, I believe, substantially correct in both his assessment of the functionalist tendencies within Marxism and his critique of those tendencies. Social reproduction should always be understood as a contingent reality in need of explanation rather than as an automatically guaranteed process. While in some cases functional *descriptions* may be heuristically useful – i.e. descriptions of how a particular institution or structure in fact does reproduce class relations – such descriptions are never in and of themselves explanations.

In spite of my agreement with the main thrust of Giddens's arguments about functionalism, I feel his discussion of the problem is in certain respects misleading. First of all, he writes as if Marxists have largely ignored this problem, whereas in fact a great deal of the critical debate within Marxism in the past fifteen years has revolved around the problem of functionalism. This has been the case in the discussions of work by Althusser and other 'structuralist' Marxists, but the problem of functionalism has been raised in numerous other contexts as well.[2]

---

[2] It is particularly surprising in this context that Giddens has completely ignored the most sustained defence of functional explanations in historical materialism, G. A. Cohen's *Karl Marx's Theory of History: A Defense* (Princeton: Princeton University Press: 1978), and the debate over functionalism and Marxism which this book inspired. See in particular Jon Elster, 'Cohen on Marx's Theory of History', *Political Studies*, XXVIII:1 (March 1980), 121–8; Joshua Cohen, 'Review of *Karl Marx's Theory of History: A Defense*', *Journal of Philosophy* (1982), 253–73; and Andrew Levine and Erik Olin Wright, 'Rationality and Class Struggle', *New Left Review*, 123 (September–October 1980).

Secondly, while I think that Giddens is correct in his suspicion of the way writers slide from functional descriptions to functional explanations, I think he is wrong to totally dismiss the term 'function' from explanations of social phenomena. While the functionality of a given institution or practice is never a complete explanation of that institution, I see no reason why arguments about functionality cannot constitute an aspect of a proper explanation. Take the problem of racism, for example. Marxists often attempt to explain racial domination in terms of its negative consequences for working-class unity (divide and conquer). This is a functional explanation in that the phenomenon – racism – is explained by its beneficial effects for capitalism. This is clearly an incomplete explanation, for the simple fact of an effect being beneficial does not guarantee that the effect will be produced. A docile and happy working class would be beneficial for the Italian bourgeoisie, but this hardly assures the production of docility. But it is also the case, arguably, that in the absence of such beneficial effects for capitalism, racism would disappear *much more easily*. Thus the consequences of racism – its beneficial effects – can be considered part of the explanation for its persistence.

Giddens, I imagine, would accept this point, but still insist that it does not imply the legitimacy of any vestiges of functionalism in social theory. If the effects of racism are beneficial to the bourgeoisie, this helps to explain its persistence only because the actions of the bourgeoisie help to support racism. The explanation, then, would be based on an analysis of the discursive and practical aspects of the consciousness of actors and the associated strategies of action, not on the functional relation as such.

The fact that racism will actually have these 'beneficial effects', however, is not a property of the consciousness of the bourgeoisie, but of the social system within which they form their consciousness. It is, to use the formulation in G. A. Cohen's defence of functional explanations, a 'dispositional fact' of the social system. This is similar to the problem of functional explanation in biology. The causal explanation for the long neck of the giraffe (Cohen's favourite example) is a series of specific mutations that changed the genes of short-necked giraffes. The sense in which a functional explanation is still appropriate here is that unless it was a dispositional fact of the situation of short-necked giraffes that their chances for reproductive survival would be enhanced by long necks, those same mutations would not have led to the gradual increase in the length of the giraffe's neck. Similarly for functional explanations in sociology: unless it were a dispositional fact about the society that racism would produce the effects that it does, then the strategies of specific actors to ensure racism would not have the effects that they do.

Such dispositional facts, it must be emphasized, are real properties of social systems and thus can legitimately figure in causal explanations of social processes and outcomes. It is of course difficult to defend empirically claims about dispositional facts, and the form of argument in support of such claims often has recourse to counterfactual analyses in the ways suggested by

Giddens. But this does not imply that such analyses have the status simply of heuristic exercises designed to point the way towards questions; claims about dispositional properties of social systems are a part of many answers. Functional arguments, thus, can at least constitute part of a legitimate social explanation.

Certain of Giddens's own arguments can be reconstructed as functional explanations based on dispositional facts about particular kinds of societies. Consider, for example, his interesting arguments about the association between 'nationalism' and the nation-state. How should we explain the fact that nationalism plays such a prominent role in modern states? Giddens argues as follows:

> With the coming of the nation-state, states have an administrative and territorially ordered unity which they did not possess before. This unity cannot remain *purely* administrative however, because the very coordination of activities involved presumes elements of cultural homogeneity. The extension of communication cannot occur without the 'conceptual' involvement of the whole community of knowledgeable citizenry ... The sharing of a common language and a common symbolic historicity are the most thorough-going ways of achieving this (and are seen to be so by those leaders who have learned from the experience of the first 'nations'). (*NSV*, p. 219)

According to Giddens, modern nation-states face a problem of social reproduction – creating the necessary conceptual community for effective co-ordination – which has to be solved in one way or another. 'Nationalism' – a common symbolic historicity – is the pre-eminent solution. It is a dispositional fact of nation-states that nationalism will contribute to social reproduction. Through a process of historical learning, leaders come to understand this, and thus the functional solution becomes generalized.

It could be objected that this is not truly an instance of 'functional explanation' because intentionality plays a key role in the feedback mechanism which establishes the functional outcome. In the case of nationalism it is implausible that nationalism would become a general ideological feature of nation-states if political actors did not recognize its cohesion-producing effects. Much of the debate over Cohen's use of functional explanation in historical materialism has centered precisely on this point. If the mechanism that explains the functional relation is the conscious beliefs of the actors in the desirability of the outcome, as Elster and others have argued, this should simply be treated as a special instance of intentional explanation rather than functional explanation.

Even if we adopt this very restrictive use of the designation 'functional explanation', Giddens's absolute injunction against functional arguments is unjustified, for there are specific situations in which fully fledged functional explanations that do not rely on the actors' belief in the beneficial consequences of a given practice are possible in social science. Jon Elster, himself a vigorous opponent of functionalism, gives a clear example in his discussion of profit-maximizing strategies of captialist firms.[3] Elster argues that it is appropriate to use a functional explanation to answer the question 'Why do capitalist firms adopt on average profit-maximizing strategies?' His argument is that the market acts as a selective mechanism which eliminates firms that adopt sub-optimal strategies. After a sufficiently long operation of the market, only those firms which happened to adopt profit-maximizing strategies will survive. Thus, even though the decision-making procedures within capitalist firms operate on 'rough-and-ready rules of thumb', only those particular rules of thumb which happen coincidentally to maximize profits will survive over time. The end result, therefore, will be a distribution of strategies among firms which are generally functional for the reproduction of those firms, even though such a distribution was not intended by any actor within the system. Of course, it may empirically happen that some capitalists consciously attempt to adopt profit-maximizing strategies. Elster's point is that we need not assume that they do so in order to understand how the functional outcome is possible. Conscious profit-maximization may improve the efficiency of the selective mechanisms, but the functional relationship is itself structurally ensured through the operation of the market.

To be sure, there are relatively few social processes which have the properties of firms acting in a competitive market, and thus it is generally not the case that completely non-intentional selective mechanisms operate to produce functional relations. Functional explanations by themselves are usually unsatisfactory precisely because no plausible mechanism for regulating the functional outcome can be posited. Giddens is therefore quite justified to be suspicious of functional explanations. His categorical rejection of any use of functional arguments within social explanations, however, is unwarranted.

Typologies of social forms

At the heart of Marxist theory lies a particular strategy for classifying societies. In one way or another, all Marxists root their typologies of social forms in the concept of class structure, which is itself based on the concept of mode of production. While there are substantial disagreements over how the concept of mode of production should be defined and precisely how class structures should be distinguished, there is a general agreement among Marxists that these concepts provide the central principle both for differentiating types of societies and for providing a road map of the historical trajectory of societal transformations. Even where Marxists allow a great deal of room for the autonomy of relations of domination other than class (for example ethnic, gender, national domination), they nevertheless characterize the overall form of society primarily in terms of its class structure.

---

[3] *Ulysses and the Sirens* (Cambridge: Cambridge University Press, 1979), p. 31.

A great deal of *A Contemporary Critique* is devoted to challenging this principle of social typology. The accusation that historical materialism is an economic or class reductionist theory is, of course, a standard criticism. What is unusual about Giddens's position is that he rejects class-based typologies of societies without challenging the importance of class analysis in general.

Giddens raises the critique of reductionism in two contexts: first, he insists that only in capitalism can class be viewed as the central structural principle of the society as a whole, and thus, in general, class structure provides an inadequate basis for specifying the pivotal differences between social forms; and second, he argues that societies are characterized by multiple forms of domination and exploitation which cannot be reduced to a single principle, class. The first of these can be termed the critique of *inter*societal class reductionism, and the second, of *intra*societal class reductionism. Since Giddens spends so much more time discussing the first of these, I will concentrate on it below.

Intersocietal class reductionism

Societies should not be primarily classified in terms of their class structures, Giddens argues, because only in capitalism is it the case that class constitutes the basic structural principle of the society. Only in capitalism does class permeate all aspects of social life. While various forms of non-capitalist society may have had classes, class relations did not constitute their core principle of social organization. This argument forms the basis of a pivotal distinction which Giddens makes between *class society* (a society within which class is the central structural principle) and *class-divided society* ('a society in which there are classes, but where class analysis does not serve as a basis for identifying the basic structural principle of organization of that society', *CCHM*, p. 108).

Giddens's defence of this proposition revolves around his analysis of *power* and *domination*. Power, in Giddens's theory of 'social structuration', is defined as a sub-category of transformative capacity, in which 'transformative capacity is *harnessed to actors' attempts to get others to comply with their wants*. Power, in this relational sense, concerns the capacity of actors to secure outcomes where the realisation of these outcomes depends upon the agency of others.'[4] This relational transformative capacity rests on specific kinds of resources which are used to get others to comply. In particular, Giddens distinguishes between *allocative* resources (resources involving control over nature) and *authoritative* resources (resources involving control over social interactions of various sorts). *Domination* is then defined as 'structured asymmetries of resources drawn upon and reconstituted in such power relations' (*CCHM*, p. 50).

On the basis of these concepts of power and domination, societies can be classified along two principal dimensions:

---

[4] Giddens, *CPST*, p. 93. Italics in the original.

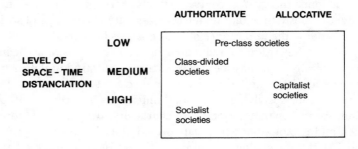

Figure 1

(1)   *Which type of resource domination, allocative or authoritative, is most important for sustaining power relations.* Giddens argues that it is only in capitalism that control over allocative resources *per se* is of prime importance. In all non-capitalist societies 'authoritative resources were the main basis of both political and economic power' (*CCHM*, p. 108).

(2)   *The magnitude of control over each of these resources in time and space.* This is the core of Giddens's complex concept of 'space–time distanciation'. The control over any resource can be specified in terms of its extension over time and space. This is easiest to understand in terms of allocative resources. Hunting and gathering societies involve rather limited control over allocative resources in both time and space: food is continually acquired in the present with relatively short time horizons, and trade over long distances (spatial extension of allocative resources) is very limited. On both of these counts, settled agriculture involves greater space–time 'distanciation'. And industrial capitalism, of course, extends this to historically unprecedented levels: production is organized globally and allocative time horizons extend over decades in some cases. In terms of authoritative resources, the central basis for the extension over time and space is the increasing capacity of a society for *surveillance*, i.e. for the gathering and storing of information and the supervising of subordinate groups. The basic institutional sites for this extension of authoritative resources in time and space are initially the city and subsequently the state.

Taking these two dimensions together produces the general typology of societal forms shown in Figure 1. This is certainly a different kind of typology from the usual Marxist typology of modes of production. But are the two really completely incompatible? Giddens certainly believes that they are. Nevertheless, I think that the distance may not be quite so great as he imagines.

The central qualitative break in Giddens's typology occurs between capitalism and all non-capitalist societies. Only in capitalism are allocative resources the central basis of power, and thus only in capitalism can class be viewed as the organizing principle of the society. This seems to run directly counter to the Marxist thesis that class structures (or modes of production) are the basic structural principle of all societies. On closer inspection, however, I think that the difference may not be quite so significant for two reasons.

First of all, we can ask: *why* is it that in non-capitalist societies authoritative resources are the basis of power, whereas in capitalism allocative resources are the basis? One answer, of course, is to say that this question is illegitimate. The authoritative/allocative resource distinction could be treated strictly as the taxonomic criterion for specifying the different types of society, and thus there would be no theoretically meaningful answer to the question (any more than there is a theoretically meaningful answer to the question why mammals nurse their young while birds do not, since in the absence of nursing a mammal wouldn't be a mammal).

Giddens, however, does not seem to reject this question, and when he does attempt to explain the differences between the two types of society, he tends to emphasize the causal importance of differences in their economic structures: the importance of agrarian production, the degree of economic autonomy of communities, the existence of free wage labour, the alienability of different forms of property, etc.[5] While Giddens clearly emphasizes non-economic factors in his explanations of the *genesis* of capitalism (for instance the specificity of the European state system), he consistently argues that it is the distinctive property relations of capitalism that explain why class becomes such a central organizing principle of capitalist societies.[6] Such an explanation, however, is symmetrical: the distinctive property relations of feudal society (in contrast to capitalism) explain why in feudalism the control of authoritative resources is the central axis of power. Or to state the problem more generally: throughout Giddens's analysis, it is *variations* in the nature of property relations which explain *variations* in the relative centrality of control over allocative or authoritative resources in the society.

This argument comes quite close to Marx's argument in *Capital* that the economic structure of society is 'determinant' even if in specific types of society other aspects of society may be 'primary':

---

[5] See, for example, *CCHM*, pp. 114–15; *NSV*, pp. 70–1.
[6] Classical Marxism, of course, sees class as central both to the problem of historical trajectories and to the problem of social structure. Thus, 'class struggle is the motor of history' is traditionally as important a formula as class structures constitute the material foundation of society. Giddens quite consistently rejects the dynamic role attributed to class struggles in Marxism. Contrary to his rhetoric, however, his arguments constitute a much more ambiguous critique of the centrality of class structures in the explanation of variations across societies.

My view is that each particular mode of production, and the social relations corresponding to it at each given moment, in short, the economic structure of society ... conditions the general process of social, political and intellectual life. In the opinion of the German–American publication this is all very true for our own times, in which material interests are preponderant, but not for the Middle Ages, dominated by Catholicism, nor for Athens and Rome, dominated by politics ... One thing is clear: the Middle Ages could not live on Catholicism, nor could the ancient world on politics. On the contrary, it is the manner in which they gained their livelihood which explains why in one case politics, in the other Catholicism, played the chief part.[7]

This idea is also at the heart of Louis Althusser's notion of societies as a 'structured totality' within which the form of economic structure determines which aspect (instance or level) of the society is 'dominant'. To be sure, Giddens emphatically, and I think correctly, rejects the functionalist logic underlying Althusser's argument. But nevertheless it appears that when Giddens tries to explain the differences in the relationship between allocative and authoritative resources in capitalist and non-capitalist societies he also relies heavily on differences in the system of property relations.

A second reason why Giddens's position may not be quite so distant from some Marxist formulations centres on the concept of class itself. Giddens very narrowly ties the concept of class to 'sectional forms of domination created by private ownership of property', where 'ownership' is taken to mean the direct control over the use and disposition of the means of production, and 'private' is meant to designate legally guaranteed individual rights of disposition over those means of production. This means that where a group appropriates surplus through directly coercive means without controlling the actual use of the means of production, this appropriation is treated as a result of the control over authoritative resources (command over military personnel and activity), not ownership of private property as such. The *result* of such coercive appropriation is still class divisions since it produces differential access to allocative resources (i.e. rich and poor), but the *basis* for the appropriation itself is not the class structure, but the structure of authoritative domination. Feudal exploiting classes, therefore, are not classes directly by virtue of property relations as such, but only by virtue of the secondary effects of the redistributive mechanisms of feudal authoritative power. It is for this reason that Giddens insists such societies should be termed class-divided rather than class societies.

---

[7] *Capital*, vol. I (London: Penguin Books, 1976), pp. 175–6. Marx's reasoning in this quote is quite elliptical. The fact that feudal society could not 'live on' Catholicism does not show why the form of production has explanatory primacy. Giddens's analyses of how particular forms of social conflict and power relations are conditioned by particular forms of property relations provide a more refined analysis. Giddens's arguments, however, do not contravene Marx's point that it is fundamentally differences in property relations – class relations/economic structures – which explain the broader structural differences between capitalist and feudal society.

This formulation by Giddens depends heavily upon his definition of 'class'. Many Marxists, myself included, define classes in terms of the mechanisms by which surplus products or suplus labour is appropriated, not by private property in the means of production as such.[8] Such appropriation of surplus always involves specific combinations of economic and political mechanisms (i.e. relations to allocative and authoritative resources in the present context). In feudal societies this mechanism involves the direct use of extra-economic coercion; in capitalist societies the political face of class relations is restricted to the guarantee of contracts and the supervision of the labour process. In both societies, however, it is the mechanisms of surplus extraction which specify the character of class relations.

What this suggests is that the disagreement between Giddens and many Marxists is at least partially of a terminological nature. Many Marxists draw precisely the same descriptive contrast as Giddens does between the economic mechanisms of class relations rooted in the labour contract of capitalist society and the extra-economic coercive mechanisms of non-capitalist class societies. And many Marxists agree completely with Giddens that this qualitative distinction between capitalist and pre-capitalist (or non-capitalist) societies is a much more fundamental break than any distinctions among the range of pre-capitalist societies (G. A. Cohen in particular stresses this point). Where they differ is in how the term 'class' is to be employed with respect to the use of authoritative and allocative resources in surplus appropriation.

Now, terminological disputes are rarely innocent. It is generally the case that drawing the boundary criteria for a concept in one way or another opens up or closes off lines of theoretical inquiry. When Marxists treat the mechanism of appropriation (exploitation of labour) as the pivot for specifying class relations they are doing so because, at least implicitly, they feel that: (1) these mechanisms determine a set of social actors or collectivities with opposing interests and thus tendencies towards struggle; (2) the typological distinctions among these mechanisms constitute the basis for distinguishing societies with different dynamics, forms of social conflict, trajectories of development; and (3) the different elements within these mechanisms do not have an autonomous logic, but instead form at least a loose kind of gestalt. The last point is, I think, the most fundamental in the present context. By combining the joint effect of control over allocative and authoritative resources in the specification of class relations, Marxists are at least implicitly arguing that these two forms of resource control are not just contingently interconnected. They are systematically linked one to the other so that only certain forms of variation can occur

---

[8] For an important dissenting view in which a narrow property relations definition of class is defended in Marxist terms, see John Roemer, *A General Theory of Class and Exploitation* (Cambridge, Mass.: Harvard University Press, 1982). This debate over the status of 'private property' in the definition of class begins to dissolve when the term 'property' is extended to include a range of productive resources other than the means of production as such.

in their forms of combination. By excluding the relation to authoritative resources from the concept of class, Giddens is, in contrast, affirming his view that the social organization of authoritative resources and their development and transformation is autonomous from allocative resources. (This is not to say, of course, that in Giddens's argument the development of forms of control of authoritative resources has no effects on allocative resource control, but simply that those effects are contingent rather than necessary.)

The implications of this difference in claims about the relationship between allocative and authoritative resources will become clearer when we discuss the problem of evolutionism below. But first we must briefly turn to the issue of intrasocietal class reductionism.

Intrasocietal class reductionism

Historical materialism is class reductionist, Giddens argues, not only in its treatment of the central differences between societies: it is reductionist in its treatment of the various forms of domination within given societies. In addition to class exploitation Giddens argues that:

> There are three axes of exploitative relationships ... which are not explained, though they may be significantly illuminated, either by the theory of exploitation of labor in general or by the theory of surplus value in particular. These are: (a) exploitative relations between states, where these are strongly influenced by military domination; (b) exploitative relations between ethnic groups, which may or may not converge with the first; and (c) exploitative relations between the sexes, sexual exploitation. None of these can be reduced exhaustively to class exploitation.   (*CCHM*, p. 242)

As Giddens points out, Marxists have often attempted to explain the existence and forms of these axes of domination or exploitation as 'expressions' of class, typically by recourse to functional explanations. If such reductionist accounts are illegitimate, then the attempt at characterizing the overall form of society strictly in terms of modes of production is clearly inadequate, since interstate, ethnic and sexual relations of domination within societies have sources of variation independent of class structures.

Many, perhaps most, contemporary Marxist theorists accept much of this argument against class reductionism. In general there is a recognition that at least ethnic and sexual domination are not simply reflexes of class domination, and some Marxists would add interstate domination to this as well. How much autonomy such relations have and precisely how their articulation with the class system should be understood are, of course, matters of considerable disagreement. While tendencies towards functional reductionism continue in the Marxist tradition, it is nevertheless the case that the thrust of much contemporary Marxist thinking has been against attempts at intrasocietal class reductionism.

Where Marxists would tend to disagree with Giddens is in the implication that such irreducibility of sex or ethnicity or nationality to class implies that these various forms of domination/exploitation are of potentially equal status in defining the differences among societies. Most Marxists would continue to argue for a general primacy of class, even if other relations are not simple reflections of class. In particular it is often argued that the class structure determines the limits of possible variation of other forms of relations, even if it does not functionally determine the specificity of those relations. If such arguments are correct, class relations do not simply 'illuminate' the analysis of sex, ethnicity or nationality, as Giddens suggests; they determine the basic structural parameters within which these other relations develop.

This kind of argument, of course, can be reversed. It can be argued, as many feminist writers have argued, that gender relations impose limits on forms of variation on the class structure. And it is certainly plausible to argue that the interstate system of political and military relations imposes real limits on the possible forms of development of class relations. If the relations of limitation are symmetrical, then it is rather arbitrary to claim any primacy for class relations.

Yet Marxists continue to argue for such primacy, if sometimes covertly or apologetically. Three kinds of arguments are used to defend the primacy of class. First, it is sometimes argued, if only implicitly, that while various non-class forms of domination are irreducible to class, class most systematically and deeply structures the subjectivity of actors. This does not imply that individuals are necessarily 'class conscious' in the sense of being aware of their class position and class interests, but simply that their forms of social consciousness are more systematically shaped by class relations than by any other relations and should therefore be accorded primacy.

A second argument for class primacy shifts the attention from the consciousness of actors to the objective constraints under which they act. Here the argument is that class relations, by structuring the access to material resources of various sorts (particularly the social surplus), most pervasively determine the limits on the capacities for action of different groups, including groups which are not directly defined by class relations as such. Thus, for example, racial domination may be irreducible to class domination, and yet the condition for blacks to struggle effectively against racial domination may be gaining control over more of the surplus product. Thus, even if the interests or motivations for struggle are irreducible to class interests, the conditions for successful pursuit of those non-class interests are fundamentally structured by class relations.[9]

---

[9] This argument rests on the distinction between the *interests* groups may have and their *capacities* for realizing those interests (see Erik Olin Wright, *Class, Crisis and the State* (London: NLB, 1978, pp. 98–108)). Functionalist attempts at reducing non-class relations to class relations typically involve a translation of non-class interests into class interests. The 'interests' whites might have in dominating blacks, for example, are explained in terms of the interests the bourgeoisie has in dominating workers: the former is functional for the latter. Here non-class interests are viewed as radically irreducible to class interests, but the capacities for realizing those non-class interests are viewed as systematically constrained by class structure.

Giddens partially endorses these two arguments in the case of capitalism –
and thus his designation of capitalism as a class society, a society within which
class permeates all facets of social life, deeply shaping the forms of subjectivity
and conditions of action of all social actors. But he rejects this kind of reasoning
as a general thesis about the effects of class in all societies. In this I think
Giddens is correct. Furthermore, even in capitalism, it is not clear that the
arguments for the *centrality* of class in the formation of subjectivity and
conditions for struggle can be extended into an argument for the *primacy* of
class. There may well be specific situations in which racial or gender
conditions more deeply stamp the subjectivity of actors than class. And while
struggle for control over material resources may be *an* essential condition
for struggle against non-class forms of domination, there are many other
necessary conditions as well, including struggles over ideology and control
of political apparatuses, neither of which can be viewed as simply effects of
control over material resources. As many people have argued, where multiple
necessary conditions of struggle exist, it is generally arbitrary to assign one of
these necessary conditions the privileged theoretical position of 'causal primacy'. These defences of the primacy of class, therefore, are at best
problematic.

The premise of this argument is that indeed class relations have internally

This, then, leads to the third argument in defence of the primacy of class.
While it may be the case that there are many processes which interact to set the
conditions of struggle, Marxists have generally argued that only class relations
have an internal logic of development, a logic which generates systematic
tendencies for a trajectory of transformations of the class structure. This
trajectory has a general directionality to it, it is argued, because of the way
class relations and class struggles are articulated to the development of the
forces of production. No such developmental trajectory has been persuasively
argued for other forms of domination. While class structures cannot be accorded any *static* primacy with respect to other social relations, they can
therefore be potentially accorded a *dynamic* primacy.

The premise of this argument is that indeed class relations have internally
generated tendencies of development. If this argument is false, then Giddens's
implicit argument for a pluralism of symmetrical forms of exploitation and
domination would be difficult to challenge. To assess this argument we must
turn to the third critique Giddens raises against historical materialism:
evolutionism.

Evolutionism

Throughout *A Contemporary Critique of Historical Materialism* Giddens attacks all
forms of evolutionary thinking in social theory. He does so for two principal
reasons, one methodological and the other primarily empirical. Methodologically, most evolutionary perspectives in sociology are based on some notion of

adaptation, particularly of adaptation of society to its material environment. But, Giddens insists, it is meaningless to talk about 'societies' adapting to anything: 'the idea of adaptation falls in the same category as the functional "needs" to which I have already objected. Societies have no need to "adapt" to (master, conquer) their material environments' (*CCHM*, p. 21). Societies are not organisms, and it is an inadmissible use of language to see them as evolving adaptively in the manner of biological organisms. The tacit teleology of such arguments must be rejected.

An alternative is to reconstruct the theory of social evolution on the basis of a theory of individual human adaptation. Human individuals, it could be argued, adapt to their environment and through such adaptation the societies within which they live may be pushed along some evolutionary path, even though the mechanism is not really lodged in 'society' per se. Such a reconstruction, Giddens argues, simply fails empirically. While it no longer rests on the methodological sin of reifying society, it is now based on a false empirical generalization, namely that there is a transhistorical tendency for human beings to improve their material conditions of existence. Furthermore, no alternative transhistorical principle of adaptation can be found: in Giddens's view there simply are no transhistorical individual drives or motives which could provide the basis for a general theory of social development.

The Marxist theory of history is thus doubly unsatisfactory. It is, in Giddens's view, empirically false. It is simply not true that there is any general tendency for the forces of production to develop throughout history, and thus the 'dialectic' of forces and relations of production could not possibly be the basis for a general trajectory of historical development. And it is methodologically flawed in its presupposition that societies have transhistorical adaptive imperatives.

In place of such evolutionary schemas, Giddens offers a view of social change in terms of what he calls 'episodic transitions', 'time–space edges' and 'contingent historical development'. 'Episodes', Giddens writes, 'refer to processes of social change that have definite direction and form, and in which definite structural transformations occur' (*CCHM*, p. 23). The critical point is that the directionality and dynamics of such change are specific to each episode, each historically specific form of social transition. There is no general dynamic or direction to social change. There are no 'episodes of episodes'. 'Time–space edges' refer to the 'simultaneous existence of types of society in episodic transitions' (p. 23). Giddens feels that evolutionary theories imply successions of societies in sequences of stages, whereas in fact social change is always a process of overlapping of different forms of society. Finally, Giddens sees the overarching trajectory of historical development as involving radically contingent factors: 'There are no "inevitable trends" in social development that are either hastened or held back by specific historical processes. All general patterns of social organization and social change are compounded of

contingent outcomes, intended and unintended . . . ' (*NSV*, p. 235).[10] Instead of
a theory of social evolution, Giddens thus envisions social change as a set of
discontinuous, contingently determined, overlapping transitions which have
no overall pattern or logic of development.

I will criticize Giddens's treatment of evolutionism on several grounds: first,
while he is correct in rejecting teleological forms of evolutionary theory, he is
wrong to characterize evolutionary theory as generally teleological; second,
when a proper specification of evolutionary theory is made, it does not have the
flaws attributed to it by Giddens; and third, Giddens's own theory of space–
time distanciation and episodic transitions should be viewed as a variety of
evolutionary theory in these terms. My conclusion will therefore be that the
challenge Giddens poses to Marxist theory is not so much anti-evolutionism
versus evolutionism, but two substantively different theories of social
evolution.

What is an evolutionary theory of social change?

Giddens is on firm ground when he rejects theories of social evolution which
are built on teleological arguments, arguments that societies inexorably develop towards some end-state of increasing adaptation to environmental or
material conditions. And he is correct that one finds such images of social
development in many social theories employing evolutionary arguments.

In contrast to Giddens's claims, however, I would argue that teleology is not
an essential part of evolutionary theory. Giddens's objections to teleological
theories of history should properly be viewed as objections to 'organic growth'
models of social change rather than evolutionary models. The distinction
between organic growth models and evolutionary models is clear in biology.
An organic growth model of the development of a given organism from
conception to death is appropriate because the genetic structure of the organism programmes such a development from the start.[11] In contrast, the theory
of biological evolution does not postulate any necessary end-state, any programmed sequence of stages. There is no inherent necessity for single-celled
organisms to evolve eventually into human beings. Evolutionary theory allows
for a retrospective explanation of the transitions and developments that occurred,

[10] Arguments of contingency play an especially important role in the analysis of *The Nation-State
and Violence*. Giddens argues, for example, that the universal scope of the nation-state in the
modern world is to be explained in part by 'a series of contingent historical developments that
cannot be derived from general traits attributed to nation-states, but which have nonetheless
decisively influenced the trajectory of development of the modern world' (*NSV*, p. 256).
Included in this list of contingencies is the long peace of the nineteenth century and the nature
of the treaties following the First World War. This is parallel, it should be noted, to the claim by
evolutionary biologists that the development of new species is to be explained in part by various
contingent events (climatic changes, mutations, etc.).

[11] It should be noted that a genetically based organic growth model of the development of an
organism from conception to embryo to birth to growth to death does not preclude the analysis
of contingencies in the life of any specific organism. Indeed, the genetic theory of inherent
tendencies of development in the given type of organism is necessary if we are to be able to
identify a contingent event – being killed by a disease – as a contingent event.

but the specific sequence and end-state involved countless contingent events that are completely outside of the theoretical purview of evolutionary biology. Giddens is quite justified in attacking theories of history that treat historical trajectories like the organic growth of an organism from embryo to maturity. But he is wrong to characterize such theories as evolutionary.

For a theory of society to be evolutionary three conditions must hold:

(1)   The theory must involve a typology of social forms which *potentially* has some kind of directionality to it. Evolutionary theories are not built simply around taxonomies of societies, but typologies capable of being ordered in a logically non-arbitrary way.

(2)   It must be possible to order these forms of society in such a way that the probability of staying at the same level of the typology is greater than the probability of regressing. The typology is thus 'sticky downward'.

(3)   In this ordered typology, there must be a positive probability of moving from a given level of the typology to the next higher level. This probability need not be greater than the probability of regressing, but once movement 'up' occurs, the probability of staying there is greater than the probability of moving back (by condition 2). This implies that there is some process, however weak and sporadic, which imparts a directionality to movements from one form to another.[12]

Several things are important to note about this way of defining evolutionary theory. First, there is no claim that societies have needs or teleologically driven tendencies towards achieving some final state. Teleological arguments would be one way of elaborating conditions 2 and 3, but not the only way. Second, this way of defining evolutionary theory does not imply that there is a rigid sequence of stages through which all societies *must* move. There is no statement that the probability of skipping a stage is zero. The only claim is that there is some positive impulse for movement and that movements can be characterized as directional. Third, it does not follow from this specification that all societies necessarily evolve. Regressions are possible, perhaps in some historical circumstances even more likely than progressions. And in most societies, long-term steady states may be more likely than any systematic tendency for movement in the typology of social forms. All that is implied in the criteria for evolutionary theory is that given enough time, *some* societies will evolve in the manner indicated by the evolutionary typology.

Finally, this definition of evolutionary theory does not imply a meta-theory of history in the sense of claims for a universal mechanism of transition from

---

[12] It should be noted that this specification of the desiderata of evolutionary theories of social change is somewhat stronger than would normally be suggested for evolutionary biology. In biology there is no general agreement that the typological forms in evolutionary development have any inherent 'directionality' other than the actual historical sequences that in fact occurred. Theorists who attempt to construct evolutionary theories of society, however, generally do accord some kind of logical ordering to the forms of society (not simply a temporal ordering). This, of course, is what makes such theories seem to be teleological.

one form of society to another. There is, to be sure, an overall logic which allows for an ordering of the typology in the evolutionary process, but the actual mechanisms which might explain movement between adjacent forms in the typology need not be the same at every stage in the typology. The theory specifies a road map of history and specifies what kinds of movements are likely to be stable or unstable, reproducible or unreproducible. But it does not necessarily postulate a universal process of transition. Indeed, as in the case of biological evolution, there may be a very high level of contingency involved in the concrete explanation of any given evolutionary development.

This specification of evolutionary theory is clearly non-trivial. There is no logical reason why every taxonomy of societies should meet these criteria. It may not be possible to order social forms in this way.

The Marxist theory of history

At least some versions of the Marxian theory of social change meet these three criteria. While it is certainly true that before capitalism there were no strong impulses for the development of the forces of production, nevertheless it was the case that (a) there was in general a positive probability of the forces of production developing, if only very slowly, and (b) the probability of regression was less than the probability of retaining given levels of productivity.

The defence of such claims need not rely at all on theses about the goals or needs of society. What is needed is a general argument for why the development of the forces of production should be 'sticky downward'. A number of such arguments can be found in Marxist writings: first, and perhaps least contentiously, there are in general no groups in a society with strong interests directly in reducing the level of productivity of labour. People may have interests which have the unintended consequence of reducing productivity (for instance they may have interests which lead them to engage in military activity which results in a destruction of forces of production), or, in specific circumstances, they may intentionally strive to reduce productivity to accomplish some other interest (for example workers may want to reduce productivity to protect their jobs). But no one has an interest in reducing labour productivity per se. This means that once a level of productivity is reached there will not in general be groups organized to reduce it.

Second, the key aspect of the development of the forces of production is the development of knowledge of productive techniques, not the physical hardware as such. As G. A. Cohen has argued, with any luck if a society can retain the knowledge of production it can restore a given level of productivity even if the physical means of production are destroyed, whereas if the knowledge is lost then those physical means of production are useless even if they are in working order. Knowledge, in general, has a 'sticky downward' character.[13] This does not mean that technical knowledge is never lost, but simply that there will be strong tendencies for it to be transmitted from one generation to the next.

[13] See Cohen, *Karl Marx's Theory of History*, p. 41.

Third, as Marx and Engels argued in *The German Ideology*, once a given level of the forces of production is reached by whatever route, it tends to engender new needs in people which are dependent upon that level of development of the forces of production. This means that in addition to there being no groups (in general) with strong interests in the reduction of labour productivity, there will be groups with strong interests in the preservation of a given level.

Fourth, specific arguments can be made for why there are also interests in enhancing labour productivity, and thus developing the forces of production (and not simply preventing their decline). Under conditions in which increases in labour productivity have the consequence of reducing the toil of direct producers, those producers will in general have interests in developing the forces of production. Direct producers may not have any particular interest in increasing the surplus product as such, but they will have interests in reducing unpleasant labour.[14] This means that in pre-class societies in which improvements in labour productivity generally imply lesser toil, direct producers will have interests in increasing productivity. This does not mean that people will feel under any great *pressure* to reduce toil, but simply that when innovations which reduce toil occur for whatever reasons and however sporadically, they will tend to be adopted.

In societies with class exploitation, however, there is no longer any necessary link between the development of the forces of production and the reduction of toil. On the contrary, in many cases technical changes may be associated with the intensification of toil of direct producers. There will thus no longer be any *universal* interests in positively developing the forces of production. Ruling classes, however, will generally have at least weak interests in adopting changes which increase labour productivity. They certainly have class interests in maintaining or enhancing the level of surplus appropriation, since this is critical to their reproduction as a ruling class. And except in peculiar circumstances where increasing productivity undermines their ability to appropriate surplus, this implies that they will have some interest in the development of the forces of production. This certainly does not mean that before capitalism ruling classes experienced systematic pressures to encourage such innovations, but simply that they will tend to adopt them when they occur.

To be sure, this is a very weak impulse throughout much of human history. It took hundreds of thousands of years of toilsome existence before some of the basic innovations which marked the transition from hunting and gathering societies to settled agriculture occurred. The argument is simply that there is

---

[14] This does not imply a transhistorical definition of what constitutes 'toil'; the content of the activities defined as toilsome undoubtedly changes radically with the development of the forces of production. The only requirement is that in the human encounter with nature, some activities are experienced as unpleasant, toilsome, painful. The weak impulse for technical innovation need not come from a transhistorical drive to 'expand the surplus product' or even to 'reduce scarcity' understood in terms of consumption, but simply to reduce toil. See Cohen, *Karl Marx's Theory of History*, pp. 302–7, for an elaboration of this argument.

at least a weak impulse for such improvement and that when such achievements are made, they are not willingly relinquished.

The Marxist theory of history, of course, is not simply a technological
typology of societies. The heart of the theory is a specific argument about the
interconnection between the tendency for the forces of production to develop
and the social relations of production within which those forces of production
are used. Two pivotal claims are made: (1) that for a given level of the forces of
production, only certain types of production relations are possible. Other
forms, if they were to occur through historical accidents, would be highly
unstable and would be more or less rapidly transformed into a 'compatible
form'. (2) With a given form of production relations, there is a limit to the
possible development of the forces of production. There is thus a relationship
of reciprocal limitation between the forces and relations of production. However, as argued above, there is at least a weak impulse for the forces of
production to develop, and this creates a dynamic asymmetry in their interconnection. Eventually the forces of production will reach a point at which
they are 'fettered', that is, a point in which further development is impossible
in the absence of transformations of the relations of production.

Now, the classic Marxist argument is that when such fettering occurs, the
relations will be transformed, and thus societies will necessarily move from one
societal form to another. As I have argued elsewhere this claim presupposes
that social actors with interests in such transformations will necessarily have
the capacity to accomplish the qualitative change in social relations of production.[15] Marxism, however, lacks an adequate theory of class capacities, and
thus the strong claims about the inevitability of progression cannot be sustained. This, however, does not call into question the argument about the
tendencies towards progression or the directionality of the ordering of social
forms. And this is all that is needed for the theory to retain its evolutionary
structure.

Giddens's evolutionary theory of history

Not only does Marxian theory generally meet the three criteria for evolutionary theory, but so does the framework elaborated by Giddens in *A
Contemporary Critique of Historical Materialism* and elsewhere. Giddens formulates a typology of social forms which has a clear quantitative ordering along
the dimension of space–time distanciation. But does this ordering meet the
second and third criteria of evolutionary theories? Giddens's explicit rhetoric
seems to reject the possibility of specifying any tendencies towards movements
through this ordered typology of social forms. He insists that the mechanisms
or dynamics of movement from one form to another are specific to each
transition, and, above all, that there is no transhistorical impulse to move from
tribal societies with low space–time distanciation to capitalist societies and
eventually socialist societies with high space–time distanciation.

---

[15] Levine and Wright, 'Rationality and Class Struggle'.

On closer inspection, however, Giddens's own detailed accounts seem to suggest a general logic to such progression. 'Space–time distanciation' is a concept which captures the ability of people in a society to control allocative and authoritative resources in time and space for use in power relations. Expanding allocative space–time distanciation involves (among other things) the development of the forces of production; expanding authoritative space–time distanciation involves developing the means of surveillance. Increases in such distanciation are human achievements: they increase the capacities of certain agents to act. But if those are indeed capacities, then it follows that the people whose capacities are enhanced by increasing distanciation will not willingly accept lower levels of space–time distanciation once a given level is achieved.

Of course, there may be other agents who would like to see the level of distanciation reduced. This is unlikely to be the case for allocative resources. As we argued earlier for the Marxist theory of the development of the productive forces, there will not in general be organized groups with interests directly in favour of a reduction of space–time distanciation with respect to allocative resources since this will typically imply increasing toil or decreasing consumption. Nothing in Giddens's analysis suggests otherwise.

The situation, however, is quite different with respect to authoritative space–time distanciation. Here we can easily identify social actors, often with potentially effective capacities for struggle, with clear interests in reducing aggregate authoritative space–time distanciation. Increasing capacities for surveillance are often a real threat to specific social categories. Territorial centralization – an aspect of expansion of spacial authoritative distanciation – is often resisted by the groups and the communities being absorbed under a central authority. Such resistance could be interpreted as a kind of 'authoritative-Luddism': the opposition is more to the unequal distribution of access to authoritative resources that accompanies the increasing space–time distanciation than to the sheer fact of increasing distanciation. However, unlike for allocative Luddism, this kind of resistance is the general pattern, rather than the exception, and frequently attempts at reducing overall authoritative space–time distanciation have been historically successful. It might appear, then, that on this dimension at least Giddens's approach is non-evolutionary.

Even here, however, I think Giddens's analysis remains evolutionary in its thrust. While there will often be contending social actors with interests in expanding/maintaining or reducing authoritative space–time distanciation, in general it will be the case that those actors with interests in expansion or maintenance will be the more powerful and will thus have the greater capacity to translate their interests into outcomes. This means that while regressions will not be historical oddities, there will still be a tendency for movement up the levels of authoritative space–time distanciation to be generally sticky downward.

What can we say about the third criterion? Is there a positive probability, however weak, of forward movement? Clearly there is in capitalist society, particularly for allocative resources, but is there any such general impulse towards increasing space–time distanciation of authoritative space–time distanciation?

I think it is possible to read such an impulse from Giddens's analysis. Essentially the impulse for expansion of space–time distanciation comes from different forms of conflict and competition in different societies. In class societies (capitalism) this is impelled primarily by conflicts over allocative resources in the form of economic competition between capitalist firms; in class-divided societies it is rooted in conflicts over authoritative resources, primarily in the form of military and territorial competition. The leading edge of such impulses towards increases in distanciation thus varies, depending upon which kind of resource is the 'basis of power' in the society, and accordingly, which dimension of distanciation will be most implicated in pervasive social conflicts. But because of the link between conflict, power, resources and distanciation, there will be at least a weak impulse for increasing distanciation throughout history. Again, this is not equivalent to claiming that there will be universal *progress*, a universal tendency for all societies to actually increase space–time distanciation along both resource dimensions; it is simply a claim that there is a universal, if often weak, impulse towards such increases, and thus a positive probability for such increases to occur.

If this reconstruction of Giddens's argument is correct, then what is novel in this argument is not that it is necessarily anti-evolutionary (although it is anti-teleological), but that it proposes a dual logic to evolutionary development: the evolutionary trajectory is animated by the autonomous impulses of the expansion of space–time distanciation with respect to allocative and authoritative resources. Stated in more conventional terms (which Giddens would probably disavow), social evolution is the result of autonomous evolutionary dynamics rooted simultaneously in political and economic structures. While in specific historical cases one may be justified in saying that one or the other of these constitutes the central locus of impulses for social change, there is no general priority of one over the other and their interconnection is best characterized as historically specific and contingent.

Contending models of historical trajectory

What we have, then, are two contending evolutionary theories.[16] The debate over these alternatives is not, I would argue, fundamentally a methodological one, but a substantive one. On the one hand there is the view, shared by most

[16] To these, a third could be added, as elaborated in the work of Jürgen Habermas (see in particular *Communication and the Evolution of Society* (Boston, Mass.: Beacon Press, 1979)): the claim that normative structures also have an autonomous logic of development producing a typology of societies based on their level of moral development (a kind of moral space–time distanciation, where 'meaning' can be seen as an action-relevant resource).

Marxists, that the developmental tendencies with respect to political power and economic structures are intrinsically linked, with economic structures having dynamic primacy. While there may be a 'relative autonomy' of one with respect to the other in the sense that a range of variations in forms of political power can co-exist with a given form of economic structure, the relation is not simply a historically contingent one. They form a loose gestalt. And within this gestalt, the most *systematically* dynamic element is rooted in the organization of production itself. Giddens, on the other hand, insists that the developmental tendencies of these two structures are autonomous and no general principles govern their interconnection. In different historically specific situations one or the other may be more important.

This debate underwrites the specification of the concept of class itself as well as the claims about the relationship between class domination and other forms of domination discussed earlier. The Marxist claim that the concept of class combines the relations of economic exploitation and authoritative domination is implicitly a rejection of the claim that these have genuinely autonomous logics of development; Giddens's restriction of class to relations of domination with respect to allocative resources affirms his view that allocative and authoritative domination are autonomous and contingently related processes. The adjudication of these contending class concepts and the typologies of social forms to which they are linked, therefore, ultimately hinges on these different substantive claims about the process of transformation of economic and political (allocative and authoritative) aspects of social relations.

It is, of course, not an easy task to build a convincing case one way or the other on this issue. Particularly once the simple functionalist version of the base–superstructure model is abandoned, it is difficult to argue systematically for the structural unity of economic and political relations within the theory of social development and the concept of class. It is tempting, therefore, to opt for Giddens's solution, to reduce the theoretical ambitions of Marxism in favour of a more contingent causal pluralism. This solution has been pursued in different ways by a number of theorists often identified as 'post-Marxist'.[17]

This temptation, I think, should be resisted. There are, I believe, compelling intuitions for why the Marxian account of evolutionary trajectories should be retained even though it is in need of modification in a number of crucial ways. I will mention only a few of these in closing:

(1)   As discussed earlier, Marxists generally share Giddens's view that in pre-capitalist societies the appropriation of surplus labour (or products) relied

---

[17] For illustrative examples of this intellectual tendency, see the work of Barry Hindess and Paul Q. Hirst in England, most notably their books with Anthony Cutler and Athar Hussain, *Marx's Capital and Capitalism Today*, vols. I and II (London: Routledge & Kegan Paul, 1978 and 1979), and the work of the American writers Robin Hahnel and Michael Albert, *Unorthodox Marxism* (Boston, Mass.: South End Press, 1980) and *Marxism and Socialist Theory* (Boston, Mass.: South End Press, 1982).

on the use of extra-economic coercion (control over authoritative resources). There is therefore no disagreement that the concrete relationship between control over allocative and authoritative resources varies across social forms. Marxists, however, insist that the explanation for the primacy of authoritative resources in pre-capitalist societies in contrast to the primacy of allocative resources in capitalist societies must be sought in the differences in the economic structure of such societies. If this is correct – and nothing in Giddens's analysis directly challenges this point – then it would be expected that the key to understanding changes in the relationship between allocative and authoritative resources lies in understanding the trajectory of development of economic structures. This does not imply that an autonomous political process of change is absent, but simply that the dynamics centered in property relations impose more fundamental limits on the overall process of social change.

(2)   Any theory of social change that recognizes the importance of social actors must contain, among other things, an account of the interests implicated in different processes of social change and the capacities of actors for translating such interests into outcomes. In these terms, there is a clearer link between interests and the evolutionary tendencies around allocative resources than around authoritative resources. Throughout most of human history, there has been a universal interest in increasing the productivity of labour in order to reduce toil (not necessarily to increase actual surplus products), and this underwrites the sustained, if often weak, impulse towards the improvement of the forces of production. There is no such universal interest in the expansion of social control over authoritative resources. Such expansion is pervasively contested, and thus there is a less sustained generic impulse for its continual development. To the extent that in spite of this contestation there is a net evolutionary tendency for 'space–time distanciation' with respect to authoritative resources, it is because the social actors supporting such expansion have greater capacities (power) to accomplish their objectives. But this greater capacity itself depends upon their control over allocative resources: the means of paying troops and retainers, of building the infrastructures of surveillance and communication, etc. Thus again, there is an asymmetry in the explanatory role of allocative and authoritative resources, with the former providing a more systematic basis for explanations of evolutionary tendencies.

(3)   Finally, the motivational assumptions underlying claims about the development of the forces of production are more plausible than parallel claims about the autonomous development of control over authoritative resources. It is easy to see why people wish to reduce toil – or at least, why they are reluctant to have toil increased (i.e. why the changes are sticky downward). But why should people want greater 'space–time distanciation' over authoritative resources? One answer is that this contributes to their material well-being, either

by increasing consumption or reducing toil even further. The beneficiaries of increasing space–time distanciation of authoritative resources are typically ruling classes who use their increased command of authoritative resources to increase their material welfare.[18] Such an answer, however, has the effect of subordinating the development of authoritative resources to motivations structured by allocative resources. This kind of subordination is more consistent with the Marxist account of their intrinsic structural interconnection.

An alternative answer is that people want power for power's sake, not because it increases their material welfare. This could then provide the motivational basis for an autonomous development of political power, of domination with respect to authoritative resources. However, while there are undoubtedly specific cases of such non-instrumental power motivations (i.e. power as an end in itself rather than as a means to some other end), this seems hardly a satisfactory motivational basis for a general argument of the autonomous logic of development of authoritative resources.

Conclusion

It is important not to overstate the differences between much of what Giddens proposes and the basic tendencies of current Marxist theorizing. While Giddens's general theory of action may run counter to mechanistic and functionalist reasoning in the Marxist tradition, it is entirely compatible with many of the substantive claims of both classical and contemporary Marxism. There is no intrinsic incompatibility between the substantive claims Marxists make about the importance of class structures and class struggle, about the role of the state and ideology, etc. and Giddens's methodological stress on the knowledgeability of actors, the 'duality of structure', the analysis of social processes in terms of the unacknowledged conditions of action and the unintended consequences of action, and so on. Many of the criticisms of functionalism and class reductionism which Giddens makes from this methodological standpoint are also accepted by many, if by no means all, contemporary Marxist theorists.

Even on more strictly substantive matters, Giddens's position is not generally the polar opposite of Marxist positions. The actual structural typology of societies Giddens elaborates is much closer to conventional Marxist typologies than either are to typologies in 'modernization' theory, for example. And on many specific topics, such as the analysis of the capitalist labour process or the structural contrast in forms of surplus extraction in capitalism and feudalism, Giddens's analysis hardly differs at all from most current Marxist formulations.

---

[18] It is interesting in this regard that many of the earliest historical advances in surveillance which Giddens stresses so heavily were advances precisely concerned with the tallying of tribute. See for example his discussion of the early forms of writing in Sumer, *CCHM*, p. 95.

What is less easily meshed with neo-Marxism is Giddens's arguments of the duality of power rooted in the autonomous logic of control over allocative and authoritative resources. This leads Giddens to reject the possibility of any general theory of history, any general principles of historical development, in favour of more limited epochal theories of particular transitions. Most Marxists retain a commitment to constructing an overall theory of historical development, based in some version of historical materialism, within which the development and contradictions of class relations provide the central framework for analysis. Giddens not only rejects the substantive propositions of this project, but rejects the project itself.

What are the stakes in Giddens's critique of the possibility of a theory of history? Some Marxists have argued that the Marxist *theory* of history can in any event be abandoned without prejudicing Marxist class analysis. In this view, Marxism may provide general abstract concepts with which to analyse historical development, but provides no general theory of that development. There are specific theories of specific social formations, but no general theory of the overall trajectory of social forms. Can the Marxist theory of history be dispensed with so easily without serious ramifications for Marxism in general?

I think not. Specifically, I think that the justification for Marxian class analysis rests in important ways on the theory of history in which it is embedded. There are three kinds of arguments for the Marxist preoccupation with class: a functional defence, a structural constraint defence and what I have termed a dynamic defence. Each of these potentially provides a defence of Marxist claims for the primacy of class in the analysis of social structure and social change. If the functional defence is rejected as generally unsatisfactory, and the structural defence is viewed as only contingently correct, then we are left with the dynamic argument: class relations have a specific primacy in that dynamics rooted in class relations provide an overall directionality to the trajectory of historical change. If this argument is also rejected, then there is no longer any general justification for Marxist class analysis as such. Without the theory of history and without a general theory of class analysis, it is hard to see what remains as the distinctive theoretical core of Marxism as such.

It would still be possible, of course, to adopt insights from Marxist class analysis, as Giddens enthusiastically does. And it would even be possible to say that in a particular instance, say the analysis of capitalism, class does have a form of primacy as characterized by Marxist theory. But there would no longer be any grounds for class analysis being the core of a general social theory. This is the central challenge posed by Giddens's critique. It is a challenge which Marxists should take seriously.

5

Capitalism, nation-states and surveillance

BOB JESSOP

In this chapter I consider Anthony Giddens's various contributions to theories of the modern state from two viewpoints.[1] I will first relate his growing interest in the state to his concurrent attempts to criticize and move beyond historical materialism and to develop a theory of 'structuration' based on the 'duality of structure'. And then I will compare his approach to the state with four other recent attempts to 'bring the state back in' to social and political theorizing. In combining an immanent critique with such comparisons, a balanced assessment of Giddens's contributions should be possible.

Early views on the state

Giddens's initial comments on the state can be found in his reviews of how classical social theorists had analysed capitalism and in his own work on the class structure in advanced societies. His comments on Marxian and Weberian state theories were largely exegetical and not particularly original. Only later did he start to criticize them for neglecting the distinctive role of warfare and military organization in the modern state (*NSV*, pp. 24–7).[2] Even in his early writings, however, Giddens made a major contribution by publicizing and reassessing Durkheim's political sociology and state theory (see especially *SSPT*, pp. 235–72; also *Emile Durkheim: Selected Writings*, pp. 17–20, 189–202; *NSV*, pp. 17–18, 23–4).

His views on neo-capitalism and the state differed little from the prevailing 'orthodox consensus' and were obviously influenced by reflections on the postwar boom. Among other features, Giddens emphasized: the price-making activities of giant firms; the rise of state involvement in contra-cyclical demand management and production to compensate for market failures, in regulating prices and incomes, and economic planning; the rise of social democracy as a natural governing party; and the emergence of concerted action among big industry, organized labour, and the state (*CSAS*, pp. 148–52, 164, 290, 315–

[1] Simon Bromley made some useful comments on the first draft and helped to improve my arguments in his usual incisive manner.
[2] To what extent classical social theorists as a whole actually ignored these issues and how far it is the contemporary neglect of theorists and/or specific works on these issues that is at fault is an interesting and controversial question too large to discuss here. But see: Mann 1984; Turner 1986; and Ashworth and Dandeker 1987.

16). More generally, Giddens argued that 'neo-capitalism' involved a shift in the mediation of control away from economic towards political elites (*CSAS*, p. 173). However, as the owl of Minerva has once more taken flight only at dusk, neo-capitalism can now be understood in more circumscribed terms. It was shaped by the mass production and mass consumption involved in the Fordist mode of growth and has been undermined by the crisis of Fordism (see Boyer 1986). Indeed, in discussing the nature of modern capitalism in these terms, Giddens had failed to anticipate one of his own sociological caveats. For he has since cautioned against over-generalizing from a short period of time and projecting current trends into the indefinite future (*PCST*, p. 164).

More durable and important were two other arguments which still inform his analyses of the nation-state and violence. He argued, firstly, that the institutional separation of the economic and the political in advanced capitalism is rooted in the nature of the capitalist labour contract; and, secondly, that this has major repercussions for the logic of market forces and the nature of liberal democracy. These ideas were by no means novel, and they remained somewhat undeveloped in Giddens's early work. Since then his growing concern with the critique of historical materialism has also involved a deeper interest in the institutional features of the state. This interest was also related to his concurrently developing interest in the theory of structuration.

The critique of historial materialism

Giddens argues that historical materialism has made positive contributions to the analysis of modern societies. This is especially true for its discussion of how capitalism is organized as a system of generalized commodity production[3] and the effects this has on other spheres of society (*CCHM*, vol. 1, p. 198; *NSV*, pp. 129–37, 167). Many ideas drawn from Marxism can be found in his own work. Thus he describes the process of accumulation as an investment–production–profit–investment cycle; stresses the importance of wage labour and control over labour-time to capital accumulation; identifies the primary contradiction of modern capitalism as the contradictory relation between private appropriation and socialized production; argues that one of the resulting secondary contradictions is that between the hegemony of the nation-state and the internationalization of capital; and, in a claim reminiscent of Althusser's views on overdetermination and ruptural unity, asserts that social conflict is more likely when contradictions coincide rather than cut across each other (*CSAS*, pp. 315–16; *CPST*, pp. 142–5, 212; *NSV*, pp. 127–40, 143–4; cf. Althusser 1969, pp. 87–128).

In this sense Giddens extends his account of capitalism well beyond the economic sphere to cover other aspects of modern societies. Indeed, he claims

[3] This Marxist concept signifies that capitalism not only involves the production of goods and services as commodities but also generalizes the commodity form to labour-power itself so that it is bought and sold as wage labour on the labour market.

that 'in capitalism, more than any other kind of social order, economic influences play a major dynamic role' (*NSV*, p. 135). But he also argues that capitalist societies cannot be fully comprehended through Marxist categories alone. For, alongside their specifically *capitalist* features, there are other distinctive features which have no intrinsic connection to capitalism (or to each other). They are also always *industrial* societies, having specific forms of *surveillance and control* over their populations, and integrated into a global *system of nation-states* (*NSV*, pp. 2–5, 135). These three features are typically neglected by historical materialism and cannot be introduced into an analysis of bourgeois society once its main outlines have been explored by Marxism. On the contrary, Giddens argues that ' "capitalist society" is "society" only because it is also a nation-state' (*NSV*, p. 141; cf. *STMS*, pp. 35, 40).

Similar arguments can be applied to the world system as a whole. For Giddens argues that this 'should be seen as influenced by several primary sets of processes, each in some part independent of the others. These are processes associated with the nation-state system, co-ordinated through global networks of information exchange, the world capitalist economy, and the world military order' (*NSV*, p. 290). Likewise, in discussing the characteristics of the capitalist state, Giddens insists these derive (in Europe at least) from the combination of three distinct organizational clusters. These are capitalism, industrialism, and certain administrative apparatuses of government; and, despite their contingent co-evolution in Europe, none of them can be analytically reduced to the others (*NSV*, pp. 141, 160). He concludes that historical materialism displays a one-sided concern with the specifically *capitalist* aspects of modern industry, modern states, modern societies and the modern world system. Because it ignores the non-capitalist aspects of these phenomena, therefore, it cannot fully understand them.

Even more damaging is Giddens's claim that historical materialism also has theoretical flaws on its own terrain. Two are especially crucial: firstly, its assumption that there is a progressive development in the forces of production; and secondly, its tendency to reduce all historical development to a resultant of class struggles (*CCHM*, vol 1, p. 198; for further criticisms, see also *CPST*, pp. 150–5).

Giddens denies that there is a general evolutionary pattern in societal development – let alone that this is determined in some mythical last instance by technological change. Indeed, whatever Marx might have argued, only in capitalism do the forces of production have an internal dynamic which stimulates continuous technological innovation and economic transformation (*CCHM*, vol. 1, p. 198; *CPST*, p. 154). Their evolutionary approach also leads Marxists to underestimate the discontinuity between capitalist societies and all preceding societies – a discontinuity which Giddens sees as fundamental and relates to a shift in the relative primacy of allocative and authoritative resources. He argues that, whereas the main dynamic of capitalist societies is, indeed, rooted in control over allocative resources (natural forces and material goods), it was the co-ordination of authoritative resources (based on dominion over social forces) which was crucial in pre-capitalist societies (*CCHM*, vol. 1, pp. 4, 210; *NSV*, pp. 7, 31–2). In turn this affects the ties between class and state power. Whereas it was state power which generated class power in pre-capitalist societies, in capitalist societies it is class power which is the key to state power (*CCHM*, vol. 1, p. 210; *NSV*, p. 62).[4]

Giddens also criticizes Marxist class reductionism. It is only under capitalism, he argues, that classes emerge as significant social and political actors. In this sense he takes issue with the claim in the *Communist Manifesto* that the history of all hitherto existing societies is the history of class struggle. In this respect too, then, Giddens stresses that a fundamental break occurred in moving from pre-capitalist to capitalist societies. This has two contrasting implications. On the one hand, it means that class analysis cannot cast much light on the dynamic of pre-capitalist societies; for capitalist societies, on the other hand, such an analysis can be used to unlock all the key institutional features of society (*CCHM*, vol. 1, p. 198; *CPST*, pp. 162–4; *NSV*, pp. 64–5). Thus class struggle is not confined to the work-place: it is also dominant in the political field (*NSV*, p. 66) and, presumably, in other spheres too.

Structuration and power relations

The theory of structuration attempts to 'reconcile a notion of structure with the necessary centrality of the active subject' (*SSPT*, p. 117; cf. *CPST*, p. 69). It aims to link 'an adequate account of (meaningful) action with the analysis of its unanticipated conditions and unanticipated consequences' (*PCST*, p. 10). It stresses the duality of structure as present both in institutional systems and in strategic conduct; and argues that structure comprises '*generative rules and resources* that are both applied in and constituted out of action' (*SSPT*, p. 117; cf. *CPST*, p. 88).

Giddens argues that all processes of structuration involve three elements: the communication of meaning, the exercise of power, and the evaluative judgement of conduct. These can be considered from the viewpoint of structures as well as of agents. Thus, as signification, structure involves semantic rules; as domination, unequally distributed resources – primarily allocative and authoritative; and, as legitimation, moral or evaluative rules (*SSPT*, pp. 132–3; cf. *CPST*, pp. 82–3, *NSV*, pp. 19–20). The theory of structuration supposedly holds for all social systems, but it is especially relevant to our present concerns. Indeed Giddens considers that authoritative resources and structures of political domination constitute crucial factors in the production and reproduction of social systems. More generally, the theory of structuration

[4] To take just one example, Giddens claims that it was the scope of military sanctions which largely determined the boundaries of economic relations within and among imperial societies. But, in the modern world system, capital's economic reach is beyond the control of even the most powerful nation-states (*CCHM*, vol. 1, pp. 197, 226; cf. *CSAS*, pp. 313–14, *CPST*, pp. 225–6, *STMS*, p. 177).

also has major implications for the analysis of power relations. These are also a central focus in theories of the state. Yet, as Giddens has correctly indicated elsewhere, the weakness of Marxist state theories is partly rooted in their failure to develop a general conception of power (*PCST*, p. 217).

Giddens argues on many occasions that power is logically entailed in the very idea of 'action' (*SSPT*, p. 347; cf. *NRSM*, p. 110, *CPST*, p. 88, *NSV*, p. 7). It is an integral element of the capacities of agents to transform their situation and secure preferred outcomes; and it is also structured into institutions with the result that it sustains domination. Its analysis must be related to resources, its location in time and space (e.g., in power containers such as the work-place, courts, cities, nation-states), the institutional mediation of power, and the dialectic of control which emerges from strategies and counter-strategies of power (*NSV*, pp. 7–10, 14–16; cf. *CS*, pp. 1–41, *STMS*, p. 162). In this sense power characterizes both the conduct of agents and the properties of structures (*CPST*, pp. 88–9, 92; cf. *SSPT*, p. 347, *NSV*, p. 7). Let us briefly consider each aspect in relation to the state.

Modern states are advanced forms of organization. They combine three sets of capacities: surveillance and supervision, specialization in intellectual labour, and military and police sanctions (*NSV*, pp. 13–16, 52, 187–9, 192). Their rise within Europe depended on their ability to concentrate and centralize authoritative resources within a national 'power container' (*NSV*, p. 47). In turn this gives nation-states the capacity to manipulate the settings in which human activities occur and thereby control their timing and spacing to a greater or lesser extent (*NSV*, pp. 46–7). It is these structural properties and their crystallization into a system of nation-states, each with its own unified administrative apparatus, which underpin the pattern of political domination in modern societies.

The resources generated in and through this power container do not, however, guarantee the reproduction of political domination. Instead, as with all resources in durable social systems, they must be mobilized by contextually located actors (*CPST*, p. 92; *CCHM*, vol. 1, p. 4; *NSV*, pp. 8–10). In general terms this involves routinized, predictable practices, but these always have an important strategic dimension within the overall dialectic of control (*NSV*, p. 11).

Thus, bringing these two aspects of power together, Giddens concludes that power relations consist in relations of autonomy and dependence which are reproduced in strategic interaction (*CPST*, p. 93; *NSV*, p. 8). We shall now see how (and how far) he actually applies these ideas to the analysis of the modern state.

The nation-state and violence

Giddens defined the nation-state in his earlier critique of historical materialism. There he argued that 'the nation-state, which exists in a complex of other nation-states, is a set of institutional forms of governance maintaining an administrative monopoly over a territory with demarcated boundaries, its rule being sanctioned by law and direct control of the means of internal and external violence' (*CCHM*, vol. 1, p. 190; cf. *NSV*, p. 125).

The Nation-State and Violence considers how the state system developed and then explores its culmination in the current global system of modern nation-states. It does not develop a theory of the state or provide a general account of its origins. Giddens rightly refuses to engage here in the debate about the state's origins (which actually vary considerably from case to case: *CPST*, pp. 246–56) and concentrates instead on the general features and consequences of state formation. Indeed, once one state has emerged, this affects other societies. It encourages the formation of an inter-state system with its own structural properties. Granted the decisive break involved in the genesis of such a system, the key typological contrast should run between traditional states and the modern nation-state (*NSV*, pp. 83–4). It is around this contrast that Giddens presents his main historical arguments.

Traditional and modern states

Giddens emphasizes that traditional states are very different, as 'social systems', from modern ones. Thus, although they could generate both authoritative and allocative resources through the intersection of city and countryside, they remained fundamentally segmental in character and could sustain only limited administrative authority. That such states had frontiers rather than boundaries indicates their relatively weak level of system integration. They are internally heterogeneous and often comprise numerous societies. Indeed traditional states did not actually 'govern', if this means to provide regularized administration of the overall territory they claimed as their own. Their polities were mainly limited to governance of conflicts within the dominant classes and/or within the main urban centres. This overall lack of administration was compensated by sporadic resort to military force. We can develop this contrast between traditional (class-divided) and modern (capitalist) societies by considering six criteria which Giddens has emphasized.

Firstly, whereas traditional societies had a ruling class (i.e., the dominant class occupied the key political positions) with limited governing capacities, modern societies have a governing elite which is relatively insulated from the economically dominant class but whose power is extensive. Secondly, although traditional societies did have classes, class conflict was not endemic. Such conflict does occur both in the work-place and in the state system of modern societies, however, and overall social development is strongly shaped by class relations. This contrast is partly related to the form of economic organization in traditional societies and partly to their lack of a broad public sphere. In the latter respect Giddens claims that they lacked a discursive space for articulating generalized policies and integrating them with systematic information; those who were excluded from the political centre therefore had limited opportunities to press their class (or other) demands. More generally, Giddens argues that the growth of a 'public sphere' of state administration was inseparable from textually mediated organization (*NSV*, pp. 178–9, 210).

Thirdly, the economic and political spheres are related in quite different ways in the two types of society. Although the economy in traditional societies was not clearly 'separated' in institutional terms from other spheres, the state itself had only limited scope for intervention. The economic life of peasant communities was conducted independently of what happened in the state and could therefore be described as 'severed' from politics. In modern societies these patterns are reversed. The economy is clearly 'separated' from other spheres because it has its own organizational principles and institutional logic. But, since the state can intervene quite widely and also derives its own revenues from the market economy, economic and political life are closely intertwined rather than 'severed'.

Fourthly, whereas private property in class-divided societies is relatively fixed and difficult to alienate, it is highly mobile and fluid under capitalism. This has contradictory effects. For, whilst this mobility and fluidity reinforce the dominance of the economic sphere in capitalism, they also mean that law and the state must be more active in protecting such property.

Fifthly, whilst labour markets are largely absent in traditional societies, modern societies have a well-organized labour market. And, sixthly, whilst the main sanction over subordinate classes in traditional societies was that of violence, in capitalist societies they are subject mainly to an economic compulsion to go to work together with close managerial supervision when there. Accordingly industrial capitalism leads to the 'doubling' (*Verdoppelung*) of surveillance into parallel economic and political channels (*NSV*, pp. 160, 191). In turn this is associated with the doubling of labour movement struggles into struggles for economic betterment and citizenship rights (unions, industrial arbitration) and for political reform and citizenship rights (labour and socialist parties, franchise and political participation) (*NSV*, pp. 207–8, 321).

Absolutism and the nation-state

Having considered Giddens's general contrasts between traditional and modern societies, we now turn to the differences between their respective state forms. Here he subscribes to the usual argument that the absolutist state was crucial in the transition from traditional to modern forms of political domination. But, in discussing absolutism, Giddens reverses normal accounts of its origins. For he focuses first on the emergence of a reflexively monitored international system of states as a key indicator of the modernity of absolutism. He also stresses that the energizing force behind this movement was change in the organization of war rather than in that of production (*NSV*, pp. 112–13). In addition, the need to finance military organization was tied to the emergence of modern monetary and credit systems (*NSV*, pp. 115–16). Having discussed its international context Giddens then considers the internal factors behind the rise of absolutism. Two are stressed. Giddens notes how the concept of sovereignty arose in association with the notion of centralized, impersonal administrative power. And he explores how the distinction between city and countryside was dissolved so that the nation-state eventually became the key 'power container' and also developed firm borders (*NSV*, p. 172).

Early capitalism was associated with absolutism, but the absolutist state was not yet fully modern. Although it clearly had some modern features (notably the rise of standing diplomacy and its accompanying forms of surveillance), it remained traditional in many other respects (lacking above all a ubiquitous, centralized administrative apparatus) (*NSV*, pp. 85, 97). The subsequent consolidation of capitalism in the nineteenth and early twentieth centuries witnessed the rise of the nation-state and its ensuing transformation into a liberal-democratic state (*CCHM*, vol. 1, pp. 184–6, 188; cf. *CSAS*, pp. 317–18, *PCST*, p. 128). This close structural tie between capitalism and the nation-state was not accidental but derived from the attempts of the bourgeoisie to consolidate capitalism within a pre-existing state system (*CCHM*, vol. 1, p. 189; *NSV*, p. 135).

Giddens identifies the key structural features of the modern state in the following terms. It is associated with (a) a centralized legal order permitting and protecting an expanding range of forms of private property and related contractual obligations, (b) centralized administration, (c) a centrally organized taxation system articulated with a rational, fiduciary monetary system, (d) major innovations in military organization reflected in the international state system and the separation of external military force from internal policing, (e) the development of the modern nation in conjunction with the nation-state, (f) the development of communication, information and surveillance possibilities, (g) internal pacification through the disciplinary society and (h) the development of democracy in the sense of a pluralist polyarchy and citizenship rights – as the reciprocal of the enhanced surveillance and the ideology of the general interest involved in the modern state.

The twentieth-century state system

In the last three chapters of *The Nation-State and Violence* Giddens considers how the nation-state system became global in the twentieth century. Among other elements which receive detailed discussion are the industrialization of war (particularly under the impact of two world wars), the world military order (with its super-power hegemony, arms trade and military alliances), the development of a capitalist world economy, the rise of intergovernmental organizations as a means of consolidating the spread of nation-states, the phenomenon of totalitarianism as an ever-present possibility in all modern nation-states, and the types of protest movement which develop in response to the four key institutional orders of modern society (capitalism, industrialism, the nation-state and military and police force). In the last respect Giddens emphasizes that no critical theory of modern society which merely poses the choice between capitalism and socialism can do justice to the complexities and problems involved in modernity.

Some alternative approaches

Giddens's recent work clearly represents a major contribution to recent moves to 'bring the state back in' as a central theme in social theory. However, as Giddens's own critique of historical materialism suggests, there is less agreement on how exactly it should be reimported. Since other texts provide exhaustive reviews of this debate this section merely provides some reference points for critically assessing Giddens's approach (useful surveys of recent state theory include: Alford and Friedland 1985; Carnoy 1984; Dunleavy and O'Leary 1987; Evans et al. 1985; Jessop 1982; Krasner 1984; and Thomas and Meyer 1984).

Marxist state theories

The resurgence of interest in Marxist state theory which began in the late sixties produced a wide variety of theoretical and methodological approaches to political analysis. These include the initial structuralist Marxism of Poulantzas (1969 and 1973); the sophisticated instrumentalism of Miliband (1968) and, from a 'state managers' versus class forces perspective, Block (1977); the various analyses of 'state monopoly capitalism' associated with communist parties throughout Europe – with the partial exception of Italy (e.g., Boccara et al. 1976; Hemberger et al. 1975; Jung and Schleifstein 1979); the *Staatsableitung* (or state derivation) approach in West Germany (e.g., Blanke et al. 1975; Gerstenberger, 1977; Hirsch 1976; Kraetke 1985); the appropriation of Gramscian perspectives in Italy, France and Britain to underpin both left and right Eurocommunist and Eurosocialist analyses (e.g., Buci-Glucksmann 1975; Ingrao 1977; Mouffe 1979); the 'autonomist' current on the Italian left with its politico-strategic reading of the capital relation in all its forms and a particular concern with working-class struggles (e.g., Bologna et al. 1972; Cleaver 1979; Negri 1974; Tronti 1977); the 'form problematizes function' approach inspired by Claus Offe (1975, 1984, 1985); and the relational approach eventually adopted by Poulantzas (1976 and 1978).

The best Marxist theorizing has greatly advanced our knowledge of the different logics of capital accumulation; the complexities of class struggle in different societies; the state's various forms – ranging from abstract features such as the rule of law or the bourgeois tax-form to more concrete types of state and regime; the tensions, dilemmas and contradictions involved in different modes of policy production; and its various economic, political and ideological contributions to capitalist reproduction. In particular Nicos Poulantzas made a crucial contribution to Marxist theory in developing the twin arguments that (a) the state apparatus, considered as an institutional ensemble, constitutes a strategic terrain with a distinct structural bias and (b) state power should be understood as the complex resultant of political class struggles occurring both on this terrain and at a distance from it (Poulantzas 1978; see also Jessop 1985). Poulantzas and other theorists also explored the nature and limits of state autonomy both in general terms and in relation to specific regimes and conjunctures. And the neo-Gramscian current has made significant advances in exploring the specific nature and dynamic of political class struggle as a struggle for political, intellectual and moral leadership.

Given his concern to build on as well as to go beyond historical materialism, it is odd that Giddens does not really confront Marxist state theories (as opposed to criticizing the general evolutionary and class-reductionist schema of historical materialism). Not all such theories are equally vulnerable to his charge of obsessive concern with the economic functions of the state or with its power of internal repression. Indeed some of his comments on specific Marxist theorists (notably concerning Poulantzas) are somewhat 'cavalier and off-hand',[5] and he completely ignores other major contributions both from classic Marxist theorists (such as Gramsci) and from postwar theorists (such as Hirsch 1976 or Tuschling 1976).

In this sense the strengths of Marxist state theory are also the weaknesses of Giddens's approach. Thus, although he agrees that political struggles in modern societies are oriented to the general interest, he has not considered questions of hegemony or the role played by political parties and the state in securing hegemony. Nor has he shown much interest in the question of how economic classes and class fractions (whose centrality to modern societies he accepts) express their interests politically and seek to promote these interests on the strategic terrain formed by the state. The role of party politics and organized interests is especially important here, but the strategic selectivity of the state itself as the 'party' of capital also needs examining. Moreover, whilst arguing that the state has been engaged in economic 'management' at least since the late eighteenth century and that state managers can better 'oversee' the system as a whole than employers or industrial managers,[6] he has largely ignored the nature, functions and limits of state intervention in the economy. Even if one cannot expect him to cover all forms of intervention, one omission is distinctly odd. For, despite the importance he allots the labour contract in modern capitalism, Giddens hardly mentions the state's role in managing the

[5] Elsewhere Giddens himself criticized Parkin for neglecting the important contributions of Althusserian Marxism to contemporary social science and suggested that Poulantzas's work in particular demands 'a much more sustained critique than the cavalier and offhand survey Parkin offers' (*PCST*, p. 191). He also notes that Lenin and Gramsci contributed significantly to the theory of the capitalist state (*CCHM*, vol. 1, p. 203). Unfortunately Giddens himself makes no attempt to provide a detailed critical assessment of classical and recent Marxist state theorists.

[6] Both arguments are implausible: the first because it ignores the changing modalities and extent of intervention, the second because it overlooks the problems arising from the global reach of capitalism and the discrepancies between state managers' models of the economy and its real operations.

wage relation. Yet this is just as central to the role of the interventionist state as its management of state credit or its structural policy.

Nor does his work provide any detailed account of how the state and economy are connected in capitalism. It is restricted to such general comments as: the modern state has a key role in maintaining the 'insulation' of economy and state; the modern state is a tax state whose tax revenues and ability to sell public debt depend asymmetrically on capital's continued productivity and profitability; politicians have an interest in securing the reproduction of capital; and the shift of state intervention from allocative towards productive activity is determined both by the contradiction between private appropriation and socialized production and by specific market failures or crises (*CSAS*, p. 152; *CCHM*, vol. 1, pp. 209–29). Thus his contributions in these areas are extremely limited and his work on *The Nation-State and Violence* ignores them altogether.

Among other concerns of Marxist theory which Giddens has so far ignored or failed to consider adequately two more can be noted. How far and in what respects does the state embody a structural or strategic selectivity in class and/or non-class terms? The theory of structuration suggests that patterns of political domination are inscribed within specific institutional and organizational structures; but Giddens does not explore this to any great extent for the capitalist state apart from noting that the separation of the economic and political spheres limits the scope of class struggle. What are the 'normal' forms assumed by the state in different stages of capitalism, and how should we analyse 'abnormal' forms? On occasion Giddens implies that liberal or social democracy are 'normal', and elsewhere he implies that there is only one abnormal form – degeneration into fascism.

In reply to these criticisms Giddens could reasonably make three claims. Firstly, it is somewhat unfair to compare the work of a single theorist whose concerns are wide-ranging with the alleged role of an entire theoretical tradition in elucidating just some of these concerns. Secondly, there is, in any case, little in Giddens's own approach which prohibits its articulation with the main Marxist contributions on economic intervention and political hegemony. And, thirdly, whatever the merits of the best Marxist state theories in these restricted areas, they all remain vulnerable to Giddens's charge of one-sidedness. For they have been overly concerned with capitalism to the neglect of industrialism; have neglected internal surveillance in the formation and dynamic of the modern state; have focused on individual nation-states and/or the economic logic of imperialism to the neglect of the reflexively monitored international state system; have been more or less enduringly class reductionist; and have failed to develop a theory of modern warfare. In all these respects Giddens has gone well beyond orthodox Marxism. But this does not mean, as we shall see, that he himself manages to avoid one-sidedness in his own treatment of the state's non-capitalist dimensions.

Bringing the state back in

Giddens has certainly contributed to the proper evaluation of the state as a distinctive institutional order in the modern world. It is therefore worth comparing his analyses with those of the 'state-centered' theorists who have been openly demanding that the state be brought back in as an independent variable in social analysis. Such theorists argue that there are *sui generis* political pressures and processes which shape the form and functions of the state and which endow it with a real and important autonomy vis-à-vis all pressures and forces located in civil society. They argue that the state is an institutional ensemble or 'structured field of action' with a unique centrality in both national and international formations. In order to define how Giddens's work differs, if at all, from these attempts to bring the state back in, we must first sketch the main themes in their work.

Six themes have been emphasized: (1) the geo-political position of different modern states within the international system of nation-states and its implications for the logic of state action; (2) the dynamic of military organization and warfare in the development of the modern state; (3) the *sui generis* powers of the modern state – especially those rooted in its capacities to produce and enforce collectively binding decisions within a centrally organized, territorially bounded society – and its strategic reach in relation to all other social sub-systems (including the economy), organizations (including capitalist enterprises) and forces (including classes) within its domain; (4) the nature of the state as a *sui generis* factor in shaping the character of institutions and social forces beyond the state in the economy and civil society – the aspect Skocpol has identified as its Toquevillean moment; (5) the distinctive pathologies of the state system and government; and (6) the distinctive interests and capacities of 'state managers' as opposed to other social forces. Different 'state-centered' theorists have emphasized different factors. But the conclusion remains the same: the state is a force in its own right and does not simply reflect the dynamic of the economy and/or civil society.

This leads 'state-centered' theorists to advocate a radically different approach to the question of state autonomy. They have drawn particular attention to two dimensions of autonomy: (a) state autonomy as the ability of state managers to exercise power independently of (and even in the face of opposition from) social forces located in civil society – a power rooted in the state's own specialized capacities and/or in the room for manoeuvre which state managers enjoy vis-à-vis a pluralistic universe of social forces; and (b) state capacities or 'infrastructural' power, i.e., the state's ability to penetrate, control, supervise, police and discipline modern societies through its specialized capacities even when these are controlled directly or indirectly by forces beyond the state (cf. Block 1977; Mann 1983; Nordlinger 1981; Skocpol 1985).

Giddens is clearly sympathetic to many of these arguments, and his own work has particularly stressed the first four factors. Indeed his account of how capitalist societies developed stresses the contributions made by the international state system, the dynamic of military organization and warfare, the unification of administrative power within individual nation-states and the state's role in shaping the institutional terrain and balance of forces beyond the state. More generally, he has noted that asking about the autonomy of the modern state involves nothing more than inquiring 'into the *sources of state power* and *the scope of the sanctions* which the state is capable of wielding' (*CCHM*, vol. 1, 217). He has also alluded briefly to the pathologies of the state system in relation to totalitarianism (*CCHM*, vol. 1, pp. 244–5; *NSV*, pp. 295–310).

Giddens emphasizes one factor above all in discussing these issues: the unrivalled infrastructural power of the modern state. He argues that this type of state enjoys immense capacities for surveillance within its own territory and can significantly structure all forms of social life and their space–time relations. His pleading for a shift of focus away from the purely repressive capacities of the state may have been partly inspired by Foucault, but Giddens develops his argument in a more complex, sophisticated and consistent manner. It is closely integrated into his historical overview of how the modern state developed as well as his account of its present and future capacities; and it is also underpinned by his more general work on the theory of structuration. It is certainly one of his most important contributions to theorizing about the state.[7]

Although Giddens has not, to my knowledge, commented directly on these 'state-centered' approaches, his own approach clearly differs from them in several respects. It differs most noticeably in his approach to the autonomy of the state and 'state managers' as political subjects. Firstly, he criticizes geopolitical accounts which treat nation-states as *real* subjects and stresses that their subjectivity is actually a socially constructed capacity (*NSV*, p. 289). He also notes that, although all states seem to have been associated with 'territoriality', their boundaries were quite imprecise in empires and most absolutist states (*STMS*, pp. 171–2). From this we can conclude that a geo-political approach could mislead if it fails to analyse the changing geo-political significance of states. This would clearly require both society- and state-centered analyses. And, secondly, Giddens notes that the dominant class in traditional societies was also a ruling class in so far as it directly staffed the state and could wield wide-ranging, often 'despotic' power over the populace (*NSV*, pp. 63–4). In contrast, since state officials in modern societies are rarely recruited directly from the dominant class, this might seem to give them independent interests and capacities as 'state managers'. However, in so far as Giddens touches on this issue (for example, in his analyses of military rule), he emphasizes that officials' scope for autonomous action is limited and that the complex power-dependence relations in modern societies always encourage polyarchic patterns of governance (*NSV*, pp. 249–51). Thus Giddens rejects not only the

[7] Simon Bromley urged this point in his comments on the first draft of this chapter, and it is one I have come to share.

geo-political concept of state subjectivity but also the idea that government officials can ever be radically autonomous.

It would still be fair to say that Giddens's work falls within the broad stream of 'state-centered' theorizing, however, as long as one important qualification is accepted. For Giddens clearly rejects the false dilemma which requires one to see either state or society as primary. He does not share the 'state-centered' theorists' tendency simply to turn 'society-centered' approaches on their head. This can be seen in his empirical inquiries, his methodological remarks and his general theoretical approach. Thus empirically he sometimes focuses on the state's role in social reproduction through its control over authoritative resources and its 'infrastructural power'; and sometimes he focuses on the role of struggles beyond the state in shaping the development of liberal democratic government and citizenship rights. In turn this reflects his methodological remark that the distinctive importance of government and politics in shaping social life as a whole no more justifies a sociological imperialism towards political science than it does a politological imperialism towards sociology (*STMS*, p. 40). What is more, in his account of structuration, the duality of structure and the dialectic of control, Giddens also provides the theoretical means to reveal the limits of any reduction of society to the state.

Autopoietic theories

A third recent approach is inspired by systems-theoretical analyses of auto-poiesis (or self-reference) in different societal sub-systems ranging from economics through law and politics to art and religion. Autopoietic theorists argue that modern societies comprise a plurality of socially differentiated, self-referential institutional sub-systems, each of which has its own indispensable function within the society and its own *sui generis* dynamic. From this they conclude that modern societies have no centre able to co-ordinate their diverse interactions, organizations and institutions and that there can be no pre-given causal hierarchy among the different sub-systems. Each sub-system responds to changes in its environment as these are reflected in its own activities; and it attempts to maintain its own functional capacities despite the perturbations and crises introduced from outside. In this sense each sub-system tends to 'drift' along through a series of stepwise changes triggered by external forces but determined in and through its own internal operations. Each sub-system can observe itself and, through this reflexive self-monitoring, engages in a recursive reproduction of its own activities. There can be no guarantee that the combined result of these recursive activities is the reproduction of society as a whole. Thus societal development merely takes the form of the 'structural coupling' (or blind co-evolution) of sub-systems.

In this context autopoietic theorists explore the specific codes and mechanisms through which different sub-systems establish their operational autonomy and reproduce themselves through their own activities. Four examples are: the modern economy as a self-perpetuating system of payments; modern law as a self-contained and self-modifying system of legally binding legal decisions; the political system as a system of collectively binding decisions which generate further political decisions; and the welfare state as a system tautologically concerned to meet welfare needs which are defined and monitored within the welfare system itself. Once sub-systems reach 'autopoietic take-off', they can only respond to problems defined in their own terms, and any others are regarded as irrelevant. This emphasis on operational autonomy does not exclude interdependencies among different sub-systems. But each sub-system can maintain its own operational autonomy in so far as it has its own operating codes and the time to implement them, faces competing demands so that it can choose which to process, and has the general legitimacy or societal trust needed to operate without having constantly to justify its specific activities on each occasion (on autopoietic theories, see: Luhmann 1982, 1984, 1986; Teubner 1984; and, for a critique, Jessop 1987).

Giddens's approach differs substantially from such theories. This is particularly clear in the contrast between their evolutionary and functionalist bias and the counter-arguments in his own work (*CCHM*, vol. 1, p. 15). But Giddens also develops some themes similar to those in autopoietic systems theory. Three are especially significant. Firstly, he insists on the distinctiveness of the different institutional orders of capitalist society and argues that modern capitalism only developed because of their 'elective affinities' in the West (*NSV*, p. 142). This is suggestive of the concept of 'structural coupling' in autopoietic theory. Secondly, Giddens notes how the modern state system accentuates 'the reflexive monitoring of system reproduction' and also considers official statistics' role in the reflexive self-regulation of the modern society/state (*NSV*, pp. 12, 17, 180). Here Giddens pursues the theme of self-reflection which is also strongly developed in autopoietic theory. And, thirdly, in arguing that the development of notions such as sovereignty and government helped to define the modern state as a political formation, he pursues ideas analogous to those of self-definition and self-reference in autopoietic systems (*NSV*, pp. 20, 94). Similar ideas also occur in his comments on the constitutive role of early economic theories, doctrines of 'natural frontiers', concepts of international relations, the production of official statistics (pp. 51, 86–90, 170, 180–1, 210, 257–66).

Giddens's concept of structuration is also reminiscent of autopoietic theory in its emphasis on the recursive reproduction of social systems. But this concept actually provides one of the key differences between his approach and autopoietic theories. For Giddens emphasizes that structuration occurs through the strategic conduct of social agents and is not simply the result of a self-reproducing social system. In contrast autopoietic theorists tend to treat actions in an autopoietic system as mere supports, serving to secure its continued reproduction; and/or as having significance only in so far as they adopt the operational code of a given system, so that their specific content and consequences are irrelevant. In this respect Giddens's emphasis on structuration is salutary and highlights the enduring problem of providing an account of the interplay among systems, structures and actions. Whether or not Giddens himself can actually provide a better account of societal evolution through this structuration approach will be considered below.

Organizational materialism

A fourth recent approach to the state focuses on middle-range concepts but applies them to macro- as well as micro-level concerns. Two recent examples are found in Mann's organizational materialism and Peter Hall's institutional analysis, but these studies simply illustrate a much broader current of work. Mann's work is extremely broad in historical and theoretical scope, and only its main analytical points can be summarized here. Hall's work is more concrete, but has also made major theoretical contributions.

Mann argues that societies are confederal rather than unitary; they consist in multiple overlapping, intersecting and rarely coincident socio-spatial networks of power; they rest on a loose confederation of stratified allies. He works on a concrete, socio-spatial and organizational level and focuses on the capacities to organize and control people, materials and territories. He sees power as rooted mainly in organization and explains the subordination of the masses in terms of their involvement in organizations controlled by others (Mann 1986, pp. 1–3, 7–9, 14, 506).

Hall is also concerned with the organizational qualities of institutions and their role in structuring power relations among individuals. He identifies two main effects in this regard. Firstly, institutional structures help to 'mobilize bias' by mediating conflicts among competing social groups and thereby influence the power of different economic forces; and, secondly, they help to define their interests. Hall also mentions two further organizational consequences: institutions affect the capacities for organizational intelligence of collective actors; and they shape state capacities in so far as the state relies on organizational resources in its policy implementation (Hall 1986, pp. 19. 232–3, 264, 277–8). Finally, since altering institutional structures is neither easy nor costless, strategy tends to follow structure more often than structure follows strategy. This involves a complex dynamic between state and society. The state is a product of cumulative social struggles and its own strategies have a cumulative impact on societal organization and the relative balance of power among social forces (Hall 1986, pp. 37, 258, 266–7).

Such arguments are similar to those developed by Giddens. Thus we could just as plausibly classify his work under an organizational materialist approach as under the movement to bring the state back in; or, as Giddens would no doubt prefer, we could classify organizational materialism as a particular application of the theory of structuration. Which of these classificatory solutions is adopted is less important, however, than noting that Giddens and Mann have developed similar accounts of the origins of the modern state as a result of working with similar theoretical frameworks. Both argue that the expansion of the international state system was heavily influenced by military organization and the impact of wars; they also agree that legal and judicial functions provided another driving force and that their fusion with military and class organization produced both absolutist states and constitutional monarchies (Mann 1986, pp. 511–12). Both also find that industrial capitalism developed in a pre-existing system of competing geo-political states and that international relations were dominated by trade, diplomacy and warfare (Mann 1986, p. 513). And, although Giddens has not addressed the same research problem as Hall, it is equally interesting to note how far Hall's studies of British and French economic management confirm not only his own institutional approach but also Giddens's ideas on structuration. Given these convergences we can now turn to some general remarks on the theory of structuration and its application to an account of the modern state.

A final assessment

My review should have revealed both the richness of Giddens's work and its interdisciplinary character. Four main points emerge from comparing it with other approaches: the apparently 'state-centered' (but actually more balanced) analysis of the immense infrastructural power of the modern state; the advantages of structuration over autopoiesis theory in dealing with the self-reflexivity and recursive reproduction of social systems and structures; the analogies between the theory of structuration and organizational materialism together with the more middle-range character of the latter; and the extent to which its greater scope is won at the price of a relative neglect of many issues central to – and well developed by – Marxist state theories. More generally we should note that Giddens provides a general account of crucial historical and/or institutional preconditions for the rise of the modern state; offers a provocative analysis of the fundamental discontinuities involved therein; takes seriously the 'nation-state' by stressing the integral relations among military violence, administrative control and the nation; and outlines four key institutional orders which shape the structures and activities of the state. Although other approaches may well give more detailed accounts of specific issues, they typically lack the breadth of his discussion and often appear one-sided.

Given the range of themes relevant to any analysis of the state system and state power, it is too easy to score debating points by accusing state theorists of having neglected key issues. This should not deter us from noting many surprising omissions and/or weaknesses in Giddens's account. But it would certainly be more useful here to note some more fundamental theoretical problems in his approach to the state apparatus and state power.

Authoritative resources and politicism

Firstly, there seems to be a 'politicist' bias in Giddens's work on the state. It represents a fundamental challenge to historical materialism and it calls for a

wider-ranging and non-reductionist analysis of the state. By widening his
focus to include surveillance and administration as well as industrialized
warfare and international relations, Giddens has significantly deepened conventional analyses of the modern state. He has also traced the implications of
economic changes (such as industrial production or information technology)
for the military and/or surveillance capacities of the state.[8] But sometimes he
seems to conclude from the mutual institutional separation of the modern state
and the capitalist economy that they have exclusive control over authoritative
and allocative resources respectively. For widening state analysis to include
surveillance and administration still keeps it within the domain of authoritative resources, and Giddens also neglects the direct role of economic capacities
in the exercise of state power.

It is worth noting here the distinction between the powers of *dominium* and
imperium which can be wielded by the state. Whereas *dominium* refers to
resources and capacities of the state considered as an economic force, *imperium*
refers to its authoritative resources and capacities (cf. Daintith 1985). The
economic resources which the modern state controls either directly or indirectly play a major role in both its domestic and international activities, and
it often acts directly as an economic force and not merely as the upholder of an
institutional order within which market forces beyond the state operate.

This qualifies any argument that, because the state depends on market
forces for access to economic resources, it is therefore subordinated to the logic
of the market. Problems arise with this argument in domestic as well as
international politics. Dominant nations in the modern world order often use
economic as well as political or military resources – witness the role played by
the politics of food, energy, trade and money. There is also great variation
across capitalist states in their economic capacities and their activities as
economic actors. This variation is not just a function of public ownership,
state-industrial complexes or *eminent domain* but is fundamentally rooted in the
forms and modalities of state intervention, ranging from the political as well as
economic nature of money and taxation up to detailed micro-economic industrial policies. Indeed arguments about the market-dependent 'tax-state' can
be misleading if they neglect how taxation (and state credit) can be structured
to encourage particular patterns of market behaviour (e.g., Przeworski 1986;
Kraetke 1985). The duality of structure as both constraint and resource
applies as much to the separation of the economic and political spheres as it
does to other aspects of social relations. Finally the distinction between
dominium and *imperium* also qualifies any argument that the power of the
modern state depends on its administrative and surveillance capacities rather
than its resort to repression. For the latter argument rests on a false dichotomy
which diverts attention not only from the ideological capacities of the state but
also from the power of *dominium*.

---

[8] In this regard he takes further the work of historical materialists such as Engels.

A capitalist state?

There is another basic problem. Nowhere does Giddens adequately establish how the state is articulated to capitalism. He provides an interesting institutional analysis of the state and carefully dissects its institutional logics as a system of administration, as a site for industrialized warfare and as a component in the international order. But these logics are not connected (even contingently) with a detailed account of their impact on the reproduction of capitalism.

This criticism is partly inspired by Giddens's own insistence that modern societies are *capitalist* societies. The priority which he seems to accord to their capitalist character fits ill with his emphasis on the need to consider their four institutional orders as distinct elements. In turn this raises the problem of how modern societies are successfully reproduced as capitalist societies. Answering this question does not entail returning to a class reductionist or functionalist 'capital logic' account. For Giddens's criticisms of historical materialism are compelling here, and he correctly emphasizes the need to consider other dimensions of the state. But, even if his criticisms are valid, it does not automatically follow that his alternative is better. This depends on how well it can explain the economic dynamic of capitalism (an issue which lies beyond the scope of this chapter) and the ways in which it imprints itself on modern societies (an issue to which we now turn).

Giddens adopts none of the usual non-reductionist Marxist approaches to explaining the capitalist character of modern societies. He has no coherent concept of bourgeois hegemony as a form of political, intellectual and moral leadership of society; no dominant institution (such as the state) acting to maintain social cohesion (and thereby indirectly reproducing capitalism and its class order); no broad-based strategies and/or 'modes of regulation' to produce a 'historic bloc' unifying the economic base with the political and ideological superstructure.[9] In avoiding such ready-made but often unsatisfactory solutions, however, Giddens adopts two contrasting positions on the nature of modern societies. One is more concerned with the systematic structuring of capitalist societies in and through class relations; the other is more concerned with the institutional development of societies which happen to be capitalist. These positions are associated in turn with contrasting views on the state itself: in the one case it is a capitalist state; in the other it is a state articulated with capitalism.

On the one hand, Giddens argues that capitalist societies are the first societies whose dynamic can be deciphered from their class relations and their roots in the primacy of allocative resources. This suggests that they are essentially capitalist societies and that other features, however distinct and

---

[9] This is not meant to suggest that hegemony, the state *qua* factor of cohesion, or a dominant mode of regulation do guarantee capitalist reproduction; it merely identifies a vacuum in Giddens's approach whose implications are traced below.

irreducible to the primacy of capitalist relations, are secondary. Yet Giddens once wrote that class, ethnic differentiation and territorial claims are the *three* basic divisions which provide the focus for schism and cohesion in the modern world (*CPST*, p. 227). And, more recently, he has claimed that there are *four* bases of social conflict organized around the four irreducible dimensions of modern societies: capitalism, industrialism, state organizations and warfare (*NSV*, pp. 313–18). In addition Giddens has suggested that capitalist societies, as nation-states, are in large part politically ordered and derive their internal cohesion through political power (*NSV*, p. 141; *STMS*, pp. 35, 40) and has criticized modern Marxist state theories for excessive concern with the state's economic and 'law and order' functions (*NSV*, p. 28). Such arguments pose serious problems for Giddens's assertion about the primacy of class relations in capitalist states and societies.

A rescue attempt which suggested that other forms of conflict are always overdetermined by class struggle would not take the argument very far: for class struggle would be overdetermined in turn by other lines of conflict. Nor would it help much to relate the primacy of the nation-state to the fluid, anarchic nature of market forces as requiring a political force to regulate them and their consequences. Thus, although Giddens himself seems to link the second pole of the main contradiction in capitalism (that between private appropriation and socialized production) with the state's role in 'unifying' or 'socializing' capitalism (*CCHM*, vol. 1, p. 238), too heavy an emphasis on this regulatory, socializing role would pose problems for Giddens's arguments in other spheres. In particular he claims that capitalism has a global reach (and thus extends beyond the boundaries of the nation-state) and that the state's nature and role cannot be reduced to any functions it might have for capital. In short, the relative primacies of class versus non-class conflicts[10] and of economic versus political power in Giddens's analysis of capitalist nation-states remain uncertain.

As if to counter this first approach, Giddens also provides a historical account of the gradual co-evolution, mutual accommodation and 'elective affinities' of four different institutional spheres to produce contemporary societies (*CCHM*, vol. 1, p. 188; *NSV*, p. 142). It is unlikely that Giddens would go as far as Luhmann in talking simply of *structural coupling*, i.e., a co-evolution and co-adaptation of structures determined through the internal dynamics of each as it reacts to changes in its environment (cf. Luhmann 1982). But

---

[10] Although he often accuses Marxism of class reductionism, Giddens frequently explains major social changes in terms of class conflict. Thus the successive struggles of the bourgeoisie against feudal lords and of organized labour against capital explain the sequential expansion of citizenship rights (*CCHM*, vol. 1, pp. 227–9; cf. *PCST*, pp. 171–2). The growth of the welfare state was also heavily shaped by class struggle; and 'the struggles of the labour movement have played a leading part in the internal metamorphosis of the capitalist state' (*CCHM*, vol. 1, p. 228). In contrast social movements receive little historical attention, and their present role is left in doubt.

Giddens does not move beyond historical accounts to explain how capitalism, industrialism, political surveillance and warfare are integrated around the specifically *capitalist* character of modern societies. If these institutional clusters are integrated around capitalism as their principal axis, we should be told why this (and not one of the other axes) is primary. Otherwise capitalism would be just one among several features of modern society. As it is, this second position seems to imply that the modern state might derive some of its features from its articulation with capitalism and others, at least equally significant, from quite different institutional clusters. In this case it is hard to understand why Giddens has devoted so much time and attention to a contemporary critique of historical materialism as opposed to alternative approaches to analysing modern societies.

Taken together these two positions suggest that Giddens is rather uncertain about the purpose behind his contemporary critique of historical materialism. Does he intend to reconstruct historical materialism by rounding it out through the inclusion of hitherto neglected institutional clusters and thereby revealing the full complexity of capitalist societies? Or does he intend to develop an account of societies whose capitalist character is merely one feature among several and is fundamentally influenced by other institutional forces? Surveying the general development of his work and the evidence from the concluding chapters of *The Nation-State and Violence*, it would seem that the latter purpose is becoming paramount. This would explain the equal weight Giddens has come to give to social and political forces mobilized against industrialism, warfare and political surveillance alongside the class forces engaged in a struggle against capitalism. It might also explain the tendency to shift from an initial concern with class struggle towards a concern with contestation over civil, political and economic citizenship rights, each linked to a distinctive type of surveillance and each having a corresponding dialectic of control (*NSV*, pp. 204–5, 209).

If we accept the logic of this apparent theoretical evolution, however, it poses major problems for Giddens's approach to the state. We are told that 'the state is best seen as a set of collectivities concerned with the institutionalized organization of political power' (*CCHM*, vol. 1, p. 220). If this power itself is not reducible to *class* power, however, we need a different explanation for their emergent patterns of action. This is where a theory of structuration should come into its own in explaining the structural selectivities embodied in the state as a system of political domination as well as the patterns of strategic conduct adopted by different social forces towards the state in a *polyarchic* (as opposed to class-polarized) political system. As yet Giddens has not directed his theory of structuration towards these key problems.

This is partly related to the form in which Giddens develops the arguments in his main monograph: through a series of largely historical narratives and/or broad theoretical descriptions of specific institutional features of the nation-state. More specific conjunctural analyses are missing. This makes it hard to grasp how nation-states fit into the overall structure of capitalist societies and help to unify and cohere them – unless it is through their powers of surveillance and disciplinary organization. Indeed, because it is concerned with the organization of the nation-state and violence, Giddens's work has largely neglected broader political processes. The linkages among economy, civil society and political authority which give substance and direction to state policies are ignored in favour of more general descriptions of polyarchy and control. Indeed the very strengths of Giddens's analysis (its one-sided concern with the state as an institutional ensemble and the specificity of its powers of surveillance and authoritative command) make it difficult to understand how the state apparatus and state power are articulated with the rest of society. In turn this suggests that it is not so much 'politicism' in general which infuses his work as a more specific tendency towards 'statism' in the sense of an exaggerated concern with problems of government resources.

Some other issues

Nowhere does Giddens really explore the problems involved in the modern state form for its functions for capital. One might expect a theorist of structuration who also emphasizes the interaction between structural properties and strategic conduct to say something about the structural contradictions and strategic dilemmas involved in the form of the modern state and its relation to the capitalist economy. It would certainly be nice to know whether Giddens still believes that state intervention is an intrinsic mechanism of mutual realignment of the polity and economy and that it never transgresses the essential character of economic activity (*CSAS*, p. 286). The dialectic of control implied in autonomy-dependence relations and the uneven access of economic and political institutions to allocative and authoritative resources would suggest that no real guarantees can be given that state power will always reproduce the capitalist market economy. And various analyses suggest that all forms of state organization (whether rational-legal, participatory or planning) pose serious strategic dilemmas for capitalists and industrial managers. All that one can say here is that Giddens's theory of structuration does not prevent a concern with such issues and may identify the terrain on which they can be fruitfully addressed. But, unless this theory is developed much further, it will remain more useful for its diacritical and heuristic character than its own positive theoretical contributions.

Moving beyond the immediate field of historical materialism it is disappointing to note that Giddens's growing interest in the modern warfare state has led him into a corresponding neglect of the modern welfare state. He has certainly suggested that the development of citizenship rights completes rather than undermines capitalism (*CSAS*, p. 158) and has also considered the emergence and contradictory nature of the welfare state in various essays (e.g., *PCST*). But a much fuller treatment of its genesis and its various functions could reasonably be expected in an extended discussion of the nation-state.[11] Moreover, given his focus on warfare rather than welfare in his recent book, it is a pity that Giddens did not discuss its economic functions. Giddens certainly emphasizes the industrialization of war, but he seems to treat this primarily in terms of its impact on military technology rather than on the relations between state and economy.

Moreover, given his emphasis on concrete analyses of structuration, it is disappointing that Giddens glosses over the many differences among modern capitalist states as well as among traditional states. He provides a typology which locates states in the international system as well as in terms of their internal structures, but this does not match up to the potential of a structuration approach. What is required here is movement beyond the abstract level of state systems to more concrete work on specific state structures. Relevant variables would include the forms assumed by the separation of powers, the relative weight of different state organs and the forms of political representation and state intervention. This would then lead to a more complex analysis of regime forms to supplement an analysis of state forms.

On a more concrete level still it is also surprising to note that, although Giddens often talks about class struggles and new social movements, he provides no real analysis of political parties or the dynamics of social movements. He neglects party organization and the role of political parties in reproducing the system of political domination or playing a role in formulating the policy and programmes of the state. In this respect his emphasis on the polyarchical nature of modern liberal democracies seems to have encouraged neglect of one of the main forms of political mobilization and policy-making in contemporary capitalism.

Given the importance of ideology and legitimation in the structures of political domination, it is also disappointing that Giddens has not developed his remarks on ideology in the context of state theory. Elsewhere he has noted that ideology can be analysed through the duality of structure; as strategic conduct it can be studied in terms of the relations between modes of discourse and reflexive monitoring of action; and as institutional analysis in terms of how symbolic orders sustain domination in the everyday context of forms of 'lived experience' (*CPST*, pp. 190–2). These remarks should be applied to the political sphere and strategies for winning hegemony in a polyarchic state.

Concluding remarks

I have now reviewed the overall development of Giddens's approach to the state, considered his monograph on the nation-state and violence in some

---

[11] That there is scope for a more nuanced analysis of the welfare state can be seen in Giddens's arguments that the welfare backlash is middle class because the welfare state predominantly connects with the interests of the working class (*PCST*, p. 176) and that its costs are largely met within that class through life-cycle redistribution (*CSAS*, p. 158).

detail, compared its arguments with four other schools, and offered some fundamental theoretical criticisms. It would also have been possible, but for lack of space, to note areas where basic omissions need correcting or minor themes merit more extended treatment. But I think enough has now been written to draw up a preliminary balance sheet.

In some respects it might be unfair to criticize Giddens's state theory. For it is an integral part of a much broader and as yet unfinished theoretical project and can only be properly assessed in relation to that project. Grand theory on this scale is rare, but it should not escape criticism on these grounds alone. Having offered some criticisms, however, we should welcome the range and complexity of Giddens's reflections. He has considered the modern state's development from absolutism and its differences from traditional state forms; he has begun to explore the dialectical interplay between the international state system, the global military order and the logic of industrialism; and he has traced its implications for the organization of the nation-state and the dynamic of class struggles and social movements. His emerging theory of structuration should also generate new insights into the institutional mediation of political domination and its implications for political strategies. At the same time there is still much to accomplish even within the terms of Giddens's own theoretical project. In a research agenda for state theory which he presented in 1983, he called for further work on surveillance as a medium of the disciplinary power of the state and other aspects of repression; on the nature and significance of the nation-state in socialism as well as capitalism; and on the implacable expansion of the means of violence (*STMS*, p. 182). These are all ways to bring the state back in – not just as an object of theoretical inquiry but also as a target of political action. One can only look forward to the final volume in the trilogy on historical materialism which promises to explore this agenda and bring Giddens's theoretical project to a (no doubt provisional) conclusion.

References

In the text I refer to Giddens's works by abbreviations indicated in parentheses after each title listed below.

Alford, R. and Friedland, R. 1985. *Powers of Theory*. Cambridge: Cambridge University Press
Althusser, L. *For Marx*. 1969. London: Allen Lane
Ashworth, C. and Dandeker, C. 1987. Warfare, Social Theory, and West European Development. *Sociological Review*, 35 (i)
Blanke, B. et al. 1975. *Kritik der politischen Wissenschaft*. Frankfurt: Campus
Block, F. 1977. The Ruling Class Does Not Rule. *Socialist Review*, 33
Boccara, P. et al. 1976. *Traité de l'économie politique: le capitalisme monopoliste d'état*. Paris: Editions Sociales
Bologna, S. et al. 1972. *Operai e stato*. Milan: Feltrinelli
Boyer, R. (ed.). 1986. *Capitalismes fin de siècle*. Paris: Maspero-La Decouverte

Buci-Glucksmann, C. 1975. *Gramsci et l'état*. Paris: Fayard
Carnoy, M. 1984. *The State and Political Theory*. Princeton: Princeton University Press
Cerny, P. 1985. Structural Power and State Theory. *Paper presented at the World Congress of the International Political Science Association, Paris, 15–20 July*
Cleaver, H. 1979. *Reading 'Capital' Politically*. Brighton: Wheatsheaf
Daintith, T. 1985. The Executive Power Today: Bargaining and Economic Control. In J. Jowell and D. Oliver (eds.), *The Changing Constitution*. Oxford: Oxford University Press
Dunleavy, P. and O'Leary, B. 1987. *Power and the State*. London: Macmillan
Evans, P. B., Rueschemeyer, D. and Skocpol, T. (eds.), 1985. *Bringing the State Back In*. Cambridge: Cambridge University Press
Gerstenberger, H. 1977. Zur Theorie des buergerlichen Staates. In V. Brandes et al. (eds.). 1977. *Handbuch 5 (Staat)*. Frankfurt: EVA
Giddens, A. 1971. *Capitalism and Modern Social Theory (CMST)*. Cambridge: Cambridge University Press
    (ed.) 1972. *Emile Durkheim: Selected Writings*. Cambridge: Cambridge University Press.
    1976. *New Rules of Sociological Method (NRSM)*. London: Hutchinson
    1977. *Studies in Social and Political Theory (SSPT)*. London: Hutchinson
    1979. *Central Problems in Social Theory (CPST)*. London: Macmillan
    1981. *The Class Structure of the Advanced Societies (CSAS)*. 2nd edn., London: Hutchinson
    1982. *Profiles and Critiques in Social Theory (PCST)*. London: Macmillan
    1983. *A Contemporary Critique of Historical Materialism (CCHM)*. London: Macmillan
    1984. *The Constitution of Society (CS)*. Cambridge: Polity Press
    1985. *The Nation-State and Violence (NSV)*. Cambridge: Polity Press
    1987. *Social Theory and Modern Sociology (STMS)*. Cambridge: Polity Press
Hall, P. A. 1986. *Governing the Economy*. Cambridge: Polity Press
Hemberger, H. et al. 1975. *Imperialismus Heute: der staatsmonopolistische Kapitalismus in Westdeutschland*. Berlin: Dietz Verlag
Hirsch, J. 1976. Bemerkungen zum theoretischen Ansatz einer Analyse des buergerlichen Staates. *Gesellschaft 8–9*. Frankfurt: Suhrkamp
Ingrao, P. 1977. *Masse e Potere*. Rome: Editori Riuniti
Jessop, B. 1982. *The Capitalist State: Marxist Theories and Methods*. Oxford: Martin Robertson
    1985. *Nicos Poulantzas: Marxist Theory and Political Strategy*. London: Macmillan
    1987. Theories of Relative Autonomy and Autopoiesis in the Economy, State, and Law. Essex Papers in Government and Politics
Jung, H. and Schleifstein, J. 1979. *Die Theorie des staatsmonopolistischen Kapitalismus und ihre Kritiker*. Frankfurt: VMB
Kraetke, M. 1985. *Kritik der Staatsfinanzen*. Frankfurt: EVA
Krasner, S. D. 1984. Approaches to the State: Alternative Conceptions and Historical Dynamics. *Comparative Politics* 16 (2), 223–46
Laclau, E. and Mouffe, C. 1985. *Hegemony and Socialist Politics*. London: New Left Books
Luhmann, N. 1982. *The Differentiation of Society*. New York: Columbia University Press
    1984. Staat und Politik: Zur Semantik der Selbstbeschreibung politischer Systeme. In *Politische Vierteljahresschrift: Sonderheft 15*, 99–125
    1986. *Die soziologische Beobachtung des Rechts*. Frankfurt: Metzner
Mann, M. 1983. The Autonomous Power of the State. *Archives européennes de sociologie*, XXV, 187–213
    1984. Capitalism and Militarism. In M. Shaw (ed.), *War, State, and Society*. London: Macmillan

1986. *The Sources of Social Power*. Cambridge: Cambridge University Press

Miliband, R. 1968. *The State in Capitalist Society*. London: Weidenfeld & Nicolson

Mouffe, C. (ed.). 1979. *Gramsci and Marxist Theory*. London: Routledge & Kegan Paul

Negri, A. 1974. *La crisi dello stato-piano*. Milan: Feltrinelli

Nordlinger, E. A. 1981. *On the Autonomy of the Democratic State*. Cambridge, Mass.: Harvard University Press

Offe, C. 1975. The Theory of the Capitalist State and the Problem of Policy Formation. In L. N. Lindberg et al. (eds.), *Stress and Contradiction in Modern Capitalism*. Lexington: D. H. Heath

1984. *Contradictions of the Welfare State*. London: Hutchinson 1985.

1985. *Disorganized Capitalism*. Cambridge: Polity Press

Poulantzas, N. 1969. The Problem of the Capitalist State. *New Left Review*, 58

1973. *Political Power and Social Classes*. London: Sheed and Ward/New Left Books

1976. *Crisis of the Dictatorships*. London: New Left Books

1978. *State, Power, Socialism*. London: New Left Books

Przeworski, A. and Wallerstein, M. 1986. Structural Dependence of the State on Capital. Mimeo

Skocpol, T. 1985. Bringing the State Back In. In P. B. Evans et al. (eds.), *Bringing the State Back In*. Cambridge: Cambridge University Press

Teubner, G. 1984. After Legal Instrumentalism? Strategic Models of Post-Regulatory Law. *International Journal of the Sociology of Law*, 12 (4), 375–400

Thomas, G. M. and J. W. Meyer 1984. The Expansion of the State. *Annual Review of Sociology*, 10, 461–82

Tronti, M. 1977. *Sull'autonomia del politico*. Milan: Feltrinelli

Turner, B. S. 1986. Review of *The Nation-State and Violence*, *Thesis Eleven*

Tuschling, B. 1976. *Rechtsform und Produktionsverhaeltnisse*. Frankfurt: EVA

6

War and the nation-state in social theory

MARTIN SHAW

The history of the twentieth century has often been written as that of a 'century of total war'.[1] Centuries are not, of course, socio-historical periods. But the idea of 'total war' expresses a dominant reality of a major period in the history of modern society: from the 1890s to the 1950s, the period of the build up to, fighting and aftermath of the two World Wars. It can also be argued that the most important group of questions about late-twentieth-century world society is whether and in what sense we have superseded, or can supersede, the period of total war.

In the history of twentieth-century social theory, however, war hardly figures. Our most important writers have continued the debates of nineteenth-century thinkers about industrialism and capitalism, recognizing war as an event external to the main processes of social change – if at all.[2] The late-twentieth-century boom in sociology, even radical and Marxist, has uncritically taken 1945 as the baseline of modernity, failing to reflect on the processes of war which determined this major rupture in social history.

This failure goes beyond sociology to encompass other disciplines and orientations in social science and the humanities. It is not a secondary or minor problem which can be met simply by partial adaptations of the social sciences, for example by developing a new sociology, geography or philosophy of war, however useful the contributions which these may make.[3] It is a central issue in the interpretation of modern societies, a key problem of social theory in general.

The virtual absence of the problem of war in any mainstream tradition of social thought has many ramifications. Its consequences are not limited to the evident weakness of the sociological contribution to problems of war and peace. Total war, in the earlier part of the twentieth century, was a fundamental process in the restructuring of state, economy and society. A social theory which has not grasped the nature and role of this mode of warfare

---

[1] See Arthur Marwick, *War and Social Change in the Twentieth Century* (London: Macmillan, 1977) and *Britain in the Century of Total War* (London: Bodley Head, 1968).

[2] Michael Mann argues that modern sociology has selected those strands of nineteenth-century theory, liberal and Marxist, which make these assumptions, while neglecting others, which he calls militarist, which challenge them: 'War and Social Theory', in *The Sociology of War and Peace*, ed. Colin Creighton and Martin Shaw (London: Macmillan, 1987).

[3] See Martin Shaw and Colin Creighton, Introduction, ibid.

historically is ill equipped to deal with the effects which its mutation, in the current period, has on economic and social life. The profound transformations of economics and politics in every part of the globe at the end of the twentieth century are only explicable against the backdrop of the changes in total war – which earlier shaped the 'postwar' world.

As an example of this, the crisis of the social-democratic welfare state since the 1960s reflects the decline of particular forms of military and socio-economic participation associated with the period of total war. Britain's acute socio-political crisis is related, not just to its sharper economic decline, but to the dramatic transition from a participatory military democracy to a nuclear state which Britain underwent between the 1940s and the 1960s.[4]

The sociology of war and the state

The re-emergence of war, war-preparation and militarism as sociological issues is partly a reflection of the new public awareness of these problems in the 1980s. A new sociology of war has widened the focus from the sociology of the military, which until the present decade was the only significant manifestation of these issues. But even this new sociology has paid insufficient attention to the nature and processes of war and war-preparation themselves. The new sociology of war, drawing many of its materials from social history, presents itself very often as a development from, and even a variant of, the historical sociology of the state. Certainly the theoretical impetus to the new interest in war has been the changing direction of thinking about the state.

It is a remarkable fact, of parallel and equally striking importance to the neglect of total war, that in the depths of the totalitarian epoch, sociology had little to say about the nature of the modern state. Even more fundamentally, of course, the issues of power and power-holding groups were hardly confronted in mid-century sociology. These issues were only slowly recovered, notably in and following Mills's *The Power Elite*; but it was not until the late sixties and even seventies that a serious debate developed about the state.

Modern state theory then emerged primarily, but never exclusively, from the rebirth of Marxism. The 1970s debate was mainly between Marxists, 'instrumentalist', 'structuralist' and 'state-derivatist'. In this debate, the key issues were the relationships between capital, classes and state power, and more specifically the forms of these relationships in modern (i.e. 'postwar') capitalism. War and militarism were never central concerns.[5]

The neglect of war and militarism in this case reflected both the theoretical origins of Marxism and the particular context of the new state theory. Marxism was itself a product of the long nineteenth-century peace: it shared the

[4] Martin Shaw, 'The Rise and Fall of the Military–Democratic State', ibid.
[5] Martin Shaw, 'War, Imperialism and the State System: A Critique of Orthodox Marxism for the 1980s', in *War, State and Society*, ed. Shaw (London: Macmillan, 1984), pp. 47–70.

characteristic of much classical social theory that socio-economic issues predominated over political and military concerns. More particularly, Western Marxism had emerged from a socio-cultural 'detour' which, as Anderson argues, avoided core political problems.[6] The core problems which it failed to grapple with were those of the epoch of totalitarianism – and total war.

Moreover, Western Marxism finally flowered in the one decade of modern times in which the actuality or fear of global war was not a dominant social theme. One should not underestimate the extent to which détente, as well as affluence, was a condition for the radicalism of the late 1960s and early 1970s, of which the Marxist revival was a product. The Vietnam War had the paradoxical effect of pushing the general issue of modern warfare, especially in its nuclear form, to one side.

Marxist critics themselves have pointed out the inadequacy of the new state theory, which neglected the 'national', 'external' and 'inter-state' dimensions of state power.[7] But as, in the later 1970s and 1980s, social theory has come to terms with these realities, the tendency has been to reject the terms of the Marxist debate. None of the major writers are hostile, politically or intellectually, to Marxism, and all wish to incorporate what are seen as the valid contributions of the Marxist discussion. But they reject the assumption that Marxism provides a sufficient framework for state theory – or for a radical politics.

Two major reference points in this debate are undoubtedly Theda Skocpol's *States and Social Revolutions* (1979) and Michael Mann's more recent *The Sources of Social Power* (1985).[8] Skocpol reversed the Marxist terms of debate by explaining social revolutions in terms of the crises of state power, themselves seen as contingent on international, war-related events. Her argument implied that the state has more than the 'relative autonomy' from capital assumed by the Marxist debate. She sufficiently impressed Ralph Miliband for him to propose a compromise between Marxism and the new state theory, in which capital and the state are seen as autonomous centres of power working in 'partnership' with each other.[9]

Skocpol's subsequent work has stressed state-centeredness, in that states must be seen as conglomerations of administrative and political power *sui generis*, irreducible to economic power. The international/military context of state power has, however, become a more subordinate theme, if we are to judge by a recent collaborative volume, *Bringing the State Back In*.[10]

Mann, on the other hand, has provided a sustained challenge to Marxist

6 Perry Anderson, *Considerations on Western Marxism* (London: New Left Books, 1976).
7 Shaw, 'War, Imperialism and the State System', pp. 47–70.
8 Theda Skocpol, *States and Social Revolutions: A Comparative Analysis of France, Russia and China* (Cambridge: Cambridge University Press, 1979); Michael Mann, *The Sources of Social Power* (Cambridge: Cambridge University Press, 1985).
9 Ralph Miliband, *Class Power and State Power* (London: Verso, 1983), p. 70.
10 Peter B. Evans, Dietrich Rueschemeyer and Theda Skocpol (eds.), *Bringing the State Back In* (Cambridge: Cambridge University Press, 1985).

assumptions, in arguments which give war and militarism a central place. For him, states are above all about military power, and there is only a contingent relationship between this and economic power. In recent essays he has challenged the view that there are necessary links between capitalism and militarism, or between domestic and international politics.[11] His arguments are constructed around a scheme of the phases of modern warfare, and so brings war back into the foreground of social theory. It remains to be seen how this will be worked through in the more contemporary volumes of his *Sources of Social Power*.

Mann's theory of warfare and society, however schematic it remains at this point, makes him unusual among state theorists. The only comparable contribution to the social theory of war comes from a writer with a very different starting point. Mary Kaldor, the defence analyst and peace movement activist, has argued for analysis of the 'mode of warfare' and its interaction with the mode of production. She argues, following Clausewitz's tantalizing remarks about the analogies between war and commerce, that we can see warfare as a social process comparable to the process of production. The central problem of war, especially modern war, is that opportunities for testing the values of weapons and strategies are far more limited and irregular than those for testing the values of commodities. This, Kaldor has argued, causes particular difficulties in the nuclear age, leading to 'baroque' military technology and an imbalance between the modes of warfare and production which may be dangerous to peace.[12]

Kaldor's argument, although using Marxist-influenced terminology, is non-reductionist and non-Marxist in its basic theoretical assumptions. She could better be described as a radical Clausewitzian, so long as it is understood that the way in which she uses Clausewitz's understanding of war is very different from that of military strategists and classical Marxists alike. She presents some of the elements of a war-centered, rather than capital- or even state-centered, social theory, but very much in outline form. (In my own work I have attempted to take this process further,[13] and some of the lines along which the arguments might be developed will be considered later in this chapter.)

Giddens on war and the state

Anthony Giddens's recent work is a particularly important contribution to this developing debate on the social theory of war, both in general and in

---

[11] Michael Mann, 'Capitalism and Militarism', in *War, State and Society*, pp. 25–46; 'War and Social Theory'.

[12] Mary Kaldor, 'Warfare and Capitalism', in *Exterminism and Cold War*, ed. E. P. Thompson et al. (London: Verso, 1982); *The Baroque Arsenal* (London: Deutsch, 1982).

[13] Martin Shaw, *Dialectics of War: An Essay on the Social Theory of War and Peace* (London: Pluto Press, 1988).

relation to the state. *The Nation-State and Violence* (1985) is by far the most complete statement, not just of Giddens's own thinking, but of these issues in relation to the main traditions of sociological thought as a whole.[14] Giddens places himself clearly alongside those, like Skocpol and Mann, who are attempting a non-economic reductionist theory of state power, and takes up the same general issues of the role of international relations and war in the analysis of states. He extends the challenge to Marxism which these writers have made, and invites the same incomprehension of Marxists like Bob Jessop, who complains that he 'curiously neglects the modern welfare state in favour of the modern warfare state'.[15] (Jessop clearly cannot accept that it is the neglect of the warfare state, notably by Marxists, that cries out to be corrected.)

Giddens's work is distinguished, above all, because it locates these issues within a synthetic sociological theory, and a generalized critique of previous positions which marginalized war and militarism (chiefly but not only Marxism). Giddens is concerned, however, with power and states, rather than with a theory of war as such. It is important to evaluate his work in this context, both to establish what he has achieved, and to identify the issues which his approach has not fully addressed.

Giddens's early work, while always identifying the state as a major problem of social theory, contains few indications of the centrality more recently afforded to the international and military context of state power. In *The Class Structure of the Advanced Societies*, for example, Giddens contrasts Marx and Weber in terms of their treatments of state and society:

> The Marxian conception . . . treats the state essentially as an 'expression' of the class relationships generated in the market . . . whereas Marx viewed the state in terms of his presuppositions about the infrastructure of society, Weber tended to view that infrastructure in terms of a paradigm derived from his analysis of the state. For Weber the 'class principle' is subordinate to the 'bureaucratic principle'.[16]

But the Weberian model, to which Giddens inclines, does not appear at this stage to be connected to any particular concern with the state-system in which states operate. In Giddens's short study of *Politics and Sociology in the Thought of Max Weber*, written in the same year, the only reference to war is a passing one:

> In the effects of the First World War upon German society, Weber saw both a vindication of his earlier analysis of the German social structure and the possibility of transforming the political order . . . He made no secret of the positive sentiments which the 'great and wonderful' war inspired in him: the passivity, and the lack of a national political sense, which he had criticised in the past, were replaced by a collective assertion of the integrity of the nation in the face of the other world powers.[17]

---

[14] *NSV*, especially chs. 1, 9–11.

[15] Bob Jessop, review of *The Nation-State and Violence*, *Capital and Class*, 29 (Summer 1986), 216–17.

[16] *CSAS*, pp. 124–5.

[17] Anthony Giddens, *Politics and Sociology in the Thought of Max Weber* (London: Macmillan, 1972), p. 21.

One will not find the terms 'war', 'militarism' or even 'violence' in the index to any of Giddens's work in the 1970s.

War and militarism appear to have become of interest to Giddens as he began to develop his own theory of power and to frame the terms of his critique of Marxism. In *A Contemporary Critique of Historical Materialism* (1981), he brings together a number of concerns in his work to focus on the nature of power and the state. He argues that power is routinely involved in the 'instantiation' of social practices: it is not a secondary characteristic of social life. Giddens also insists that 'power was never satisfactorily theorised by Marx, and that this failure is at origin of some of the chief limitations of his scheme of historical analysis'.[18]

In this volume, Giddens introduces some of the principal axes of his current approach to the state. Modifying Foucault's view of power, he argues that 'surveillance', the capacity for 'storage of authoritative resources', is a key attribute of modern states. 'Lack of analysis of the phenomenon of surveillance ... is one of the major limitations of Marx's interpretation of the state.'[19] Surveillance is not just a feature of late, computerized, capitalist society, but integral to the history of capitalism.[20] He quotes Foucault: 'the traditional, ritual, costly, violent forms of power ... were superseded by a subtle, calculated technology of subjection'.[21]

The concept of surveillance is linked by Giddens, however, to a number of other theoretical propositions. On the one hand, it is argued, in terms quite compatible with Marx, that 'the insulation of economy from polity involves ... the extrusion of the means of violence from the principal axis of class exploitation, the capital/wage-labour relation'.[22] On the other, Giddens attacks 'the prevalence in nineteenth-century social thought of the notion that capitalistic economic enterprise is essentially non-violent in nature'. This apparent paradox is explained by the fact that 'Such a view ignores the processes that led to the internal pacification of states ... And it ignores the fact that the capitalist state has been the purveyor of violence externally ...'[23]

The opposition of 'surveillance' and 'violence' thus assumes a signal importance in Giddens's thought. The growth of state surveillance corresponds to the reduction of violence within societies ('pacification') and in particular within class relations. But – and this is perhaps the most radical element of Giddens's argument – the pacification of societies by states does not imply a general pacification of social life. The reason for this, once the violence of the initial pacification process itself has subsided, is the *external* violence of the state. Here, given the theoretical importance accorded to violence in society, is to be found the source of the growing theoretical importance of war to Giddens. When he remarks, later, that

---

[18] *CCHM*, p. 3.   [19] Ibid., p. 5.   [20] Ibid., p. 175.
[21] Michel Foucault, *Discipline and Punish: The Birth of the Prison* (London: Allen Lane, 1977), pp. 220–1.
[22] Giddens, *CCHM*, p. 11.   [23] Ibid., p. 12.

I have long contended that the neglect of what any casual survey of history shows to be an overwhelmingly obvious and chronic trait of human affairs – recourse to violence and war – is one of the most extraordinary blank spots in social theory in the twentieth century.[24]

Giddens is not simply making a ritual comment on a lack in social theory. He is pointing to a force which, his theory suggests, is directly related to the main trends of contemporary society.

The changing balance of internal and external violence, and the changing role of the state, implies a major change in the character of military power. 'In class-divided societies', Giddens suggests, 'open class struggle is generally very sporadic, though it may be very violent.'[25] Because of this violence, and the lack of developed surveillance,

Military power has normally placed a decisive role in the integration of class-divided societies ... The use or the threat of the use of violence in sustaining system integration is ever present in class-divided societies. This is of major importance to the conceptualisation of the state ...[26]

In capitalism, by contrast, class struggles are a chronic feature of the organization of production, but they are correspondingly less violent, and they are regulated by surveillance rather than violence. Military power no longer plays a decisive role in system integration. The growth of military power continues, however, and can only be explained by external conflict.

It is clear that Giddens differs sharply from Marxists who have tended to present the growth of military power as a result of the sharpening of class contradictions, often neglecting in the process the more obvious war-related explanations for the growth of military power. If he considers the role of military power within capitalist societies, he is more likely to see it as cause than consequence. For example, he makes the point that military organization anticipated the organization of the factory:

In the army barracks, and in the mass coordination of men on the battlefield (epitomised by the military innovations of Prince Maurice of Orange and Nassau in the sixteenth century) are to be found the prototype of the regimentation of the factory – as both Marx and Weber noted.[27]

Giddens also now presents the state specifically as a 'nation-state'. He sees 'the period of triumph of capitalism as a "world capitalist economy"' as 'also a period eventuating in the world-wide triumph of the nation-state as a focus of political and military organisation'.[28] And he argues that it is 'not necessary (nor is it legitimate) to suppose that one has to unearth how it came to be that capitalism "needed" the nation-state for its development, or in which, *per contra*, the nation-state "needed" capitalism'.[29] Nor is nationalism the direct

[24] Ibid., p. 177.   [25] Ibid., p. 130.   [26] Ibid., pp. 163–4.
[27] Ibid., p. 125.   [28] Ibid., p. 182.   [29] Ibid., p. 183.

product of nation-states (still less of capitalism): this too needs to be specifically explained, perhaps as a result of war. War-mobilization disrupts the
social fabric – 'the relatively fragile fabric of ontological security may become
broken. In such conditions regressive forms of object-identification [national-
ism] tend to come to the fore.'[30]

In this volume, therefore, Giddens outlines many of the positions on state
and society which mark him off not just from Marx but also from others who
acknowledge Weber as the major figure in social theory. What Giddens takes
from Weber is quite clearly a world away from Parsons's interpretation, for
example:

> Neither Weber's sombre view of modern capitalism, nor his emphases upon the
> centrality of military power and violence more generally in history, survive
> prominently either in Parsons's representations of Weber's work, or in Parsons's
> own theories.[31]

The centrality of war, military power and violence had not been so apparent in
Giddens's earlier work, either, but now these are becoming the cutting edges of
his theory of state and society.[32]

The Nation-State and Violence

Not surprisingly, the second volume of the 'contemporary critique of historical
materialism' bears directly on these themes and contains a full exposition of
his views. The more radical theoretical developments were, arguably, made in
the first volume, but *The Nation-State and Violence* integrates them in a broad
theoretical and historical statement. The gap between his theory and Marxism
is also clarified.

At the centre of Giddens's theory, now, is the nation-state, presented not
just as a major institution or set of institutions, but as *the* defining and
integrating institution of modern societies. 'Modern societies', he writes, 'are
nation-states, existing within a nation-state system.'[33] Societies were not previously co-extensive with administrative units, since traditional states lacked
clearly defined boundaries and means of social control. It is a result of
'distinctive forms of social integration associated with the nation-state' that
this has come about.[34]

'Capitalism' needs, in Giddens's view, to be 'prised free from the general
framework of historical materialism, and integrated in a different approach to
previous history and to the analysis of modern institutions'.[35] It becomes

---

[30] Ibid., p. 194.   [31] Ibid., p. 206.
[32] Curiously, however, the indexing of these terms remains incomplete: only violence is – rather
briefly – annotated in *A Contemporary Critique*, while 'war' and 'military' are unlisted. Even in
The Nation-State and Violence there is no entry under 'military', while that under 'war' simply
refers to other headings.
[33] *NSV*, p. 1.   [34] Ibid., p. 2.   [35] Ibid., p. 1.

instead one of four ' "institutional clusterings" associated with modernity: heightened surveillance, capitalistic enterprise, industrial production and the centralised control of the means of violence'.[36] These clusterings are irreducible, the one to the other, but reflect different forces which are at work in modern societies. Two of these clusterings, of course, directly appertain to the nation-state (surveillance and military violence); the other two, which are more commonly used to define modern societies (industrialism and capitalism) 'intersect with' the development of the nation-state system.

States in general can be defined, following Weber rather than Marx, according to violence and territoriality, but Giddens wishes to qualify his definition. Traditional states, he argues, could 'claim' a legitimate monopoly of violence within a given territory, but only modern nation-states have really achieved it.[37] Traditional states were characterized by specialized military forces, but the distinction between external and internal war was not always very clear. The monopoly of violence eluded the central state, and much warfare was the result of attempts by states to establish and maintain as well as to extend the scope of their power. On the other hand, states did not 'govern' their populations in a regular sense, and so had periodically to resort to military force as a substitute for administration.

The fundamental transition, according to Giddens, is from the traditional state to the modern nation-state. The absolutist state is a stage in this development, but is still basically a traditional form. This transition is not determined by a single socio-economic process, or indeed by socio-economic processes in general. Giddens is determinedly non-reductionist in his explanation for changes in state forms, and one of the most interesting points in his account is where he argues that 'there were three sets of military developments that decisively influenced (but were also influenced by) the rise of the absolutist state'.[38] He refers to technological changes in armaments, the emergence of modern military discipline and the development of naval strength. He goes on to assert that

> Various main features of European state development were shaped in a decisive way by the contingent outcomes of military confrontations and wars. Nothing shows more clearly how implausible it is to regard the emergence of modern societies as the result of some sort of evolutionary scheme that inexorably led from the alluvial dirt of Sumer to the factory shop-floor of latter-day Europe.[39]

A crucial analytical issue in this assertion is whether military events should be regarded as purely 'contingent' or whether there is a major category of factors which need to be incorporated into the explanation of social change. Should military factors as such, or only the outcome of particular battles and wars, be regarded as 'contingent'? Giddens pursues his analysis of military developments, such as the development of standing armies and discipline, in a way

---

[36] Ibid., p. 5.   [37] Ibid., pp. 19, 27.   [38] Ibid., p. 105.   [39] Ibid., p. 112.

which suggests that these are significant general factors. Repeating the historical point already made in *A Contemporary Critique* he writes that through the interventions of Maurice of Nassau,

> there is a very real sense in which . . . the techniques of Taylorism became well embedded in the sphere of the armed forces several hundred years before, in industrial production, they came to be known by that label.[40]

The development of modern nation-states, aided by military organization and technology, involves in Giddens's view the establishment of monopolies of violence. Nation-states as 'bordered power-containers' achieve more and more effective surveillance of their societies and are able to eliminate or marginalize violence within them. Civil wars in modern nation-states are, according to Giddens, less common than were the internal armed struggles of traditional states and societies. Where they do occur, the fact that armed movements are invariably concerned with the assumption of state power testifies to the centrality of the state in the modern world.

Giddens is 'principally concerned with the means of violence associated with the activities of organised armed forces, not with violence as a more blanket category of doing physical harm to others', and hence can discount (though he denies wishing to underplay) 'violence that takes place in small-scale contexts in modern societies'.[41] He mentions violent crime and domestic violence; it is obviously crucial to his theory that it should be possible also to discount class, industrial, political and racial violence.

The elimination of violence, or 'pacification' of societies by nation-states and their surveillance activities, are necessary conditions for the expansion of capitalism and industrialism. Indeed capitalism, according to Giddens, involves

> a novel type of class system, one in which class struggle is rife but also in which the dominant class . . . do not have or require direct access to the means of violence to sustain their rule. Unlike previous systems of class domination, production involves close and continuous relations between the major class groupings. This presumes a 'doubling-up' of surveillance, modes of surveillance becoming a key feature of economic organisations and of the state itself.[42]

Marx, of course, was aware of how the 'dull compulsion' of economic relations, rather than violence, was the main mechanism of capitalist power; but according to Giddens, 'he does not ask what happens to the means of violence "extruded" from the labour contract'.[43]

This 'admittedly crude formulation' echoes closely words used in *A Contemporary Critique*, already quoted, and expresses one of Giddens's most radical ideas. It is almost as though he is suggesting that the violence which is squeezed out of society, and notably economic relations, is directly expressed

---

[40] Ibid., p. 113.   [41] Ibid., p. 121.   [42] Ibid., pp. 159–60.   [43] Ibid., p. 160.

in externally directed military violence, i.e. in war. It is not, surely, that he believes that there is a fixed amount or level of violence in any society. What he is arguing is that the pacification of social relations occurs primarily through the accumulation of power in the nation-state. Although the mature form of a pacified society is one in which surveillance is paramount, the initial pacification occurs partly through military power, and leads to a standing army as the foundation of the modern nation-state. At the same time, Giddens argues that nation-states exist only in and through the nation-state system. He attacks Wallerstein's concept of a world system, arguing that a world system 'is not only formed by transnational economic connections and dependencies, but also by the global system of nation-states, neither of which can be exhaustively reduced to the other'.[44]

This argument gives Giddens a novel angle on an old debate. Mann, for example, has argued that, contrary to both the nineteenth-century 'optimistic theory of pacific capitalism' and the early-twentieth-century Marxist 'theory of militaristic capitalism', industrial capitalism is instrinsically neither pacific nor militarist.[45] Giddens, by contrast, argues that industrial capitalism is 'pacific' – but only internally, within a nation-state:

> What it involves, however, is not the decline of war but a concentration of military power 'pointing outwards' towards other states in the nation-state system.[46]

Pacification and militarism are not alternatives, but two sides of the same process. This implies, however, that military power itself has undergone immense change.

Giddens devotes a chapter to the historical sociology of military power, outlining the development of armaments and military technology. Locating these within his four 'institutional clusters', he rejects the common assumption that capitalism lies behind the growth of arms, insisting instead that 'Industrial capitalism provided the means for the industrialisation of war, but the activities and involvements of nation-states are at the origin of the phenomenon.'[47] He also emphasizes the link between military duty and citizenship rights in political democracy. In discussing the two World Wars, he stresses the impact of war on industrial organization, the institutionalization of class conflict and the political structures of the combatant states. 'My main point', he argues, 'is to emphasise that the impact of war in the twentieth century upon generalised patterns of change has been so profound that it is little short of absurd to interpret such patterns without systematic reference to it.'[48]

It is obviously of critical importance to discover how far this impact continues beyond the period of the two World Wars. 'Do we', Giddens asks, 'still, in fact, live in military societies?' 'How far are Western nation-states currently

[44] Ibid., p. 169.   [45] Mann, 'Capitalism and Militarism', pp. 44–5.
[46] NSV, p. 192.   [47] Ibid., p. 226.   [48] Ibid., p. 244.

dominated by military imperatives in terms of their basic economic organisation? Are patterns of military rule likely to become more, rather than less
common . . .?'[49] He deals mainly with the economic issue, arguing that despite
the specific weight of military industries, economies as wholes are not generally dominated by a 'military–industrial complex'; and with the political
aspect, maintaining that even where the military take power, rule is not
generally carried out through military means. Consistent with his main argument, Giddens argues that military power as such is of declining importance in
social control. Repressive military regimes are examples of the more general
phenomenon of totalitarianism, which is inherent in the surveillance state.
Giddens concludes that only in the sense that our nation-states are part of a
world military order, in which the means of waging industrialized war are
widely diffused, do we live today in 'military societies'.

The system of nation-states – rather than capitalism or industrialism – is,
then, the key to understanding the problems of military power. The role of the
military in the newer 'state-nations' depends on the same twin features of
centralized, bureaucratized military power and a historically high level of
internal pacification which are found in nation-states generally. Despite the
extent to which some states are militarily and politically subordinate to others,
and despite elements of international organization, world society is more than
ever composed of competing nation-states with the means to wage industrialized war.

This analysis leads Giddens to largely pessimistic conclusions. 'In terms of
historical agencies of change,' he writes, 'there is no parallel in the sphere of
weaponry to the proletarian in the area of industrial labour. No plausible
"dialectical counterpart" to the progressive accumulation of military power
seems to exist.'[50]

Peace movements are likely, in Giddens's view, to be of limited effect. Hope
is sought, however, in resistance to militaristic values – old-style militarism is
seen as in decline, new-style militarism as no more than a propensity to seek or
accept military solutions. In the absence of a dialectic of change, we must look
to 'a renewal of utopianism, mixed with the firmest form of realism' to resist
the war-propensities of nation-states.[51] This utopianism 'can (not *must*) negatively affect tactical decisions relevant to coping with a heavily militarised
world'.[52]

Dialectics of total war

It will be evident that *The Nation-State and Violence* has a very wide scope and
offers an impressive range of generalizations – matched, it should be stated, by
the breadth of its author's historical knowledge. In its restoration of the issues

---

[49] Ibid., p. 245–6.   [50] Ibid., p. 326.   [51] Ibid., p. 334.
[52] Ibid., p. 339. Italics in the original.

of war and militarism to the centre of social theory in general, and state theory in particular, it is far and away the most important text yet published. Its basic theoretical approach has been questioned, however, by Jessop, who argues that

> we seem to be faced with the concept of a gradual co-evolution of four different spheres without any serious attempt to move beyond an historical account to an analysis of system integration around the *capitalist* character of modern societies.[53]

There seem to be two separate issues here. One is whether Giddens has adequately identified, and explained the relationships of, his 'institutional clusterings'. It is possible to argue, as this chapter does in relation to war and militarism, with the way the four are specified and to suggest better explanations for their interactions. But Jessop clearly wants to go further than this. As a Marxist, forced to admit that Giddens has made 'compelling' criticisms of historical materialism, he feels obliged to insist that it is around the 'capitalist' character of modern societies that system integration must be identified.

Giddens has, however, given compelling reasons for structuring our explanations of social integration – and social change – around the nation-state rather than around capitalism. It is not an oversight that prevented him from arguing as Jessop suggests. As our preliminary discussion has indicated, his argument brings together main points which are increasingly common ground among state theorists. *The Nation-State and Violence* is a persuasive statement of the new theoretical consensus based on the widely perceived inadequacies of Marxist state theory.

It is perhaps surprising that Jessop hinged his criticism on the relation between capitalism and the state, rather than examining the more novel parts of Giddens's argument such as his use of violence, war and militarism. A great deal, after all, hinges on the argument about pacification and surveillance. Giddens is adopting very broad historical standards when he dismisses class, industrial, political, racial, criminal or personal violence in contemporary societies as not amounting to significant violence for his purposes. When he accepts the Marxist concept of class struggle, but denies there is significant class violence, he identifies violence very narrowly with organized, armed fighting and killing.

The distinction between what is commonly described as 'social violence' in contemporary societies, and violence in this more fundamental sense, is valid and important. But it is still unclear that Giddens is on strong historical ground. It would have been difficult for him to put forward his argument at an earlier stage in the development of nation-states and capitalism. In the first half of the twentieth century organized class violence – for example, the paramilitary formations of communist and fascist parties – was all too commonplace. Class struggle appeared as likely to culminate in political

---

[53] Jessop, p. 219. Italics in the original.

violence as it did in pacification and integration. It is not so clear, then, that these are features of nation-states as such, rather than of the more industrially advanced nation-states since the Second World War. May not pacification also be regarded as a contingent military outcome?

What this demonstrates is that while *The Nation-State and Violence* presents itself as a synthesis, it is often raising fundamental historical and analytical issues rather than resolving them. If this is true of its observations on social violence, it is even more true of the analysis of war and militarism. These themes are in reality far more problematic than Giddens allows. For him, they are a means of explaining important features of the modern nation-state, but they are still not treated coherently from a theoretical point of view. Because of the new importance accorded to military power as one of the core institutional clusterings of modern societies, it is necessary to develop a social theory of war and militarism.

Despite many assertions of the striking effects of war on society, Giddens never enters into the theory of war: to seek, for example, the sociological meaning of Clausewitz, whose concept of war could be set alongside the ideas of Marx and Weber as an intellectual landmark for the modern era. He therefore lacks a general explanation for the facts which in so many ways he finds of startling importance for understanding modern societies.

There is a broad similarity between Giddens's concept of military power as an institutional cluster and Kaldor's of a 'mode of warfare'. The difference is that where Giddens offers us a series of historical accounts of military technology, organization, etc., Kaldor argues for seeing warfare as a set of social processes flowing from the contest of violence between states. Giddens writes of the concentration of outward-pointing military violence in the state, but he does not discuss the logic of its use in actual war. This is where, as Kaldor recognizes, Clausewitz is essential.[54]

Clausewitz's main contribution is not to be sought, as Marxists have believed, in his dictum that 'war is the continuation of policy by other means'. The core of his work is his concept of warfare as a contest of force, to which there is no necessary limit. War may be limited, by the political aims of the combatants and also by what Clausewitz calls 'friction', i.e. constraints such as geography, climate, logistics and technology. But the essence of war is the contest of force which *tends* to become absolutely destructive. 'Absolute war' is not therefore merely one type of war, but the logical culmination of the inner meaning of war. 'Absolute war' can therefore be seen as an 'ideal type' or a 'maximum possible concept' of war in general. Clausewitz may not have envisaged that absolute war would ever be fully realized in practice: but as Howard points out, nuclear war threatens to abolish friction and make war instantaneously absolute.[55]

[54] Kaldor, 'Warfare and Capitalism'.
[55] Michael Howard, *Clausewitz* (Oxford: Oxford University Press), 1982.

The absolutism of war is a fact of general sociological interest. It is this which accounts for the tendency of war to cut through established patterns of social relations. The logic of violence dwarfs other social concerns, so that both formal and informal social institutions undergo change in response to the demands of warfare. Wars are often major periods of social change: this has long been true, but the nature of modern warfare and its relationship to society have given the point new significance. Twentieth-century industrialized war raises the stakes in the military determination of social relations. Giddens recognizes the manifestations of this process, but his theory does not fully explain it.

The concept of the mode of warfare is extremely important here. Kaldor lays emphasis on the way in which the form of war being waged or envisaged in strategic planning becomes embedded in military technology and economy and hence in social relations. Her study of contemporary military technology stresses the way in which it reflects historically outmoded strategic concerns, thus rendering itself militarily obsolescent and economically retarding.[56]

What is needed is a more general account of the 'mode of warfare' which developed as a result of the rise of the nation-state system and of industrial capitalism, and of the way this has changed over time. I have suggested that we need to develop the sociological concept of *total war* to describe this mode of warfare, incorporating both Clausewitzian and socio-historical insights.[57] On the one hand, the development of military technology, under the impact of the industrialization of war, led to warfare which increasingly realized the ideal type of 'absolute war'. On the other hand, capitalist organization of an industrial work-force, combined with the mobilizing power of the nation-state (a form of what Giddens calls surveillance), created the potential not just for mass armies but for total socio-economic and political war-mobilization.

These two dimensions combine to define the mode of total war which dominated the economic, social and political life of the first half of this century, and which was realized in the two World Wars. Total war was not of course a single form of war, but was constantly changing. Between two World Wars, developments in strategy and technology changed national labour forces from the suppliers of total war to its targets. Revolutionary ideologies, by-products of the First World War, became motive forces of the Second. These and other changes marked inner transformations of total war and its relationship to society.

Much of Giddens's analysis could be further explicated by a dynamic concept of total war, attempting to relate the international, military, political-ideological and socio-economic processes involved. Total war was, moreover, a deeply contradictory process, leading to both revolutionary and reformist social movements. Giddens is wrong to deny the significance of revolutionary violence in capitalist societies in the first part of the twentieth century. A more

---

[56] Kaldor, *The Baroque Arsenal.*   [57] Shaw, *Dialectics of War.*

satisfactory argument against Marxism is that revolutionary contradictions were much more apparent in mobilization for total war than in the capitalist economic crisis which Marxists have seen as determining. Total war was also, however, the context for much of the consolidation of the power of nation-states of which Giddens writes. Indeed, and this again is a question-mark against Marxism, the outcome of class, as much as military, violence in the epoch of total war has invariably been to centralize state power.

The criticism of Giddens is that while he recognizes many of the effects of total war, he does not explain what total war is or has been. The nature of military power, as a basic institutional cluster of modern society, is explained only *ad hoc* and not theoretically (on a par with capitalism, industrialism or even surveillance). Military power tends to be presented as a resource of states; it is not clear that Giddens has quite come to terms, theoretically at least, with the destructive logic of actual war. He has not thought through an answer to the question, why and how is it that modern war has such a transformative effect on social relations?

Just as Giddens lacks a clear concept of the mode of warfare and its development historically, he only skirts around the changes which have taken place since 1945. He grasps, with his seemingly unerring sense for the historical tendency, the demise of classical militarism which accompanied the passing of classical total war. He puts his finger on the paradox of societies which, while producing an ever more destructive outward-pointing militarism, are not inwardly militarist in most obvious senses. He does not, however, discuss either the causes of this in the nuclear mutation of total warfare, or the consequences for nation-states. In this respect Giddens has less to offer than Mann, who has recently outlined a scheme of the stages of modern warfare.[58] (Mann's threefold classification – 'Clausewitzian', 'citizen' and 'nuclear' war – is, however, open to question both on interpretation and argument.[59])

What cannot be in doubt is that the period since the end of the Second World War has seen a fundamental transition, in the advanced industrial societies, from mass-mobilization to high-technology militarism. Nuclear weaponry was the first, is still the dominant, but is by no means the only technology of this new form of war-preparation. Warfare has in general moved beyond the stage in which quantities of men and weapons are crucial, to the supremacy of technological sophistication – in electronics as well as nuclear physics.

The transformation of modern warfare clearly has major implications for the relationship of war and society. Nuclear militarism clearly requires general ideological mobilization, in the context of Cold War rivalry, and this can give the impression of societies which are still highly militarized. At the same time

---

[58] Mann, 'The Roots and Contradictions of Modern Militarism', *New Left Review*, 162 (March–April 1987), 35–50.
[59] Shaw, *Dialectics of War*, ch. 4.

there is a need for specialized military industries of a high order of technological sophistication, which lie behind the concept of a 'military–industrial complex'. Indeed, these two characteristics, taken together, have led E. P. Thompson to assert that societies in the Cold War 'do not have military–industrial complexes; they are military–industrial complexes'.[60]

This view, understandable in view of the danger which war-preparation poses is, however, misleading. Ideological mobilization accompanies practical demobilization: populations are no longer mobilized *en masse* in war-preparation, nor will they be required to fight and produce in nuclear war. The concentration of military industry in high technology means that it has less direct impact on advanced economies as wholes. In order to prepare for possible wars, nation-states no longer require much of the direct and detailed control over economies and societies which they took in the epoch of classical total war.

Giddens clearly appreciates some of this change, but his analysis cannot pinpoint the issues decisively enough. The difficulty is that his concepts are at too high a level of generality to explain specific phases and forms of the relationships of nation-state and society. The relationships of military power, surveillance, industrialism and capitalism are changing in ways which are descriptively acknowledged, but cannot be accounted for theoretically. For example, Giddens is right to argue that modern nation-states rule through surveillance rather than military power. But surveillance takes many forms: the fact that nuclear nation-states like the US and the UK can dispense with much of the direct control which they assumed forty years ago is of immense political importance. More sophisticated forms of surveillance, monitoring and manipulating without postwar 'intervention' and controls, have opened up a new economic and political era in advanced Western nation-states. The ideology of Thatcherism, with its twin totems of nuclear weapons and the market, actually expresses the new relationship of the nuclear state to economy and society. The state may retain overall direction of the national economy while abdicating much of its detailed intervention to private agencies. Giddens offers us little with which to define these changes, or their relationship to military power.

One point on which Giddens is clear is his denial that there are dialectics of change in military power and war. It has been argued here, against this, that there certainly have been radical contradictions in the mode of warfare. Total war (very ironically from the point of view of Marxism) was the context of socialist advance in the first half of this century. It is common ground, however, that contemporary nuclear militarism will not generate any internal agency for change: the radical contradictions of war-mobilization have been closed off. It is not so clear, however, that the changed relation of war and

[60] E. P. Thompson, 'Exterminism: The Last Stage of Civilization', in Thompson et al., *Exterminism and Cold War* (London: Verso, 1982).

society is so hopeless for radical politics. The decline of classical militarism, and the *de facto* demilitarization of late industrial societies, creates a space in which ideals of a more peaceful world can flourish.

Similarly, although the retreat of the nuclear state from much direct socio-economic control is designed to create new opportunities for private capitalism, it also creates new space for a decentralizing politics of democratic control. It may make it possible, for almost the first time in this century, to define socialism free from the distortions of statism induced by total war. This may be, as Giddens insists, largely a utopian exercise, but the link with historical possibility is still there to be shaped.

7
Only half the story: some blinkering effects of 'malestream' sociology

LINDA MURGATROYD

Introduction

In writing a chapter about Giddens on women and gender in society, I must first express disappointment that, along with so many other social theorists even today, he has largely ignored these from his field of study. This chapter therefore starts with a critique of what he has omitted, and of some of the consequences of this omission, rather than of a substantive body of Giddens's writings. However, it also shows how the omission of women and gender relations from a supposedly broad social theory, and associated with this, the omission of spheres of social activity particularly associated with women, results in other fallacies and limitations of as great importance, and which have been less commented upon elsewhere. Not only is half of society (and the relationship between that half and the other half) virtually omitted from his analysis, but also, partly by association, half of the activities carried on in that society. I then explore how some of the concepts elaborated by Giddens might usefully be developed further for analysing these areas as well as pointing to how some of the shortcomings in Giddens's work might be made good. Rather than discussing gender relations and 'women' in general terms, I have limited my comments here to specific areas of social activity: those that take place in the domestic sphere, and more generally activities concerned with the production of people. These both illustrate some of the more general problems of ignoring women and gender in sociological analysis, and stand in their own right as core areas of social activity which theoretical texts such as those produced by Giddens ought to encompass. I shall show how Giddens's theory of structuration, in particular, could – with the addition of some important new perspectives – be adapted to provide a strengthened framework for analysis of these areas, with implications for a wide range of social investigation.

I am grateful to Michelle Stanworth for her comments on a draft of this chapter. The views expressed are only my own, however.

Giddens: continuing the 'malestream' of sociological tradition

Many of the sociological consequences of dismissing women, and hence gender, from the field of mainstream sociological inquiry have by now often been spelled out.[1] However, the fact remains that Giddens has continued to fail to deal seriously in the main body of his work with either the gender dimension of social relations or any of the areas of social activity in which women typically participate more. He is not alone in this, and this indicates that some reiteration is needed. An approach which leaves women out of the main field of study not only draws a lop-sided picture of the societies being analysed, but also produces a theoretical analysis which is blinkered. As a result, inconsistencies and mistakes are made. This is, of course, not a fault unique to Giddens,[2] but at a time when the pitfalls of a male-centered sociology are increasingly widely understood, when the study of women has begun to redress that balance, and when a sociology of gender has become well established, continued ignoring of this dimension of social systems in mainstream social theory is inexcusable. It would appear that Giddens is prepared to recognize this limitation in his work,[3] yet his comments are confined to assertions which are added on as afterthoughts instead of being developed as an integral part of his analysis.

A *Contemporary Critique* provides a good example of this cavalier approach. It is a volume which ignores the gender dimension to social systems, but which nonetheless asserts that there exist 'exploitative relations between the sexes', which 'do not originate with capitalism or even class divisions more generally'[4] (an assertion that is not backed up by arguments within the book and that some would contest). Soon after, Giddens continues 'The creation of everyday life in capitalist time–space, with its characteristic separation of home and work-place, together with other aspects of the commodification of social relations, have decisively influenced the relations between the sexes, and at least in certain respects served to intensify the exploitation of women.'[5]

It seems therefore that Giddens recognizes the relations between the sexes as a significant area of sociological inquiry, which – if addressed – would yield insights of fundamental importance for critical sociology. Yet his comments are confined to asserting that some other dimensions of social life affect the relations between the sexes, without investigating either what effects they have had or (more significantly) whether and how the relations between the sexes might have effects on other areas of social life – such as the particular forms of

[1] See, for example, J. Acker, 'Women and Social Stratification: A Case of Intellectual Sexism', *American Journal of Sociology*, 78 (1973), 936–45; D. E. Smith, 'Women's Perspective as a Radical Critique of Sociology', *Sociological Enquiry*, 44.1 (1974), 7–13, and Dale Spender, *Male Studies Modified* (Oxford, Pergamon Press, 1981).
[2] See, for example, the discussion of such problems and inconsistencies in relation to occupational grading in Linda Murgatroyd, 'Women, Men and the Social Grading of Occupations', *British Journal of Sociology*, xxxv.4 (1984), 473–97.
[3] Anthony Giddens, *Sociology: A Brief but Critical Introduction*, 2nd edn (London, Macmillan, 1986).
[4] Giddens, *CCHM*, p. 242.   [5] Ibid., p. 243.

the division of labour, developments of state institutions or commodification of social resources more generally. The main thrust of Giddens's theory of structuration, as developed in *Central Problems in Social Theory*[6] and *A Contemporary Critique of Historical Materialism* could in my view provide an excellent theoretical context for analysing the social relations of gender in contemporary Western societies once the sexist blinkers were removed and if it were reworked accordingly; the more so because these cannot adequately be analysed without considering other dimensions of the social system, such as the economic order, the class structure and the state.

Domestic work: an area for sociological inquiry

There are a number of aspects of domestic work that a sociological theory needs to be able to encompass. These have by now been well documented in a variety of empirical studies, ranging from time-budgets through interview surveys and observation about both the nature and amount of domestic work, and attitudes to it and reasons for particular people doing it in particular ways.

However, the principal traditions in mainstream sociological theory have only touched on a few (if any) aspects of domestic work. It is an area of human social activity in which many of the problems of functionalist and Marxist sociological approaches quickly became apparent, and which therefore poses fundamental theoretical problems for sociologists working within these traditions.

The development, in industrial societies, of places of work that are outside the home has led social analysts to consider work as itself being something that happens outside the home. The way this is described varies according to the sociological tradition, but in general, 'the family' is described as a sphere which stands in contrast to the world of 'work'. By implication, the work done within the family, or in the domestic sphere, is not considered to be work. Hence, social relations within the household are not considered to be 'relations of production'. By some, they are perceived in terms of kinship or affective ties, to the exclusion of the economic and productive element. This approach has been common within anthropological traditions, where the different kinship ties and the patterns of marriage, residence and intergenerational transfer of wealth in different communities have been the subject of intense inquiry, but where the sexual distribution of labour (especially that taking place within the home) has (until recently, at least) attracted far less academic interest.[7]

Functionalist sociologists have tended to identify 'the family' as a unit whose functions include the 'socialization of children' and the 'stabilization of adult personalities' and which, in industrial society, does not have direct functions in relation to the economy. Within this 'unitary unit' the division of

---

[6] Giddens, *CPST*, esp. chs. 1–5.
[7] Shirley Ardener (ed.), *Perceiving Women* (London: Dent, 1975).

labour is described in terms of 'a characteristic conjugal segregation of roles'. In addition to the general problems with functionalist approaches that Giddens has tackled in his theory of structuration this tradition shares with many Marxist approaches a difficulty in relating the empirical specificity of particular conditions to the broader theoretical overview.

More recently, feminist-inspired sociologists have made a number of contributions to this field. Again, however, one finds some difficulty in explaining many of the specific findings in the more empirical studies in relation to the broad theoretical approaches taken by writers such as Rubin, Hartmann or Delphy.[8] Each of these makes important contributions to the analysis of gender relations in general, and those obtaining within the domestic sphere in particular, but each attempts to theorize some kind of social 'system' (or set of systems), within which it is not clear how the conditions of change might be specified, or how particular institutional or cultural forms appearing at different times are to be explained. Conversely, more empirical (often feminist-inspired) sociology has documented a wide range of specific conditions of domestic activities and relationships which have a gender dimension. A number of these studies have looked at the circumstances under which certain actions are likely to obtain rather than others, and investigated aspects of the relationship between the domestic sphere and other institutions such as the state or elements of the labour market, and between class and gender dimensions of social relationships.

As a result, there is now a substantial and accepted body of work in the social sciences which has documented aspects of domestic work which an overarching sociological theory needs to be able to take on board. Roughly summarized, these include the following:

There are a number of tasks which, even in today's highly commodified societies, are usually done within the home and characterized as 'housework', typically done by 'housewives'. The amount may have fallen (on some measures), and its nature varies, but there is still a substantial amount of 'housework' done, and women take responsibility to a remarkably consistent extent.[9]

The social relations under which this work is characteristically done are qualitatively different from the social relations pertaining outside the home, in a number of respects. Most obviously, most of this domestic labour is unpaid

[8] Gayle Rubin, 'The Traffic in Women, Notes on the "Political Economy" of Sex', in *Towards an Anthropology of Women*, ed. R. R. Reiter (New York: Monthly Review Press, 1975); Heidi Hartmann, 'The Unhappy Marriage of Marxism and Feminism', *Capital and Class*, 8 (1979), 1–33; C. Delphy, *Close To Home* (London: Hutchinson, 1984).

[9] Ann Oakley, *The Sociology of Housework* (Oxford: Martin Robertson, 1974); Graham Thomas and Christine Zmoroczek, 'Household Technology: The "Liberation of Women from the Home"?', in *Family and Economy in Modern Society*, ed. Paul Close and Rosemary Collins (London: Macmillan, 1985), and Ray Pahl and Clare Wallace, 'Household Work Strategies in Economic Recession', in *Beyond Employment: Household, Gender and Subsistence*, ed. Nanneke Redclift and Enzo Mingione (Oxford: Basil Blackwell, 1985).

(though some is paid, and this too is generally done by women)[10]; most tasks done in the home are mainly done by women – especially those which are repeated frequently, or are concerned with physical cleaning of the home and its inhabitants, as opposed to childcare tasks;[11] and most unpaid domestic labour (that is done for someone else, rather than purely for the person themself) is done by women for a member of their family, usually their husband, child, or parent.

This situation is largely sustained by normative means. The very close cultural association between domestic work, the 'housewife' and the roles and images of wife and mother are inextricably intertwined. These are all closely connected also with gender roles and sexuality, and a link is thus established with fundamental elements in personal identity and psychological make-up.[12]

The workings of the state also sustain this situation, through the legal, economic and institutional context in which domestic work is done. For example in Britain (despite some struggles and recent changes) the operation of tax and benefits discourages both an equal participation in the labour force by a married couple and the taking on by a woman of a 'breadwinner' role, with her male partner instead becoming responsible for domestic tasks. The rules for allocating social services resources have also made it harder for women to avoid certain types of domestic work (for example care of sick or elderly relatives) and for men to take this on instead.[13] There are also, of course, a number of other economic, political, physical and normative ways in which women's performance of most domestic work is maintained, though again these are not always found acceptable.

There are a number of economic and distributional aspects of the domestic division of labour and domestic relations of production which are of considerable importance, as Delphy has argued, and Morris and others have demonstrated.[14] In addition, there are many effects on the division of labour and economic life more generally: women do less paid work than men; participation and hours have a direct relationship with sex, marital status and presence of children. On re-entry to the labour force, after a 'family' break,

---

[10] Office of Population Censuses and Surveys, *Census of Population, 1981* (London: HMSO, 1984), Economic Activity Tables (10% sample).

[11] Oakley, *The Sociology of Housework*; Charlie Lewis and Margaret O'Brien (eds.), *Reassessing Fatherhood* (London: Sage, 1987).

[12] Nancy Chodorow, *The Reproduction of Mothering: Psychoanalysis and the Sociology of Gender* (Berkeley: University of California Press, 1978).

[13] Hilary Land, 'Sex-role Stereotyping in the Social Security and Income Tax Systems', in *The Sex-Role System: Psychological and Sociological Perspectives*, ed. J. Chetwynd and O. Hartnett (London: Routledge & Kegan Paul, 1978). See also, for example, Clare Ungerson's discussion, in 'Paid Work and Unpaid Caring: A Problem for Women or the State?', in *Family and Economy in Modern Society*, ed. Paul Close and Rosemary Collins (London: Macmillan, 1985).

[14] Christine Delphy, 'Sharing Bed and Board? Consumption and the Family', in *The Sociology of the Family*, ed. C. C. Harris et al. (Keele: Sociological Review Monographs, 1979), and Lydia Morris, 'Redundancy and the Pattern of Household Finance', *Sociological Review*, vol. 32, no. 3 (1984).

women tend to have a lower occupational status.[15] The tasks done by women in the home are seen as 'women's work', and where done outside the home they continue to be done mainly by women; this has directly affected the occupational structure. However, women's distinctive position in the paid labour-force is not entirely due to the division of domestic labour, but rather to perceptions of gender (and power relations) more generally, which are linked intrinsically with the way the division of labour (and hence occupational structure) develops. I have discussed this point more fully elsewhere.[16]

The character of domestic work and the amount done has not remained unchanged over time; neither are the nature and quantity of domestic work homogeneous across society. There are variations in both the physical tasks carried out and the social relations under which they are done. While some changes over time have been documented,[17] there has been less systematic investigation into differences across society.[18] There is, however, a considerable amount of evidence from secondary sources which indicates, for example, that there are class-related elements which differentiate between domestic work in different families, according to the economic and labour market situations pertaining to the members of the household/family.

While some of these features of domestic work are now well documented, few of them can be directly addressed within the theoretical framework constructed by Giddens as it stands. Indeed, in his characterization of social institutions and types of social relations, one is hard pressed to imagine where institutions such as families or households fit into his conception. Similarly, his presentation of the characteristics of power relations in terms of control over allocative and authoritative resources is, while applicable to certain economic issues (for instance the immediate allocation of goods and income among family members) of little use, at first sight, in addressing other aspects of the mesh of kinship, gender and other relations in the domestic sphere. Thus, despite the development of the theory of structuration, even the later edition of *The Class Structure of the Advanced Societies* retains, as the only comment on domestic work, the assertion that '[insofar as it is the fact] that women still have to await their liberation from the family ... female workers [remain] largely peripheral to the class system'.[19]

---

[15] See Jean Martin and Ceridwen Roberts, *Women and Employment, A Lifetime Perspective* (London: HMSO, 1984), and Shirley Dex, *Women's Occupational Mobility* (London: Macmillan, 1987).

[16] For a fuller discussion, see Linda Murgatroyd, 'Gender and Occupational Stratification', *Sociological Review*, vol. 30, no. 4 (1982), 574–602.

[17] Ruth Schwartz Cowan, 'A Case Study of Technological and Social Change: The Washing Machine and the Working Wife', in *Clio's Consciousness Raised*, ed. M. Hartmann and L. Banner (New York: Harper & Row, 1974); Elizabeth Garnsey, 'The Rediscovery of the Division of Labour', *Theory and Society*, vol. 10, no. 3 (May 1981), 337–58; J. I. Gershuny, *After Industrial Society: The Emerging Self-Service Economy* (London: Macmillan, 1978).

[18] A notable recent exception is Leonore Davidoff and Catherine Hall, *Family Fortunes* (London: Hutchinson, 1987). For an overview of some of the evidence in relation to later periods, see Linda Murgatroyd 'Gender and Class Stratification', D.Phil. thesis, University of Oxford, 1982, ch. 5.

[19] *CSAS*, p. 288.

I shall investigate some of these issues in the remainder of this chapter, arguing that far from being an area of social activity which is marginal to, and unconnected with, other spheres which have traditionally been more central areas for social investigation, the social relations embodied in the domestic sphere, the interactions which take place in the course of it, and the physical goods and social structures produced through the routine carrying-on of domestic work are in fact crucially inter-twined with events and structured patterns of social relations that are outside the domestic sphere and which are widely considered to be core elements that any macro-sociological theory needs to address. By combining some of the insights of this – largely feminist – body of empirical and theoretical work with the main elements in the theory of structuration, and making some necessary additions and adaptations to both, I shall argue that a strengthened sociological approach could be produced: one capable of taking on gender and incidentally also contributing more to an understanding of other non-class-based social relations (as well as giving a more complete and less one-sided view of class itself). In order to do this, however, it is first necessary to sketch out another area of activity which both Giddens and many feminist sociologists have by-passed. This is an area which partly overlaps with the domestic sphere, but which also under certain conditions (themselves of interest), and with important consequences, spills over into the 'public' sphere: namely the production of people.

Domestic work and the production of people

The Marxist tradition and 'reproduction'

For Marx, the characterization of the domestic arena as the sphere of reproduction is intrinsically connected with his identification of the 'public', economic sphere as the arena of production. Production is defined as the application of human labour-power to the natural environment and the appropriation of nature for human ends. In *Capital*, Marx's analysis of the social relations of material production is confined to the production of the means of subsistence and takes place within the market sphere. His main concern was to demonstrate how the mediation of money served to camouflage the exploitative relations of production and distribution under capitalism, as shown in his labour theory of value. Insofar as this relationship is distinctive to and (Marx would argue) defining of capitalism, this was the crucial area to focus on, as other areas of social relationships depended on it. However, when it comes to domestic work, and social relations in the home and family, the Marxist approach has fallen short. Three strands of Marxist writings touch on the area, none of them in itself adequate. The domestic sphere is seen as the sphere of social reproduction, women's domestic activities are seen as preventing their full participation in social production (i.e. paid work in the labour market), and there has been a debate about the status of domestic labour in capitalist society, and how it relates to the labour theory of value.

To the extent that Giddens has touched on the edges of the subject (albeit often only by implication), he has followed this Marxist approach, including its pitfalls. However, the approach taken in his theory of structuration could, in combination with some of the insights gained (largely through the investigations of feminists in recent years) be developed to offer a framework for a much more constructive and exciting approach. It is worth looking at each of these three areas in more depth.

Giddens's theory of structuration has extricated the critical tradition from the sterile debate regarding the degree to which and manner in which other social relations are 'determined' by that between capital and labour, under capitalism. However, he has fallen into some of the pitfalls of a Marxist approach. Implicitly, if not explicitly, he appears to assume that domestic work does not involve material production in any significant way (which might for example affect power relations) and that 'the family' is a major site of social reproduction, without there being social relations involved which are sufficiently important to warrant consideration in any of his prolific writings. If, however, we examine more closely the nature of this 'social reproduction' or 'domestic' work, it then becomes possible to investigate some of the 'contingent and historical' conditions of reproduction referred to by Giddens.[20] One important element in this work is the production of people. This is an area of production by no means confined to the domestic sphere, but consists of a number of activities whose organization in most known societies is nonetheless rooted in a domestic environment as the norm.

Anthroponomy and the production of people

The production of people can be counterposed to the sphere of economic production in much the same way as the private domain (generally non-waged, domestic labour) can be counterposed with the public domain of production, which generally involves wage labour. I have discussed these distinctions in greater depth elsewhere.[21]

Daniel Bertaux has posited the existence of what he calls an 'anthroponomic process' which operates in parallel with the economic process.[22] Through it, the production of people is organized, as is their distribution to different 'places' in society, and their 'consumption', in the same way that economic goods are produced, distributed and consumed in the economic system. Bertaux is primarily concerned with the distributive aspects of this process, discussing especially the formation of classes at a macro-historical level and the allocation of individuals to them. Through the anthroponomic process, relative advantage and disadvantage are transmitted across generations. Ber-

---

[20] *CCHM*, p. 27.

[21] Linda Murgatroyd, 'The Production of People and Domestic Labour Revisited', in *Family and Economy in Modern Society*, ed. Paul Close and Rosemary Collins (London: Macmillan, 1985), pp. 53–6.

[22] Daniel Bertaux, *Destins personnels et structure de classe* (Paris: Presses Universitaires de France, 1977).

taux argues that different strategies must be pursued by families according to the specific advantages that they have, in order to transmit this capital (be it financial, intellectual, business, land or cultural capital) in a form which will be profitable to their descendants.

Giddens picks up this notion of anthroponomy in his discussion of power and resources, identifying the distributive aspect of this anthroponomic system as one of 'the major forms of authoritative resource to be found in any society'.[23] However, neither Giddens nor Bertaux himself pays attention to the production element in the anthroponomic process. Both of them have gone along with the Marxian view that, in broad terms, 'production' refers to the application of human labour power to the natural environment and to the appropriation of nature for human ends. Both then concentrate on the production and distribution of material goods in the economic sphere to the exclusion of the physical production of people. While the distribution of people attracts considerable interest, this is primarily the case because of their interest in the patterns of social institutions and the re-production (albeit in changing forms over time) of the class structure and of the conditions for production of material goods. However, this ignores the fact that just as production of the means of subsistence, of articles for human consumption (and perhaps for use in further productive activities), involves the cultivation and manipulation of the natural environment, so the production of people involves the cultivation of biological human animals. This happens through feeding and physically caring for them from birth (or conception) and also transforming their biological urges into culturally meaningful (in a particular cultural context) and socially acceptable forms. It is the work involved in this set of activities which may be said to be the production of people, by contrast with that involved in the manipulation of the natural environment, which contributes to the production of goods.

Social relations in the production of people

While, as I have said, the analyses of Bertaux and Giddens have omitted to consider the actual work of producing people (implying, like others before them, some magic 'reproduction'), there is no reason why the concept of anthroponomy cannot be built upon to incorporate both an analysis of the social relations of anthroponomic production and a gender dimension. The recognition that the production of people in a class society implies producing people embodying different characteristics according to their class of origin may be combined with similar insights regarding the production of gendered individuals. There are a number of systematic elements in this process, which can be described and analysed in various ways, while it is recognized at the same time that contingent and historical factors also affect the conditions and manner of this production throughout, and hence the particular characteristics of the individuals produced. Combining these insights with the fact that

[23] *CCHM*, pp. 51, 52.

the production of people involves work, we are well on the way to providing a conceptual framework within which to analyse the social relations of production and the division of labour as a whole.

We may consider 'people-producing work' to be that which involves the direct manipulation of people in such a way that they embody more (or a different quality) of energy or productive capacity from that previously embodied. Those who nurture, procreate, feed, educate, give physical care (medical or otherwise) or manipulate others psychologically in such a way as to increase the amount or ameliorate the quality of human energy and potential labour-power by directly manipulating people are doing people-producing work. This applies regardless of whether and how that potential is ultimately used. Those engaged purely in harnessing this labour-power are not producing people. Managers engaged in directing workers' activities at the point of production of goods are contributing to economic production and to the consumption of labour-power. Managers engaged in training others to become managers or to do some other work task are engaged in people-work: they are affecting the quality of the labour-power embodied in the trainees. Although the purpose of their activity may ultimately be further production of objects, the direct result of their work is embodied in people, and it is only at a later stage that the trained workers may apply their labour-power to the production of objects, whether directly or indirectly.

This definition permits us to suggest how the social relations of the production of people might be analysed further, especially with regard to appropriation and control. Since the production of people, directly or indirectly (for example through childcare, education, care of the sick and generally looking after household members) makes up a large portion of the productive work done in the domestic sphere, this is a crucial element in the analysis of domestic production relations and any analysis of power relations within the home or family. It could in theory be combined with other aspects of domestic productive activities and power relations to provide an analysis of the relations of domestic production, although in practice there has to date been a split across disciplines and the way subjects have been addressed between the distinct elements, and few connections have been made between, for example, studies of 'housework' and psychological studies of 'child development' – let alone incorporating these into more macro-sociological studies of social mobility, for example. However, the analysis of the production of people is also an important focus for analysing patterns of interaction and structures of power outside the domestic sphere, and helps fill a big lacuna still current in sociological theory.[24]

Medical sociologists and economists, for example, have done some useful work in elucidating the social relationships in health care; these epitomize

---

[24] Margaret Stacey, 'The Division of Labour Revisited, or Overcoming the Two Adams', in *Development and Diversity: British Sociology, 1950–1980*, ed. Philip Abrams et al. (London: George Allen & Unwin, 1980).

many of the relationships in the production of people more generally.[25] We
need, however, to link an analysis of the production of people with an analysis
of the relations of reproduction in the production of objects, in order to
understand the social relations of people-producing work. The link between
these two is labour-power. People-work (together with material objects, food
and other resources) produces people who embody labour-power of various
kinds. This labour-power may be put to productive use, either to produce
more people, or to produce goods, but this will not necessarily happen. In so
far as people have a certain degree of autonomy, they may choose to work or
not to work, within a structured set of options constituted by social arrange-
ments at a particular time. Even within advanced capitalist societies, the
nature of tasks in people-producing work, the location of it and the social
relations involved in it can vary widely. Where it takes place in the private,
domestic, sphere, it may be coupled with a certain degree of autonomy in
relation to the tasks done, within well-defined limits (themselves to some
extent structured socially[26]). In addition a certain amount of power may be
exercised over those to whom people-work is being done. Thus, mothers gain
influence over their children, for example, and wives may be able to influence
husbands, through the very processes of nurturing, servicing work that they do
for them. At the same time, people-production in the home is subject to various
controls. These may come from other members of the household, and the
physical strength they have (which is available to enforce their will if they
wish), or the economic power they acquire by selling their labour-power (and/or
owning property), or they may come from outside, from the state, church, local
community or extended family. Either way, the relationships are more personal,
and of a different quality from those encountered in other spheres of production.

The importance of the influence of power relationships within the family on
the psychological development of children and their learning of culturally
appropriate behaviour patterns (as well as skills) and class and gender identi-
ties has been widely demonstrated within the fields of psychoanalysis, child
psychology and education. I am suggesting that these might be considered as
part of the wider process of the production of people, and that the power
dimensions of such processes should be more fully integrated into general
analysis of power structures and relationships within sociology. Such an
analysis could also encompass the important influences of people who have
contributed to personal growth, through their structured roles as carers,
nurturers, teachers, etc. – both through professional relationships and those of
kinship or affective ties.

[25] See, for example, Margaret Stacey and Marion Price, *Women, Power and Politics* (London:
Tavistock Women's Studies, 1981); W. J. M. Mackenzie, *Power and Responsibility in Health Care:
The National Health Service as a Political Institution* (Oxford: Oxford University Press, 1979); and
M. Carpenter, 'Left Orthodoxy and the Politics of Health', *Capital and Class*, 11 (1980), 73–98.
[26] See Julia Brannen, 'The Re-entry of Women into the Labour Market: The Point at which the
Youngest Child Starts School', M.Sc. dissertation, University of Surrey, 1978, and Jan Pahl,
'Patterns of Money Management within Marriage', *Journal of Social Policy*, 9.3 (1980), 313–36.

Where production takes place in the public, market, sphere the division of labour generally tends to be more refined and fragmented, and this is true of people-producing work as well as of that concerned with making material objects. In particular, the hierarchical forms of organization produce concentrations of power and responsibility and relations of authority and deference among the workers, as well as between them and the object of their work (or 'patient', 'pupil' or social work 'client'). The removal of people-producing work from the home into public spheres (or back into 'the community') has been combined with changes in organization and in technology. Capitalist or bureaucratic principles of organization are introduced, and the nature of the work relations and the forms and standards of care alter accordingly. The relationship between worker and client/work-object also changes, and the amount of work done by the latter as well as the former may alter. Such changes are not necessarily smooth; on the contrary, they are increasingly often the focus of considerable social tension and struggle. Many disputes about tax policy or the public provision of services (such as health, education, social services) can be interpreted as being about the location and control of people-producing work, which involve both the workers and those for (or on) whom the work is being carried out (or their representatives, parents, etc.).

Some examples of the types of changes involved have been well documented in the literature on the medicalization of various kinds of health care.[27] In the management of childbirth, for example, the movement from community care in the home to medical and professional care, first in the home and then increasingly in hospitals (which, in turn, have become increasingly centralized), has involved not only geographical concentration and 'rationalization', but also shifts in power and control – away from both the mother and the person doing most work on her or to her (the neighbour/midwife/nurse). Technological changes and bureaucratic/capitalist forms of organization of the process of birth management (a specific element in the production of people) have transformed the mother from an active participant who puts a lot of work into the production process, with a certain amount of control over her own labour and the conditions of place of birth, to a passive recipient of 'care' (though recent efforts of groups such as the National Childbirth Trust and the Association of Radical Midwives have changed this trend in some areas). Expectant mothers wait in increasingly long queues for ante-natal care, which is administered with increasing impersonality and lack of continuity. The time and place of birth may be dictated largely by the convenience of the medical staff and organization, with technology being used in such a way as to deprive the mother of control and to transform the experience of birth; presumably this also has some impact on the experience for the baby being born. Such changes in the process of production of people mirror similar developments in the

[27] B. Ehrenreich and D. English, *'For Her Own Good': 150 Years of the Experts' Advice to Women* (London: Pluto, 1979); Ann Oakley, 'Wisewoman and Medicine Man', in *The Rights and Wrongs of Women*, ed. J. Mitchell and A. Oakley (Harmondsworth: Penguin, 1976).

production of objects; the organization of work, the forms of technology used are similar, and the economic and other criteria which determine the form of production are essentially the same.

The social relations of the production of people are inextricably connected with a number of other aspects of the social relations of gender, and also with a structuring of society in other ways, for example along class and ethnic lines. 'Who does what, to whom, and in what way' varies systematically along all three dimensions. Any single activity may in fact be contributing to production of more than one kind at the same time, and may be contributing to the reproduction of the conditions of production, in the same form as previously or in a modified form. (This point itself has close parallels with others embodied in Giddens's conception of the duality of structure, which could usefully be applied further here.) The different ways male and female children are handled right from birth, and taught in subtle or direct ways how different kinds of behaviour are expected of them – at home, at school, and more widely – are now well documented.[28] The Newsons, for example, have shown variations according to social class in the way children are treated,[29] and the connections between childcare styles and methods, schooling and the acquisition not only of skills but also of particular behaviour and language forms and values associated with different social classes have also been well documented. Differences along ethnic lines too have been the subject of empirical study. Yet the information available from empirical studies in these areas has yet to be incorporated into the wider-ranging sociological theories at the level at which Giddens, for example, is writing.

The production of people in a classed society

It may be helpful at this point to give some examples of the way the production of people is structured in a classed society, and the impact it has on some of the aspects of social life to which more attention has traditionally been given (indeed by Giddens himself, among others). In general terms, people-producing work is done under different relations depending on its location within or outside the domestic sphere. Even within the home, though, the conditions and relations of people-producing work vary according to the position of the household and its members in the wider class structure. To conceptualize this adequately, it is necessary to classify a number of wider aspects of class analysis, to take full cognizance of the distinction between individuals, families and households in the class structure, and how these elements are related.[30] People-producing work is directly related to the class structure through the current labour-market position and work situation (outside the household) of household members, and indirectly through contributions it can make to the

[28] See, for example, Sue Sharpe, *Just Like a Girl: How Girls Learn to Become Women* (Harmondsworth: Penguin, 1976).

[29] For example, J. Newson, and E. Newson, *Infant Care in an Urban Community* (London: Allen & Unwin, 1963).

[30] See Murgatroyd, 'Gender and Class Stratification', ch. 6.

maintenance of social closure (both in the short term and across generations). In addition, the balance between economic and anthroponomic production by household members, between paid work outside the home and unpaid work within it, and the very division of that labour and the manner in which decisions are made and resources shared within the houshold, are themselves structured by class as well as by gender.

More specifically, within the domestic sphere, people-producing work can be related to the current occupational class structure, in a number of ways. For example:

(1)   in the maintenance work necessary to produce the domestic worker's own labour-power;

(2)   in that work needed to reproduce the labour-power of other family members;

(3)   and work that is required of a spouse as part of her (or his) spouse's market work (career or business).

To some extent, there are choices that exist as to how much of this work is done within the home, by whom and on what terms, and also how much can be substituted for goods and services available in the market (or provided by the welfare state); I am suggesting that these choices are affected by structural factors, both economic and social (such as value-systems, cultural pressure) which are intrinsically connected with the class system. For example, the decision for a married woman with children whether to do a paid job will thus depend on a combination of:

(a)   Her own position in the labour market – whether she could get a job at all, whether she would find it worth while (financially and in other ways);

(b)   Her husband's work – whether he has work and what kind; how well he is paid, and what demands it makes of him and also of her (for example, is he often away from home? Is she expected to entertain for his business or to accompany him?);

(c)   The sort of day-to-day maintenance work needed, which may be affected by work – for example type and amount of washing, cooking, psychological nurturing, or the provision of a quiet (or entertaining) environment;

(d)   The attitude of both partners to the roles of women and men, and how this is reflected in the division of labour in the home;

(e)   The number and ages of their children, what sort of aspirations they have for them, and what they see as most important to provide for them (for instance education, a mother at home, expensive toys, smart clothes, a particular sort of social life, the 'right connections', etc.);

(f)   The availability of services (and, to a lesser extent, goods) of an acceptable quality and at an acceptable price, to substitute for some of the mother's domestic labour;

(g) Wider institutional factors, such as tax structures, social childcare provisions, etc.

Each of these factors will vary to some extent with broader social structures of the society in which the household lives, for example the occupational structure, the positions of women and men in the broader division of labour, and the way class-related advantages are transmitted from one generation to another,[31] not to mention the norms and ideological positions dominant among different groups (often structured along class, ethnicity, gender, age and other lines). Of course, a variety of other factors are also important, including the personalities and personal histories of the people involved, and the particular local and historical circumstances in which they are living. Without an analysis of the processes and social relations of domestic work, or one of the class structure which encompasses gender, it is impossible to see how such questions can be seriously addressed by sociologists. Yet the outcome of these decisions (relating to the employment of mothers and wives) crucially affects the way the class structure develops, as well as influencing the broader relationship between men and women, and more generally, the sort of people produced in that society.

Conclusion

For all the strength of Giddens's work, and the way he has taken sociological theory a large step forward in establishing a theoretical framework which allows systematic and structured social processes, and the specific conditions under which change occurs to be considered at a number of levels, he is still only telling half the story. Not only are the crucial dimensions of gender and ethnicity omitted from his analysis of power and exploitation, but so are important areas of productive activity and social interaction. The processes of producing people are central to the division of labour in a number of ways, and only by bringing analysis of these processes into the mainstream of sociological anaylsis can many of the deficiencies of the latter be made good. As well as having major significance in their own right, the division of labour and the social relations of the production of people have a crucial impact on the division of labour outside this sphere, and must be taken on board in any analysis which purports to study continuity and change in the class structure. I suggest that the theory of structuration is an approach which both needs to be extended in this direction and is capable of such development, though some modifications would be needed, as I have pointed out. It would then also become both necessary and possible for the theory to deal with some of the vast areas of social life (in particular the gender and ethnic dimensions) that Giddens acknowledges he has completely ignored in the main body of his writing, and the omission of which constitutes a major flaw in his work to date.

[31] See, for example, Bertaux, *Destins personnels*, and D. Bertaux and I. Bertaux-Wiame, 'Artisanal Baking in France: How it Lives and Why it Survives', in *The Petit Bourgeoisie; Comparative Studies of an Uneasy Stratum*, ed. F. Bechofeer and B. Elliott (London: Macmillan, 1981).

8
Citizenship and autonomy

DAVID HELD

In this chapter, I wish to cut a particular path through Anthony Giddens's work by focusing on the way in which he interprets the relationship between citizenship, capitalism and the possibilities of a new 'progressive' politics. I believe this to be a particularly fertile domain in which to assess his writings because it is in exploring the interconnections between class, citizenship and related phenomena that Anthony Giddens analyses some of the key features of modern society and evaluates some of the key contributions of the major traditions of political and social theory: above all, those of liberalism and Marxism. It will be my contention that there are ambiguities at the very heart of Anthony Giddens's project. While he unquestionably makes a major contribution to rethinking social and political theory today, there are a number of essential questions which remain unanswered in his work – questions which cast doubt on the coherence of central parts of his project as it is currently formulated.

The chapter has a number of sections. In the first part, I examine T. H. Marshall's classic study, 'Citizenship and Social Class'.[1] In a number of his works Giddens focuses attention on Marshall's contribution; for Marshall's work is a – if not the – classic treatment of the relationship between class and citizenship, capitalism and democracy (see *CCHM*, pp. 226–9; *PCST*, pp. 164–80; *NSV*, pp. 198–209). In the second part I shall argue that Giddens is right to focus attention on Marshall, but that many of Giddens's specific criticisms of Marshall are misconceived. After elaborating elements of Giddens's attempt to move beyond Marshall's views in the third part, I will contend in the fourth that the entire framework through which Marshall and Giddens examine the relationship between class and citizenship is partial and limited. The terms of reference of their analysis are such that they exclude from view a whole range of substantive problems, conflict areas and struggles. In the fifth and final part, I will explore some of the implications of this position. Focusing in particular on Giddens's recent work, I shall show that the failure to examine class and citizenship in broader terms has created ambiguities in his characterization of rights, of the political realm, of social structure, and

---

[1] T. H. Marshall, 'Citizenship and Social Class', in Marshall, *Class, Citizenship and Social Development* (Westport, Conn.: Greenwood Press, 1973), pp. 65–122. Marshall's later work altered some of the emphases of his earlier essay. See, for instance, 'The Welfare State – a Comparative Study', in the same volume, pp. 277–95.

finally of the political choices that face us today. I shall argue that there are fundamental ambivalences in Giddens's account of central elements of contemporary society.

Citizenship and class

By citizenship, Marshall meant 'full membership of a community', where membership entails *participation* by individuals in the determination of the conditions of their own association.[2] Citizenship is a status which bestows upon individuals *equal* rights and duties, liberties and constraints, powers and responsibilities.[3] While there is no universal principle that determines what exactly the citizen's rights and duties shall be, societies in which citizenship is a developing force create, Marshall contended, an image of an 'ideal citizenship' and, thereby, a goal towards which aspirations can be directed. Within all such societies, the urge to attain the ideal is 'an urge towards a fuller measure of equality' – an enrichment of the stuff of which citizenship is made and an increase in the number of those upon whom the status of citizenship is bestowed.[4] If citizenship is a principle of equality, class, by contrast, is a system of inequality anchored in property, education and the structure of the national economy.[5] According to Marshall, class functions, among other things, to erode and limit the extent to which citizenship creates access to scarce resources and participation in the institutions which determine their use and distribution. Class and citizenship are contrary principles of organization: they are basically opposed influences.

The concept and reality of citizenship are, Marshall argued, among the great driving forces of the modern era. There has been a long, uneven, but persistent trend towards the expansion of the rights of citizenship which for analytical purposes can be broken down into three 'bundles' of rights: civil, political and social.* Essentially, he maintained, political reform in each of these domains can modify the worst aspects of economic inequality and can, therefore, make the modern capitalist system and the liberal polity more equal

---

* *Terminological note*: By civil rights Marshall meant 'rights necessary for individual freedom', including liberty of the person, freedom of speech, thought and faith, the right to own property and enter into contracts and the right to be treated equally with others before the law. Political rights refer to those elements of rights which create the possibility of participation in the exercise of political power 'as a member of a body invested with political authority or as an elector of the members of such a body'. Social rights are defined as involving a whole range of rights 'from the right to a modicum of economic welfare and security to the right ... to live the life of a civilized being according to the standards prevailing in ... society'.[6] The adequacy of Marshall's categories will be discussed in several places in the chapter, and additional rights categories – the economic, reproductive and those deriving from international law – will be examined. The meaning of the latter categories will be set out as they are introduced.

[2] Marshall, 'Citizenship and Social Class', p. 70.
[3] Ibid., p. 84.   [4] Ibid, p. 84.   [5] Ibid., pp. 84–5.   [6] Ibid., pp. 71–2.

and just, without revolutionary activity. The dynamic of class inequalities stemming from the capitalist market system can be moderated to some degree: the excesses of class inequality can be contained, or in his word 'abated', through the successful development of democratic citizenship rights. Citizenship can remould the class system.

Marshall's discussion is explicitly focused on Britain and, although he sometimes generalizes beyond this context, he does not claim that his argument can be applied with equal cogency to other countries.[7] With respect to Britain itself, his argument is that the three elements of citizenship developed at different rates over the past two or three centuries. He sought to show that civil rights were the first to develop, and were established in something like their modern guise before the first great Reform Act in 1832. Political rights developed next, and their extension was one of the main features of the nineteenth century, although it was not until 1928 that the principle of universal political citizenship was fully recognized. Social rights, by contrast, almost vanished in the eighteenth and early nineteenth century, but were revived in the latter part of the nineteenth century.[8] Their revival and expansion began with development of public elementary education, but it was not until the twentieth century that social rights in their modern form were fully established. Marshall's principal evidence for this is the history of the modern welfare state. The great redistributive measures of the postwar welfare state, including measures introducing the health service, social security, new forms of progressive taxation and so on, created better conditions and greater equality for the vast majority of those who did not flourish in the free market. And they provided a measure of security for all those who are vulnerable in modern society, especially those who fall into the trap of the 'poverty cycle'. Marshall's proposal is that social rights form a vital element in a society which is still hierarchical, but which has mitigated the inequalities – and mellowed the tensions – deriving from the class system.

While Marshall interpreted the development of modern citizenship rights as an uneven process, he conceived each bundle of rights as a kind of step or platform for the others.[9] The eighteenth century was the main formative period for civil or legal rights, when the rights of liberty of the individual, and full and equal justice before the law, became firmly established. Civil rights created new freedoms – although initially, of course, it was the male property-owning individual who was to benefit from them directly. The new freedoms gradually allowed the male citizen liberty from subservience to the place in which he was born and from the occupation to which he was typically tied by custom or statute. While these freedoms (and others relating to them) threatened the traditional forms of power and inequality imposed by feudal society,

---

[7] Ibid., p. 72.   [8] Ibid., p. 83.
[9] See ibid., pp. 71–83, 95–6. See also Giddens, *NSV*, pp. 203–5, for a succinct statement of this issue.

they did not strain the new forms of inequalities created by the emergence of the competitive market society; on the contrary, Marshall argued, they were 'indispensable to it'.[10] The fundamental reason for this is that the new rights 'gave ... each man ... the power to engage as an independent unit in the economic struggle'. They created individuals who were 'free and equal in status' – a status which was the foundation of modern contract. Paradoxically, then, 'the single uniform status of citizenship', in its early form, 'provided the foundation of equality on which the [modern] structure of inequality could be built'.[11]

The slow but progressive achievement of civil rights was a prerequisite for the secure establishment of the liberty of the subject. It was also an indispensable first stage in the development of political rights; for, as Giddens usefully explains it, 'only if the individual is recognised as an autonomous agent does it become reasonable to regard that individual as politically responsible' (NSV, p. 203). The establishment of political rights belongs above all to the nineteenth century and involves a growing interest in equality as a principle to be applied to a range of domains. It involves, moreover, an appreciation of a tension between, on the one hand, the formal recognition of the individual as 'free and equal' in civil matters and, on the other, the actual liberty of the individual to pursue his interests free from political impediment. Political rights were gradually recognized as indispensable to guaranteeing individual freedom. Since there is no good reason for believing that those who govern will act ultimately in anything other than a self-interested way (as will those who are governed), government must, to avoid abuse, be directly accountable to an electorate called upon regularly to decide if their objectives have been met.

The establishment of 'political liberty' involved a process whereby the political rights which had previously been the monopoly of the privileged few were extended to the adult population as a whole. The rise of the trade union movement and of the labour movement more generally was a critical factor in the development of political citizenship. If citizenship was an entitlement, it had to be an entitlement to full political membership of society. Thus, the search for citizenship became the search for the conditions under which individuals could enjoy a sense of equal worth and equal opportunity. The scene was set for struggle over the enactment of political rights, and of social rights as well.

The ascendance of industrial capitalism created massive disparities in wealth, income and life conditions. Those who were unsuccessful in the marketplace experienced profound inequalities in all aspects of their lives. With the establishment of the universal franchise, the organized working class was able to secure, Marshall argued, the political strength to consolidate

---

[10] Marshall, 'Citizenship and Social Class', p. 87.   [11] Ibid., p. 87.

welfare or social gains *as rights*. While citizenship and class have been 'at war' in the nineteenth and twentieth centuries, the labour movement has succeeded in imposing modifications on the capitalist class system. In the twentieth century, demands for social justice have, in Marshall's words, 'contained contract'.[12] The preservation of economic inequalities has been made more difficult by the expansion or enrichment of the notion of citizenship. Class distinctions certainly survive, Marshall recognized, but there is less room for them today, and they are more under pressure and are more likely to be challenged. As he eloquently put it, the expansion of social rights

> is no longer merely an attempt to abate the obvious nuisance of destitution in the lowest ranks of society ... it is no longer content to raise the floor level in the basement of the social edifice, leaving the superstructure as it was. It has begun to remodel the whole building, and it might even end by converting the sky-scraper into a bungalow.[13]

Contract has been challenged by status, and the rule of market forces has begun to be subordinated to social justice.[14] Marshall's view of the likely progress of social democratic reforms (unsurprisingly perhaps, given that many of his ideas were formulated in the late 1940s) is decidedly optimistic.

Giddens versus Marshall

While Anthony Giddens affirms the significance of Marshall's analysis of citizenship for contemporary social and political theory, he has a number of criticisms to make (see *CCHM*, pp. 226–9; *PCST*, pp. 171–3; *NSV*, pp. 204–9). In the first place, he is critical of what he sees as the teleological and evolutionary elements in Marshall's analysis (see especially *PCST*, p. 171). Giddens criticizes Marshall for treating the development of citizenship as if it were something that unfolded in phases according to some inner logic within the modern world. In Giddens's account, Marshall tends to overstate the extent to which citizenship rights can be understood in terms of a threefold staged process. In addition, Giddens sees in Marshall's account an over-simplification of the role of politics and the state. Marshall, according to Giddens, understood the unfolding of citizenship rights from the eighteenth to the twentieth century as a process which is supported and buttressed by 'the beneficent hand of the state'. In Giddens's analysis, Marshall seriously underestimated the way 'citizenship rights have been achieved in substantial degree only through struggle' (*PCST*, p. 171). Furthermore, Giddens argues, Marshall underestimated the degree to which the balance of power was tipped to the underprivileged only during times of war, particularly during the periods of world war.

---

[12] Ibid., p. 111.   [13] Ibid., pp. 96–7.   [14] Ibid., p. 111.

These criticisms are, in my view, misleading in a number of respects.[15] Far from suggesting a general evolutionary framework for the explanation of the development of citizenship rights, Marshall, in my assessment, takes a more contingent view of historical change.[16] There seems little, if any, evidence to suggest that his scheme rests on the assumption of an evolutionary logic. Marshall emphasized that institutions and complexes of rights developed at their 'own speed' and under the direction of varying forces and principles.[17] The development of rights by no means followed, he stressed, a linear path in any one time period; there were often losses as well as gains. Further, the chief factor which he saw underpinning the development of rights was, in fact, struggle – struggle against hierarchy in its traditional feudal form, struggle against inequality in the market-place and struggle against social injustice perpetuated by state institutions. Rights had to be fought for, and when they were won they had to be protected. At the root of these processes was (and is) the delicate balance between social and political forces. When Marshall discussed citizenship and class, and when he described the relationship between the two as one of 'warfare', he was addressing himself explicitly to some of the major social movements which have shaped the contemporary world. In writings after 'Citizenship and Social Class', Marshall is even more explicit about the formative role of political and social conflict.[18]

A second area of criticism voiced by Giddens concerns Marshall's treatment of the expansion of citizenship rights as a purely 'one-way phenomenon' (*PCST*, p. 173). Marshall is criticized for regarding the development of citizenship as an 'irreversible process'. There are passages in Marshall which certainly justify this criticism. However, it seems in general to be misplaced. For instance, Marshall documented the way in which primitive forms of social rights – rooted in membership of local communities and functional associations (guilds) – existed prior to the eighteenth century and yet practically vanished in the latter half of the eighteenth century and the early nineteenth century. He argued that their revival began with the development of public elementary education, but that this process of revival itself had by no means a stable history, and depended on the particular strength of the various social

---

[15] I am by no means the first to make this observation. See Bryan S. Turner, *Citizenship and Capitalism: The Debate over Reformism* (London: Allen & Unwin, 1986), pp. 45–6 for a particularly helpful discussion.

[16] This is not the emphasis, it should be acknowledged, which has generally been put on Marshall's work in recent times. The chief reason for the discrepancy lies in the way Marshall's ideas were incorporated and popularized by writers who dominated sociological thought in the 1950s and 1960s such as Seymour Martin Lipset, Reinhard Bendix and Daniel Bell. Some of the latter's concerns and perspectives, in my view, distorted the reception of Marshall's key notions. While Marshall's writings are not without some ambiguity on these matters, they cannot, for reasons set out below, simply be interpreted as offering an 'evolutionary' account of citizenship rights.

[17] Marshall, 'Citizenship and Social Class', pp. 73–4.

[18] See, for example, *The Right to Welfare and Other Essays* (London: Heinemann, 1981), particularly pp. 104–36.

movements supporting reform.[19] More fundamentally, Marshall pointed to the emergence of nationalism – 'modern national consciousness', as he put it – as a critical factor in the stimulation of the demand for the recognition of equal social worth.[20] Nationalist movements inspired a direct sense of 'community membership' and the aspiration that all nationals become full and equal members of the community. Marshall did not develop this insight, and he did not provide a detailed analysis of the international context within which the demands for citizenship rights developed. Nonetheless, he did not ignore this context, and in various writings stressed the significance of nationalism and warfare to the history of rights, particularly social rights.[21] Moreover, Marshall concluded his reflections on class and citizenship by arguing that the balance achieved between these two great forces in the twentieth century by no means promised a simple stable future. In Marshall's view, how long the current balance lasts cannot easily be determined. And, he concluded, 'it may be that some of the conflicts within our system are becoming too sharp for the compromise to achieve its purpose much longer'.[22] Marshall appears to have been quite sensitive to the potential instabilities which might wreck any period of social equilibrium. Written four decades before the epoch of Reagan and Thatcher, and the New Right's attack on welfare rights, this certainly was an insightful observation.

A third set of criticisms Giddens makes is concerned with Marshall's threefold classification of rights. Giddens objects in particular to Marshall's treatment of civil rights as a homogeneous category. He emphasizes that the civil rights of individual freedom and equality before the law were fought for and achieved in large part by an emergent bourgeoisie. These rights helped consolidate industrial capitalism and the modern representative state. As such, they are to be distinguished from what Giddens calls 'economic civil rights' (or 'industrial citizenship', as Marshall put it). This latter group of rights had to be fought for by working-class and trade union activists. The right to form trade unions was not gracefully conceded, but was achieved and sustained only through bitter conflicts. The same applies to the extension of the activities of unions in their attempt to secure regularized bargaining and the right to strike. All this implies that there is 'something awry in lumping together such phenomena with civil rights in general' (*PCST*, p. 172). If individual civil rights tended to confirm the dominance of capital, economic civil rights tended to threaten the functioning of the capitalist market.

More fundamentally, Giddens maintains that each category of citizenship right should be understood as an arena of contestation or conflict, each linked to a distinctive type of regulatory power or surveillance, where that surveillance is both necessary to the power of superordinate groups and an axis

---

[19] Marshall, 'Citizenship and Social Class', pp. 79–83, 95ff.   [20] Ibid., p. 92.
[21] See Marshall, *Social Policy in the Twentieth Century* (London: Hutchinson, 1975), especially part 1.
[22] Marshall, 'Citizenship and Social Class', p. 122.

Table 1. *Rights, surveillance and locales*

Types of right	Civil	Economic civil	Political	Social
Type of regulatory power or surveillance	Policing	Control of work-place	Political	'Management' of population
Institutional centre or locale where rights are championed and fought over	Law courts	Work-place	Parliament or legislative chamber	(State administrative offices?)[a]

[a] This category is particularly underdeveloped in Giddens's writings.

around which subordinate groups can seek to reclaim control over their lives (see *NSV*, pp. 205ff). For instance, he writes,

> Civil rights are intrinsically linked to the modes of surveillance involved in the policing activities of the state. Surveillance in this context consists of the apparatus of judicial and punitive organizations in terms of which 'deviant' conduct is controlled ... [Like the other kinds of rights] civil rights have their own particular locale. That is to say, there is an institutionalized setting in which the claimed universality of rights can be vindicated – the law court. The law court is the prototypical court of appeal in which the range of liberties included under 'civil rights' can be both defended and advanced. (*NSV*, pp. 205–6)

Table 1 shows the type of classificatory scheme of rights, and the modes of power and institutional sites to which they are related, which is suggested in Giddens's writings.

It is hard to be sure that the scheme in Table 1 is exactly what Giddens has in mind because he is inconsistent in his use of key terms. In some publications, for example, economic civil rights figure prominently, while in others they do not; in some writings social rights are themselves referred to as economic rights, although in others they are not. The same can be said about the treatment of the locale of rights (see *PCST*, ch. 12 and *NSV*, ch. 8). In addition, while Giddens recognizes that the struggle for types of rights is not restricted to one particular setting, the precise connections that are drawn (and the significance of them) remains vague. For instance, the category of civil rights includes a variety of important rights ranging over matters as diverse as marriage, religion and economic affairs. This involves 'bundles' of rights which have quite different origins, conditions of existence and institutional mechanisms of support, from the local community to the courts or Parliament.[23] Why, and in what particular ways, types of rights are linked to particular forms of power and locale is not sufficiently elaborated. And while there is much to recommend Giddens's emphasis on the achievement of rights through contestation, it does not separate him as decisively from Marshall as

[23] I shall return to this point at some length below.

he claims: Marshall does grant conflict a central place in the achievement of rights.

However, underpinning Giddens's concern with conflict, and the domains in which it is located, is a wider concern to develop a new explanatory framework for the development of rights. It is worth dwelling on this for a moment; for it has a number of advantages over Marshall's account although, as I shall show, it is itself by no means fully satisfactory.

The roots of modern citizenship

In Giddens's view, the development of citizenship and of modern democracy in general has to be linked to the expansion of state sovereignty or the build-up of administrative power from the late sixteenth century. The development of the state's 'apparatus of government' was made possible to a significant extent by the extension of the state's capacity for surveillance; that is, the collection and storing of information about members of society, and the related ability to supervise subject populations (*CCHM*, pp. 169ff.). As the state's sovereign authority expanded progressively and its administrative centres became more powerful, the state's dependence on force as a direct medium of rule was slowly reduced. For the increase in administrative power via surveillance increased the state's dependence on co-operative forms of social relations; it was no longer possible for the modern state to manage its affairs and sustain its offices and activities by force alone. Accordingly, greater reciprocity was created between the governors and the governed, and the more reciprocity was involved, the more opportunities were generated for subordinate groups to influence their rulers. Giddens refers to this 'two-way' expansion of power as 'the dialectic of control' (*NSV*, pp. 201f.)

The struggle for rights, Giddens argues, can be understood in this context. The expansion of state sovereignty helped foster the identity of subjects as political subjects – as citizens. As Giddens puts it, 'the expansion of state sovereignty means that those subject to it are in some sense – initially vague, but growing more and more definite and precise – aware of their membership in a political community and of the rights and obligations such membership confers' (*NSV*, p. 210). Nationalism is a critical force in the development of this new identity. In fact, Giddens contends, nationalism is 'the cultural sensibility of sovereignty' (*NSV*, p. 219). The conditions involved in the creation of the modern state as a 'surveillance apparatus' are the same as those that help generate nationalism. Nationalism is closely linked to the 'administrative unification of the state'. And citizenship mediates this process. The development of citizenship, as pertaining to membership of an overall political community, is intimately bound up with the novel (administrative) ordering of political power and the 'politicization' of social relations and day-to-day activities which follows in its wake (see *NSV*, ch. 8).

The pursuit of equal membership in the new political communities reconstituted the shape of the modern state itself. Although the struggle for citizenship took a variety of forms, the most enduring and important was, Giddens claims, class conflict: first, the class conflict of the bourgeoisie against the remnants of feudal privilege; and, second, the class conflict of the working classes against the bourgeoisie's hold on the chief levers of power. These conflicts shaped two massive institutional changes, respectively. The first of these was the progressive separation of the state from the economy. It was the establishment of civil and political rights by the bourgeoisie which first and foremost helped free the economy, and more generally civil society, from the direct political interference of the state. The 'separation' of the state from the economy remoulded both sets of institutions. As Giddens explains it, the new rights and prerogatives

> should not be seen as being created 'outside' the sphere of the state, but as part and parcel of the emergence of the 'public domain', separated from 'privately' organised economic activity. Civil rights thus have been, from the early phases of capitalist development, bound up with the very definition of what counts as 'political'. Civil and political citizenship rights developed together and remain, thereafter, open to a range of divergent interpretations which may directly affect the distribution of power.   (*NSV*, p. 207)

The development of polyarchy (rule by the many, or liberal democracy as it became in the West) can be understood against this background. The new 'public' domain became concerned in principle with protecting the space for citizens to pursue their activities unimpeded by illegitimate state action and with ensuring the responsiveness of government to the preferences of its citizens considered as political equals.[24] The 'public' and the 'private' spheres were formed through interrelated processes.

The second massive institutional change was linked, after the general achievement of the franchise, to the success of the working classes in the late nineteenth and twentieth century struggling for 'social rights', or for what Giddens sometimes prefers to call 'economic rights'. This second set of struggles produced the welfare order – the modern welfare interventionist state. Social or economic rights cannot be regarded as a mere extension of civil and political rights, for they are in part the creation of an attempt to ameliorate the worst consequences of the worker-citizen's lack of formal control of his or her activities in the work-place.

In sum, in Giddens's assessment, class conflict has been and remains the medium of the extension of citizenship rights and the basis of the creation of an insulated economy, polyarchy and the welfare state. The forging of state

---

[24] *NSV*, pp. 198–201. Giddens's conception of polyarchy is directly informed by Dahl's and Lindblom's views. See R. A. Dahl, *Polyarchy* (New Haven: Yale University Press, 1971) and Charles E. Lindblom, *Politics and Markets* (New York: Basic Books, 1977).

sovereignty was a critical impetus to the struggle for rights and to the remould-ing of citizenship. The increase in state administrative power led to the creation of new aspirations and demands, and to the development of insti-tutions which were responsive to them. These were major historical changes. But there is nothing inherent about them, Giddens notes, which would prevent their erosion in different political or economic circumstances. They remain fragile achievements.

There is much that is compelling about this position. In particular, Gid-dens's emphasis on the way in which an increase in state power led to the progressive reliance of the state on new relationships with its subjects – relationships based on consent, rather than force – has much to recommend it as a basis for explaining why new forms of political relations were called into being in the modern era. Likewise, his emphasis on the contingent nature of these developments has much to be said for it, especially if one is seeking to explain the different forms citizenship has taken, and the complex articulation of these forms with industrial capitalism.[25] Nonetheless, it is my view that the value of Giddens's analysis is weakened considerably by a number of difficult-ies. It will be my contention that problems in Giddens's position derive from accepting too much of Marshall's initial terms of reference, and from lack of precision in central formulations. The upshot of these problems is a funda-mental underestimation of the complexity of citizenship: its multidimensional roots and the way the struggle for different types of rights is 'inscribed' into, or embedded in, changing conceptions of citizenship. A few reflections on the nature of citizenship provided a useful starting point from which to highlight these shortcomings.

Citizenship, rights and obligations

From the ancient world to the present day, all forms of citizenship have had certain common attributes. Citizenship has meant a certain reciprocity of rights against, and duties towards, the community.[26] It has entailed member-ship, membership of the community in which one lives one's life. And membership has invariably involved degrees of participation in the com-munity. The question of who should participate and at what level is a question as old as the ancient world itself. There is much significant history in the attempt to restrict the extension of citizenship to certain groups: among others, owners of property, white men, educated men; men, those with particular skills and occupations, adults. There is also a telling story in the various

---

[25] See Göran Therborn, 'The Rule of Capital and the Rise of Democracy', *New Left Review*, 103 (1977), 3–41; and Michael Mann, 'Ruling Strategies and Citizenship', *Sociology*, 21, 3 (1987), 339–45.

[26] See Carl Brinkmann, 'Citizenship', in *International Encyclopaedia of the Social Sciences* (New York: Macmillan, 1968), pp. 471–4.

conceptions and debates about what is to count as citizenship and in particular what is to count as participation in the community.[27]

If citizenship entails membership in the community and membership implies forms of social participation, then it is misleading to think of citizenship primarily in relation to class or the capitalist relations of production. Citizenship is about involvement of people in the community in which they live; and people have been barred from citizenship on grounds of gender, race and age, among many other factors. To analyse citizenship as if it were a matter of the inclusion or exclusion of social classes is to eclipse from view a variety of dimensions of social life which have been central to the struggle over citizenship. In the light of this fact, the debate about citizenship initiated by Marshall requires elaboration and modification.[28]

The argument against Marshall and Giddens can, thus, be put as follows. Class conflict may well be an important medium for the development of citizenship rights, but it is by no means the only one which requires detailed examination. If citizenship involves the struggle for membership and participation in the community, then its analysis involves examining the way in which different groups, classes and movements struggle to gain degrees of autonomy and control over their lives in the face of various forms of stratification, hierarchy and political oppression. The post-Marshall debate needs to extend the analysis of citizenship to take account of issues posed by, for instance, feminism, the black movement, ecology (concerned with the moral status of animals and nature) and those who have advocated the rights of children.[29] Different social movements have raised different questions about the nature and dimensions of citizenship. As one commentator aptly put it, 'citizenship rights are the outcome of social movements which aim either to expand or to defend the definition of social membership ... The boundaries which define citizenship ... ultimately define membership of a social group or collectivity.'[30] The struggle over the nature and extent of citizenship has *itself* been a, if not the, central medium of social conflict – the medium through which various classes, groups and movements strive to enhance and protect their rights and opportunities. The very meaning of particular rights cannot be adequately understood if the range of concerns and pressures which have given rise to them is not properly grasped.

Now, it is the case that Giddens does acknowledge a range of movements which have been significant in shaping the struggle for citizenship rights. But this acknowledgement has come 'late' in the sense that it leaves the impression of being tacked on to his existing explanatory framework. This is the case for at least two reasons. First, whenever Giddens offers substantive explanations of the development of citizenship, class conflict is the major determining factor

---

[27] For an account see my *Models of Democracy* (Cambridge: Polity Press, 1987).
[28] This argument has been stated very usefully by Turner. See his *Citizenship and Capitalism*, especially chs. 1, 2 and 4.
[29] Ibid., pp. 88–9 and pp. 85–92 for a fuller discussion of these issues.
[30] Ibid., pp. 92, 85.

(*PCST*, pp. 171–2; *CCHM*, pp. 227–9; *NSV*, ch. 8). Second, little attention is devoted to understanding the nature and activities of social movements, and particular movements' advocacy of certain rights is not properly explained.[31] Giddens's attempt in his most recent work to provide a 'conceptual map' that links together diverse sources of social protest with particular sets of institutions and particular forms of rights does not solve the problems (*NSV*, pp. 310–25). Significant movements are missed out altogether (such as the anti-racist movements),[32] and the connections between those that are there and particular struggles for rights seem tenuous. For example, many would argue with the view taken within Giddens's scheme that social rights[33] are the prime objective of the labour movement, that political rights are the prime concern of the 'free-speech movement' (a dubious catch-all category itself), that civil rights are the main focus of the peace movement and that 'moral imperatives' are the preoccupation of the ecological movement. Moreover, different movements changing orientations over time (from civil concerns to perhaps wider political and social issues), their different institutional locations at any given moment (economy, polity, local community, etc.) and their different views of the meaning of rights cannot be accommodated on a map which essentially plots static relations between phenomena. In short, although Giddens acknowledges different clusters of movements and rights in the struggle for citizenship, this is not elaborated into a coherent framework. If Giddens is serious about the necessity to encompass a diverse range of groups and movements in his account of citizenship, then he will have to depart decisively from the terms of reference of his debate with Marshall, which affirms class as the key variable affecting, and the determining influence on, citizenship rights.

It is important to be clear about the meaning of rights if a more adequate account of citizenship is to be developed. The type of rights which are central to the Marshall–Giddens discussion can be defined as *legitimate spheres of independent action (or inaction)*.[34] Accordingly, the study of rights can be thought of as the study of the domains in which citizens have sought to pursue their own activities within the constraints of community. If the early attempts to achieve rights involved struggles for autonomy or independence from the

---

[31] The women's movement, for example, typically gets half a paragraph in *NSV* (p. 321). In addition, the contemporary women's movement is connected, without explanation, to concerns with civil and political rights. Some of the difficulties involved in such a view – above all, the neglect of the struggle for reproductive rights – are discussed below.

[32] Giddens would counter this criticism by arguing that all social movements can in principle be located on his 'map' (see *NSV*, p. 318). It is quite unclear, however, how movements concerned with matters such as racial prejudice or sexual freedom can be fitted into his categories. The same kind of consideration is raised in the note above about the prime orientation of the women's movement.

[33] Giddens actually uses the term 'economic rights' here instead of 'social rights'. I have stayed with Marshall's term in order to help keep clear the key concepts under discussion.

[34] Not all types of rights can, of course, be reduced to this conception. But it is, I believe, the pivotal notion underpinning the issues raised by Marshall and Giddens. I discuss this and related conceptions of rights further in my *Foundations of Democracy* (Cambridge: Polity Press, forthcoming).

locale in which one was born and from prescribed occupations, later struggles involved such things as freedom of speech, expression, belief and association, and freedom for women in marriage. The autonomy of the citizen can be represented by that bundle of rights which individuals can enjoy as a result of their status as 'free and equal' members of society. And to unpack the domain of rights is to unpack both the rights citizens formally enjoy and the conditions under which citizens' rights are actually realized or enacted. Only this 'double focus' makes it possible to grasp the degrees of autonomy, interdependence and constraint that citizens face in the societies in which they live.[35]

There is insufficient space in this chapter to elaborate fully a new classificatory scheme of rights which would do justice to the range of rights which have been established or advocated in the struggle for citizenship. But it is important at least to indicate that the set of rights compatible with citizenship in modern societies has to be conceived more broadly than either Marshall or Giddens has allowed. The broad cluster of rights Marshall refers to under the headings 'civil', 'political' and 'social', and Giddens refers to as 'civil', 'economic civil', 'political' and 'social', can usefully be thought of as pertaining to four distinct spheres which I prefer to call civil, economic, political and social. Giddens's reasons for not lumping together civil and economic civil rights are sound, but little is gained by retaining the label 'civil' in this category. Accordingly, economic rights means all those rights which have been won by the labour movement over time and which create the possibility of greater control for employees over the work-place. Removing this category from civil rights distinguishes usefully those rights which are concerned with the liberty of the individual in general from those sub-categories of rights which seek to recover elements of control over the work-place, and which have been at the centre of conflicts between labour and capital since the earliest phases of the Industrial Revolution.[36] The category of political and social (or welfare) rights can, following Marshall and Giddens, be treated as fairly unproblematic for the purposes of this chapter.

But apart from these broad sets of rights, there are other categories which neither Marshall nor Giddens develops, linked to a variety of domains where, broadly speaking (non-class specific) social movements have sought to re-form power centres according to their own goals and objectives. Among these is the area of struggle for reproductive rights – at the very heart of the women's movement.[37] Reproductive rights are the very basis of the possibility of effective participation of women in both civil society and the polity. A right to reproductive freedom for women entails making the state or other relevant political agencies responsible not only for the medical and social facilities

[35] For an elaboration of the issues underpinning the necessity of a 'double focus' in the analysis of citizenship rights see my *Models of Democracy*, ch. 9.

[36] Separating these categories in this way also helps illuminate why certain types of rights may not always be complementary (as illustrated, for instance, in recent controversy over whether 'the closed shop' undermines the individual's freedom of choice).

[37] Cf. Rosalind P. Petchesky, *Abortion and Women's Choic* (London: Verso, 1986).

necessary to prevent or assist pregnancy, but also for providing the material conditions which would help make the choice to have a child a genuinely free one and, thereby, ensure a crucial condition for women if they are to be 'free and equal'. Giddens's lack of attention to reproductive rights is symbolic of his disregard of the whole question of the social organization of reproduction, and of women and gender relations more generally.[38] He has not made the latter an integral component of his work and the inevitable result, I believe, is major lacunae in his conception of the conditions of involvement of women (and men) in public life.

Marshall's and Giddens's accounts of rights suffer, in addition, from a further limitation: a strict focus on the citizen's relation to the nation-state. While this is unquestionably important, the whole relation of rights to the nation-state has itself become progressively more problematic in the twentieth century. For a gap has opened up, linked to processes of globalization, between the idea of membership of a national political community, i.e. citizenship, and the development of international law which subjects individuals, non-governmental organizations and governments to new systems of regulation.[39] Rights and duties are recognized in international law which transcend the claims of nation-states and which, whilst they may lack coercive powers of enforcement, have far-reaching consequences. For example, the International Tribunal at Nuremburg (1945) laid down, for the first time in history, that when *international rules* that protect basic humanitarian values are in conflict with *state laws*, every individual must transgress the state laws (except where there is no room for 'moral choice'). The legal framework of the Nuremburg Tribunal marked a highly significant change in the legal direction of the modern state; for the new rules challenged the principle of military discipline and subverted national sovereignty at one of its most sensitive points: the hierarchical relations within the military.[40] In addition, two internationally recognized legal mainstays of national sovereignty – 'immunity from jurisdiction' and 'immunity of state agencies' – have been progressively questioned by Western courts. While it is the case that national sovereignty has most often been the victor when put to the test, the tension between citizenship, national sovereignty and international law is marked, and it is by no means clear how it will be resolved.

A satisfactory account of the meaning and nature of citizenship today must transcend the terms of reference which Marshall and Giddens have set down. The study of citizenship has to concern itself with all those dimensions which allow or exclude the participation of people in the communities in which they live and the complex pattern of national and international relations and processes which cut across these. Neither Marshall nor Giddens has provided an adequate basis for such a study.

[38] On this point see the chapter by Linda Murgatroyd in this volume.
[39] See R. J. Vincent, *Human Rights and International Relations* (Cambridge: Cambridge University Press, 1986).
[40] For an excellent discussion of these issues see Antonio Cassese, *Violence and Law in the Modern Age* (Cambridge: Polity Press, 1988).

Rights, states and societies

The restricted conception of citizenship in Marshall's and Giddens's work has serious sociological and political implications for central areas of inquiry. The section below will explore these implications in relation to Giddens's treatment of the ideological nature of rights, the critical dimensions of the state, the social structure of postwar society and contemporary political directions.

Rights: sham or real?

When setting out the meaning of citizenship rights, Giddens criticizes Marshall from a Marxist perspective and then uses Marshall against Marxism, pursuing the question: are rights an ideological sham or of real significance? In recent writings, Giddens has affirmed that capitalism is, as Marx argued, a class society. Pivotal to Giddens's analysis is the capitalist labour contract, the basic concept, he suggests, for analysing the class structure of capitalism from the eighteenth century to the present time.

The creation of a marketplace for both labour power and capital involved two fundamental developments. The first of these was the progressive separation of the economic from the political, referred to earlier. The creation of a distinctive sphere of the political was established by the overthrowing of feudal, courtly power, and by its progressive replacement by parliamentary representative government (*PCST*, p. 173). The struggle for civil and political rights consolidated this development, giving distinctive form to the public domain. While the separation of the economic from the political was in many respects a progressive development in political terms, it served also to undercut the new-won freedoms. For although the new freedoms were universal in principle, they favoured the dominant class in practice. The rights of the citizen to elect or stand as representatives were not extended to work and, accordingly, the sphere of politics was not extended to industry. Once citizens entered the factory gates, their lives were fully determined by the dictates of capital. To quote Giddens: 'the capitalist labour contract ... excludes the worker from formal rights over the control of the workplace. This exclusion is not incidental to the capitalist state, but vital to it, since the sphere of industry is specifically defined as being "outside politics"' (*NSV*, p. 207). 'In substantial degree', Giddens argues, 'Marx was surely right' (*PCST*, p. 173; *NSV*, p. 207). Many of the new freedoms were 'bourgeois freedoms' (*CCHM*, p. 228; *PCST*, pp. 173–4).

In prior types of society it was taken for granted that the worker or peasant had a significant degree of control over the process of labour. But with the birth of industrial capitalism this substantial degree of control was lost and had to be won all over again. The formation of the labour movement, and of trade unions in particular, created a minimum basis of power for workers in the industrial sphere. Labour and socialist parties were able to build on this despite often bitter opposition. Together, unions and socialist parties took advantage of and

fought for the development of political and social rights. It is very important,
Giddens concludes from this, to see the different kinds of citizenship rights
distinguished by Marshall as – contra Marx and Marxism – 'double-edged'.
Citizenship rights do serve to extend the range of human freedoms possible
within industrial capitalist societies; they serve as levers of struggle which are
the very basis on which freedoms can be won and protected. But at the same
time they continue to be the sparking points of conflict. In the final analysis,
therefore, citizenship rights have not simply been bourgeois freedoms. To use
Marshall against Marx is, according to Giddens, to recognize that Marxism
has failed to understand, and anticipate, the very way in which certain types of
citizenship rights have been actualized within the framework of liberal industrial capitalist society. As he puts it:

> Among the industrialized societies at least, capitalism is by now a very different
> phenomenon from what it was in the nineteenth century and labour movements
> have played a prime role in changing it. In most of the capitalist countries, we
> now have to speak of the existence of 'welfare capitalism', a system in which the
> labour movement has achieved a considerable stake and in which economic
> [social] citizenship rights brook large.   (*NSV*, p. 325)

Citizenship rights helped cement the industrial capitalist order while at one at
the same time creating new forms of politics linked to new rights for all its
citizens.

There is a fundamental ambiguity in Giddens's analysis. This ambiguity
derives from his attempt to reconcile three different positions. First, he wants
to argue that Marx was right: citizenship rights have been so much ideology –
a sham (*CCHM*, p. 228). Giddens affirms the view that citizenship rights have
for long periods largely been the province of the bourgeoisie and can legitimately be referred to as 'bourgeois freedoms' (*CCHM*, pp. 227–8). Secondly,
he argues that Marx was only partially right. Marx was right about the extent
to which citizenship rights served to legitimate and cement the industrial
capitalist order. But Marx was wrong as well, because citizenship rights have
proven to be 'double-edged'. Thirdly, Giddens argues that Marx was simply
wrong about the nature of rights. The fact that rights are double-edged – the
fact that citizenship rights can be actualized within the framework of liberal
democracy – seems to him to imply that the revolutionary socialist project is
quite unjustified. To support this view Giddens singles out the fact that
citizenship rights have been actually developed and extended within the
sphere of industrial capitalism modifying and altering industrial capitalism
itself. Giddens's overall equivocation on this issue, and the consequences this
equivocation has, can be highlighted by considering his appraisal of the
political significance of the separation of the 'political' and 'economic'.

For Giddens, the separation of the political and economic is linked fundamentally to the nature of modern domination – the rule of capital. While he is
surely right to stress the way the institutionalized separation of the economic

from the political creates the very basis for the development and expansion of capital – and secures the interests of the capitalist class – his analysis fails to explore systematically the ways in which this separation also creates a significant space for the realization of political rights and freedoms. The relative separation of the political and economic means that there is a realm in which the citizen can enjoy rights unavailable to those in societies where this separation has not been established. What this amounts to, among other things, is the necessity to recognize the fundamental liberal notion that the 'separation' of the state from civil society is (and must be) a central feature of any democratic political order; for without it, a number of critical modern political innovations – concerning the centrality, in principle, of an 'impersonal' structure of public power, of a constitution to help guarantee and protect rights, of a diversity of power centres within and outside of the state, of mechanisms to promote competition and debate between alternative political platforms – cannot be enjoyed.[41] While one consequence of the differentiation of the economic and political is to give the economy relative freedom and, thereby, to produce and reproduce massive asymmetries in income, wealth and power, as Giddens rightly maintains, another is to create a space for the enjoyment of civil and political rights.[42] The significance of this requires detailed comparative investigation (between countries West and East, North and South) which is missing in Giddens's work.

An additional problem of analysing and assessing citizenship rights primarily in terms of their ideological significance for class relations and capitalist society is that the very diverse origins of rights and the distinctively modern conception of citizenship get put aside. The modern conception of citizenship is inseparable from a series of multiple and complexly overlapping conflicts. Struggles between monarchs and barons over the domain of rightful authority; peasant rebellion against the weight of excess taxation and social obligation; the spread of trade, commerce and market relations; the flourishing of Renaissance culture with its renewed interest in classical political ideas (including the Greek city-state and Roman Law); the consolidation of national monarchies in Europe (England, France and Spain); religious strife and the challenge to the universal claims of Catholicism; the struggle between church and state – all played a part in the emergence of the modern idea of the state, the citizen and citizenship.[43] The idea of the individual as a citizen is, more-

[41] I trace the importance of these issues at some length in *Models of Democracy*, chs. 2, 3, 8 and 9.
[42] See Turner, *Citizenship and Capitalism*, pp. 37–44. Turner offers an illuminating discussion of some of the key theoretical issues involved here.
[43] See, for example, Gianfranco Poggi, *The Development of the Modern State* (London: Hutchinson, 1978); Charles Tilly, 'Reflections on the History of European State-making', in C. Tilly (ed.), *The Formation of National States in Western Europe* (Princeton: Princeton University Press, 1975); Theda Skocpol, *States and Social Revolutions: A Comparative Analysis of France, Russia and China* (Cambridge: Cambridge University Press, 1979); Reinhard Bendix, *Kings or People* (Berkeley: University of California Press, 1980); S. I. Benn and R. S. Peters, *Social Principles and the Democratic State* (London: Allen & Unwin, 1959); John Keane, *Public Life and Late Capitalism* (Cambridge: Cambridge University Press, 1983), essay 6; and my *Models of Democracy*, ch. 2.

over, an idea deeply connected with the doctrine of freedom of choice, a doctrine which raises questions about choice in matters as diverse as marriage, economic and political affairs.[44] If the modern idea of citizenship crystallized at the intersection of a variety of struggles, it did so in the context of struggles concerned with rights which are fundamental to most aspects of choice in everyday life. The significance of these rights goes far beyond that which can be embraced in an analysis which simply places class first.

Giddens's emphasis on separating out the formal rights that people enjoy from the actual capacities they have to enact rights is important. But this insight is not original, and his use of it is marred by terms of reference which are too narrow and do not permit the adequate specification of the diverse range of rights that emerge with the development of modern citizenship. The right to freedom of choice in marriage, the right to choice about one's religion – these and many other rights cannot simply be understood or their meaning explicated within the framework of concerns: rights – sham or real? They suggest a diversity of issues, and a diversity of conditions, which need much more careful analyses than Giddens has hitherto provided. They also require a much more sophisticated classificatory scheme of rights if many of them are to be given adequate treatment at all. A satisfactory theory of rights, which attends to the diverse range of rights which have been essential to the shaping of the modern world, will require an analysis which goes far beyond that provided by Marx, Marshall or Giddens.

State: capitalist or modern?

In modern Western political thought, the idea of the state is often linked to the notion of an impersonal and privileged legal or constitutional order with the capability of administering and controlling a given territory.[45] While this notion found its earliest expression in the ancient world (especially in Rome), it did not become a major object of concern until the late sixteenth century.[46] It was not an element of medieval political thinking. The idea of an impersonal and sovereign political order, i.e. a legally circumscribed structure of power separate from ruler and ruled with supreme jurisdiction over a territory, could not predominate while political rights, obligations and duties were closely tied to religious tradition and the feudal system of property rights. Similarly, the idea that human beings were 'individuals' or 'a people', with a right to be citizens of their state, could not develop under the constraining influences of the 'closed circle' of medieval intellectual life.

These notions are sometimes argued to be constitutive of the very concept of the modern state. There are passages in which Giddens seems to share this view, and as a corollary an emphasis on the extraordinary innovatory power of

[44] Cf. C. B. Macpherson, *The Real World of Democracy* (Oxford: Oxford University Press, 1966), ch. 1.
[45] See Quentin Skinner, *The Foundations of Modern Political Thought* (2 vols., Cambridge: Cambridge University Press, 1978).
[46] See ibid., vol. 2, pp. 349–58.

these notions, recognizing that they provided a critical impetus to the form (constitutional, representative) and limits ('separation' of state and civil society, division of powers) of the modern 'apparatus of government' (see *CS*, ch. 6). From this perspective it follows that an understanding of the state requires a detailed appreciation of its institutional and legal bases – a 'state-centered' perspective.[47] While Giddens sometimes seems to recognize this, there are other passages in his work where the very idea of the modern state is eclipsed by the idea of the 'capitalist state'.

By the 'capitalist state' Giddens means, following Claus Offe, a state 'enmeshed' in class relations (see especially *CCHM*, pp. 210–14, 219–26).[48] The following points are central to the position:

(1)   The state in capitalism 'is a state in a class society' – a society in which class relations (via control over allocative resources) enter into the very constitution of the productive process; class struggle is a chronic feature of everyday life, and class conflict is a 'major medium' of the internal transformation of society (*CCHM*, pp. 214, 220–1).

(2)   Unlike other ruling classes in history, 'the ruling class does not rule' in capitalism; that is, the 'capitalist class does not generally compose ... the personnel of the state' (*CCHM*, p. 211). Nonetheless, 'the state, as a mode of "government", is strongly influenced by its institutional alignments with private property and with the insulated "economy"' (*NSV*, p. 136).

(3)   The state is dependent upon the activities of capitalist employers for its revenues and, hence, operates in the context of various capitalist 'imperatives' (*CCHM*, p. 211). It has, accordingly, to sustain the process of accumulation and the incentives for the private appropriation of resources while not undermining belief in itself as an impartial arbiter of all class interests, thereby eroding its power base.

(4)   The state is 'directly enmeshed in the contradictions of capitalism'. In so being, it is 'not merely a defender of the status quo' (*CCHM*, p. 220). For if it is enmeshed in the contradictions of capitalism, it can in some part be seen as a force able to shape the very nature of interests and policies.

In this analysis, the explanatory and political axis 'class/state' is once again granted the central role. Class and state power are directly linked and class power is held to be the basis of political power. Such a position clearly grants primacy to the capitalist nature of modern societies *and* states.

While there is some scope within this framework for understanding the political or strategic intelligence which government and state agencies often display, the general emphasis is one which denies what is central to the idea of the modern state, i.e., that the state apparatus itself has sufficient primacy over

---

[47] For a discussion of this perspective see Peter B. Evans, Dietrich Rueschemeyer and Theda Skocpol (eds.), *Bringing the State Back In* (Cambridge: Cambridge University Press, 1985).

[48] Cf. Claus Offe, *Contradictions of the Welfare State* (London: Hutchinson, 1984).

social classes and collectivities that the nature and meaning of political outcomes – constitutional forms, particular institutional structures and the like –
cannot be inferred directly from the configuration of class relations. Giddens's
account of the capitalist state sits uneasily with his recognition of the *sui generis*
powers of the modern state, and of the necessity to see the state as 'a set of
collectivities concerned with the institutionalized organization of political
power' (*CCHM*, p. 220). Further, it sits in some tension with his own argument
that Marx's treatment of the capitalist state is deficient because it generally
ignores the non-capitalist features of the state and fails to separate out the
institutional elements of modern politics from the broad pattern of social
relations (see *NSV*, pp. 141, 160).

Giddens's equivocation on the critical dimensions of the modern state is
related to his equivocation about rights. It is one thing to argue that the
modern state has (as do civil and political rights) central 'functions' for the
reproduction of capital – an argument, however, that would need very careful
elaboration (see the contribution by Jessop in this volume). But it is quite
another thing to stress the capitalist character of the state to the point at which
the significance of the institutional, constitutional and legal innovations of the
modern state tends to be eclipsed from view altogether. A systematic treatment of the idea of rights, and of the new freedoms they formally allow, and a
systematic understanding of the relationship between formal rights and the
actual possibilities of their realization require a much more substantial account of the modern state that can be found in Giddens's work. Only such a
treatment could do justice to the fact that the modern state developed partly in
response to the demand to articulate and protect a range of rights and interests
which cannot be reduced to issues of property and property relations.

Society: pluralist or class-ridden?

In *A Contemporary Critique of Historical Materialism* and other texts, Giddens
argues at length that capitalism is a class society. In fact, it is his view that
capitalism is the only social formation to which the concept of 'mode of
production' is applicable. As he puts it, 'I do . . . want to claim that capitalism
is the first and only form of society in history of which it might be said with
some plausibility that it both "has" and "is" a mode of production' (*NSV*, p.
134).

However, there are many other places in Giddens's work where he rejects
(even in the case of capitalism) the direct connection Marx made between the
history of classes, exploitation, conflicts of interest and the political power of
the state. Here he argues that there are multiple routes of domination and
different types of exploitation within and between classes, states, the sexes and
ethnic groups. He suggests it is a mere delusion to imagine that the end of
capitalism means the end of oppression in all its forms. In a typical passage he
writes,

The validity of much of what Marx has to say in analysing the nature of capitalist production need not be placed in doubt ... However, Marx accords undue centrality to capitalism and to class struggle as the keys to explaining inequality or exploitation, and to providing the means of their transcendence.

(*NSV*, p. 336)

The difficulty here is that ultimately Giddens has not resolved the issues posed by the debate between Marxism and pluralism – and no amount of elaborate syntheses seems to have resolved the matter.[49] Giddens wishes to affirm the centrality of class in the determination of the character of contemporary society while at the same time recognizing that this very perspective itself marginalizes or excludes certain types of issues from consideration. This is true of all those issues which cannot be reduced, as Giddens himself recognizes, to class-related matters. Classic examples of this are the domination of women by men, of certain racial and ethnic groups by others and of nature by industry (which raises ecological questions). Other central concerns include the power of public administrators or bureaucrats over their 'clients' and the role of 'authoritative resources' (the capacity to co-ordinate and control the activities of human beings), which build up in most social organizations.

Giddens's affirmation of class analysis is certainly not unqualified; he argues strenuously on behalf of class analysis in social theory, but does not grant class relations primacy over many critical areas: from ecology to the military. Further, he recognizes, of course, the social and political significance of a number of social movements (*NSV*, ch. 11). But how exactly these movements are to be linked into the overall emphasis on class is not clarified. As one critic has remarked: 'Giddens wants to affirm the centrality of class while not giving up pluralist insights.'[50] Earlier equivocations and ambiguities are reflected in the decisive issue of how he characterizes the very nature of contemporary society. There are fundamental unresolved tensions in Giddens's account of the core relations and conflicts of modern life.

Political choices: liberalism or socialism or ... ?

These problems are carried over into the political dimension of Giddens's work. Giddens does not see himself as a champion of liberalism, but neither does he stray far from some of liberalism's central prescriptions. He does not straightforwardly advocate socialist positions, but neither does he wish to jettison central socialist ideals. He is critical, in addition, of a variety of intermediate positions, for example pluralism, and of 'reformist' political views like those of Marshall's. Yet he shares some of the terms of reference of the 'middle ground'. In *The Nation-State and Violence*, Giddens appears to advocate the necessity to go beyond liberalism, pluralism and Marxism. The

---

[49] See Gregor McLennan, *Pluralism, Marxism and Beyond* (Cambridge: Polity Press, 1989) for an excellent discussion of this issue.
[50] Ibid., ch. 6.

contemporary world, he argues, is far more complex than any of these doctrines anticipated, and it has left none of them with their 'hands clean' (*NSV*,
ch. 11). He maintains, moreover, that there are trends at work in the late
twentieth century – particularly global trends – which render incoherent most
contemporary conceptions of the political good (*NSV*, pp. 325ff.).

Traditionally, concepts of the political good have been elaborated at the
level of state institutions, practices and operations; the state has been at the
intersection of intellectually and morally ambitious conceptions of political
life.[51] The challenge facing these traditional concepts is daunting today, as
Giddens stresses. The dynamics of a world economy which produces instabilities and difficulties within states and between states and which outreach
the control of any single 'centre'; the rapid growth of transnational links which
have stimulated new forms of collective decision-making involving states,
intergovernmental organizations and an array of international pressure
groups; the build-up of military arms and the general means of warfare as a
'stable feature' of the contemporary political world – all these developments
raise, I believe, fundamental questions about the terms of reference of liberalism, pluralism and Marxism. It is, of course, important to recognize the new
questions on the political agenda. But it remains a, if not the, central task of
political and social theory to think them through. One cannot be wholly
optimistic about Giddens's future contribution in this area while there is such
ambiguity at the heart of his critique and reconstruction of social and political
theory. On the other hand, if Giddens fails here, we will all almost certainly be
the losers, for there are very few with his scope and range of insight.

---

[51] See John Dunn, 'Responsibility without Power: States and the Incoherence of the Modern
Conception of the Political Good', lecture delivered to the IPSA, Paris, July 1985. Forthcoming
in M. Banks (ed.), *The State in International Relations* (Hassocks, Sussex: Wheatsheaf).

9
Presences and absences: time–space relations and structuration theory

DEREK GREGORY

Introduction

In this chapter I consider the incorporation of time–space relations within structuration theory: the way in which Giddens conceives of what he calls the time–space constitution of social life. There are obvious dangers in disentangling one thread from such a dense and developing argument, and so I want to begin by putting some limits around my own discussion.

A number of commentators are evidently uncomfortable about the status of structuration theory. They claim that its first formulations were pitched at forbidding heights of abstraction, whereas its later arguments have moved towards a more concrete terrain. In consequence, they say, it has become difficult to determine the scope of structuration theory with any precision.[1] In my view, however, it makes most sense to treat Giddens's writings as a *research programme* developed through a continuous dialogue between the theoretical and the empirical. The term derives from Lakatos, of course, but I use it in a somewhat different sense because Giddens's project is not linear: one proposition does not succeed another in a unidimensional, unidirectional sequence. What I have in mind is closer to Hesse's network model of science. Structuration theory then appears as a loose-knit web of propositions, some more central than others, some spun more tightly than others. In contradistinction to networks in the natural sciences, structuration theory is clearly not directed towards the discovery of 'laws'; but, as Hesse suggests more generally, its development has been determined – though less formally than some of its critics seem to think – by both coherence rules (relating to the structure of the network) and correspondence rules (relating to empirical observations). These have required a constant reworking of its conceptual fabric, so that structuration theory has, of necessity, been developed unevenly. In saying all this, I do no more than take Giddens at his word: in wanting to fire 'conceptual

I am grateful to Chris Philo and John Thompson for their comments on a draft of this chapter.

[1] See, for example, N. Gregson, 'Structuration Theory: Some Thoughts on the Possibilities for Empirical Research', *Environment and Planning D: Society & Space*, 5 (1987), 73–92; N. Thrift, 'Bear and Mouse or Bear and Tree? Anthony Giddens's Reconstitution of Social Theory', *Sociology*, 19 (1985), 609–23.

salvoes into social reality', he is, I think, refusing to detonate the single, spectacular explosion of a Grand Theory.[2]

Yet Giddens's project is not without direction, and for my present purposes there is one particular sense in which his research programme may be counted as *progressive*. In his first attempts to elucidate the connections between 'human agency' and 'social structure' Giddens paid some considerable attention to questions of temporality. This was, in part, the product of a critical engagement with phenomenology and hermeneutics; but it was also more obviously the result of his attempt to work out the implications of Marx's famous claim that people make history but not just as they please and not under conditions of their own choosing. This is the pivot around which much of mainstream social theory can be made to move too, of course, and Giddens draws freely upon Marxist and non-Marxist writings. I see nothing exceptional in that. Like many others concerned with these issues, Giddens was sceptical of the division of labour between sociology and history. It made little sense, so he believed, to separate synchronic and diachronic analysis – 'statics' and 'dynamics' – and, as Abrams argued in an influential commentary on these matters, structuration theory thus had important things to say to sociologists and historians alike.[3] In common with most other writers, however, Giddens paid little or no attention to questions of spatiality. In describing his research programme as 'progressive', therefore, I mean to indicate the way in which Giddens gradually mapped time–space relations into structuration theory, until he could claim – as he had already done for history – that there are no logical or methodological differences between sociology and human geography either.[4]

His earliest discussion of any consequence is contained in *Central Problems in Social Theory*. It derived from his continuing interest in phenomenology and hermeneutics, particularly Heidegger's treatment of time–space as 'presencing', now combined with a critical appraisal of concepts of 'spacing' found in structuralism and post-structuralism. But it is in the first volume of *A Contemporary Critique of Historical Materialism* that these themes are developed in detail. In bringing time–space relations within the core of structuration theory in this way, Giddens tacitly supplied another reason, in addition to all those which he spelled out *en clair*, for regarding his project as a 'deconstruction' of historical materialism. For when Marx spoke about the 'annihilation of space by time'

---

[2] M. Hesse, *The Structure of Scientific Inference* (London: Macmillan, 1974). I have taken Giddens's rejection of Grand Theory from two interviews: J. Bleicher and M. Featherstone, 'Historical Materialism Today: An Interview with Anthony Giddens', *Theory, Culture & Society*, 1 (2) (1982), 63–77; D. Gregory, 'Space, Time and Politics in Social Theory: An Interview with Anthony Giddens', *Environment and Planning D: Society & Space*, 2 (1984), 123–32. For all that, I do not find Giddens's account of the relations between structuration theory and empirical research especially satisfactory: see *CS*, ch. 6.

[3] P. Abrams, 'History, Sociology, Historical Sociology', *Past & Present*, 87 (1980), 3–16.

[4] *CS*, p. 368.

his remarks were unusually prophetic: historical materialism, in both its classical and modern versions, turned out to have remarkably little room for the historical geography of capitalism.

Conversely, human geography was itself distanced from historical materialism. In the English-speaking world at any rate, it was probably the last of the social sciences to take Marxism seriously. But it soon made up for lost time. One of the most prominent figures in its new intellectual landscape was Harvey, who was adamant that 'one of the extraordinary failures of an otherwise powerful Marxist tradition' was the way in which it had licensed 'the study of historical transformations while ignoring how capitalism produces its own geography'. His own account of *The Limits to Capital* has to be read in a double sense, therefore, marking both the bounding contours of capitalist development and an important silence in Marx's master work.[5] But Harvey's vision of geography was framed within a particular horizon of meaning which placed concepts of spatial structure at its very centre. Other perspectives would change the composition. I make this point because Giddens would obviously object to Harvey's attempt to fashion an 'historico-geographical materialism', since he does not think that Marx can be redeemed in this (or any other) way. Whatever reservations he has about Harvey's invocation of a Marxist tradition, however, Giddens does not, I think, dissent from the *geographical* tradition that he represents: and this puts important limits around structuration theory too. In particular, and as I will seek to show, it means that structuration theory in its present form remains close to the analytics of spatial science. It has little to say about senses of place and symbolic landscapes in the reproduction of social life, and it continues to theorize the problem of order as in large measure a problem of pattern. And yet where Harvey does move beyond the problematic of spatial science, Giddens does not: structuration theory is virtually silent about 'the production of space'. These objections may seem opaque at the moment, but they ought to become clearer as my argument proceeds: so let me now indicate the direction I propose to take.

The time–space constitution of social life

I have provided a rough map of my argument in Figure 1. Giddens draws a basic distinction between social integration and system integration, but he formulates it in terms strikingly different from conventional social theory. The only scheme of comparable scope is, I think, Habermas's theory of communicative action. But even Habermas – whose forays across the field of social theory are just as wide-ranging as Giddens's – fails to engage with the

[5] D. Harvey, *The Limits to Capital* (Oxford: Basil Blackwell, 1982).

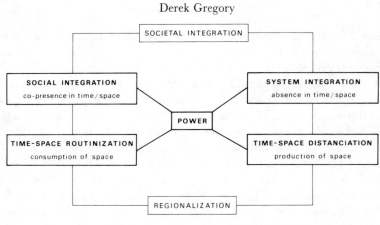

Figure 1

spatiality of social life: with what Giddens calls time–space routinization and time–space distanciation.[6]

Giddens argues that the continuity of everyday life depends, in large measure, on routinized interactions between people who are *co-present* in time and space. This is what he means by *social integration*, but it is also what 'society' meant before the eighteenth century: simply the company of others. Although Giddens is critical of several of Hägerstrand's theorems, and rightly so, he nevertheless suggests that his time-geography provides an exemplary notation through which the characteristic shapes of *time–space routinization* can be captured.

Hägerstrand describes time-geography as a *contextual* approach – and one which is by no means confined to the social sciences – which seeks to 'grasp things together' in time and space. 'Being a geographer', he once wrote,

> basically means to appreciate that when events are seen located together in a block of space–time they inevitably expose relations which cannot be traced any more, once we have bunched them into classes and drawn them out of their place in the block.[7]

The contextual approach partitions the world on the basis of proximity, therefore, in contrast to *compositional* approaches, whose categorizations are based on similarity. The distinction is essentially Kantian. In his Königsberg lectures, Kant distinguished between physical classifications containing phenomena which 'belong to the same time [history] or the same space [geography]' and logical classifications containing phenomena 'even though

---

[6] I have elaborated the comparison between Giddens and Habermas in my *The Geographical Imagination: Social Theory and Human Geography* (London: Unwin Hyman, in press).
[7] T. Hägerstrand, 'Commentary', in A. Buttimer, *Values in Geography* (Washington: Association of American Geographers, 1974).

they are to be found in widely separated places'. Hägerstrand develops his argument in a radically non-Kantian direction, however, because in its traditional form Kant's physical classification was used to underwrite a cellular regional geography conspicuously uninterested in general theoretical claims and preoccupied with the differences between particular places.[8] 'How was everything held together?' Hägerstrand asked. 'The answer is simple: it was not.' For this reason, his own programme was directed towards the elucidation of contextuality through the construction of a system of general concepts.[9]

But there is, of course, quite another sense in which things may be held together. In the closing decades of the eighteenth century, when Kant was delivering his lectures, the friction of distance was being transformed: 'pockets of local order', as Hägerstrand calls them, were being bound in to extra-regional and extra-national systems. This is precisely what Marx was referring to less than a hundred years later when he spoke about the 'annihilation of space by time'. The process was complicated, fractured and far from homogeneous, and it did not undermine the importance of areal differentiation: but it required a conjoint analysis of spatial integration. For social life increasingly depended on interactions with others who were *absent* in time or space. This is what Giddens means by *system integration*, and it is also what 'society' came to mean after the eighteenth century: the larger world stretching away from the human body and the human being. Giddens calls this process of 'stretching' *time–space distanciation* and uses it to indicate the ways in which social systems are embedded in time and space. The modern world system, so he says, 'is, for the first time in history, one in which absence in space no longer hinders system co-ordination'. One of the basic objectives of structuration theory is thus to show how 'the limitations of individual "presence" are transcended by the stretching of social relations across time and space'.[10]

The only account which approximates to these distinctions is Schutz and Luckmann's (brief) discussion of the 'spatial arrangement of the everyday life-world'. They distinguish between the *primary zone* of operation – 'the province of nonmediated action . . . the primary world within reach' – and the *secondary zone* of operation, 'the world within potential reach' which 'finds its limits in the prevailing technical conditions of a society'.[11] But they are self-evidently concerned with the structures of the life-world and develop their argument in the vocabulary of constitutive phenomenology, whereas Giddens points to the persistent failure of approaches of this sort to recognize the importance of power to the production and reproduction of social life. Power,

[8] Cf. R. Hartshorne, *The Nature of Geography* (Lancaster, Pa.: Association of American Geographers, 1939).

[9] T. Hägerstrand, 'In Search of the Sources of Concepts', in A. Buttimer, *The Practice of Geography* (Harlow: Longman, 1983), pp. 238–56.

[10] *CS*, pp. 35, 185.

[11] A. Schutz and T. Luckmann, *The Structures of the Life-World* (London: Heinemann, 1974), pp. 36–44.

so he claims, is a chronic feature of social life, and its exercise is logically implicated in the transformative capacities of human agency.[12]

Power and space are linked in Giddens's writings in a number of ways, but they are of pivotal importance in elucidating the connections between social integration and system integration. Giddens suggests that these can be traced through the various modes of *regionalization* which 'channel, and are channelled by, the time–space paths that the members of a community or society follow in their day-to-day activities'. Regionalization is thus of decisive significance to social theory. For in so far as modes of regionalization are typically formed through a hierarchy of locales – which, in Hägerstrand's terms, means a hierarchy of domains entrained by a hierarchy of projects – then, so Giddens argues, time–space paths will be 'strongly influenced by, and also reproduce, basic institutional parameters of the social systems in which they are implicated'. He claims that this makes it possible to explicate the interconnection of routinized and repetitive social action with long-term, large-scale institutional development in a depth which is denied to both conventional social theory and historical materialism.[13]

Time–space routinization

I think it necessary to expose the composite logic behind Giddens's model of time–space routinization in order to see how it is wired in to circuits of social reproduction.

The logics of routinization

Giddens locates time–space routinization within a series of overlapping claims about the intermingling of 'presence' and 'absence' in the conduct of social life. These can be divided into three sets.

(1)   Saussure, Lévi-Strauss and Derrida all point in various ways to the significance of 'spacing through difference' in the constitution of both language and society. Giddens is sharply critical of structuralism, of course, and rejects the view that 'society is like a language': but he nevertheless accepts that language exemplifies some aspects of social life as a whole. In particular, the 'structure' of language is *absent*, a 'virtual order of differences', *present* only in its instantiations in the constituting moments of speech. In much the same way, Giddens distinguishes between the syntagmatic and paradigmatic dimensions of social life. The first refers to social relations considered as systems, to the 'patterning' of interaction between individuals and groups which is a commonplace of social theory and spatial science. What these two perspectives characteristically overlook, however, and from opposite

----

[12] See in particular *NRSM*.   [13] *CS*, pp. 142–3.

directions, is that 'patterning' implies the reproduction of social practices in time and space. Giddens suggests that this involves structures of rules and resources which are drawn upon by actors in the production of interaction, and which have a 'virtual existence': 'present' only in their instantiations in the constituting moments of social systems. The second dimension thus refers to 'the recursive connection between "presencing", constituted by human activities, and structural properties which are the medium and outcome of such activities'. This is a relation between moment and totality quite distinct from that between part and whole in functionalism, Giddens argues, because it involves 'a dialectic of presence and absence which ties the most minor or trivial forms of social action to structural properties of the overall society' – just as every speech act is bound in to the structural properties of language.[14]

(2)   The linguistic model has considerable limitations, however, and Saussure's work was in fact directed towards the singularity of language: towards everything that separated it from other social practices. But Giddens's conception of 'presence' and 'absence' is more than a model, because it is also strongly influenced by Heidegger's treatment of being and time. Giddens is as critical of phenomenology and hermeneutics as he is of structuralism, but he considers Heidegger's writings to be essential to the elaboration of his own ideas. In his view, Heidegger shows that time and space cannot be treated as 'frameworks' within which social life is spun out: the Kantian legacy which bequeathed 'time', 'space' and 'society' to nominally separate disciplines and thereby impoverished all of them. Instead, Heidegger argues that in its most fundamental form time–space connotes *modes of presencing* which enter into the constitution of Being itself. He clearly acknowledges the force of conventional parametric conceptions of time and space:

> To the calculating mind, space and time appear as parameters for the measurement of nearness and remoteness, and these in turn as static distances. But space and time do not serve only as parameters; in this role their nature would soon be exhausted – a role whose seminal forms are discernible early in Western thinking, and which then, in the course of the modern age, become established as the standard conception.[15]

Giddens says much the same. Measurable time–space is imposed on time–space relations in Western culture and is deeply implicated in the commodification of time and space: it is historically and geographically specific, therefore, and should not 'be confused with the nature of time–space as such'. This is, in part, why Giddens attaches so much importance to Foucault – who was himself no stranger to Heidegger's writings – and for whom discipline depended upon the 'calculative division' of time and space.[16] But the import-

---

[14] *CPST*, ch. 1; *CCHM*, ch. 1.
[15] M. Heidegger, *On the Way to Language* (New York: Harper & Row, 1971), p. 102.
[16] *CCHM*, p. 33; *CS*, pp. 145–58; M. Foucault, *Discipline and Punish: The Birth of the Prison* (London: Allen Lane, 1977).

ance of Heidegger to structuration theory is more basic. Whatever reservations Giddens has about some aspects of Heidegger's philosophy, it allows him to develop a *non*-parametric conception of time–space through which he is able to claim that time–space relations enter as deeply into the most stable forms of social reproduction as they do into the most volatile moments of social change. Heidegger's views about the relations between temporality and spatiality altered between *Being and Time* and *On Time and Being*, but in his later writings he argued that 'prior to all calculation' and indeed independent of it is 'the mutual reaching out and opening up of future, past and present'. This does not imply that time is three-dimensional ('future, past and present'), however, because there is also a fourth dimension: 'the "presencing" which brings them together and holds them apart'. Time–space is, thus, not a 'contentless form' in which objects exist: *it expresses the nature of what objects are*.[17] Giddens does not discuss Heidegger's writings in much more detail than this, and he is (properly) cautious about folding them directly into social theory. But their importance is surely unmistakable: they provide structuration theory with an ontological rather than a merely analogical foundation.

I do not propose to discuss the limitations (or otherwise) of these two sets of claims here, though both of them are open to objection in the form in which Giddens expresses them. I am more concerned about the connections which can be established between them and the third set of claims, which relate specifically to time-geography. Giddens does not elucidate these connections in any systematic fashion, and I think this is unfortunate. His silence implies that his interest in time-geography is largely methodological: that it provides a 'useful notation' and little else. It would not be difficult to find textual support for an interpretation of this sort, which has allowed some critics to assume (wrongly, as it happens) that the time–space relations embedded in routinization are somehow incidental to structuration theory and that they can be pulled out without damaging the integrity of the project as a whole. But the absence of a connecting discussion is more serious than that, because in reducing the contribution of time-geography in this way Giddens restricts the scope of structuration theory too. I do not, of course, mean to exempt time-geography from criticism, and I have expressed my reservations about some of Hägerstrand's formulations in detail elsewhere;[18] but time-geography amounts to more than a series of templates for tracing trajectories in time and space. That would be to treat it as another version of spatial science, whereas Hägerstrand's vision is clearly *ecological* and his project is better described as a

[17] *CCHM*, pp. 30–4. Giddens does not, I think, properly distinguish between Heidegger's early and later writings in this respect.
[18] D. Gregory, 'Suspended Animation: The Stasis of Diffusion Theory', in D. Gregory and J. Urry (eds.), *Social Relations and Spatial Structures* (London: Macmillan, 1985), pp. 296–336.

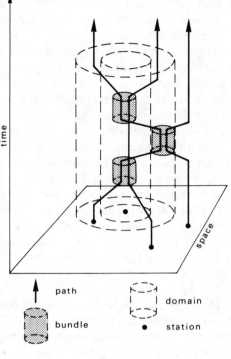

path   domain

bundle   station

Figure 2

time–space ecology.[19] I will confine my discussion to a clarification of these remarks.

(3)   There are several affinities between time-geography and structuralism on the one hand and phenomenology on the other. Hägerstrand's web model (Figure 2) portrays a social system as a series of time–space paths flowing through a set of stations. The paths on the display can be seen as a concrete realization of a whole repertoire of possible trajectories enclosed by an under-lying structure of capability, coupling and steering constraints. One of Häger-strand's co-workers has claimed that the distinction between 'realization' and 'repertoire' (the terms are mine, incidentally, not Hägerstrand's) is formally equivalent to the distinction between speech and language I noted earlier, and so he seeks to develop time-geography into what he calls a 'time–space structuralism'. In anything other than analogical terms, this would sharply separate time-geography from structuration theory; but in those terms the project is plausible enough. Although Hägerstrand himself does not say

[19] T. Hägerstrand, 'Ecology under One Perspective', in E. Bylund, H. Linderholm and O. Rune (eds.), *Ecological Problems of the Circumpolar North* (Lulea: Norrbottens Museum, 1974), pp. 271–6.

anything about structuralism, he does talk about time-geography as a means of registering the 'momentary thereness' of things in a constant flow of 'interrelated presences and absences'.[20]

But he is also concerned, as I have said, to grasp the 'togetherness' of things, and this suggests that there are rather deeper resonances between time-geography and phenomenology. By 'deeper', I mean that they go beyond the analogical. There may well be a superficial resemblance between Heidegger's time–space and the four-dimensional time–space of post-Newtonian physics, as Giddens says, and similar comparisons can be found in several commentaries on the way in which 'process takes shape as four-dimensional form' in Hägerstrand's time-geography; but I do not find them especially illuminating.[21] More to the point is that both Heidegger and Hägerstrand are concerned in some substantial sense with finitude: and when Hägerstrand insists that the finitude of time and space is one of the most 'fundamental devices for giving shape to the world' he is not, I think, speaking parametrically at all. His ideas are usually interpreted in that way, I realize, and it is easy to see how his diagrams could be viewed as Kantian 'frameworks' within which social life is simply spun out in time and space. But read differently they are symptomatic of a much more fundamental time–space ontology. For Hägerstrand as for Heidegger, time–space relations are constitutive. Heidegger suggests that human spatiality has the character of a 'situating' enterprise in which we 'make room' for things in ways which 'allow them to be the things that they are'.[22] In much the same way, I think, time-geography can properly be interpreted as a 'situational ecology' (the term is Hägerstrand's this time) directed towards an elucidation of the finitude of 'room'.[23]

Hägerstrand makes it plain that when he talks about 'ecology' he does not intend the term as a 'superficial analogy' but instead means to get at 'the fundamental bonds between life, time and space'.[24] Indeed, in an analogical sense there would be nothing very novel about representing social life as a web. Parsons developed his account of The Structure of Social Action around the 'unit act', for example, which he described as:

---

[20] See T. Carlstein, Time Resources, Society and Ecology, vol. 1, Preindustrial Societies (London: Allen & Unwin, 1982), 56–60; cf. T. Hägerstrand, 'Presence and Absence: A Look at Conceptual Choices and Bodily Necessities', Regional Studies, 18 (1984), 373–80.

[21] CCHM, p. 30; D. Harvey, Explanation in Geography (London: Edward Arnold, 1969), p. 226; C. Rose, 'Reflections on the Notion of Time Incorporated in Hägerstrand's Time-Geographic Model of Society', Tijdschrift voor Economische en Sociale Geografie, 68 (1977), 43–50.

[22] J. Pickles, Phenomenology, Science and Geography: Spatiality and the Human Sciences (Cambridge: Cambridge University Press, 1985), pp. 158–70.

[23] T. Hägerstrand, 'Space, Time and Human Conditions', in A. Karlqvist, L. Lundqvist and F. Snickars (eds.), Dynamic Allocation of Urban Space (Farnborough: Saxon House, 1975), pp. 3–14; A. Karlqvist, L. Lundqvist and F. Snickars (eds.), 'Survival and Arena: On the Life-history of Individuals in Relation to their Geographical Environment', in T. Carlstein, D. Parkes and N. Thrift (eds.), Timing Space and Spacing Time, vol. 2, Human Activity and Time-geography (London: Edward Arnold, 1978), pp. 122–45.

[24] Hägerstrand, 'Ecology under One Perspective'.

A 'knot' where a large number of ... threads come together only to separate
again, each one to enter, as it goes on, into a variety of other knots into which only
a few of those with which it was formerly combined enter with it.

The parallel with Hägerstrand is very close, but Parsons insisted that his was
an abstract schema in which 'relations in space are not as such relevant'.[25] One
of the few sociologists to have recognized the significance of the spatiality of
social life was Simmel. His *Sociology* contained a remarkable chapter on 'Space
and the Spatial Structures of Society', and he had previously claimed that one
of the distinguishing features of modernity was the way in which its webs of
social interaction were spun out of fleeting and fragmentary threads.

> On every day, at every hour, such threads are spun, are allowed to fall, are taken
> up again, replaced by others, intertwined with others. Here lie the interactions
> ... between the atoms of society which bear the whole tenacity and elasticity, the
> whole colourfulness and unity of this so evident and so puzzling life of society ...
> We can no longer take to be unimportant consideration of the delicate, invisible
> threads that are woven between one person and another if we wish to grasp the
> web of society according to its productive, form-giving forces.

Again, the parallel with Hägerstrand is close, but Simmel thought these
interactions were 'only accessible through [a] psychological microscopy'
which would recover the 'inner life' of human beings. Space was simply 'a form
which had to be filled with social and psychological energies'.[26]

In contrast to these two writers, Hägerstrand claims that time–space relations enter directly into the constitution of social life and that it is possible to
provide a conceptual grid which shows how this comes about. He argues that
social practices of every sort depend upon a series of time–space discriminations within and between their various projects. When a project is moved
forward, suspended or abandoned, all of these things happen within a web of
competing claims to paths, stations and domains. These time–space dependencies are the means through which social life is given a precarious coherence
– what Hägerstrand sometimes calls a 'grain structure' – because, so he says,
social practices are inescapably *collateral processes* which take place within
bounded regions: that is to say, they are processes which cannot 'unfold freely'
but which 'have to accommodate themselves under the pressures and opportunities which follow from their common existence in terrestrial space and
time'. This makes it of the utmost importance to identify the time–space
modalities which enable projects to hook up in particular configurations.
Hägerstrand refers to these as capability, coupling and steering 'constraints',
but since he clearly recognizes that they are enabling as well as constraining –

[25] T. Parsons, *The Structure of Social Action* (New York: McGraw-Hill, 1937).
[26] These passages are cited in D. Frisby, *Fragments of Modernity: Theories of Modernity in the Work of
Simmel, Kracauer and Benjamin* (Cambridge: Polity Press, 1985), pp. 55–6; D. Frisby, *Georg Simmel*
(London: Tavistock, 1984), pp. 126–31. Hägerstrand's early studies of innovation diffusion
were indebted to social psychology too, and his concept of the information field owed much to
Moreno's vision of the bonds between 'social atoms': see Gregory, 'Suspended Animation'.

something which Giddens consistently misunderstands – I prefer to call them modalities. They forge a vital conceptual link between the social and the spatial.[27]

Many of them have concrete form, of course, as institutional projects chronically enclose individual paths to reproduce the time–space routines which give social life its characteristic shape. But these routines are not, as Giddens seems to think, the 'starting-point' of time-geography. Although Hägerstrand acknowledges the importance of routinized and repetitive conduct – projects cut from 'standard patterns' – he is equally interested in 'crashed projects' (which create holes in the web) and innovations (which knit the fabric into a different design). 'Intentions have a high death rate', he concedes, and 'surviving ones have to adjust'; but the web model enables him to trace all of these morphologies of strategic intentionality – I can think of no better description – as they evolve in time and space. It is this, as much as anything else, which makes time-geography a situational ecology. Hägerstrand is concerned to tease out the time–space dependencies as they vary across the web as a whole and to track the competition between the four-dimensional shapes of different projects as they encounter one another in time and space.[28] If this makes time-geography a much more inclusive model than Giddens allows, however, it is still primarily an interaction model, and its principal objective remains what Habermas calls instrumental action rather than communicative action. In saying this, I do not mean to imply that the web model is a *danse macabre* of disembodied movements; whatever reservations one might entertain about Hägerstrand's first formulations, in his later writings he has, I think, done much to meet that particular objection. But his landscapes are not – or not yet – *symbolic* landscapes. In particular, the competition between projects which he envisages is essentially a struggle for space rather than a struggle over (the meaning of) *place*.[29]

Routines and reproduction

Let me now connect these comments to Giddens's discussion of the relations between routinization and reproduction. His argument can be reduced to four basic propositions.

---

[27] T. Hägerstrand, 'What about People in Regional Science?', *Papers of the Regional Science Association*, 24 (1970), 7–21; T. Hägerstrand, 'The Domain of Human Geography', in R. J. Chorley (ed.), *Directions in Geography* (London: Methuen, 1973), pp. 67–87. Cf. *CS*, p. 117.

[28] T. Hägerstrand, 'Time-geography: Focus on the Corporeality of Man, Society and Environment', in S. Aida (ed.), *The Science and Praxis of Complexity* (Tokyo: United Nations, 1985), pp. 193–216; see also T. Hägerstrand, 'On Socio-technical Ecology and the Study of Innovations', *Ethnologia Europaea*, 7 (1974), 17–34.

[29] Cf. A. Pred, 'Structuration and Place: On the Becoming of Sense of Place and Structure of Feeling', *Journal for the Theory of Social Behavior*, 13 (1983), 157–86. It is only fair to add that some of Hägerstrand's later essays display a greater sensitivity to these questions; see in particular the evocative descriptions in T. Hägerstrand, 'Diorama, Path and Project', *Tijdschrift voor Economische en Sociale Geografie*, 73 (1982), 323–39.

(1)   Routinization is deeply implicated in the sustentation of 'ontological security'. It is, in effect, a mode of self-reassurance brought about by the agent's involvement in the conduct of everyday life. Giddens argues that 'the familiar is reassuring' in a quite basic sense, and that time–space routines are therefore of vital importance in maintaining a stable psychological existence. They are directly related to the so-called 'stratification' of the agent, since they are, for the most part, cognitively established rather than directly motivated. They rely on tacit rather than discursive knowledge – on *practical consciousness* – and as such 'drive a wedge between the potentially explosive content of the unconscious and the reflexive monitoring of action which agents display'.[30]

(2)   Time–space routines also thread out into wider skeins of social reproduction: they are integral to 'the institutions of society which *are* such only through their continued reproduction'. Giddens therefore treats time–space routines as the 'material grounding' of the *recursiveness* of social life, and it is for precisely this reason that several writers have commended Hägerstrand's graphical displays as a means of demonstrating the 'material logic' of structuration: what Pred calls the 'cement' binding individuals and institutions into a coherent matrix.[31]

(3)   The dislocation of routines – and, by implication, of social reproduction – depends upon *critical situations* in which 'the established modes of accustomed daily life are drastically undermined or shattered'. Some of these are more or less predictable, especially where they intersect with the life-cycle, but others are 'radical disjunctures of an unpredictable kind which affect substantial numbers of individuals, situations that threaten or destroy the certitudes of institutionalized routines'.[32]

(4)   Critical situations are of immense importance in modern capitalist societies, Giddens asserts, where a series of time–space transformations has fundamentally undermined trust in 'the continuity of both the object world and . . . the fabric of social activity'. In the maelstrom of modernity – Marx's world (and Simmel's) where 'all that is solid melts into air' – tradition has lost its normative force: its ability to authorize social practices. In consequence, many time–space routines have become purely habitual, 'stripped of both a *moral* and a *rational* content' for those who participate in them, and their 'emptiness' testifies to what Giddens regards as 'the fragility of ontological security in the wasteland of everyday life'.[33]

Using a parallel notation, I want to make four overlapping observations about these claims.

---

[30] *CS*, pp. xxiii, 60.
[31] *CS*, p. 60; A. Pred, 'Social Reproduction and the Time-geography of Everyday Life', *Geogr. Annaler*, 63B (1981), 5–22.
[32] *CPST*, pp. 123–4, 219–20; *CS*, pp. 60–1.   [33] *CCHM*, pp. 11–13, 153–5, 193–4.

(1)   Giddens is surely right to recognize the importance of routinization and to connect it to practical consciousness. But such an emphasis runs the double risk of minimizing strategic intentionality and muting discursive consciousness. There are three areas in which these dangers are particularly acute.

(a)   The reproduction of capitalism has always depended, in some substantial degree, upon technical change, and Giddens is not unaware of its extraordinary importance in the late twentieth century. But his only detailed discussions concern the time–space convergence brought about by changes in media of communication and transportation and the geopolitics of the world military order sustained by changes in the means of waging industrialized war. The significance of these developments can hardly be minimized; but Giddens says remarkably little about technical change outside these spheres (though often closely connected to them) and, in particular, next to nothing about the diffusion of innovations in time and space. I have reservations about Hägerstrand's early discussions of these matters – and his distance-bound models obviously have a limited bearing on spatial diffusion in nominally 'advanced' societies – but I am puzzled at Giddens's reluctance to explore the themes which loom so large in his later writings. As Hägerstrand shows with an exemplary clarity, the spread of innovations *outside* the spheres of communication and transportation not only depends upon the structure of the time–space web: it can radically transform the web by restructuring capability, coupling and steering modalities and thereby enabling (on occasion requiring) projects to hook up in new configurations. Studies of innovation diffusion are not confined to Hägerstrand's contributions, however, and Massey has opened up a markedly different perspective. She links technical change to a cluster of industrial strategies shaped by the dynamics of capital accumulation. Changing divisions of labour over space are thus imbricated in successive rounds of investment over time. Objections can be registered against Massey's model too, of course, but – like Hägerstrand – she accentuates the way in which projects are embedded ('sedimented') in time and space. Production systems are woven into a 'structured coherence' at local and regional scales and bound in to a wider mesh of dependencies at national and international scales: the incorporation of a local area into the web is likely to produce both local and extra-local dislocations. This is not the place to adjudicate between these approaches, and there are in any case several connections that could fruitfully be established between them. But a sustained theorization of spatial structures of technical change would, I think, convert Giddens's scattered accounts of the uneven development of capitalism from the perfunctory to the persuasive. This is not an argument for a technological determinism, let me say, and neither is it to suggest that the consequences of technical change are fully enclosed by the contours of discursive consciousness. But any account of the modern world which fails to explicate the novel, non-routine projects which course through its turbulent landscapes of production is surely materially incomplete.[34]

(b)   The diffusion of innovations cannot be reduced to the circulation of information, as Hägerstrand once supposed, but the discursive mobilization of information is of strategic importance in the rise of the so-called 'service class'. Lash and Urry claim that its members have created 'a space for their own class formation' by appropriating – to a greater or a lesser extent – specific forms of discursive knowledge to themselves. This has involved them in the expansion of higher education, professional institutions and the like and in the deployment of arguments 'justifying their position in terms of superior education and expertise'. Although the rise of the service class is related to the growth of the knowledge–education–science nexus, it cannot be reduced to some transcendent 'logic of technology', and Lash and Urry accentuate both the *contingency* of these developments and their *complexity* over space. Indeed, Lyotard identifies the commodification of knowledge as a vital moment in the production of a 'post-modern' network of social relations that is supposedly more complex, more heterogeneous and more mobile than ever before. Whatever one makes of Lyotard's specific theses (and I am unhappy about many of them) the general importance of discursive knowledge in accounting for class structuration in the late twentieth century is, I think, unimpeachable. Giddens would presumably not dissent from many of these claims: in his early writings he provided a discussion of 'the new middle class' which intersects with them. But they remain undeveloped in his subsequent formulation of structuration theory, where discursive knowledge is discussed in most detail in relation to the surveillance capabilities of the nation-state. These are of tremendous significance, of course, and many fractions of the service class are deeply involved in the state apparatus. But contemporary class structuration requires (among other things) a more nuanced account of the changing geographies of discursive knowledge than Giddens currently provides.[35]

(c)   Discursive knowledge is confined neither to the state nor to the service class, and the formation of social movements depends upon the ability of their members (whatever their social location) to make sense of what is happening around them and to formulate their views discursively. I am not starry-eyed about this: discursive penetration is both limited and differentiated, and a

[34] See, for example, D. Massey, *Spatial Divisions of Labour: Social Structures and the Geography of Production* (London: Macmillan, 1984); A. J. Scott and M. Storper (eds.), *Production, Work, Territory: The Geographical Anatomy of Industrial Capitalism* (Boston: Allen & Unwin, 1986).

[35] Arguments about the relations between the 'service class' and discursive knowledge are contained in S. Lash and J. Urry, *The End of Organized Capitalism* (Cambridge: Polity Press, 1987); their presentation derives from (and considerably simplifies) the theses proposed in N. Abercrombie and J. Urry, *Capital, Labour and the Middle Classes* (London: Allen & Unwin, 1983). Lyotard's own claims will be found in J.-F. Lyotard, *The Postmodern Condition: A Report on Knowledge* (Minneapolis: University of Minnesota Press, 1984). For the intersections between these arguments and Giddens's early attempts to rethink the theory of class, see his *The Class Structure of the Advanced Societies* (London: Hutchinson, 1973; 2nd edition, 1981).

major task of structuration theory must be to map what Thrift calls, more generally, 'geographies of social knowing and unknowing'. But a critical theory with practical intent cannot neglect the ways in which, as Bourdieu puts it, the undiscussed is brought into discussion. I return to this below. In his later writings, however, Giddens does acknowledge the basic importance of social movements – and in particular their orientation to 'novel projects' – but his account of them is, I think, profoundly unsatisfactory. It renders them to all intents and purposes placeless. In contradistinction to organizations, so Giddens claims, social movements do not 'characteristically operate within fixed locales'. I am not sure what this is supposed to mean (or what consequences follow from it). It appears to limit the concept of locale to an architecture of power – to the built forms of palaces, temples, barracks, offices and so on – yet elsewhere Giddens categorically (and I think correctly) rejects any such restriction. Social movements evidently have their own historical geographies, and many of them have a coherent territorial identity which is not incidental to their discursive and strategic evolution. This is true not only of obvious 'struggles for place', like the urban social movements which Castells and others have described in such detail, but also of (say) traditional labour movements which are often closely identified with particular regions. The rise and fall of Luddism and Chartism in the nineteenth century and trade unionism in the twentieth century provide clear examples of these tendencies.[36]

(2)   In insisting on the importance of strategic intentionality, I do not mean to imply that structuration theory is a model of a 'programmed society' in which routines mesh smoothly with social reproduction and time–space paths are spun over an endlessly recursive plain. Power may well be at its most intense 'when running silently through the repetition of institutionalized practices', as Giddens puts it, but structuration theory (unlike structural functionalism) turns on a vital distinction between the 'taken-for-granted' and the 'accepted-as-legitimate'. Just because actors are bound in to time–space routines, it does not automatically follow that they internalize the values of the social institutions which are reproduced through them. If this allows Giddens to claim that a theory of routine need not be a theory of social stability, however, it also requires him to show how the separations between the taken-for-granted and the accepted-as-legitimate can be widened in the course of established routines: and so far he has not done so. This is partly an empirical question, of course, but to accentuate the recursiveness of time–space routines without opening a conceptual space for de-routinization 'from

---

[36] N. Thrift, 'Flies and Germs: A Geography of Knowledge.' In D. Gregory and J. Urry (eds.), *Social Relations and Spatial Structures* (London: Macmillan, 1985), 366–403; *CS*, pp. 204–5; *NSV*, pp. 313–25; *STMS*, pp. 48–50. For a more general discussion of the importance of discursive consciousness, see M. Storper, 'The Spatial and Temporal Constitution of Social Action: A Critical Reading of Giddens', *Environment and Planning D: Society & Space*, 3 (1985), 407–24.

the inside' is, I think, to short-change the transformation model embedded within structuration theory.[37]

Anderson's account of colonial nationalism provides a particularly vivid example of what I have in mind. He argues that the colonial state was routinely experienced by both the native functionaries who filed behind its desks and the native children who filed into its classrooms as a 'looping flight' in time and space. Individual postings and promotions followed an 'established skein of journeys' which wound inwards and upwards towards the colonial capital (but no further), and these provided the territorial basis for what Anderson calls an 'imagined community' in which 'natives' would eventually come to see themselves as 'nationals'.[38] It would be possible to represent these journeys on one of Hägerstrand's diagrams, I suppose, but their interpretation would evidently require a greater sensitivity towards communicative action and the symbolic landscape than is ordinarily found in time-geography. Giddens provides his own account of nationalism, but he is primarily concerned with Europe where, so he claims, nationalism can be directly related to the disruption of ontological security.[39] The significance of Anderson's example is that it suggests precisely the opposite. The two cases are, of course, different, and it is not a matter of choosing between two competing explanations. But it is necessary to look beyond them to see how, in some circumstances, routines can become progressively disengaged from circuits of reproduction. To overlook this possibility is to imply that social life oscillates between stasis and spasm and that social change is a purely *discontinuous* process of sudden and spectacular transformation.

(3)   Even so, Giddens is right to predicate structuration theory on a 'discontinuist' conception of modern history – if that means on the overlapping series of changes which distinguishes the modern world from anything that preceded it. He thus pays some considerable attention to the time–space transformations that undermined the ontological security afforded by tradition: namely, the commodification of labour; the realignment of daily time–space paths around a sphere of work separate from and superordinate to the household; and the commodification of land as part of the 'created space' of modern urbanism.[40] But these transformations span, very roughly, the end of the sixteenth through to the beginning of the twentieth centuries. They have little immediate purchase on the distinctive features of social life at the end of the twentieth century. The dislocation of routines is now bound in to the emergence of regimes of 'flexible accumulation' and the installation of 'disorganized capitalism'. Neither of these is a neutral term, of course, and neither should be accepted without critical scrutiny. But it is not the absence of the

---

[37] *CCHM*, pp. 64–6.
[38] B. Anderson, *Imagined Communities: Reflections on the Origin and Spread of Nationalism* (London: Verso, 1983), pp. 105–11.
[39] *CCHM*, ch. 8; *NSV*, pp. 215–21.   [40] *CCHM*, pp. 152–4.

concepts that is at issue: the process of continuous transformation that they represent is barely registered in existing formulations of structuration theory. It is not only the temporal scope of Giddens's argument that is foreshortened in this way. These same perspectives reveal, for all their differences, the heightened significance of spatiality in the late twentieth century. Yet, as I have already indicated, Giddens's discussions of the uneven development of capitalism are, at best, gestural.[41]

Changes of this sort are usually wired to the explosion of critical situations by a concept of *crisis*. The term may be overloaded – and it is one which Giddens himself rarely uses – but it is nevertheless indispensable to any critical social theory. Habermas reverts to its original, medical meaning to suggest that crises are both 'objective' and 'subjective', both 'caused' and 'experienced', and Bourdieu claims that it is for exactly this reason that crises can 'bring the undiscussed into discussion' and so 'call the habitus into question'.[42] But Giddens (like Simmel?) is concerned largely with their inward 'subjective' side. Critical situations are sparked off by interruptions in circuits of social reproduction, but their wider implications are never properly illuminated. Their pathologies remain psychological rather than fully social, largely disconnected from Giddens's outline diagram of 'crisis tendencies', and the sense in which they may be 'moments of opportunity' is never satisfactorily elucidated.

That this is *conditional* requires some emphasis. One of the most persistent features of the uneven development of contemporary capitalism and its correlative geography of mass unemployment has been the intensification of competition between territorially defined groups for new rounds of investment and new jobs. As Hudson, Sadler and others have shown, the characteristic response to redundancies and plant closures has been to defend 'the right to work' and, effectively, to 'market' localities: to set one place or one region against another. Strategies of this sort present not so much a challenge to the legitimacy of the labour contract as an acceptance (however tactical) of the decisive and dominant rationality of capitalism.

> Accepting the competitive ethic of capitalism in this way as a legitimate terrain, and fighting on a territorially defined basis within it, rather than posing broader questions as to why restructuring is regarded as either necessary or justified given its extensive social costs, has the precise (albeit unintended) effect of reproducing the basic structural relations of capitalism.[43]

41 See, for example, *CPST*, pp. 226–8; *CS*, pp. 130–2.
42 J. Habermas, *Legitimation Crisis* (London: Heinemann, 1976), pp. 1–8; Habermas here draws a distinction between social integration and system integration, but in very different terms to those provided by Giddens. In his later writings, of course, Habermas talks instead of the connections between life-world and system: see D. Ingram, *Habermas and the Dialectic of Reason* (New Haven: Yale University Press, 1987). See also P. Bourdieu, *Outline of a Theory of Practice* (Cambridge: Cambridge University Press, 1977), pp. 168–9.
43 R. Hudson and D. Sadler, 'Contesting Closures in Western Europe's Old Industrial Regions: Defending Place or Betraying Class?', in Scott and Storper (eds.), *Production, Work, Territory*, pp. 172–93.

Indeed, Habermas has himself qualified his earlier theses about the salience of
legitimation crisis in advanced capitalism, and Harvey, Scott and others have
identified an increasing disparity between theoretical expectations which
seemed to have some purchase on events in the 1960s (like Habermas's) and
the changed material circumstances of capitalist societies in the 1980s.[44] All of
this may be so, and certainly anyone writing about advanced capitalism today
must take the rise of the New Right and the advance of neo-conservatism with
all possible seriousness. But none of this denies the existence of *multiple* and
competing possibilities for change within a crisis: rather, it requires an account
of their conditionality. This would be perfectly consistent with the protocols of
structuration theory, of course, and would not entail the provision of 'guarantees' of any kind.[45]

(4) In his later writings, Castells offers a glimpse into Giddens's 'wasteland
of everyday life' in terms which are broadly congruent with the foregoing
considerations. In the modern world, Castells claims, the twin revolutions in
communication systems and micro-electronics which, as I will show shortly,
are so important to time–space distanciation – to the articulation of the world
economy and the surveillance capabilities of the nation-state – have transformed places into 'flows and channels'.

> What tends to disappear is the meaning of places for people. Each place, each
> city, will receive its social meaning from its location in the hierarchy of a network
> whose control and rhythm will escape from each place and, even more, from the
> people in each place ... The new space of a world capitalist system ... is a space
> of variable geometry formed by locations hierarchically ordered in a continu-
> ously changing network of flows ... Space is dissolved into flows ... Life is
> transformed into abstraction, cities into shadows.[46]

This may be a caricature, but it is a recognizable one. Many writers are
unwilling to confine these pulsing transformations to modernity, I know, and
represent post-modernity as another 'political economy of social dislocation' –
a decadent trope of modernism – stretching social interaction into the vastness
of what Jameson calls 'hyperspace'. It has to be said, of course, that the

[44] For lucid accounts of Habermas's recent writings, see Ingram, *Habermas*; S. White, *The Recent
Writings of Jürgen Habermas: Reason, Justice and Modernity* (Cambridge: Cambridge University
Press, 1988). Harvey and Scott do not refer explicitly to Habermas's earlier work, but the
theory which they describe as being overtaken by events is, to all intents and purposes,
Habermas's model of legitimation crisis. They do not, however, register the development of
Habermas's views since then. See D. Harvey and A. Scott, 'The Practice of Human Geography:
Theory and Empirical Specificity in the Transition from Fordism to Flexible Accumulation', in
W. Macmillan (ed.), *Remodelling Geography* (Oxford: Basil Blackwell, in press).
[45] See S. Benhabib, *Critique, Norm and Utopia: A Study of the Foundations of Critical Theory* (New York:
Columbia University Press, 1986); J. O'Connor, *The Meaning of Crisis: A Theoretical Introduction*
(Oxford: Basil Blackwell, 1987).
[46] M. Castells, *The City and the Grassroots: A Cross-cultural Theory of Urban Social Movements* (London:
Edward Arnold, 1983), p. 314; M. Castells, 'High Technology, Economic Restructuring and
the Urban–regional Process in the United States', in M. Castells (ed.), *High Technology, Space
and Society* (Beverly Hills: Sage, 1985), pp. 11–40.

post-modern city, if one can call it such, is hardly stripped of symbolic content: its streets are overflowing with signs (though their authenticity may well be questionable).[47] Still, most commentators would, I think, agree on the critical importance of collective opposition to these deformations: whatever their origins, they are not uncontested. So, for example, Castells maps the rise of urban social movements which seek to defend autonomous local cultures and democratic local governments, and Ley heralds the precarious emergence of a 'post-modernism of resistance' which celebrates diversity and difference and seeks 'to restore meaning, rootedness and human proportions to place'. All of these campaigns are vulnerable to co-option and compromise, as I have already implied, and it would be foolish to pretend otherwise or, for that matter, to exaggerate their abilities to secure concessions or carry through significant changes. But Giddens's wasteland may yet be greened at the grassroots in ways which, as yet, literally have no *place* in structuration theory. Giddens himself substitutes 'locale' for 'place', but this is not an exchange of equivalents. 'Place', as Relph and others have shown with great sensitivity, usually connotes a depth of meaning, even belonging, which the instrumentalities of 'locale' are quite unable to convey.[48]

Time–space distanciation

The concept of time–space distanciation is closely connected to that of time–space routinization. It is clearly consistent with Giddens's generalized model of presence and absence, but it has a number of other thematic affinities which need to be spelled out.

Media of distanciation

Giddens offers few clues about the intellectual genealogy of time–space distanciation. It has its immediate origins, I think, in Ricoeur's discussion of the transformations through which writing 'distanciates' a text from speech (which he regarded as a paradigm for the interpretation of social action more generally). 'In living speech, the instance of discourse has the character of a fleeting event', Ricoeur observed, and is addressed to a specific, co-present audience. In writing, however, discourse is fixed and 'in escaping the momentary character of the event . . . escapes the limits of being face to face'. Giddens says (writes!) much the same.

---

[47] F. Jameson, 'Postmodernism or the Cultural Logic of Late Capitalism', *New Left Review*, 146 (1984), 53–92; M. Dear, 'Post-modernism and Planning', *Environment and Planning D: Society & Space*, 4 (1986), 367–84; D. Harvey, 'Flexible Accumulation through Urbanisation: Reflections on "Post-modernism" in the American City', *Antipode*, 19 (1987), 260–86.

[48] Castells, *The City*; D. Ley, 'Modernism, Post-modernism and the Struggle for Place', paper presented to the seminar series on 'The Power of Place', Syracuse University, 1986; M. Castells, 'Styles of the Times: Liberal and Neo-conservative Landscapes in Inner Vancouver, 1968–1986', *Journal of Historical Geography*, 13 (1987), 40–56; E. Relph, *Place and Placelessness* (London: Pion, 1976).

Whereas spoken discourse is by its very nature evanescent, its duration being limited to the circumstances of its production, texts assume a fixity that endures across time and space.

Unlike Ricoeur, however, Giddens draws attention to the spatiality of the transformation from oral to scribal and literate cultures. This was an uneven and jagged process, but Giddens is interested in its generic features and, in particular, in the ways in which social interaction was opened out in time and space by the invention of writing. Like Goody and others, he represents the development of writing as being of pivotal importance in the transition from cyclical to linear conceptions of temporality and claims that it was almost everywhere closely bound up with the formation of states and the extension of authoritative power in time and space. These tendencies reach their climax, so he suggests, in the generalized surveillance of the modern nation-state.[49]

But Giddens is clear that Ricoeur's textual model cannot provide a paradigm for social life in general and that social interaction entails more than communication. He therefore offers an account of other media of time–space distanciation: most notably money. Although his discussion is still linked to Ricoeur's theses, it is also sufficiently removed from them to provide the basis for a more satisfactory conception of power.

> The development and universalisation of money, Marx points out, in a definite way parallels the emergence of writing, since both trace out a progressive distanciation from the objects to which they 'refer'. Writing, one might argue, manifests such a distanciation in the movement from pictures to abstract marks that have an 'arbitrary' relation to the object-world. Money also begins as objects or products that have use-values which become implicated in exchange; but it progressively becomes detached from the use-value of its content ... Money becomes a commodity only because it represents or symbolises the exchange-value of all other commodities.

Again, Giddens is concerned to expose the spatiality of these transformations and, in particular, to draw attention to what Simmel called 'the power of money to bridge distances' and what Lukács described as 'the magical enlargement of the radius of human action by means of money'. The development of money is not, of course, coincident with the emergence of capitalism, but some of the most important features of the capitalist economy (and, in particular, the formation of a capitalist *space*-economy) can undoubtedly be connected to the cascades through which money is transformed into commodities and back into money again. It is the universalization of this process, Giddens declares, which is the cutting-edge of the commodification of everyday life. It enables an unprecedented extension of allocative power in

---

[49] P. Ricoeur, *Hermeneutics and the Human Sciences: Essays on Language, Action and Interpretation* (Cambridge: Cambridge University Press, 1981), 198–203; J. Goody, *The Logic of Writing and the Organization of Society* (Cambridge: Cambridge University Press, 1986); *NSV*, p. 42.

time and space and is, so he claims, 'the condition of emergence of capitalist society'.[50]

Even from this abbreviated presentation the two main limitations of Giddens's discussion should be obvious. First, space is theorized as a 'gap' to be overcome. This explains why Giddens draws upon Janelle's concept of time–space convergence, which closely parallels the concept of time–space distanciation: the constitution of ever wider systems of interaction and, ultimately, of inter-societal systems entails a progressive reduction in the friction of distance on human affairs. But conceiving of space in this way means that Giddens takes no account of what Harvey, Lefebvre and others call the 'production of space'. This is a complex notion, and Lefebvre gives it a wider meaning than Harvey ordinarily does. He includes not only the production of material spatial structures ('spatial praxis') – which has long been the central concern of Harvey's historico-geographical materialism – but also the production of 'representations of space' and 'spaces of representation'. These last two terms connote various symbolic and normative dimensions of spatial organization which are also occluded in Giddens's presentation.[51] Second, and closely connected to this, time–space distanciation is theorized in terms of the generation of power and the extension of structures of domination in time and space. This means that Giddens effectively brackets the structures of signification and legitimation which he otherwise insists are of co-equal importance in structuration. These symbolic and normative dimensions are not, of course, separable from the concrete installations of power, but neither are they merely mirrors of them. Conceptions of space – images, graphical representations – are not epiphenomenal: they enter fully into the time–space distanciation of social life.

Let me take these objections in turn.

Power and the production of space

In recent years several writers have insisted on the close conjunction between power and space, and I have no quarrel with the claim that authoritative and allocative resources are generalized media of time–space distanciation which interlace in different ways in different types of society (Figure 3). It may well be that their contours ought to be drawn more finely: that the distinctions between 'oral' and 'literate' cultures are far from clear cut and that what matters is the mix between the two; that writing is not the dramatic innovation it seems to be until its stabilization and mechanical reproduction through printing; and so on. But qualifications of this sort are hardly surprising – Giddens is not providing a detailed historical sociology – and they do nothing to diminish the importance of the concept of time–space distanciation itself.

---

[50] *CCHM*, pp. 116–17.
[51] D. Janelle, 'Spatial Reorganization: A Model and Concept', *Annals of the Association of American Geographers*, 59 (1969), 348–64; H. Lefebvre, *La Production de l'espace* (Paris: Anthropos, 1974); Harvey, 'Flexible Accumulation'.

Giddens clearly intends the concept to signal the *complexity* of societies: they are much less coherent than conventional social theory assumes, and time–space distanciation makes both their extension and their closure profoundly problematic. In practice, however, and as I now want to show, Giddens draws back from the implications of his own argument: so much so, in fact, that he risks over-totalizing social life.

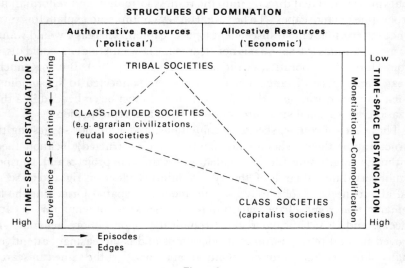

Figure 3

Giddens treats time–space distanciation as essentially progressive, entailing the gradual widening of systems of interaction. But in doing so he minimizes the volatility of these extensions. The landscapes of contemporary capitalism provide some of the most vivid examples. They are riven by a deep-seated tension between polarization in place and dispersal over space. On the one side, constellations of productive activity are pulled into a 'structured coherence' at local and regional scales, while on the other side these same territorial complexes are dissolved away through the restructuring and resynthesis of labour processes. The balance between them – the geography of capital accumulation – is drawn through time–space distanciation as a *discontinuous* process of the production of space.

It is here, I think, that Harvey's account of *The Limits to Capital* – whatever other reservations one might have about it – has much to offer. Within a capitalist space-economy Harvey argues, like Giddens, that space appears in the first instance as a barrier to the circulation of capital: as a 'gap' to be overcome. But it can only be transcended, he continues, through the production of fixed and immobile spatial configurations. In the second instance, therefore, we encounter the contradiction: spatial organisation is necessary to overcome space.

This is an elementary theorem, but its implications are far-reaching because they help to explain why regional configurations are chronically unstable. Harvey claims that there is a fundamental tension within the geography of capital accumulation 'between fixity and motion, between the rising power to overcome space and the immobile structures required for such a purpose', and that this is translated directly into 'the restless formation and re-formation of geographical landscapes'. To be sure, Harvey continues to explain this turbulence in terms of some transcendent logic of capital, whereas I would want to be more cautious (although it is not clear to me how far Giddens would dissent from Harvey's elaboration of the labour theory of value). But this much *is* clear: time–space distanciation is now closely connected to spasmodic sequences of valorization and devalorization and must be embedded in a theorization of locational structures of production and reproduction.[52]

These are, of course, skeletal formulations, and I am not suggesting that structuration theory should incorporate a (reconstructed) location theory within its programme: they are evidently very different projects and, I suspect, entail very different kinds of 'theory'. Certainly, Giddens is right to be sceptical about the value of purely abstract models of spatial form. But the fact remains that some of the most interesting work in contemporary location theory, and in urban and regional political economy more generally, has moved beyond purely formal considerations and is increasingly attentive to many of the central claims of structuration theory. Yet the same can scarcely be said in reverse. For the most part, structuration theory has been directed towards the elucidation of systems of interaction, and Giddens has displayed little interest in location. He constantly talks about locales as settings whose properties are *drawn upon* by actors and emphasizes their *substantially given* character. This is how actors routinely encounter locales in the conduct of everyday life, no doubt, but any genuinely critical theory must surely go beyond these mundanities to show how particular places and spaces are *produced*. It would be peculiarly ironic if a programme so concerned to transcend the dualism between human agency and social structure that skewered classical social theory should tacitly incorporate the dualism between 'interaction' and 'location' that confounded so many early contributions to classical spatial theory.

That said, Giddens does accord a central place to 'dominant locales'. These are physically demarcated settings for interaction, 'power containers' where allocative and authoritative resources are stored, and which generate

---

[52] D. Harvey, *The Urbanization of Capital* (Oxford: Basil Blackwell, 1985); D. Harvey, 'The Geopolitics of Capitalism', in Derek Gregory and John Urry (eds.), *Social Relations and Spatial Structures* (London: Macmillan, 1985), pp. 128–63; Scott and Storper (eds.), *Production, Work, Territory*.

the major structural principles implicated in the constitution of different types of society. But Giddens is more interested in the generic change from the city as the dominant locale of class-divided societies to the nation-state as the dominant locale of modern class societies. This singular focus means that he fails to clarify the *hierarchy* of locales involved in these societies (and beyond them): the ways in which, in Hägerstrand's terms, domains nest within one another, overlap and confound one another, in a changing web of interactions. In placing so much emphasis on the central pinnacles of power – in providing, in effect, what Foucault once called a 'descending' analysis of power – Giddens ignores the importance of *differential* distanciation. Mann's careful discrimination between the various 'sources of social power' provides an instructive contrast. Like Giddens, he refuses to treat society as an unproblematic, unitary totality and instead prefers to think in terms of 'multiple, overlapping and intersecting socio-spatial networks of power'. Unlike Giddens, however, he refuses to box these networks into a portmanteau 'power container':

> State, culture and economy are all important structuring networks; they almost never coincide.

In other words, their different geographies can rarely be reduced to a single spatial structure. Yet Giddens has no hesitation in declaring that 'modern "societies" are nation-states' and that 'understood as a bounded entity, [modern] "society" refers to the nation-state'.[53]

Conceptions of space

I think it fair to say that Giddens pays much more attention to changing conceptions of time and temporality than he does to changing conceptions of space and spatiality. Conceptions of time enter directly into the constitution of societies; but so too do conceptions of space. They too are *media* of time–space distanciation.

The production of printed maps – to take only the most obvious example – was a pivotal moment in the passage to modernity. If by the early seventeenth century, as Eisenstein suggests, 'navigators and explorers *could be seen* to be moving in a different direction', then the burden of the phrase falls exactly where I have marked it. The geographical imagination was enlarged and enhanced by the codification of these astonishing discoveries in spatial form, and a revitalized history of cartography is now beginning to reveal the ways in which these new world pictures were intrinsically politico-economic visions which helped shape the constitution of the modern world system and the consolidation of nation-states. 'Pictures of Europe's political geography became a familiar sight not just to those who administered governments and

---

[53] *NSV*, pp. 1, 13–17, 22; M. Mann, *The Sources of Social Power*, vol. 1, *A History of Power from the Beginning to A.D. 1760* (Cambridge: Cambridge University Press, 1986), ch. 1.

dominated economic life', Mukerji remarks, 'but also to those subject to them.'[54]

But maps are ever-vulnerable to competing interpretations. Saxton's county maps of Elizabethan England were designed to convey the image of a bureaucratic and centralized state, and yet the county gentry had little difficulty in converting them into the mirror image of an insistent regionalism in which the claims of the county community were reflected with a special clarity. Even so, these paper landscapes represented the administrative apparatus of the state with an apparently indelible authority, revealing the steady encroachment of surveillance into still more spheres of social life, and in this sense, Harley reminds us, 'as a regulator of human affairs', 'the map is rather like a clock'. Unlike the clock, however, the map is not a mechanism. It is, in the fullest of senses, a discourse, and one which articulates that abstracted conception of space which Sack and others see as characteristic of both class-divided and class societies. Indeed, many of these maps concerned representations of property rights, and from the sixteenth century they became vital instruments in that progressive commodification of space which Giddens portrays as focal to the emergence and expansion of European capitalism. It may be an exaggeration to believe, with one historian of geography, that 'la carte possède un pouvoir sensiblement plus fort que l'écrit', but there can be little doubt that the graphical representation of space was immensely important in its own right.[55]

If the critical reading of maps poses problems which cannot be directly assimilated to the semiotics of written texts, they cannot be altogether separated from them. Cartographic conventions, for all their seeming 'naturalness', were part of a wider cultural universe whose deconstruction requires an interrogation of multiple, intersecting and overlapping discourses. As Cosgrove has shown, there were numerous attempts in sixteenth- and seventeenth-century Europe, across the whole field of the visual arts, to clarify 'a

---

[54] E. L. Eisenstein, *The Printing Press as an Agent of Change: Communications and Cultural Transformations in Early-modern Europe* (Cambridge: Cambridge University Press, 1979), p. 193; C. Mukerji, *From Graven Images: Patterns of Modern Materialism* (New York: Columbia University Press, 1983), p. 128; C. Mukerji, 'Visual Language in Science and the Exercise of Power: The Case of Cartography in Early Modern Europe', *Studies in Visual Communication*, 10(3) (1984), 30–45.

[55] R. D. Sack, *Conceptions of Space in Social Thought: A Geographic Perspective* (London: Macmillan, 1980); R. Helgerson, 'The Land Speaks: Cartography, Chorography and Subversion in Renaissance England', *Representations*, 16 (1986), 50–85; J. B. Harley, 'Maps, Knowledge and Power', in D. Cosgrove and S. Daniels (eds.), *The Iconography of Landscape: Essays on the Symbolic Representation, Design and Use of Past Environments* (Cambridge: Cambridge University Press, 1988), pp. 277–312. Harley treats the map as 'pre-eminently a language of power', but insists that this derives as much from 'its representational force as a symbol as through its overt representations'. In some measure following Foucault, he therefore draws attention to 'the "hidden rules" of cartographic discourse whose contours can be traced in the subliminal geometries, the silences and the representational hierarchies of maps'. For a much fuller treatment, see his *The Map as Ideology: Knowledge and Power in the History of Cartography* (London: Routledge, forthcoming). I am indebted to Professor Harley for allowing me to read a preliminary version of his argument.

new conception of space as a coherent visual structure into which the actions of human life could be inserted in a controlled and orderly fashion'. Cosgrove claims that these experiments were not simply framed by capitalism: they were part of its dynamic. Their conventions, incorporated in landscape painting and in the (symbolic) landscape itself, enunciated and endorsed the alienation and objectification which were hall-marks of the new social order, and their entry into commodity markets through patronage, commission and sale exported the abstracted and distanciated conceptions of space which they embodied.[56]

All of this may be granted; my comments can be connected to the episodes which Giddens singles out without in any way compromising his formulation of structuration theory. But the previous paragraphs all relate to the *knowledge-ability* of human agents, and in seeking to theorize time–space distanciation without making these connections explicit Giddens risks obscuring the modalities through which power enters into the constitution of human subjects. These are, of course, Foucauldian concerns, but Giddens misreads (or at any rate misrepresents) them. While he evidently does not conceive of the human subject as somehow 'pre-formed', as Callinicos seems to think,[57] Giddens undoubtedly offers an account of the constitution of human subjects which is, at bottom, a-historical. Giddens treats subjectivity in strictly developmental terms, drawing on the ideas of Erikson, Freud, Lacan and others to establish the transformation of the body into an instrument of acting-in-the-world, and subsequently using Goffman, Hägerstrand and others to emphasize the significance of time–space routinization for sustaining the stratification of personality. In doing so, however, he fails to draw attention to the *different* ways in which human subjects are constituted in *different* types of society. This cannot be achieved, I think, by focusing on time–space routinization alone: as I now want to show, a project of this kind is strategically incomplete without a conjoint analysis of time–space distanciation.

Time–space distanciation and the constitution of human subjects

In fact, the consequences of stretching social relations across time and space for the constitution of human subjects can be discerned in each of the episodes which Giddens identifies. While it would be wrong to privilege the spoken over the written word as somehow more real and more personal, as what Hirst and Woolley call 'the true evocation of the speaking subject' – since it is precisely this notion of trans-historical authenticity which is being contested – it seems likely that the invention of writing marked the inauguration of new concepts of human being, and that the invention of printing provided the basis for the development of still other conceptions of personal identity and, in particular,

[56] D. Cosgrove, *Social Formation and Symbolic Landscape* (London: Croom Helm, 1984); D. Cosgrove, 'Prospect, Perspective and the Evolution of the Landscape Idea', *Transactions of the Institute of British Geographers*, New Series, 1 (1985), 45–62.

[57] A. Callinicos, 'Anthony Giddens: A Contemporary Critique', *Theory & Society*, 14 (1985), 133–66.

of the status of 'person-as-proprietor'. Indeed, Ong claims that typography enforced a doubly spatial coding, fixing words in space and fragmenting the oral world into 'privately claimed freeholdings'.[58] The systematic collation of information about individuals lowered the threshold of description even further. As Foucault remarks,

> For a long time ordinary individuality – the everyday individuality of everybody – remained below the threshold of description. To be looked at, observed, described in detail, followed from day to day by an uninterrupted writing, was a privilege ... The disciplinary methods reversed this relation, lowered the threshold of describable individuality and made of this description a means of control and a method of domination ...

Foucault shows in some considerable detail how this depended on a spatial analytics in which 'each individual has [their] own place, and each place its individual'.[59] But the introduction of electronic media, which has dramatically refined these systems of surveillance, has also, more generally and less formally, blurred what Meyrowitz calls the 'situational geography' of everyday life. Electronic media have overridden the boundaries and definitions of situations supported by physical settings, Meyrowitz claims, and in consequence conceptions of the self and of inter-personal relations are being radically revised: so much so, indeed, that Lash and Urry connect these developments to a post-modern 'decentring of identity' symptomatic of the 'disorganization' of contemporary capitalism.[60]

Monetization and commodification have had equally powerful effects within the sphere of 'organized' capitalism. On the one hand, as Simmel noted, these processes became embedded in

> the extension of means of transport which ... progressed from the infrequency of the mailcoach to the almost uninterrupted connections between the most important places and to the telegraph and telephone which [made] communication possible at any time ...

This declining distance in 'external' relationships was counterpointed by a 'growing distance in genuine inner relationships'. 'The most remote [came] closer at the price of increasing the distance to what was originally nearer', Simmel wrote, so that 'an inner barrier develop[ed] between people' and 'penetrate[d] even more deeply into the individual human subject'. On the other hand, therefore, Simmel observed how the 'enlargement' of the money economy

> places us at a distance from the substance of things; they speak to us 'as from afar'; reality is touched not with direct confidence but with fingertips that are immediately withdrawn.

[58] P. Hirst and J. Woolley, *Social Relations and Human Attributes* (London: Tavistock, 1982); W. J. Ong, *Orality and Literacy: The Technologizing of the Word* (London: Methuen, 1982).

[59] Foucault, *Discipline and Punish*, p. 191.

[60] J. Meyrowitz, *No Sense of Place: The Impact of Electronic Media on Social Behavior* (New York: Oxford University Press, 1985); Lash and Urry, *The End of Organized Capitalism*, pp. 296–300.

Here, surely, are the clearest intimations of Castells's cities 'transformed into shadows' (and, of course, Simmel had much to say about social life in the modern metropolis too).[61]

All of these examples could be qualified in various ways; I have drawn them from diverse and by no means unassailable theoretical traditions. But even as they stand they suggest that a purely abstract account of human subjectivity is inadequate for any critical theory with practical intent. For, as Callinicos argues, such an account must necessarily fail to clarify the *different* 'modalities of resistance' – the spaces for collective human agency – in *different* types of society. Giddens has so far not shown how the transformative capacities of human beings vary according to the specific circumstances in which they find themselves *and through which they are constituted as knowledgeable and capable human subjects*. His preoccupation with an abstract account of human subjectivity, Callinicos concludes, thus 'prevents him from following through the consequences of his own insight into the way in which social structures enable as well as constrain'.[62]

Conclusion

Let me now draw the threads together. I should say at once that I have learned a great deal from Giddens's writings. If I am sceptical about some of the claims that have been made about structuration theory – by advocates as much as by critics – that does not mean that I am in any sense dismissive of its importance. Gaps remain, of course, as they do in any worthwhile research programme, and I have tried to mark some of them. But these absences do not, of themselves, crash the programme. They help to provide its momentum.

Even so, doubts remain. My fear is that Giddens makes social life seem more coherent than it is by failing to realize the full implications of the incorporation of time–space relations into structuration theory. But that is to say things too quickly (and, perhaps, to make too many concessions to the currents of post-modernism).[63] In my discussion of time–space routinization, I showed that routines need not feed smoothly into social reproduction and that Giddens's model *could* be made to yield all sorts of transformations. In practice, however, many of them remain undeveloped, and it is easy to see why structuration theory is sometimes mistaken for a reproduction model in which power freezes routines in place. The same could be said, in a rather different way, of Giddens's account of time–space distanciation. The stretching of social

[61] G. Simmel, *The Philosophy of Money* (London: Routledge, 1978).
[62] Callinicos, 'Anthony Giddens'; Callinicos offers a more detailed discussion in his *Making History: Agency, Structure and Change in Social Theory* (Cambridge: Polity Press, 1987). See also M. Carrithers, S. Collins and S. Lukes (eds.), *The Category of the Person: Anthropology, Philosophy, History* (Cambridge: Cambridge University Press, 1985).
[63] D. Gregory, 'Postmodernism and the Politics of Social Theory', *Environment and Planning D: Society & Space*, 5 (1987), 245–8.

life over time and space implies, in Mann's splendid phrase, that 'societies are much *messier* than our theories of them':[64] and yet all too often Giddens over-systematizes these extensions and boxes them into discrete power-containers. What this points towards, I think, is the need for a series of meso-level concepts which are capable of linking Giddens's more abstract propositions about time and space to more detailed investigations of the specificities of history and geography.

[64] Mann, *The Sources of Social Power*, p. 4.

10
Space, urbanism and the created environment

PETER SAUNDERS

In this chapter I consider the significance which Giddens attributes to space in the organization of social life. The first part consists of a relatively detailed exposition of Giddens's treatment of the concepts of space, the city, urbanism and the created environment. These concepts are familiar to those working in areas such as urban sociology and human geography, but the significance of Giddens's analysis of them is that he seeks to place them at the heart of sociology as a whole. The first part of this chapter therefore tries to clarify why he believes these concepts are so crucial. I then follow this exposition in the second part with a critical evaluation, by means of which I conclude that his work does not establish the case for the centrality of spatial concepts to sociological theory.

Space and urbanism in Giddens's social theory

Giddens's concern with spatial organization as in some way significant as a factor entering into social organization begins with his analysis of class relations in *The Class Structure of the Advanced Societies*.[1] In that work he addressed the question of how variations in people's market situations came to form the basis of distinct social groupings, and hence of how social classes came to be 'structured'. He suggested that class structuration was accomplished in two ways – first through a process of 'mediate structuration', in which different groups sought to close off entry to others, and second, through a process of 'proximate structuration', in which social differences were reaffirmed by maintaining physical and social separateness.

According to Giddens, the principal factors entailed in the process of proximate structuration were the division of labour and authority hierarchies within work organizations, and residential segregation outside of work in the organization of consumption. The fact that different classes tended to live in different areas and neighbourhoods was, in his view, of crucial significance for the development of class awareness and consciousness, especially among the

---

[1] The concepts of mediate and proximate structuration are discussed in ch. 6 of *CSAS*.

215

working class, for whom 'the influence of neighbourhood and regional segregation has been fundamental'.[2] But having made this point (which had, of course, been made many times before, not least by Marx and Engels,[3]) he developed the insight no further. In this early work, in other words, space was treated simply as a factor or variable to be taken into account along with other factors or variables in the analysis of how specific forms of consciousness may be enabled or shaped by different types of social contexts.

It was in *New Rules of Sociological Method* that Giddens first explicitly began to outline his general theory of structuration, and it is here that we find introduced many of the key concerns and concepts – the concern with social reproduction, the assertion of a 'duality of structure', the definition of structure as involving rules and resources – which still form the building-blocks of his theoretical work today. What is striking about this book, however, is the absence of any particular concern with space as in any way crucial to the process of social reproduction which he is attempting to theorize. Thus, in the third chapter, where he explicitly discusses the problem of reproduction, we find only passing references to what he sees as the rather 'obvious' point that the situated context of interaction entails a spatial as well as temporal dimension. Similarly, in the concluding chapter, where he distils his 'new rules' (which represent the basic elements of his theory of structuration), there are a couple of references to the 'historically located' context of action, but no reference is made to the significance of spatial location.

This relative neglect of space in the early formulations of the theory of structuration is significant for three reasons. First, it is apparent that Giddens did not at that time feel compelled by the logic of his analysis to address the problem of space as anything other than a relatively minor aspect of the overall context of action. Second, and related to this, he was even in his early work inevitably sensitized to the importance of time in the process of reproduction. A theoretical concern with temporality, in other words, was from the outset inherent to his project in a way that was not true of space. The concern with space emerged much later as a logical corollary to the concern with time rather than as a necessary feature of the concern with structuration. In my view it remains the case, even in his latest works, that the treatment of space seems almost gratuitous, an appendage to the theory rather than an essential component of it (notwithstanding Giddens's own repeated protestations to the contrary). Third, and most significantly, this neglect of space in the early work is important for what he says in his later writings about the tendency of sociology *as a whole* to ignore the spatial aspect of action. I shall suggest later in this chapter that *empirical* sociology has not generally been blind to spatial

---

[2] Ibid., p. 199.

[3] See especially: Frederick Engels, *The Condition of the Working Class in England* (St Albans: Panther Books, 1969).

variations. Rather, social *theory* has tended to ignore the question of space, as Giddens himself did until quite recently, but having 'discovered' the significance of spatial location in social life, Giddens now accuses the whole of sociology of being space-blind, and in the process risks exaggerating the importance of place to such an extent that his work is likely to encourage the re-emergence of a spatial fetishism from which empirical investigation has only just made good its escape.

Giddens's concern with space as a central aspect of the theory of structuration dates from 1979, when he published *Central Problems in Social Theory*.[4] He starts by taking sociology to task for treating space merely as a backdrop against which social action unfolds:

> Most forms of social theory have failed to take seriously enough *not only the temporality of social conduct but also its spatial attributes*. At first sight, nothing seems more banal and uninstructive than to assert that social activity occurs in time and in space. But neither time nor space have been incorporated into the centre of social theory; rather, they are ordinarily treated more as 'environments' in which social conduct is enacted.[5]

Against this view of space as a passive environment, Giddens then argues that space forms part of the 'setting' of interaction. A setting, he tells us, 'is not just a spatial parameter, and physical environment, in which interaction "occurs": it is these elements mobilised as part of the interaction'.[6] He illustrates the point by returning to his earlier concern with class structuration, for spatial separation is held to be a 'major feature' of class differentiation. The geographical separation of the classes (which is in part an intended effect of human action but is also partly an unintended consequence of an ecological process of social sifting and sorting) helps foster and reproduce regionalized class cultures. This means that different classes come to act in different 'locales' which entail different situational constraints and possibilities which are then embedded in individuals' practical knowledge and actions. In short, it is impossible to begin to explain how and why the working class, or presumably any other class, acts as it does in particular situations without understanding how those situations are in part constituted in terms of peculiarities of space and time.

The significance of this argument, as I see it, is that we cannot talk of, still less theorize, 'the' working class (or any other social entity) without first appreciating that the individuals designated by this term act in a physical and social context which affects (and in turn reflects) what they do (by specifying the resources and rules available to them). The division which appeared during the 1984/5 miners' strike in Britain between, say, the Yorkshire and

---

[4] See especially ch. 6 of *CPST*.
[5] Ibid., p. 202; italics in the original.   [6] Ibid., p. 207.

Nottinghamshire areas provides an obvious example of what Giddens is getting at, for where a miner was located (both in terms of the availability of physical resources – in this case, accessible and abundant coal reserves – and social resources (such as the cultural traditions and norms of the different regions) was evidently a crucial factor in influencing how he saw the dispute and whether or not he was prepared to follow the national leadership of the union. As this example makes clear, any sociological analysis of *why* and *how* things happen will need to take account of *where* (and when) they happen.

It is this theme which recurs time and again in Giddens's subsequent work. For the sake of brevity, I shall concentrate here on three of his major books to have appeared since 1979 – namely, *A Contemporary Critique of Historical Materialism* (volume 1), *The Constitution of Society* and *The Nation-State and Violence.*[7]

In this work, Giddens repeats his earlier complaint that sociology has neglected the crucial significance of space. Indeed, in all three books he suggests that urban sociology, being that branch of the discipline which has articulated most closely with geography and which has most explicitly recognized the interrelation between social and spatial organization, should be seen, not merely as one sociological specialism among many, but rather as pivotal to the sociological enterprise as a whole. Having represented something of an unfashionable backwater of the discipline for most of the twentieth century, urban sociologists themselves may well be gratified by this unexpected plaudit from one of our generation's leading social theorists, especially since human geography and urban sociology alike have for some years now been racked by self-doubt as to whether space has any social significance, and hence whether their specialist fields have any coherent intellectual rationale at all! For years we have resigned ourselves to being ugly ducklings, and now Giddens announces that we are swans. It would be surprising if at least some of the ugly ducklings did not believe him.

The reason why Giddens seeks to elevate urban sociology to a position of eminence within the social sciences has to do with his belief that space, and in particular 'urban space', is crucial to the 'problem of order' which lies at the heart of all social theory. As he sees it, the problem of order can be conceptualized as the problem of how social systems are bound or integrated over time and across space. Following familiar terminology, he distinguishes between 'social integration' and 'system integration', the former having to do with social interaction at a face-to-face level (i.e. in situations of 'co-presence' or

---

[7] Giddens has summarized his key arguments regarding the social significance of space in his essay 'Time, Space and Regionalisation', *Social Relations and Spatial Structures*, ed. Derek Gregory and John Urry (London: Macmillan, 1985).

'high presence availability'), and the latter referring to the reproduction of social systems across temporal and spatial distance (i.e. in situations where social relations are maintained between actors who are not co-present – or, as Giddens puts it, in conditions of high time–space distanciation).

Space is for Giddens constitutive of both social and system integration. As regards social integration (the reproduction of social relations at a face-to-face level), he draws attention to the way in which actors are 'positioned' in relation to one another through everyday routines which are embedded in particular locales such that the meaning of any given interaction depends upon the time–space co-ordinates in which it occurs. In everyday life, we move through 'time–space paths' (a concept he takes from the time–space geography of Hagerstrand) which are generally familiar and reassuring to us, and in the process our lives intersect with those of other actors on their time–space paths such that particular 'regions' of our lives assume a pattern in terms of the social relations which are appropriate to them. This accomplishment of routines through regionalization is, according to Giddens, enormously significant as a factor making for a sense of 'ontological security' in the world, for in most aspects of our lives, we are not called upon to act intentionally or to reflect consciously upon our actions – we simply get on with the business of doing whatever it is we do in particular places at particular times in interaction with others whom we regularly expect to find there.

It is through these concepts of 'locale' and 'region' that Giddens believes it is possible to link the process of social integration with that of system integration. His argument rests on the fact that individuals' time–space paths are repetitive (for instance we start the day from home in the morning, follow a familiar time–space path through the day in which we interact in specific ways with specific others in specific contexts, and end up back at home in the evening, where we follow another familiar time–space path leading us to bed, whence we emerge next morning to start the process anew). This means that action is channelled (and, given his theory of structuration, itself contributes to this channelling) through regions of life which then become institutionalized. As he puts it:

> Social integration has to do with interaction in contexts of co-presence. The connections between social and system integration can be traced by examining the modes of regionalisation which channel, and are channelled by, the time–space paths that members of a community or society follow in their day-to-day activities. Such paths are strongly influenced by, and also reproduce, basic institutional parameters of the social systems in which they are implicated.[8]

In traditional or 'tribal' societies, most of this routine activity takes place within a common physical setting in a situation of 'high presence availability'. In other words, most of those who comprise the social system in which you live are in face-to-face interaction with you, their time–space paths coinciding for

[8] *CS*, pp. 142–3.

the most part with your own. In this sense, says Giddens, social integration cannot be distinguished from system integration – if interpersonal routines are maintained, then the social system is reproduced. In this type of society, it therefore follows that there is no marked structural problem of integration, and Giddens suggests that the contradiction which lies at the heart of such a society is more existential (i.e. the contradiction between the society and nature) than structural.

As humankind extends its control over nature (i.e. over what Giddens terms 'allocative resources'), and hence also extends its capacity for controlling its own social organization (through the development of 'authoritative resources'), so this 'existential contradiction' recedes. However, this very process of development of allocative and authoritative resources enables a 'stretching' of the social system over time and across space, and such time–space distanciation means that co-presence is gradually whittled down. There emerges, in other words, a problem of system integration which cannot be guaranteed through face-to-face interaction. The structural principle which emerges as the linchpin of system integration in this ('class-divided') type of society is the division between city and country.

Giddens's argument here is that allocative and authoritative resources can only grow to any significant extent when the capacity for storing them has been developed. The notion of 'storage' when applied to material goods is self-explanatory, but as applied to authoritative resources, Giddens means mainly the ability to store information (for example through the development of writing). Given that power, according to the theory of structuration, is a function of control over rules and resources, it follows that the place where resources are stored will also be the location of greatest power in the social system. This place, according to Giddens, is the city. Thus, the city in 'class-divided' societies represents a 'power-container', a centre of economic, political and military strength and intelligence, which occupies a contradictory relationship with its surrounding rural hinterland, at once interdependent and antagonistic. It follows from this that the principal locales in which social action in class-divided societies is embedded are those of city and countryside; the social system is stretched across both, while social integration is restricted to within each.

This process of 'stretching' across time and space is given added impetus with the development of capitalism from the eighteenth century onwards. Capitalism breaks out of the city–country framework by further developing allocative and authoritative resources on a world scale. Time–space distanciation is thus massively increased with innovations in transport, communications, monetary systems and so on. In such a situation of extreme 'low presence availability', system integration depends on ties of economic interdependency between people who may rarely, if ever, come into personal contact. The link between social activity and spatial location becomes ever more tenuous (hence disrupting regional routines and heightening a sense of ontological insecurity) and space itself becomes commodified (i.e. land is bought and sold just like any other commodity) and its use dissociated from its natural form (e.g. as in the city block pattern of American urbanization, where land use and lay-out make little concession to factors such as topography and fertility). In such a society, the existential contradiction of tribal systems has been all but overcome, and is replaced by a structural contradiction between the private and public spheres (private appropriation and socialized production).

The extension of allocative and authoritative resources in these 'class societies' enhances the central power of the state, organized across a national territory. Although the city is still generally the headquarters of the modern nation-state, it is no longer the crucible of power. The nation-state, not the city, is the crucial power-container of class societies, and it extends its scope of control across time and space through sophisticated surveillance and storage systems. In this world system of nation-states, the city–country tension is dissolved and the city itself ceases to be a significant 'locale':

> With the advent of capitalism, the city is no longer the dominant time–space container or crucible of power; this role is assumed by the territorially-bounded nation state . . . The development of capitalism has not led to the consolidation of the institutions of the city, but rather to its eradication as a distinct social form.[9]

It is important to emphasize this point, partly because it certainly qualifies (and arguably undermines) what Giddens says about the centrality of the city to social theory, and partly because it should not be overlooked by those who would seek in Giddens's work a justification for urban sociology as the study of cities in the modern period. What is clear in Giddens's work is that, like many writers before him,[10] he recognizes the crucial role played by cities in the social organization of pre-capitalist, pre-industrial, 'class-divided' societies, and he correctly identifies the town–country relation as fundamental in structuring these societies; but he is also fully aware that in contemporary industrial–capitalist–class societies, *the city has ceased to be the significant unit of social, economic or political life*. As Giddens clearly argues, the era of the city passed some five hundred years ago when military technology rendered the city wall redundant as a defensive fortification.

In class societies, according to Giddens, the principal 'locale' or setting within which social action occurs is the 'created environment':

> The old city–countryside relation is replaced by a sprawling expansion of a manufactured or 'created environment'.[11]

---

[9] *CCHM*, pp. 147–8.
[10] This is certainly true of Marx, Weber and Durkheim: see my discussion in ch. 1 of Peter Saunders, *Social Theory and the Urban Question*, 2nd edn (London: Hutchinson, 1986).
[11] *CS*, p. 184.

Thus, just as social life has to a large extent transcended the temporal constraints of day and night, or winter and summer, so too it has transcended the spatial constraints of physical distance (conquered by new transportation technologies and electronic communications media) and natural topography. In the modern world, where we work, sleep or take our leisure depends more on the created spaces we have manufactured – the factory, the semi-detached house, the seaside resort – than on the natural or inherent character-istics of different locations. Today, what happens in a particular place is largely determined, not by the character of the place itself, but by the oper-ation of the market for land as a commodity. Where there is no natural harbour we build one; where there is poor fertility we use agricultural chemicals; where a hill blocks our path we force a cutting; and where there is no sun to tan our bodies we create a solarium: and all such decisions will be dictated by the dull logic of the marketplace (and, I would add, political or bureaucratic expediency).

For Giddens, the changes wrought by this development of the created environment are of enormous sociological significance. In terms reminiscent of Talcott Parsons, he outlines what he calls the four principal 'institutional clusters' associated with modernity, and he includes the created environment as one of them (the others being the class system, the political order of 'polyarchy' and the concentration of industrialized military power). It is, he suggests, our experience of living within a created environment which explains the sense of 'ontological insecurity' which pervades the modern world. Indeed, he goes on to relate Durkheim's concept of 'anomie' to all this, arguing that the created environment generates an anomic crisis tendency in contemporary societies in which 'hostility or aversion to the main patterns of conduct involved in modern social and economic life' threatens a 'withdrawal of legitimacy' as 'major cultural values ... lose their grip upon the day-to-day lives of individuals'.[12] Not surprisingly, ecological movements which aim to reshape this created environment are seen by Giddens as one of the most important forms of social movement in the modern period, the others being the labour movement (arising out of the class system), free-speech movements (oriented towards the system of polyarchy and political surveillance) and the peace movement (which confronts the awesome issue of military violence). The created environment, in short, is set up by Giddens as one of four fundamental dimensions of social analysis in the current period.

But what, exactly, does all this mean? What does it mean to identify the created environment as a crucial 'institutional cluster' associated with mod-ernity? What is it that is being designated by this term?

The created environment, says Giddens, is everywhere. It is the countryside with its carefully tended pastures, planted woodlands and preserved national parks, just as much as it is the office blocks and multi-storey car parks of the

[12] *NSV*, p. 323.

city. 'The created environment of modern urbanism', he says, 'is neither confined to the areas in which constructed human habitations exist nor a matter primarily of the spread of such areas. Rather, it involves transformations in the relations between the habits of day-to-day social life and the *milieux* in and through which they are ordered.'[13] Urbanism, therefore, is not to be equated with cities, nor is the created environment to be equated with the built environment. The created environment of modern urbanism is everything and everywhere.

Giddens also makes it clear, however, that this environment is not uniform. It is different in different places. Industry and the division of labour are unevenly distributed, as is population, and variations between places exist at all spatial levels from the distinctiveness of local streets and neighbourhoods through to the differentiation of nation-states. Thus, although the subordination of nature means that geographical divisions are not as marked as they once were – downtown Melbourne does not seem that different from central Manchester and Lloret de Mar is much the same as Southend – this does not render spatial location unimportant. As he puts it, the created environment consists of different 'locales' which are the sites for different kinds of activity, and each locale may itself be divided into 'regions' associated with particular kinds of activity at particular times in the day, week or year.

The concepts of 'locale' and 'region' are fundamental to Giddens's analysis of the social significance of space and the created environment. Locales, which he says 'may range from a room in a house, a street corner, the shop floor of a factory, towns and cities, to the territorially demarcated areas occupied by nation-states',[14] are associated in everyday life with particular routinized patterns of interaction, and the way space is 'packaged' in particular locales may be crucial in reproducing relations of power (for instance by facilitating the capacity for information storage and surveillance, by affecting the possibilities for mass assemblies to form, by influencing ideology through the symbolism of the environment, and so on). For Giddens, it is the routinization of social life within regions and locales which is the secret to the analysis of social reproduction. Little wonder, then, that he seeks to pluck the concern with space from the disciplinary specialism of urban studies and erect it as a central feature of mainstream social analysis. Little wonder, too, that he wishes to install the created environment as one of the four 'institutional clusters' of modernity.

Anti-urbanism and spatial fetishism

For the remainder of this chapter, I shall develop a critique of Giddens's discussion of space and the created environment. In doing so, it is not my

---

[13] Ibid., p. 313.   [14] *CS*, p. 118.

intention to attack his theory of structuration,[15] nor to undermine his developing analysis of the contemporary social order. My comments do not, I think, damage the theory of structuration, since I do not believe that the spatial dimension is an inherent or necessary component of that theory. Similarly, they do not undermine the analysis of the contemporary social order, since the role that the created environment plays in that analysis is in my view obscure, undeveloped and tangential. The point of these comments, then, is not to develop a critique of Giddens' programme for a critical sociology, but is simply to suggest that a concern with space should not play a central part in that programme. Given the influence which Giddens's work is having in urban studies, this is obviously an important conclusion as regards the development of future work in this field.

My criticisms are twofold. First, I do not believe that Giddens has demonstrated the significance of the created environment as the source of ontological insecurity or as one of four 'institutional clusters' of modernity. His comments are in my view simply the most recent example of the romantic anti-urbanism of the Anglo-Saxon intellectual tradition, and the argument which arises out of these sentiments cannot be sustained. Second, I suggest that Giddens fails to explain *how* space enters into the constitution of society and *how* locales and regions are entailed in the process of social reproduction. His concepts are in my view unclear and undeveloped, and his analysis is almost wholly formalistic. I shall explain and elaborate these two criticisms in turn.

The created environment and ontological security

For Giddens, the created environment is the product of the fusion in Europe from the sixteenth century onwards of the two great forces of industrialism and capitalism, and as it has developed, so it has fundamentally altered the relation between human beings and nature:

> When capitalism is conjoined to industrialism, as it has been in the European societies, the outcome is the initiation of a massively important series of alterations in the relation between human beings and the natural world ... In class divided societies, production does not greatly transform nature, even where, for

---

[15] I find the theory of structuration interesting and potentially fruitful, though like other commentators, I have my doubts about its empirical applicability. As Gregory puts it in an interview with Giddens: 'It's one thing to grasp what the theory of structuration entails, it seems to me, but apparently quite another to incorporate its theorems into substantive accounts ...' – Derek Gregory, 'An Interview with Anthony Giddens', *Environment and Planning D: Society and Space*, 2 (1984), 129. It is interesting that the main example which Giddens himself gives of empirical work which utilizes a structurationist position is Paul Willis, *Learning to Labour* (Farnborough: Saxon House, 1977), for as he recognizes, this study was accomplished without benefit of Giddens's theoretical innovations. In *The Constitution of Society*, he confronts this problem, posing the rhetorical question, 'Why bother with cumbersome notions like "structuration" and the rest if first-rate social research can be done without them?' (p. 326). But his answer (just like his response to Gregory in the interview) is disappointing. He admits that empirical research does not need to take on his 'array of abstract notions' and concludes that the theory of structuration is no more than 'a sensitizing device'.

example, major schemes of irrigation exist. The city is the main power-container and is clearly differentiated from the countryside but both partake of the 'content' of the natural world, which human beings live both 'in' and 'with', in a condition of symbiosis. The advent of industrial capitalism changes all this ... radically altering the connections between social life and the material world.[16]

Now clearly it is true that over the last three or four hundred years, industrial capitalism has massively reshaped our environment and has to a large extent freed our activities from dependency upon nature. But why should this extension of the created environment generate ontological insecurity and anomie? Why, if day-to-day activity is routinized and takes place through familiar time–space paths, should it make any difference whether the space through which we move is natural or created? If Giddens's argument was that modern life is not routinized, then one could see how this might disrupt ontological security, but the theory of structuration is premised on the recognition that it is routinized. Why, then, should people feel a deep sense of desperation, fatalism, meaninglessness or whatever when they go to work every morning on the same train, but not when in the past they walked to the fields every morning along the same footpath? Why should a regular pattern of drinking lager in the pub in the evenings deeply disturb our sense of security when a regular pattern of drinking mead in the tavern apparently reassured our forebears that all was well with their world?

Further related questions arise out of this. Is nature – the nature of failed crops, fatal diseases and untamed wilderness, as opposed to the romanticized nature of Monet's paintings or radio soap operas – not at least as threatening and disturbing of ontological security as any created environment? As Giddens recognizes in his discussion of tribal societies, the principal 'contradiction' for people living under such 'natural' conditions is 'existential'. Does it really make sense to see people in their caves or mudhuts or primitive shacks as enjoying a 'symbiotic' relationship with nature, when half the time they were threatened with extinction? Is not the likelihood of imminent demise likely to raise in particularly acute form the issue of one's ontological security?

And how far back do we need to look to find nature in the raw? Giddens believes that the created environment is a modern phenomenon, a product of the industrial capitalist period, but was not the environment of 'class-divided' European society also to a large extent created? Were not forests cleared, fields tilled, roads cut and buildings constructed? Giddens stresses that the created environment should not be equated with the built environment, and that the existence of cities in class-divided societies should not be confused with modern urbanism. But did not most people – peasants as well as urban craftsmen, merchants and the rest – live their lives in a created environment in medieval Europe? And if the humanly transformed landscape of those times is not to count as a created environment, then what is the definition of this crucial

[16] *NSV*, p. 146.

concept? How is the existence of a created environment to be recognized if not by the existence of buildings and modified landscapes? One suspects that, in reserving the concept for modern times, Giddens is really referring to the dramatic switch away from agricultural work that occurred with the onset of industrial capitalism, but if this is so, then it is not people's experience of their environment which is important to his theory but their experience of industrialism.

My main point, however, is not simply that what Giddens sees as a natural environment in class-divided societies was in fact created. It is, more importantly, that there is no reason to assume that a natural environment is supportive of ontological security while a created one disturbs it. In reiterating this all too familiar lament, Giddens is contributing just one more chapter to the long intellectual history of anti-urbanism in Britain.[17] His reference to the symbiotic bond in earlier societies between human beings and their natural habitat is little more than nostalgic romanticism, and his blunt assertion that 'modern urbanism profoundly affects the character of human day-to-day social life'[18] wilfully ignores the long series of failed attempts in urban sociology to substantiate just such a claim.

The association of urbanism with social malaise is familiar in Western social thought. Marx and Engels saw in the great industrial cities the concentrated expression of the evils and horrors of their time, and Durkheim similarly recognized that rates of social pathology were highest in the urban centres. Where these writers differ from Giddens, however, is that they were clear that the causes of the phenomena they were observing lay not in the environment but in the social order. For Marx and Engels, the problem was not urbanism – the created environment – but capitalism, just as for Durkheim it was the social organization of industrialism, in the form of an abnormal division of labour, and not the city per se, which explained the high rates of suicide, crime and divorce.

In his discussion of the social significance of the created environment, Giddens completely confuses the factors which Marx and Durkheim in their different ways sought to distinguish. His approach is strangely reminiscent of Simmel's analysis in 'The Metropolis and Mental Life'.[19] Both Giddens and Simmel construct a chaotic concept which is never systematically defined (the 'created environment' for Giddens, 'metropolis' for Simmel). Both see this concept as explaining the characteristic psyche of the modern age ('ontological insecurity' for Giddens, emotional indifference, individualism and 'the blasé

[17] For the classic statement on the anti-urban tradition in British social thought, see Ruth Glass, 'Urban Sociology in Great Britain', *Readings in Urban Sociology*, ed. Ray Pahl (London: Pergamon Press, 1968). Much the same point is developed in relation to literature by Raymond Williams, *The Country and the City* (London: Chatto & Windus, 1973).

[18] *NSV*, p. 341.

[19] Georg Simmel, 'The Metropolis and Mental Life', *The Sociology of Georg Simmel*, ed. Kurt Wolff (Glencoe: Free Press, 1950).

attitude' for Simmel). And they both try to develop explanations by equating their explanatory variable of urbanism with a confusion of industrialism (or the division of labour), capitalism (or the money economy) and urbanism (or large population size).

Simmel's essay, published at the turn of the century, helped send urban sociology off on a wild-goose chase from which it has only recently returned, empty handed but hopefully a little wiser. His idea that the social and psychological traits of modernity could be explained by the material environment in which we live was sharpened up thirty years later by Louis Wirth in his celebrated paper, 'Urbanism as a Way of Life'. Wirth rightly criticized Simmel for confusing the effects of industrial capitalism with those of urbanism, and in his paper he tried to identify something in the nature of urbanism itself which might produce certain distinctive patterns of social life. But despite the enduring attraction of this paper to subsequent generations of commentators, Wirth's critics have shown time and again that the urban environment itself is actually rather insignificant as an explanation of ways of life.[20] It was not until the 1960s, however, that urban sociologists finally began to accept that in the modern world, the spatial context has little effect on social action. As Pahl suggested, it was one's social location rather than geographical location that was fundamental in explaining patterns of social life:

> It is clear it is not so much *communities* that are acted upon as groups and individuals at particular places in the social structure. Any attempt to tie particular patterns of social relationships to specific geographical milieux is a singularly fruitless exercise.[21]

Pahl's views have been supported by much empirical and theoretical work in urban sociology since the sixties. Empirically, for example, it has been shown that social phenomena like poverty and deprivation which are generally associated with urban areas (for instance the so-called 'inner city problem') are in fact concentrated in social positions and are little influenced by physical location. Thus, indicators such as unemployment, poor housing, educational disadvantage and so on are in Britain often spread across space proportional to the distribution of different social groupings, in which case where you live may not make much difference to how you live.[22]

[20] See ch. 3 of my *Social Theory and the Urban Question* for a discussion of Wirth and his critics.
[21] Ray Pahl, 'The Rural–Urban Continuum', in *Readings in Urban Sociology*, ed. Ray Pahl (Oxford: Pergamon Press, 1968), p. 293.
[22] See, for example, Gordon Cameron, 'The Future of the Conurbations', in *The Future of the British Conurbations*, ed. Gordon Cameron (London: Longman, 1980). It is true that people with similar social characteristics do sometimes act differently according to where they live, but even this so-called 'neighbourhood effect' is probably better explained in terms of social, rather than geographical or physical, factors. Evidence on voting behaviour, which shows that people's political orientations may reflect the politics of those around them, is almost certainly better explained by social-psychological theories of 'reference groups' and 'relative deprivation' than it is by resorting to concepts like 'locale'. For a recent discussion of the geography of voting behaviour, see M. Savage, 'Understanding Political Alignments in Contemporary Britain: Do Localities Matter?', *Political Geography Quarterly*, 6 (1987), 53–76.

Just as significant as this sort of work has been the theoretical critique of urban sociology mounted by Castells and others in the 1970s. Although his epistemology was certainly questionable and his own theory was open to criticism, Castells did succeed in demonstrating to most of those working in urban studies at that time that space could not constitute a theoretically coherent object of study.[23] According to Castells, the characteristic preoccupation of urban sociology with space in general, and with urban space in particular, had misled analysts into believing that what they saw happening in cities was a product of cities. Urban sociology, in other words, had failed to understand what Marx (and Durkheim) had understood – that an explanation of what goes on in cities cannot be achieved through a theory of urbanism. It was Castells's achievement to demonstrate that it is not the city or space or the urban environment which is important in sociological explanation, but rather the processes which occur in cities, across space and against the context of the urban environment.

Giddens's approach flies in the face of this conclusion, however, for as we have seen, he berates sociologists for having dismissed space as simply the backdrop against which action unfolds. Where Castells accused urban sociology of spatial fetishism, Giddens accuses the rest of sociology of spatial blindness. Where Castells believed the task was to identify the underlying processes which become manifest in the urban environment, Giddens sees the urban environment as a major factor in constituting social processes. And where Castells succeeded in revolutionizing urban sociology by liberating it from its traditional preoccupation with the city and spatial forms, Giddens now threatens to lead a counter-revolution by reasserting the centrality of the city to social theory and by re-emphasizing the importance of space to social life. The way in which he seeks to establish this essentially retrograde step is by asserting the significance of space in the routine reproduction of social life, and it is to this issue that I now turn.

Locales, regions and the social significance of space

At a time when urban sociology has at last moved away from its traditional concern with the city as its distinctive object of analysis, Giddens has announced that the city is, after all, of fundamental sociological significance:

> An essential thesis of this book is that the city cannot be regarded as merely incidental to social theory but belongs at its very core.[24]

The statement, however, is misleading, for as we know from the way he subsequently qualifies it, Giddens does not see the city as in any sense at the

---

[23] Manuel Castells, 'Is There an Urban Sociology?' and 'Theory and Ideology in Urban Sociology', both in *Urban Sociology: Critical Essays*, ed. Chris Pickvance (London: Tavistock, 1976). Also, Manuel Castells, *The Urban Question* (London: Edward Arnold, 1977) especially parts 2 and 3.

[24] *CCHM*, p. 140.

core of a sociological analysis of modern 'class societies'. Indeed, he goes on to argue that:

> The development of capitalism has not led to the consolidation of the institutions of the city, but rather to its *eradication as a distinct social form.*[25]

What he is actually saying, therefore, is not that the city is a fundamental concept in sociology – how can it be if it has been 'eradicated'? Rather, the argument is that cities played a central role in pre-capitalist societies as 'power containers', but that this role was gradually taken over by the emergence of nation-states. This, essentially, is entirely consistent with what Weber, Marx and Durkheim all argued,[26] as well as with Castells's position outlined above. We may, therefore, with no further ado jettison the city as an important concept in contemporary sociology and proceed to what Giddens says about space.

As we have seen, Giddens believes that sociology has been neglectful of the significance of space in social life. His complaint must immediately be qualified, however, for empirical sociology has consistently displayed an awareness of the importance of space. The case-study method is premised upon a recognition of the sociological significance of spatial variations. Why did the authors of the 'affluent worker' study in the 1960s select Luton, as opposed to Gateshead or Glasgow, as their research site? Why did Rex and Moore choose to locate their study of race and housing in inner Birmingham rather than the suburbs of Guildford? Why did Wilmott and Young go to Bethnal Green, or Norman Dennis and his colleagues go to Fetherstone, or, more recently, Ray Pahl select the Isle of Sheppey?[27] In my current research, I am studying the economic, political and cultural significance of the growth of home ownership in England by going to three different towns – Slough in the South-East, Derby in the East Midlands and Burnley in the North-West. Why bother travelling to such scattered places? The answer in all these cases is that anybody who comes to do empirical research is very soon sensitized to the peculiarities of place. Phenomena which develop in one area may not develop, or may develop in a very different way, in another. It is a long, long time since Lloyd Warner made his rash claim that Yankee City (the pseudonym for Newburyport) was all

---

[25] Ibid., p. 148 (my italics).

[26] Max Weber, *Economy and Society* (New York: Bedminster Press, 1968), chapter 16; Karl Marx and Frederick Engels, *The German Ideology* (London: Lawrence & Wishart, 1970); Frederick Engels, 'The Housing Question', in Marx and Engels, *Selected Works*, vol. 2 (Moscow: Progress Publishers, 1969); Emile Durkheim, *The Division of Labour in Society* (Toronto: Macmillan, 1933).

[27] John Goldthorpe, David Lockwood, Frank Bechhofer and Jennifer Platt, *The Affluent Worker in the Class Structure* (London: Cambridge University Press, 1969); John Rex and Robert Moore, *Race, Community and Conflict* (London: Oxford University Press, 1967); Michael Young and Peter Willmott, *Family and Kinship in East London* (London: Routledge & Kegan Paul, 1957); Norman Dennis, F. Henriques and C. Slaughter, *Coal Is Our Life* (London: Eyre & Spottiswoode, 1956); Ray Pahl, *Divisions of Labour* (Oxford: Basil Blackwell, 1984).

America and all America was in Yankee City, and most empirical researchers today are highly attuned to the spatial specificity of their research site.[28]

None of this, though, is taken into account by Giddens. When he complains that sociology has ignored space, he actually makes little if any reference to this long case-study tradition. Rather, his attention is focused on social theory. What he is demanding, it seems, is that sociologists should begin to *theorize* space, and the way they should do it is by means of the concepts of 'locale' and 'region'.

As we have seen, Giddens refers to locales as the 'settings' of social life, and he argues that these settings are themselves 'regionalised'. He then asserts that locales, and the regions within them, enter into social reproduction by creating and sustaining the taken-for-granted meanings of everyday routines. They are, as Thrift puts it, 'The meeting place of social structure and human agency'.[29] But in what sense are locales and regions crucial in setting social life? If they are more than a backdrop to action, then how exactly do they enter into the reflexive constitution of action? We know that the theory of structuration is antithetical to any explanation couched in terms of physical determinism; so how do actors derive meanings from their physical environment? How does the context situate the action? What is the mechanism and where is the explanation for how it all works?

I cannot find any answers in Giddens's work to any of these quite basic questions. There are references all through his work to the significance of space and the importance of locales, but he very rarely provides illustrations of what he means, and when he does they are profoundly disappointing. In *The Constitution of Society*, for example, he discusses the home as a locale. He informs us that the home is 'regionalised' so that different rooms are associated with different activities at different times of the day, and he notes that space within the home is structured into core and peripheral regions (for example the kitchen and the spare bedroom respectively). The discussion then closes with a comparison between the home and other, larger, locales which are also found to be structured into core and periphery regions – for instance the division of the city between the central business district and the suburbs, or the division of the world system between the metropolitan core countries and the less developed nations.

Now, what are we meant to make of this? The observations themselves are commonplace, the comparisons between different locales are exceedingly formalistic (once again putting one in mind of Simmel), and the explanatory power of the analysis is never made manifest. We learn that we move through the home in definable and repetitive time–space paths, washing in the bathroom in the morning, eating in the dining-room in the evening and sleeping in

[28] W. Lloyd Warner and Paul Lunt, *The Social Life of a Modern Community* (New Haven: Yale University Press, 1941).
[29] Nigel Thrift, 'On the Determination of Social Action in Space and Time', *Environment and Planning D: Society and Space*, 1 (1983), 38.

the bedroom at night. But so what? Where is the causal (or, if you prefer, dialectical) link between what we do and the place that we do it in? Would it make any difference if I cleaned my teeth in the kitchen or slept on the couch in the lounge?

I can understand how people may invest meanings in places – we feel comfortable in one place, threatened in another, alienated in a third – but surely these meanings do not inhere in the spaces we occupy but in the social relations which are realized within them? How can space per se mean anything or do anything? Notwithstanding Giddens's argument to the contrary, what I am therefore suggesting is that social theory has been quite right to treat space as a backdrop against which social action takes place. Unlike time, which is inherently caught up in, and constitutive of, social action, space does not 'enter into' what we do in any meaningful sense, because mere space can have no causal properties and is quite incapable of entering into anything. It is passive; it is context.

This does not mean, of course, that location is unimportant in the explanation of social phenomena. Giddens is surely right, for example, when he points out that 'the' working class, far from being a uniform or homogenous entity, is actually constituted and reproduced differently in different places.[30] But to explain this, we do not need to start theorizing space. Rather, we need a theory of class and class consciousness which can explain the conditions under which this or that kind of working-class culture and identity is likely to develop. As John Urry has suggested, localities vary on a number of significant factors which are likely to affect local class structures – the size of the public-sector workforce, the proportion of women employed, the presence of intermediate classes, and so on. Different combinations of these and other factors may be expected to generate different local class cultures.

The point about this is, as Urry himself emphasizes, that space is not something we can sensibly theorize about:

> It is impossible and incorrect to develop a general science of the spatial . . . This is because space *per se* has no *general* effects. The significance of spatial relations depends upon the particular character of the social objects in question.[31]

Space, in other words, refers simply to a specific combination of objects. Different things come together in different combinations at different places and with different effects. And as Sayer suggests:

> Because spatial forms are contentless abstractions, until we specify what kinds of objects with what kinds of causal powers actually constitute spatial relations, there can be no abstract general theory of space that is applicable to all objects.[32]

---

[30] This is a point which is forcefully developed by Doreen Massey, *Spatial Divisions of Labour* (London: Macmillan, 1984). Massey also shows how the spatial dimension of the restructuring of capital has significant implications for changing gender relations in different parts of the country.

[31] John Urry, 'Localities, Regions and Social Class', *International Journal of Urban & Regional Research*, 5 (1981), 458.

[32] Andrew Sayer, 'Defining the Urban', *Geojournal*, 9 (1984), 282.

As Sayer goes on to recognize, it follows from this that empirical analysis will necessarily take the spatial context (i.e. the contingent interrelationships of things in a particular place) into account. Theory, however, will be indifferent to the spatial context, for its concern lies in developing generalizable knowledge which transcends the particular conditions of any one specific place. Theory, in other words, is not interested in the contingent questions of whether or how specific combinations of factors come together in particular places, but is concerned rather to explain how those factors themselves might account for this or that phenomenon or tendency.

It is for this reason, I would argue, that Giddens finds such an absence of theoretical work on the sociological significance of space, even though empirical sociological research has clearly been sensitive to spatial variations. The explanation, quite simply, is that there is nothing for theory to say about space! This also explains why his theoretical discussion of concepts like 'locale' and 'region' is so undeveloped, vague and 'poorly articulated'.[33] Again, the explanation is that there is nothing for theory to say about places until we know what kinds of combinations of objects fill them. The 'contentless abstractions' which litter Anthony Giddens's theoretical discussions of the question of space are thus, in themselves, devoid of any analytical power.

Conclusion

In this chapter, I have considered Giddens's treatment of a range of essentially geographical or territorial concepts in his recent theoretical work. I have suggested, first, that his identification of *the created environment* as a key 'institutional cluster' in modern societies is misleading. The created environment is a chaotic concept which, like *Gesellschaft*, 'metropolis' or even 'urbanism', confuses questions of capitalism and industrialism with those of territoriality and spatial differentiation. In Giddens's theory, furthermore, it supports a rather conservative romanticism which assumes without proof or argument that a routinized existence in a 'natural' environment (whatever that is) generates harmony and 'symbiosis', while a routinized existence in a humanly transformed or created environment generates anomie and disrupts ontological security.

I have suggested, second, that Giddens's statements to the effect that *the city* is central to the concerns of social theory are similarly misleading since he himself is aware that cities have long since ceased to be the structuring units of social organization. The classic social theorists were right – we cannot in the modern period take the city as an explanatory variable. What goes on in cities cannot be explained through an analysis of cities.

Third, I have disputed Giddens's view that sociology has ignored *the significance of space*, for I have suggested that empirical sociology is fully sensitized to

---

[33] Andrew Kirby, 'Pseudo-random Thoughts on Space, Scale and Ideology in Political Geography', *Political Geography Quarterly*, 4 (1985), 9.

the importance of spatial variation. I have, furthermore, criticized Giddens's own spatial concepts of 'locale' and 'region' on the grounds that he offers no explanation of how these 'enter into' the constitution of social action. This failure, I have suggested, is inherent in any attempt to theorize spatial forms which, following Urry and Sayer, I see as 'contentless abstractions' devoid of meaning or significance. If space is simply the contingent interrelation of objects, then it follows that spatial abstractions such as 'locale' will necessarily remain 'poorly articulated'.

Where does all this leave Giddens's theory, and where does it leave urban studies?

Giddens's theories, as I suggested earlier, are left virtually intact. The elaborated concern with space was a relatively late addition to the theory of structuration and in my view it never was an essential component of it. Similarly, the identification of the created environment as a key factor of modernity is little more than an 'add-on' to the theory developed in *The Nation-State and Violence*.[34]

But what of urban sociology? Giddens, it will be recalled, has several times flattered this branch of the discipline by suggesting that it is in fact central to sociology's concerns as a whole. Now this may indeed be the case, but not for the reasons which Giddens gives. The logic of my argument in this chapter is obviously that urban sociology should not take 'space' as its distinctive object of analysis, nor should it focus on spatially defined units such as the city. Thus, we need to look at the substantive concerns of the subject in order to assess its importance.

As I have argued elsewhere,[35] one such key concern over recent years has been the focus on the social organization of consumption. This is revealed in a literature on issues to do with welfare provision, consumer movements, domestic self-provisioning, consumption sector cleavages, privatized consumption

---

[34] This is clearest in respect of the discussion of the four 'institutional clusters' in the final chapter of the book. In this highly formalistic schema, Giddens identifies the 'transformation of nature' (which produces a created environment), together with private property (which he believes gives rise to class), surveillance (associated with polyarchy) and military violence, as one of the four key dimensions of modernity. He then relates each of these to a form of social movement (labour, free speech, peace and ecological movements respectively). This has the effect of overemphasizing the importance of ecological movements while neglecting a whole host of other, potentially far more important movements (he lists some of them on p. 318) which do not neatly fit into the four axes of the model. Worse is to come, for he then tries to map Marshall's typology of citizenship rights on to his model. He manages (not without some ingenuity!) to equate social rights (which he redefines as economic rights) with the property system, political rights with surveillance and civil rights with the military dimension, following which he has to invent a fourth category, which for some reason gets labelled 'moral imperatives', to attach to the created environment. The schema, which by this stage has become a more chaotic version of the Parsonian AGLI model, is then given a Habermasian gloss by tagging various 'crisis tendencies' on to the four categories, as a result of which the created environment gets associated with anomie.

Why the created environment should be considered a basic 'institutional cluster' in the first place is unclear, but with each subsequent taxonomic innovation, its inclusion in the model becomes even more obtrusive.

[35] *Social Theory and the Urban Question*, 2nd edn, ch. 8.

and much else. This chapter does not provide the opportunity to outline and discuss such developments. In my view, however, the significance of the analysis of consumption has for too long been neglected in mainstream sociology, for the consumption sphere is increasingly important in the modern period in influencing life chances, shaping cultural values, structuring political alignments and enabling the pursuit of central life interests.[36]

Thus, when Giddens asserts the centrality of contemporary urban sociology, he is in my view right, but for the wrong reasons. The potential of urban sociology over the next few years will be realized through its escape from its traditional concerns with space and the city and in its pursuit of its substantive concerns with the question of consumption. It is something of a paradox, therefore, that in his discussions of urban sociology, Giddens should be so concerned to reaffirm the former while totally overlooking the latter.

[36] There are signs that a sociology of consumption may now be developing. See, for example, Herbert Moorhouse, 'American Automobiles and Workers' Dreams', *Sociological Review*, 31 (1983), 403–26; Herbert Gans, 'American Urban Theories and Urban Areas', in *Cities in Recession: Critical Responses to the Urban Theories of the New Right*, ed. Ivan Szelenyi (London: Sage, 1984); Pahl, *Divisions of Labour*, ch. 12.

11

On the (ir)relevance of structuration theory to empirical research[1]

NICKY GREGSON

Introduction

In recent years one of the most hotly debated issues in social science, particularly in human geography, has been the nature of the relationship between theory and empirical work.[2] In human geography at least two views have prevailed. Thus, for those who see theory as an ordering framework, theory acts as a type of 'filing system' for classifying empirical events, whilst for those who see theory as a way of conceptualizing something, theory provides an explanation for empirical events, but is also itself interrogated in terms of its practical adequacy by these events.[3] It is within this second strand of thinking that interest has grown in human geography in the relationship of social theory first to empirical research, and secondly to human geography more generally. Here various arguments have been put forward, but it is primarily the latter to which most attention has been directed. Thus, some individuals have provided straightforward outlines of ideas current in social theory and made suggestions as to what these entail for human geography, whilst others have argued strongly for the importance of space to social theory.[4]

However, thus far in this debate there has been a marked reluctance on the part of human geographers to address one key issue head-on; namely, whether the work of social theorists is critical to the conceptualization of empirical research projects and the explanation of the empirical events with which they are concerned.

To an extent it is impossible to pose this question beyond a consideration of individual social theorists: different social theorists are often working at different levels of abstraction and so there can be no cast-iron guarantee that social theory in general will be of use to empirical research. However, one broad

---

[1] An earlier version of this chapter appeared as N. Gregson, 'Structuration Theory: Some Thoughts on the Possibilities for Empirical Research', *Environment and Planning D: Society and Space*, 5 (1987), 73–91. I would like to thank David Held for his suggestions about revisions. However, the usual disclaimers apply.

[2] For discussions of this in human geography see the various contributions to D. Massey and R. Meegan (eds.), *Politics and Method: Contrasting Studies in Industrial Geography* (Aldershot: Methuen, 1985) and A. Sayer, *Method in Social Science* (London: Hutchinson, 1984).

[3] Sayer, *Method*, pp. 48–9.

[4] See D. Gregory and J. Urry (eds.), *Spatial Relations and Spatial Structures* (London: Macmillan, 1985).

235

point can be made, and this is that for any genuinely critical social theory the connection to empirical research is fundamentally important, for without this the links both to explaining the events which occur in the social world and to intervening to change this world disappear.

In this chapter the concern is with evaluating the relevance of one particular form of social theory to empirical research, that of Anthony Giddens's structuration theory.[5] The reasons for this focus are two-fold: first, because Giddens's arguments are in all probability those which have attracted most attention from human geographers,[6] and secondly because this line of debate has been neglected thus far in the critical evaluation of Giddens's work.[7]

A number of possible reasons can be put forward to account for why so few commentators have addressed the question of the relationship between structuration theory and empirical research. For example, it may be that this situation reflects the relative lack of space which Giddens himself has given over to the issue in his work, in contrast say to the problems of social structure and human agency, time and space and conceptualizing agency. Alternatively, it may be that the situation does little more than mirror the current shortage of empirical work actually informed by structurationist ideas as opposed to work which urges this.[8] A third possibility also exists: that Giddens's readership is, almost certainly, dominated by those whose principal interests are theoretical, or philosophical, rather than empirical. However, whatever the reasons, and there may well be more, this is an issue which can no

[5] Structuration theory itself is outlined in the following: Giddens, *NRSM, CPST, CCHM* and *CS*.
[6] Giddens and Foucault are the only modern social theorists to have attracted prolonged recent interest in human geography. For discussions of Giddens's work by human geographers see: T. Carlstein, 'The Sociology of Structuration in Time and Space: A Time-Geographic Assessment of Giddens's Theory' *Svensk Geografisk Årbok*, 57 (1981), 41–57; D. Gregory, 'Human Agency and Human Geography', *Transactions of the Institute of British Geographers*, 6 (1981), 1–18; N. Gregson, 'On Duality and Dualism: The Case of Time Geography and Structuration', *Progress in Human Geography*, 10 (1980), 184–205; A. Moos and M. Dear, 'Structuration Theory in Urban Analysis 1: Theoretical Exegesis', *Environment and Planning A*, 18 (1986), 231–52; N. Thrift, 'On the Determination of Social Action in Space and Time', *Environment and Planning D: Society and Space*, 1 (1983), 23–57.
[7] For a selection of critiques of Giddens's work see: M. S. Archer, 'Morphogenesis Versus Structuration: On Combining Structure and Action', *British Journal of Sociology*, 33 (1982), 455–83; M. Bertillson, 'The Theory of Structuration: Prospects and Problems', *Acta Sociologica*, 27 (1984), 339–53; D. Gregory, J. Bleicher and M. Featherstone, 'Historical Materialism Today: An Interview with Anthony Giddens', *Theory, Culture and Society*, 1 (1982), 63–77; A. Callinicos, 'Anthony Giddens: A Contemporary Critique', *Theory and Society*, 14 (1984), 133–66; D. Gross, 'Time–Space Relations in Giddens's Social Theory', *Theory, Culture and Society*, 1 (1982) 83–8; P. Hirst, 'The Social Theory of Anthony Giddens: A New Syncretism?', *Theory, Culture and Society*, 1 (1982), 78–82; G. McLennan, 'Critical or Positive Theory? A Comment on the Status of Anthony Giddens's Social Theory', *Theory, Culture and Society*, 2 (1984), 123–9; B. Smart, 'Foucault, Sociology and the Problem of Human Agency', *Theory and Society*, 11 (1982), 121–41; J. Urry, 'Duality of Structure: Some Critical Issues', *Theory, Culture and Society*, 1 (1982), 150–6; E. O. Wright, 'Review Essay: Is Marxism Really Functional, Class Reductionist and Teleological?', *American Journal of Sociology*, 89 (1983), 452–9.
[8] For examples of attempts at this see: Gregory, 'Human Agency'; Moos and Dear, 'Structuration Theory'; C. Smith, 'A Case Study of Structuration: The Pure-Bred Beef Business', *Journal for the Theory of Social Behaviour*, 13 (1983), 3–18; Thrift, 'On the Determination of Social Action'.

longer be either marginalized or ignored by those intending to engage critically with Giddens's work. A strong and weak justification can be provided in
defence of this assertion. First, the weak; and an argument adduced many
times by Giddens. This is the line that social science, whether written as social
theory or as empirically based studies, has the same primary objective, namely
to illuminate and explain the concrete processes of social life. Given this, if
structuration theory is to offer anything of value to social science, it must
ultimately 'help to illuminate problems of empirical research'.[9] In other
words, if it fails to enhance our understanding of what happens 'out there' in
the social world, it will have failed in terms of the main objective of social
science. It follows therefore that even on the basis of this argument, an
evaluation of the relevance of structuration theory to empirical research
becomes a key component of the critical assessment of structuration itself.
However, a stronger justification for this emphasis can be made and relates to
the nature and objectives of critical theory, against which, as a self-confessed
critical theorist, Giddens's work needs to be assessed. Clearly a central element, if not the central element, of critical theory turns on its ability not just to
explain what exists but to indicate what might exist and how the transformation from what is to what could be might be achieved. Given this, the
connection between theory and practice assumes paramount importance; and
embedded within this is the concrete social world, that which critical social
theory seeks both to explain and to transform. Ultimately, then, any form of
critical social theory must engage with the concrete social world; and in a
permanent rather than transitory, glancing manner. On this basis one of the
'acid tests' of structuration theory as critical theory is its ability to 'touch
ground', that is, to connect with the concerns of empirical research. A major
task in the critical evaluation of structuration theory therefore must be either
to demonstrate or refute its relevance to empirical research projects.

In the light of the above, the central task of this chapter is to establish the
relevance or irrelevance of structuration theory as currently constituted to
empirical research. This is pursued through three main sections. In the first
two sections Giddens's comments on structuration theory and empirical research are explored in depth, with structuration theory's potential applicability to empirical work being a prime area for consideration. In the third
section the focus shifts to an examination of the tension between Giddens's
statements that structuration theory should help illuminate empirical research and its patent inability to do so. Finally, some of the implications of
these conclusions are considered. Here two points are stressed, the importance
of the connection between abstract and concrete levels of abstraction for any
form of critical social theory and the collapse into relativism implied by the
absence of such links. As will become evident, structuration theory, as currently presented and in spite of stated intentions, falls well short on connection
and, consequently, becomes snared in the trap of the latter.

[9] *CS*, p. xxix.

I

In a fairly recent interview Giddens makes the following comments:

> The sense in which one theory is better than another has still to do in my opinion with the facts of the matter. I don't accept that theory is intractable to the facts, it seems to me that there is, as it were, a dialogue between theory and fact which is the basis of doing any kind of sociological analysis or political analysis or whatever.[10]

More recently he has written:

> social theory has the task of providing conceptions of the nature of human social activity which can be placed in the service of empirical work.[11]

Such remarks indicate a strong commitment on Giddens's part to the importance of empirical research in social science. Furthermore, they reiterate two points: that the relationship between social theory and empirical research is an issue of key importance to Giddens and, correspondingly, that the relationship between structuration theory and empirical research is an important area for debate.

However, until the appearance of *The Constitution of Society*, one of the major gaps in Giddens's writing had been his failure to expand on these points. For this reason, much of the discussion in this section focuses on the chapter in *Constitution* on structuration theory and empirical research, although references back to earlier work are made where appropriate. More specifically, the section focuses on three issues. Two concern the observations made by Giddens in *Constitution*: these are his guidelines for empirical research in the social sciences and examples of the use of structuration theory. A third section concentrates on evaluation.

1

There are three guidelines which Giddens offers for empirical research in the social sciences. First, all social research is argued to involve an 'anthropological' or 'ethnographic' moment.[12] Since social research is an activity conducted by some people (usually academics) about others, it necessitates the mediation of one set of concepts – for example, those drawn from sociology or geography – with those used by individuals in the course of their everyday lives. Part of the research process in social science, then, and a vital one according to Giddens, is the learning of what these individuals know, and have to know, in order to get on with their everyday activities. It is this which constitutes the 'ethnographic' moment. A second guideline relates to Giddens's concern with the complexity of skills which individuals show in daily social life.[13] This is seen to

---

[10] Bleicher and Featherstone, p. 74.
[11] *CS*, p. xvii.   [12] Ibid., p. 284.   [13] Ibid., p. 285.

be of key importance to institutional analysis; and particularly in analyses of their reproduction. Last, Giddens maintains that empirical research must recognize the 'time–space constitution of social life'.[14] Thus, instead of presenting time and space as the unproblematical dimensions within which action occurs, it is argued that researchers should see temporal and spatial structures as integral to the production and reproduction of social life.

These three guidelines reflect many of the themes which have recurred in Giddens's work since 1976. More specifically, they are presented as deriving from the ten 'structurationist' points which Giddens isolates in *Constitution* as impinging on the concerns of empirical research in social science.[15] These points represent facets, but no more, of structuration theory and are an emphasis on (1) the knowledgeability of human agents (practical and discursive consciousness) and (2) the significance of the unintended consequences of action for the reproduction of social systems; the study of (3) day-to-day life in terms of the reproduction of institutionalized practices and (4) routine activities; (5) situating social interaction within the contexts central to social and system reproduction, and emphasizing within this the importance of (6) socially sanctioned roles and (7) various types of constraint; (8) isolating structural principles and considering the degree of 'closure' within societies; (9) the importance of the analysis of power struggles, and (10) trying to integrate sociological concepts within social life.

Two major problems are suggested by the above material. These are, first, that it is unclear how the three guidelines derive from the ten listed points and, second, that the guidelines themselves are of dubious worth for empirical research projects.

Regarding the first of these: it would appear that the ten specific points suggest, at the very least, ten specific guidelines for empirical work (i.e. that empirical research projects should be sensitive to the knowledgeability of human agents, the unintended consequences of action etc.) rather than the three guidelines which Giddens isolates. Indeed, if anything, these guidelines are derived not from the ten points but from their origin, that is from Giddens's resolution of certain ontological issues. This can be seen from the following. One of the points which Giddens has stressed recently is that a primary objective in his work is to establish an ontology of human society.[16] In this three issues have been central. These are: working out the implications of the 'double hermeneutic' for social science; developing a theory of action which neither repeats the flaws of voluntarist theories of action nor, as in determinist theories, relegates action to the inconsequential; and considering how to put time and space in at the heart of social analysis from the start.[17] It is with this objective that the ideas and themes expressed in the theory of structuration,

---

[14] Ibid., p. 286.   [15] Ibid., pp. 281–4.

[16] D. Gregory, 'Space, Time and Politics in Social Theory: An Interview with Anthony Giddens', *Environment and Planning D: Society and Space*, 2 (1984), p. 124.

[17] Ibid., p. 124.

particularly those concerning human agency, social structure and time and space, are bound up and it is to this same objective and its resolution that the three guidelines connect. Thus, whilst the guidelines are manifestly not the same thing as Gidden's ideas concerning the double hermeneutic, theories of action and conceptualizing time and space (in that they offer methodological and content-pointers for empirical research, rather than concepts integral to an ontology of human society), their substance is indicative of his views on the ontology of human society. For example, the ethnographic moment is a guideline which encourages social researchers to be sensitive in their empirical work to the pre-interpreted status of the world with which they are concerned (i.e. to be sensitive to the double hermeneutic) and argues correspondingly that individuals' knowledge and understanding is not just alluded to but elucidated in the course of empirical research projects. Similar arguments apply to the guidelines concerning the complexity of individuals' skills and the importance of time and space. For instance, the first reflects many of the ideas which appear in Giddens's stratification model of human agency. Indeed, discursive consciousness, practical consciousness, the unconscious and the unacknowledged conditions and unintentional outcomes of action are all implicated in the phrase 'the complexity of skills shown by individual agents'. This particular guideline then suggests that empirical work be alive to all that is contained within the stratification model of agency. Finally, with respect to time and space, the same general principles hold. Thus, the argument that empirical research should situate action spatially and temporally and examine the various spatial and temporal structures within societies is one which is indicative of Giddens's concern to put time and space in at the heart of social theory. As far as our guidelines go, then, two points can be made immediately. First, it is clear that the source of these guidelines lies in Giddens's concern with establishing an ontology of human society, rather than with the ten structurationist points which are presented in *Constitution*, although the two points must inevitably be seen as connected. Second, the precise nature of the guidelines owes much both to Giddens's views of what is central to an ontology of human society and to his conceptualization of these.

The second major difficulty with the three guidelines concerns their potential use in empirical research, and reflects the conclusions reached above. It is also the more serious of the two problems. As has been shown, the guidelines stress the importance of the ethnographic moment, agents' skills and time and space to empirical research. It would, however, be hard to convince anyone engaged in empirical research of the intrinsic value of these points. This is because there is nothing about them which enables them to be used actively in an empirical research context. Quite simply, they lack the degree of specification required for empirical work. Thus, whilst few would disagree that social research has an ethnographic moment, that people demonstrate a vast number of skills in the course of daily life and that temporal and spatial structures are critical, for the purposes of empirical research the key questions concern *which* 'actors', *which* skills and *which* temporal and spatial structures we choose to investigate; and *how* we investigate these, *where* and *when*. Indeed, it is only by addressing precisely these questions that the objectives of theoretically informed empirical research (explaining or accounting for the events which happen in the social world) can be achieved. Empirical research then needs guidelines, but it requires guidelines which stem from theory which, as it were, 'touches ground'. It follows therefore that one of the main problems with the guidelines which Giddens presents us with is that they are incapable, in their current form, of acting *as guidelines*: they isolate three very broad categories of potential interest, but provide neither precise indications of content nor methodological directions. Indeed, the most these guidelines allow currently is either for empirical research to point to issues of ontological interest or for social theorists to see things of ontological interest in empirical research. Regardless of from which side of the fence we approach this, the situation is clearly one which stems from the ontological origins and overtones of the guidelines discussed above. Fundamentally, the guidelines which Giddens presents in *Constitution* reflect ontological rather than empirical concerns and, as such, are of limited use to empirical research.

2

The examples which Giddens uses to illustrate the connections between structuration theory and empirical research are Willis's study, *Learning to Labour*, Gambetta's research on educational opportunity and employment, Bourdon's and Elster's work on contradiction and Ingham's study of the role of the City in British industry.[18] Each study is presented as exemplifying certain aspects of structuration theory. Thus, Willis's work is used as an example of three things: first, of strategic conduct – that individuals know a great deal about their situation, position, prospects, actions and reasons; second, of the unintentional consequences of action, by which Giddens means that 'the lads'

> having effectively left school with no qualifications and entered a world of low-level manual labour, in work which has no career prospects and with which they are intrinsically disaffected . . . are effectively stuck there for the rest of their working lives[19]

and third, of the duality of structure. In the last case, those working-class attitudes to work and school which are critical to the creation of a school counter-culture are also seen to lead (unintentionally) to the reproduction of

---

[18] P. Willis, *Learning to Labour* (Aldershot: Gower, 1977); D. Gambetta, *Were they Pushed or Did they Jump?* (Cambridge: Cambridge University Press, 1987); R. Bourdon, *The Unintended Consequences of Social Action* (London: Macmillan, 1982); J. Elster, *Logic and Society: Contradictions and Possible Worlds* (Chichester: Wiley, 1978); G. Ingham, *Capitalism Divided? The City and Industry in Britain* (London: Macmillan, 1984).

[19] Willis, *Learning to Labour*, p. 293.

the unskilled male labour-force necessary for a dwindling number of sectors of capitalist production. The other pieces of research are used in a similar way. Gambetta's work, for instance, is used to indicate that human knowledge-ability provides an important dimension to the analysis of structural constraint; Elster's and Bourdon's work is used to relate structural contradictions to the unintentional consequences of action; and Ingham's study is quoted as an example of institutional analysis.

There are two sets of comments which can be made about the above. First, there is, title notwithstanding, nothing very new about what Giddens offers here; it is only reiteration, albeit on a more extensive scale than hitherto. Comments of this nature, in which brief illustrations of particular aspects of structuration theory are given, appear fairly frequently in Giddens's work. In both *New Rules* and *Central Problems* they are rather sporadic in occurrence, providing little more than a thumbnail sketch example of the more abstract ideas which Giddens wishes to convey. *Contemporary Critique*, although on the face of it a text which has rather more to say at the concrete level than either *New Rules* or *Central Problems* (particularly with respect to the emergence of capitalist society) is also characterized by this same use of existing empirical work to illustrate specific structurationist points: witness, for example, the marshalling of the arguments of Jacob, Mumford, Sjoberg, Wheatley etc. around the theme of the time–space organization of the city in history. What follows in *Constitution*, then, is but more of the same; or what Gane refers to as 'an evocation of concreteness in the midst of a survey critique of elite theory'.[20]

The second set of comments are evaluatory. They focus on a major issue, namely what precisely we are to make of a situation in which the connections between structuration theory and empirical research are all rather strained; in which, rather than structuration theory being used to inform empirical work, it is certain isolated aspects of a range of projects which are used to illustrate certain aspects of structuration theory. If we use Giddens's comments on Willis's study as our example, three points would seem to be in order. First, the representation of *Learning to Labour* which appears in *Constitution* is a travesty of the real thing which, rather than focusing simply on unintentional consequences, people's awareness of their circumstances and the duality of structure, is concerned with examining the role of cultural forms in social reproduction (generally) and the role which specific cultural forms (in particular the school counter-culture and working-class culture) play in the reproduction of labour-power. Secondly, manifestly Willis did not need the insights provided by structuration theory to produce his study. Instead, it is the work of Gramsci, Lukács, Althusser and Marx which pervades this research. Perversely then, the situation is one in which, on the one hand, Giddens needs work such as Willis's to demonstrate that structurationist concepts can be illustrated in an empirical context but, on the other, Willis (and the empirical

[20] M. Gane, 'Anthony Giddens and the Crisis of Social Theory', *Economy and Society*, 11 (1983), 389.

research he conducted) has no need of structuration theory whatsoever. This leads to a third point, namely what does all this suggest about the type of empirical research which structuration theory might produce, assuming that the problem of lack of specification referred to previously could be overcome? The answer to be inferred from *Constitution* is that it is hard to see just what the distinctive characteristics of empirical work informed by structuration theory might be. Moreover, the fact that empirical work informed by different theoretical perspectives can illustrate structurationist points suggests two further possibilities: either that the concepts which constitute structuration theory are not specific to structuration theory or that they are so general as to be compatible with different social theories. This leads us back to the conclusions reached previously: given the ontological concerns of structuration theory it is far from surprising that echoes of structurationist points appear in a host of different social research projects. However, at the same time it is hardly on for Giddens to imply that the insights contained within structuration theory would have produced similar studies to the ones selected for discussion in *Constitution*. Manifestly they would not, since for one, the structurationist programme in its current form does not enable the specification of empirical research projects and, for two, the work thus inspired would be unable to proceed beyond the limits of point-by-point illustration.

3

Thus far two major points have been established, first that the ontological concerns reflected in the guidelines offered for empirical research renders them virtually useless for such research and, second, that the concepts contained within structuration theory itself have little distinctive or new to offer to either the conceptualization of empirical research projects or their existing content. The conclusion which must therefore follow is that for the purposes of empirical research, its conceptualization and objectives, structuration theory is of little direct use. Clearly, there is a degree of tension between a conclusion of this nature and the points made by Giddens about the necessity for structuration theory to illuminate empirical research issues. This is resolved in this section, first, through a discussion of Giddens's views on the nature of the theory–empirical research relationship and, second, through a consideration of the implications for this relationship of different levels of abstraction.

In *Constitution* Giddens makes the following comments about the nature of the relationship between theory and empirical research in the social sciences:

> There is, of course, no obligation for anyone doing detailed empirical research in a given localised setting, to take on board an array of abstract notions that would merely clutter up what could otherwise be described with economy and in ordinary language. The concepts of structuration theory, as with any competing theoretical perspective, should for many research purposes be regarded as sensitising devices, nothing more. That is to say, they may be useful for thinking about research problems and the interpretation of research results. But to

suppose that being theoretically informed ... means always operating with a welter of abstract concepts is as mischievous a doctrine as one which suggests that we can get along very well without ever using such concepts at all.[21]

The view of theory being forwarded here consists of two main parts. First, Giddens clearly sees theory in terms of concepts which make their strongest claims at the abstract level, a view which is shared by Sayer.[22] Second, he makes a very clear distinction between theory and empirical work; all of which is fairly uncontroversial stuff in terms of the debate over these questions in the social sciences. However, there is one major difficulty here. This concerns the extent of the separation between the theoretical and the empirical in this passage. In terms of the current debate a polarity of this degree appears defective: not only because it reduces the ideally reciprocal dialogue between the theoretical and the empirical to a caricature of dialogue but because it goes against Giddens's arguments elsewhere for a contextual social theory. Thus, in place of the anticipated argument for the latter, here Giddens provides an entirely different picture: one in which theory acts in a *potential* service role for empirical work; in which it is empirical research questions alone which determine the use of theoretical arguments; and in which no place seems to exist for the interrogation and development of theory through empirical work. However, any doubts about these points are removed by Giddens's examples of the use of structuration theory in empirical research, in which it is the nature of the empirical work which conditions the specific structurationist concepts referred to, in which large chunks of structuration theory remain unconsidered in the empirical work discussed, and in which the role of the empirical work is clearly to illustrate structurationist concepts rather than to interrogate structuration theory. Within his lengthy discussion of the relationship between structuration theory and empirical work in *Constitution* then, Giddens, is consistent: the nature of the theory–empirical research relationship may seem defective but it at least tallies with the discussion of the use of structurationist concepts in empirical research. However, what is less comprehensible, certainly immediately, is the mismatch between this view of the relationship between theory and empirical research in social science and the more conventional view implied by Giddens, where he refers to structuration theory being of little value unless it aids empirical research projects.

This problem revolves around different levels of analytical abstraction and the place of structuration theory within these. As has been emphasized, structuration theory is concerned essentially with developing an ontology of human society. What this means in terms of the concepts which Giddens provides in structuration theory is that, for the most part, these will be specific to the ontological level; they will relate more to the nature of being, or existence, in human society generally than to the contingencies of how this might work out in particular periods or places. This can be seen from just a few

---

[21] *CS*, pp. 326–7.   [22] See Sayer, *Method*, p. 131.

examples of structurationist concepts. Take, for instance, the concept of locale, defined as follows:

> Locales refer to the use of space to provide the *settings* of interaction ... Locales may range from a room in a house, a street corner, the shop floor of a factory, towns and cities, to the territorially demarcated areas occupied by nation states. But locales are typically internally *regionalised*, and the regions within them are of critical importance in constituting contexts of interaction.[23]

Quite clearly, then, the concept of locale refers to a basic condition of human society, that all action and interaction takes place within, uses and structures space. It does not, however, make any factual or specific claims about the nature, form or content of this setting. Indeed, this seems to be the point which Giddens is trying to emphasize through his indication of the range of potential locales. Similar conclusions can be reached from a look at other concepts which Giddens works with, for example, the duality of structure, which is used to try to capture the fulcrum between human agency and social structure. Here, as with locales, no comprehensive attempt is made to specify particular structural properties and the practices implicated in their reproduction. Instead, the point seems more to acknowledge that this recursive relationship between agency and structure, individuals and society is a universal feature of human society. We could go on and on here, but a final example will suffice to reinforce the point. This concerns human agency. Agency is unpacked by Giddens into three distinct but interrelated components: the stratification model, linking the reflexive monitoring of action, its rationalization and motivation with the unacknowledged conditions and unintended consequences of action: a three-tier model of consciousness comprising discursive consciousness, practical consciousness and the unconscious; and the occurrence of action within the *durée* of everyday life. The emphasis therefore is once more on teasing out the universal characteristics of human agency, rather than on examining the content of agency in, say, the context of a Birmingham school.

Given all this, we can label structuration theory a second-order theory: its concerns are not with theorizing the unique (i.e. with explaining the events or contingencies of particular periods or places) but with conceptualizing the general constituents of human society (i.e. agency, structure, time, space, power...).

This conclusion has important implications, not least for the nature of the theory–empirical research relationship at this level. Many of the theoretical concepts used in empirical research in social science, especially in human geography and sociology, are first-order: they suggest concepts which can be transferred immediately into an empirical setting (for instance wage labour, the labour process, industrial restructuring, masculinity/femininity ...).

---

[23] *CS*, p. 118.

Moreover, such concepts are often used to structure empirical research projects and are themselves modified frequently in the course of such work. With second-order theory the situation is very different. Indeed, in these circumstances empirical research as such is largely irrelevant; the theoretical is distinct from the empirical and, if it uses the latter at all, does so for one of two reasons, either to sensitize empirical work to ontological concerns, or to develop ontological arguments through illustration. Clearly, then, when Giddens refers to structuration theory and empirical research in *Constitution*, he is referring to the nature of this relationship at the latter level of abstraction, and not to the more familiar first-order use.

The conclusions reached at the end of the previous section obviously need qualification. Clearly, whilst both the guidelines offered and the concepts contained within structuration theory are useless for conducting empirical research in social science, we can now see why: as a second-order theory concerned with developing second-order issues, structuration theory clearly has a different relationship to the empirical from that of first-order theory. Moreover, both the guidelines suggested and the use of structuration theory in empirical research projects in *Constitution* reflect this. Indeed, whilst they may not be performing a first-order role here, they are operating at a second-order level, enabling Giddens both to utilize existing first-order work for the purposes of developing his ontology of human society and to illustrate ontological concerns in specific empirical contexts. As to the tension which exists between certain of Giddens's comments on the nature of the theory–empirical research relationship in social science and his more lengthy discussion in *Constitution*, it is evident that the view presented will vary according to the level of abstraction under consideration.

II

In the light of the above, two initial conclusions can be drawn concerning the relationship between structuration theory and empirical research, at least as presented in *Constitution*. These are first, that it would be unreasonable to expect structuration theory to generate either empirical research questions or appropriate categories for empirical analysis and, second, that to transfer structurationist concepts directly into empirical analysis is misconceived. This, quite simply, is because within structuration theory it is ontological issues which are at a premium. Given this, the questions and categories which structuration theory generates are more to do with the appropriateness and validity of its ontological claims than with empirical research issues. Furthermore, attempts to transplant any, or some, of the concepts contained within structuration theory into specific empirical projects both negate much, although not all, of the initial points of these concepts and run the risk of leading to the dismissal of structuration theory on false grounds. Second-order concepts relate primarily, although not exclusively, to second-order issues: at best they may alert first-order work to broader conceptual issues but, at worst, this type of exercise could either encourage the reduction of structuration theory to a few basic concepts, or even lead to its rejection (falsely) on the grounds that it fails to inform empirical work. Our first major conclusion therefore has to be that whilst structuration theory itself is, by and large, irrelevant to doing empirical research, this in turn would be an unfair criticism to level at structuration theory. Indeed, *given its terms of reference* it would be unrealistic to expect structuration theory to be of direct relevance to empirical research in social science. Such conclusions are confirmed with the appearance of *Nation-State*. Here, and for the first time, Giddens makes no explicit reference to the tenets of structuration theory, although structurationist overtones permeate the text. If nothing else this silence attests to the two points stressed in conclusion here, first that structurationist concepts themselves cannot specify issues or categories for historical/empirical investigation (for instance as here, the development of the nation-state) and correspondingly that structurationist concepts lack content (thus whereas the nation-state might be described in structurationist terms as a 'locale' or 'power container', to unpack the nation-state Giddens needs to go to historical work in both the Marxist and non-Marxist traditions). The second point, of course, is that silence speaks volumes: *Nation-State* does not begin to attempt either to transfer structurationist concepts into an empirical context or to use these concepts in unravelling modernity. Instead, it is only in the ontological implications of what is discussed that the influence of structuration theory is felt. A clearer indication of the precise nature of structuration theory is hard to envisage.

A second conclusion, however, is less charitable. It questions the terms of reference of structuration theory and turns the above comments on their head. So far, whilst it has been established that structuration theory, given its concerns, has (i) no direct relevance for empirical work and (ii) should not be expected to be of such relevance, no comment has been made as to whether it *ought* to be of relevance. The answer to this question depends on one's view of what a critical social theory entails. If, as most would accept, emancipation is at the heart of critical social theory, then obviously theory, even that couched in purely ontological terms, has at some point to cut into the empirical world: if it does not, then the link between theory and practice which is so central to emancipation is broken. In my view, then, the link between the abstract concerns of social theory and the concrete reality of the modern capitalist and patriarchal social world is of paramount importance. Indeed, without these links we would remain extremely uncertain about both the nature of this world and the processes and events occurring within it, and possible alternatives to it. In the case of structuration theory we are now in a position to state three points which in this respect are of immediate relevance. First, as established above, the nature of the theory–empirical research relationship is that to be found within second-order theory; it is one of thumbnail sketch illustration, and no more. Secondly, and following on from this, it is evident that whilst couched purely in these terms, structuration theory itself cannot provide a purchase on the structural conditions which pertain in the modern social world, i.e. it cannot add anything to the analysis of advanced capitalism, current forms of patriarchy, and so on and so forth. Indeed, so much is confirmed by Giddens's work in *Nation-State*, where structuration theory per se takes a definite back seat. The third point is that on these grounds structuration theory does not constitute a critical social theory: in its current form it has no direct connection with practice and, consequently, no notion of possible alternatives.[24]

Besides all this there is one further implication of structuration theory's existence as a purely second-order theory. This is that without a means of increasing historical specificity, of moving from the abstract to the concrete, structuration theory falls into the trap of theoretical relativism: it is just one more voice in a theoretical sea. However, if structuration theory is to extricate itself from this sea and in so doing offer a genuinely critical social theory, as opposed to simply an ontology of society, it is to the concrete, the particular, that it needs to move, but it would need to do so with a clear idea of the world between agency and boys in schools, locales and nation-states or street corners ... In other words, before structuration theory could help to illuminate empirical research in the conventional sense, it would need to specify for itself a middle ground in which structures such as capitalism, patriarchy and racism or their equivalents exist, and from which empirical research could proceed.[25] This is the magnitude of the task which confronts Giddens if he wishes to construct a critical social theory out of structuration theory. It is also what is required before most social researchers need begin to look to structuration theory for any form of guidance in their empirical research.

[24] For a similar criticism of Habermas see D. Held, 'Crisis Tendencies, Legitimation and the State', in *Habermas: Critical Debates*, ed. J. Thompson and D. Held (London, Macmillan), pp. 194–5.

[25] Gregory, 'Human Agency', p. 124.

12
A reply to my critics

Reasoned criticism is the life-blood of any scholarly discipline. Most people, whatever their level of commitment to their intellectual endeavours, probably find it easier to provide criticism rather than to receive it. But everyone working in an academic milieu must be prepared to be the subject of critique as well as offering critical appraisals of the writings of others. Of course, criticism can be shrill and dismissive, in which case it may very easily block rather than further the debates upon which the evaluation of ideas depend. I am fortunate indeed that all the contributors to this volume have produced critical assessments of my writings which, hard-hitting though some of them are, form positive contributions to discussion of the position and prospects of the social sciences. Few authors are privileged enough to be the subject of such sympathetic, yet exhaustive, examination from their critics, and I am grateful to all of the contributors for the diligence with which they have pursued their inquiries. I hope I can respond with the same degree of competence and seriousness of intent which they have displayed.

The chapters of this book range over many issues, and raise a diversity of objections to my views. If I were to reply to every point made, the result would inevitably be a quite superficial survey – or would result in a work as long as all the chapters put together. Instead of adopting such a tactic, I shall concentrate upon themes which one or more contributors have made central to their papers, and try to deal in at least some depth with the major questions posed. In some cases, criticism is aimed at what the various authors believe to be notable, and possibly inherent, limitations in my writings. On other occasions, the objections concern the fact that, in the critic's view, I have not developed my ideas as fully as I ought to do. Some criticisms of the first type seem to me to rest upon a misinterpretation of my views, or an inability on my part to express my position clearly; in other instances, they force me to think again about notions which stand in need of modification. No body of thought can cover all problems to which it might be deemed relevant, but in response to the second type of objection I shall take this opportunity to sketch in ways in which I think my conceptions could be further developed and new work undertaken.

Among the many observations made by the critics, a number of overriding themes are prominent. I shall focus my rejoinder upon seven such themes: how the concept of 'structure' should best be used in social analysis (raised in particular by Thompson and Bauman); the logic of functionalism, Marxism and the problem of evolution (Wright); the nature of the state, and its relation to the waging of wars (Held, Jessop and Shaw); the interpretation of time–space, and ontological security and urbanism (Saunders and Gregory); the significance of gender relations, in relation to social theory (Murgatroyd); the role of critical theory (Bernstein); and the connections between social theory, or my version of it, and empirical research (Gregson).

Some background observations

A brief autobiographical sketch might help tie together my comments on these themes, which otherwise look rather disparate. Although I have ventured – perhaps unwisely – into quite a number of different areas of social science, I would see my writings, certainly of the past fifteen years or so, as concerned with a single overall project. Let me try to describe what this is. To do so, I have to begin by mentioning some characteristics of the early development of the social sciences. The social sciences had their first formation somewhere around the mid eighteenth century in Western Europe. Emerging as a set of concerns having claims to universality, they were from their beginnings confined by perspectives and emphases reflecting their contexts of origin. The leading figures in 'classical social theory' of the nineteenth and early twentieth centuries were all preoccupied with the transformation of the 'traditional' into the 'modern' – in some sense – and with the implications of this for likely future developments. In interpreting such processes of change, they established numerous different positions. But certain overall parameters of thought were taken for granted by all or most of them – and these have tended to remain important in social science right up to current times.

1.   Impressed by the achievements of natural science, they looked to the physical sciences (or the then prevalent interpretations of them) to provide a model for their own endeavours. Even those who reacted against the idea that a 'natural science of society' is possible did so by reference to such views. That is, they proposed a 'humanistic' or 'interpretative' social science, set out in disjunction from the natural science model.

In formulating a basic conceptual approach in social science, several major traditions of thought – most notably that associated with Durkheim and his followers – saw 'society' as pre-eminent over the 'individual'. According to this view, society has a primacy over individual action, and the constraining properties of 'social facts' form the chief terrain for social analysis. Proponents of the contrasting standpoint laid emphasis upon the distinctive properties of 'individuals', seeing 'society' as the outcome of a multiplicity of discrete activities. The debate between the two sides was set up in such a way that it became virtually impossible to resolve.

2.   The transition from the 'traditional' to 'modern' was first of all understood
in terms of changes internal to Europe (and later the United States). The
major patterns of change seemed to be endogenous – springing from phenomena located within these societies themselves. Most of the more prominent
analyses therefore placed an emphasis upon generic models of transformation,
based upon the idea that certain typical processes of change 'unfold' in any
system which has reached the given level of development.

3.   To the prevalence of endogenous interpretations of change was added a
concentration upon certain institutional characteristics of 'modernity'. These
were characteristics associated above all with capitalism or industrialism.
Although some thinkers saw modern systems as essentially shaped by capitalism, while others emphasized industrialism, both tended to look for a
dominant transformative force in accounting for the extraordinary social
changes they witnessed. Against this backdrop, it is not surprising to find that
the state was either accorded only a relatively minor role in social organization
and change, or was understood mainly in relation to the maintenance of
internal social order, rather than being seen in the context of wider geo-
political involvements.

Having their origins in 'classical social theory', most of these emphases have
remained prominent in the social sciences until recently. In other words,
traditions of social thought pioneered mostly in the nineteenth century still
loom large in the present day. Put quite simply, the project which underlines
my writings is that of sifting through this residue, disregarding what was
always suspect or has become obsolete in the late twentieth century, and
working out what new perspectives might be introduced. In hindsight, we can
see that opposition drawn between naturalistic and humanistic social science
was misleading, particularly where it contrasted 'explanation' and 'interpretation' or 'understanding'. Natural science is an interpretative endeavour,
involving a hermeneutic framework. Conversely, explanation remains a key
objective of social science. The chief – although of course not the only –
distinguishing feature separating the social and natural sciences is that while
the hermeneutics of natural science concern only the discourse of scientists
themselves, in the case of the social sciences we always work in the context of a
double hermeneutic. This observation is fraught with implications, as I have
tried to demonstrate in various parts of my writings. For not only is it the case
that social scientists seek to interpret a pre-interpreted world; lay members of
society routinely reincorporate social science concepts and findings back into
the world these were coined to illuminate or explain. In my view, this phenomenon explains a great deal about the seeming inability of the social sciences to
match the cumulative knowledge produced by natural science. The conceptual innovations and empirical discoveries of social scientists routinely 'disappear' back into the environment of events they describe, thereby in principle

reconstituting it. But this very fact makes social science of much more fundamental importance in modern society and culture than has been ordinarily
supposed. Modernity is inseparable from *the constitutive role of social science*, and
reflection upon social life more generally, which routinely orders and reorders
both the intimate and more impersonal aspects of the lives people lead.

The debate between those who believe that the social sciences should 'start'
with society, versus those who favour the 'individual', increasingly became a
sterile one. The starting-point for theoretical thinking and empirical work in
the social sciences should rather be understood as the analysis of *recurrent social
practices*. This is fundamental to structuration theory as I have sought to
develop it, and connects closely to the essential importance of the recursive
features of social life. The discovery that the 'individual' is not a preformed
entity is often attributed to structuralism and post-structuralism, but in fact
should be regarded as a convergent emphasis of various different theoretical
perspectives in the social sciences today. This goes along with the concurrent
emphasis that 'society' is not a clearly given entity either. As most commonly
used, the term 'society' represents a particular interpretation of the nation-
state, largely stripped of its political and territorial aspects. Seeing the subject-
matter of the social sciences as concerned with the recursive ordering of
practices – and, therefore, institutions – across time and space is again of acute
importance for analysing the nature of modernity. For the globalizing tendencies inherent in the dynamics of modernity connect the local and the
intimate with events far flung in time and space – in much more complex
fashion than ever was the case in previous history.

Other perspectives associated with the residue of 'classical social theory'
also need a substantial re-examination and revision. In place of an undue
reliance upon endogenous models of change, we should substitute an outlook
which precisely focuses upon the relationship between the local and the
distant. 'Society' – as nation-state – still must command a good deal of our
attention, but we should learn to see that the 'parts' or regions of societies are
for some purposes better regarded as enmeshed in systems which have little
directly to do with the boundaries of states. This was *always* true: pre-modern
cultures and civilizations virtually never had clear-cut boundaries in the sense
in which nation-states do. But of course the observation has become particularly important with the globalizing tendencies that are now everywhere
apparent in the late twentieth century. These tendencies, I argue, are inherent
in the nature of modernity – but they are complex, and cannot be explained by
reference to changes occurring within any single institutional sector. Modernity is institutionally multi-dimensional, and the relations and tensions
between its various institutional components are fundamental to understanding our current social situation and the dilemmas which face us for the future.
At least four prime institutional aspects of modernity can be distinguished,
none of which is wholly reducible to any of the others: capitalism (the production of commodities for markets, based upon a cycle of investment and profit,

and involving the sale of wage labour as well as goods and other services); industrialism (the transformation of nature through the systematic use and continual revision, in the light of scientific and technological advances, of the instruments of production); surveillance (control of information, plus the direct supervision of people's activities, on the part of organizations and state authorities); and military power (control of the means of violence in the context of the 'industrialization of war').

Although I have spoken of my work as forming a single project, clearly the concerns just mentioned both are very wide-ranging and raise numerous problems and difficulties. I claim only to illuminate some features of these issues, not, of course, to provide a comprehensive coverage of them. I mention them here in order to give some general sense of the connections between my various writings. While I am not either by inclination or in practice primarily an empirical researcher, I do think of myself as working upon theoretical and more substantive issues simultaneously. Thus although the ideas I have grouped under the generic label 'structuration theory' have general method-ological significance, I worked them out as part of an attempt to think through questions of a more substantive kind. There is necessarily a gap between theory and empirical research, as I shall point out below. But 'pure theorizing' is likely to be as vacuous and unilluminating as the 'mindless empiricism' which C. Wright Mills so effectively criticized many years ago.

Let me, then, turn to the themes of the critics' articles, beginning with the idea of 'structure' and associated notions.

The concept of structure

Bauman and Thompson offer several critical observations about my use of 'structure' and other concepts closely associated with it. As Bauman rightly points out, one of my concerns in social theory has been to provide an account of human agency which recognizes that human beings are purposive actors, who virtually all the time know what they are doing (under some description) and why. At the same time, I have been concerned to justify the traditional insight of naturalistic social science, that the actions of each individual are embedded in social contexts 'stretching away' from his or her activities and which causally influence their nature. Grasping the recursive nature of social practices –the duality of structure – seems to me the key to achieving this.

In developing this viewpoint, I felt it crucial to move the concept of structure away from its conventional usage in Anglo-Saxon social science, although without abandoning that usage altogether. Structure, in its broadest sense, I argued, should be understood as rules and resources, recursively drawn upon and reconstituted in processes of interaction. While this idea has found sup-porters, it has also provoked some disquiet. Bauman and Thompson each register reservations about this approach, echoing in some degree the feelings of other critics. For Bauman, the concepts I propose compare unfavourably with somewhat parallel notions set out by Norbert Elias. Elias's conception of 'figuration', Bauman suggests, captures interdependencies of actors in processes of interaction more effectively than the concepts of structuration theory. Moreover, he adds, my notion of structure is too abstract and 'fixed' to be able to grasp 'structuring' potentialities of agents. Structure here, he goes on to say, appears as a determining element of action, being invoked to explain why people act as they do. A further point Bauman makes is that 'structuring' and 'being structured' are distributed unevenly in actual social life: some people are more able to 'structure' events, while others have to accept an already structured social world.

Thompson's reservations overlap in some part. He concentrates his criticisms upon the thesis that structure can be equated with rules, making several points about this. In his view I do not give the term 'rules' sufficient precision, and in any case it is misleading to relate structure to rules (or resources). The study of structural differentiation, he asserts, cannot be carried out in terms of analysing rules, because such differentiation presupposes structural qualities which are not themselves rules. The ways in which I seek to cope with this issue, such as invoking the idea of structural principles, Thompson says, are wanting. A structural principle is not a rule, nor are many of the characteristics which social scientists have in mind when they speak of structural differentiation. The difficulties he diagnoses, he believes, derive in some substantial part from the comparisons I make between social life and the use of language.

I should be the first to admit that I have not always expressed my ideas as clearly as I might have done, and that the views I set out in the first account of structuration theory, in *New Rules of Sociological Method*, have undergone some mutation since then. But the observations which Bauman and Thompson make do not persuade me to alter the main features of my viewpoint.

As I employ it, in a generic way, 'structure' does not refer to descriptive features of social life, situated in specific contexts of time and space. When we look for the stabilities or the 'continuities of form', which the notion of structure usually brings to mind, in my view we are analysing the reproduction of human social practices. It is misleading to link this conception of structure at all closely to Elias's notion of 'figuration'. I make a basic distinction between 'structure' and 'system', the second of which refers to the patterning of social interaction and social relationships across time and space. It is in terms of the concept of *system* that I would wish to grasp the interdependencies of which Bauman speaks. The term 'figuration', in fact, seems to be a substitute for the term 'system'. Elias wishes to emphasize the open-ended nature of social interdependencies, their lack of complete closure. But so long as one does not see social systems as similar to biological systems, or to systems in nature which are highly integrated and clearly defined, I cannot see that the idea of figuration offers any particular advance over that of system.

Thompson says that, as I employ it at any rate, the idea of 'structure' is 'vague' and ambiguous, largely because the concept of 'rule' is ill formulated. It is true that both notions, since they relate to social life in all its diversity, are necessarily very general. Generality, however, is not the same as vagueness. Part of the problem with the term 'rule', probably, is that it conjures up an image of a fixed and clear prescription. When we learn the rules of a game, for instance, we may think of mastering the rule-book which sets out how the game is to be played. But most of the rules involved in the structuration of social life do not have this character. I liken them to formulae, not because they can be expressed in a quasi-mathematical way, but because they specify 'generalizable procedures' or if one prefers, conventions, which agents follow. Perhaps some examples will help, although these are necessarily taken somewhat at random.

First, take the procedures or conventions involved in 'displaying agency', such as those analysed by Erving Goffman. Goffman points out that to be a human agent is not just to be in command of what one is doing (in some sense or another), but is also routinely to *display* to others that one has such command. Displaying agency is not itself a rule or procedure, but is accomplished through a whole variety of conventions which agents adopt. These govern control of bodily posture, gesture, modulation of voice, 'repairing' slips of the tongue or bodily lapses like inadvertently knocking something over, and many other aspects of behaviour. The display of agency, and its interpretation by others, affect not only the personality of the individual concerned, but conditions very deep-rooted features of day-to-day social life. The maintenance of what Goffman calls 'civil inattention', for instance, depends upon the very subtle but extremely influential conventions involved in agency display.

As a second example, take procedures of voting. It might seem as though here we are dealing with rules which more closely resemble the rules of games, because some of the procedures involved are highly formalized, such as 'one person, one vote'. However, to discover how voting actually 'works' – i.e., is produced and reproduced as concrete practices – we would need to analyse numerous tacit conventions also. Where formalized rules exist, the problem normally is to ascertain how far political participation actually conforms to what the 'rule-book' says. A third example: rules governing styles of dress. These might be represented as defining who wears what, when and where. There are some contexts in which rules affecting styles of clothing are very carefully and formally defined, as in the case of the uniforms of the military or of prison inmates. But most of the formulae people follow in the clothes they wear from day to day express less rigid prescriptions.

In all of the above examples, the rules involved not only specify constitutive features of the conduct to which they relate, but are also *sanctioned*. That is why I distinguish the two aspects of rules to which Thompson refers, the construction of meaning and the normative sanctioning of conduct. Of course, the sanctions involved may be very diffuse, as would be true of many aspects of agency display. On the other hand, if Goffman is correct, the failure to follow even some of these prescriptions might be a defining feature of insanity – in respect of which formal sanctioning mechanisms exist.

In each of the contexts referred to, the rules agents draw upon to produce and reproduce their activities organize practices that are deeply sedimented in space and time. That is, they are directly relevant to what are sometimes called the 'macro' characteristics of social systems. In the case of voting, this is obvious enough, given the part that voting plays in modern democratic orders. The other two contexts might at first sight seem to be more trivial, but in fact they are not. Procedures for the display of agency, as Goffman shows, probably underlie some of the most pervasive aspects of social institutions – and sustain, for instance, trust in and respect for others, these in turn being the precondition of most regularized forms of social relationship. The rules involved in styles of dress also contribute to quite fundamental aspects of institutions, such as those involved in the constitution of gender relationships.

In criticizing my viewpoint, Bauman and Thompson, in somewhat varying ways, pose the question: 'what are the rules which *comprise* social structure?' (Thompson's phrase); but this is not a question which makes any sense in terms of the notions I have proposed. I usually avoid using the term 'social' structure, because this conforms too closely to a position I want to avoid, in terms of which structure appears as something 'outside', or 'external', to human action. In my usage, structure is what gives *form* and *shape* to social life, but it is not *itself* that form and shape – nor should 'give' be understood in an active sense here, because structure only exists in and through the activities of human agents.

I do not claim, as Bauman says, that structure is 'exempt from the "structuring" potentialities of human agents'. Indeed, that observation also is more or less without meaning in terms of my viewpoint. 'Structure' has no descriptive qualities of its own as a feature of social life, because it exists only in a virtual way, as memory traces and as the instantiation of rules in the situated activities of agents. When Thompson uses the phrase 'social structure', he has in mind what I mean in speaking of the structural properties of social systems. As reproduced across space and time, systems of interaction and social relationships have a 'fixity' deriving from their institutionalized character. Social *systems* are certainly marked by what Thompson calls 'differentiation'. They involve imbalances of power, regional disparities, divisions of interests between groups and so forth. The study of such phenomena, of course, forms a major element of social science research. The structural properties of social systems, however, are not themselves rules, and cannot be studied as rules.

In the course of their contributions, Bauman and Thompson place a good deal of emphasis upon the point that, in any given social context, some rules are more important than others; a criterion of importance cannot be derived from rules alone. But although they clearly regard this observation as a damaging one, I do not feel in any way uncomfortable with it. The phenomena involved here are to do with relationships of differential *power*, and I have consistently stressed that power is an elemental characteristic of all social systems (although its analysis is complex, and it has both generative and distributive aspects). The fact that some actors are more able, as Bauman puts it, to 'structure' their social environments than others is also a matter of power, and has no direct bearing upon either the concept of 'structure' or that of 'system'. To develop these points further, let me refer to the examples Thompson uses in questioning the equation of structure with rules and resources. Consider how the noun 'the Left' is used in day-to-day discourse in a contemporary society. One could study how the notion appears in the talk of certain situated groups (say, trade union leaders). While one could not subsume this under any specific rule, the semantic content of the phrase, as used in such talk, is no doubt rich and varied; the term is sometimes used in a pejorative way, while among other individuals, or in other contexts, it has more positive meanings. Analysing the texture of such usages would help us understand aspects of the production and reproduction of unions as organizations, their relation to managerial strata and business firms, and more besides. It would at the same time sensitize us to aspects of the power relations within and between such collectivities. It would not be a 'part' of the systemic relationships involved, but rather a contributing element in their institutionalized reproduction – a 'structuring feature', which is all I mean by my generic use of the notion of structure.

Thompson's second example concerns restrictive entry to organizations such as schools or universities. Such barriers to entry, Thompson says, cannot be adequately understood as being composed of either rules or sanctions, but are aspects of the differential life chances which affect individuals in various social categories. What connection does 'structure', in my sense, have to such a situation? I would reply in the following way. We could not answer such a question by looking for a social rule which is somehow responsible for this phenomenon. Rather, we would be looking at certain forms of *system reproduction*, in which complexes of rules and resources are implicated. For instance, Bernstein's distinction between restricted and elaborated codes, as characteristic of the modes of language use of individuals from different class backgrounds, would certainly be relevant to understanding such differentials in life chances.

Thompson also offers critical comments about the notion of 'structural principles', which I introduced to refer to the co-ordination of institutions within overall social systems. A structural principle, he points out, is not a rule: it is not in any sense a formula expressing agents' knowledge about how to go on in the contexts of social life. This observation is entirely correct, but I do not think I ever suggested that a structural principle was equivalent to a rule. Perhaps this derives from a lack of clarity in exposition, but I take the concept of structural principle to cover at least some of the features of social systems with which Thompson is preoccupied. In analysing the significance of structural principles, I connect them with *institutional orderings* and with *time–space-*

distanciation. A structural principle is a mode of institutional articulation. An example is the institutional alignment of city and countryside in what I call 'class-divided societies'.

It might be worth while concluding this section with a few remarks about structural constraint, since this issue has often been raised by critics, and Thompson also makes reference to it. In *The Constitution of Society*, I distinguish three senses of constraint. First, there are physical constraints upon activity, deriving from the human body and the material environment. Second, there are constraints involved with the operation of power (which concern the resource/sanction aspects of social systems). Third, there are structural constraints, originating in the 'fixity' or 'objectivity' of social systems in relation to the individual agent. With regard to the latter two types, I interpret constraint as meaning the setting of limits upon the feasible range of options that an actor in a given circumstance or type of circumstance can follow.

Thompson registers two objections to this formulation. On the one hand, he claims, constraint in the second and third senses cannot be adequately reconciled with the idea that structure should be understood in terms of rules and resources. On the other hand, he goes on to argue, this position also effectively denies what I have always been concerned to stress – the centrality of agency as the 'possibility of doing otherwise'. For when constraint reduces the options of an individual to one, there are by definition no other courses of action to be followed and therefore the agent could not in fact have 'done otherwise'. Where structural constraint of such a form exists, therefore, structure and agency once again appear as the twin sides of a dualism, not a connected duality.

I have to say that I do not think either of these points is valid. Structural constraint derives from the institutionalized nature of social practices in a given context of action in which an agent finds himself or herself. Examining the nature of such institutionalization is inseparable from analysing the recursive characteristics of structure, but the constraining elements themselves have to be seen as expressing the 'givenness' of social environments of action to particular agents. It seems to me that this is usefully expressed in terms of sets of feasible options open to individuals or groups, and I think there is good reason to insist that where there is only a single feasible option, or type of option, this in no way undermines the significance of agency itself. Thompson thinks this point is merely a definitional one, and is, as he puts it 'for all *practical* purposes, irrelevant'. An individual who is 'forced' to gain a livelihood through the sale of his or her labour-power, as a consequence of being rendered propertyless, in the early days of the development of modern capitalism, had no other choice except to go hungry. Why insist that agency, the chance of 'doing otherwise', is still fundamental in such a situation?

The reason can be made clear by contrasting structuration theory with naturalistic versions of sociology. In these versions, regularities of action produced by structural constraints have causal properties of an invariant kind supposedly parallel to those characteristic of the physical world. What I refer to as a single feasible option, in other words, is treated only as a single option, which really *does* mean no option at all. There are no circumstances in social life, in fact, save perhaps certain marginal cases where an individual is completely drugged and simply manhandled by others, which are like this. The point is not a purely logical one, but is fraught with substantive implications. What describes a given option as the 'only feasible option' always presumes a certain range of wants or motivations on the part of the person or persons concerned. Where such wants or motivations become redefined, there may no longer be only one feasible option, but several potential courses of action. Many forms of contestation, opposition and active attempts at transformation stem from this circumstance, which I have tried to conceptualize using the idea of the 'dialectic of control'.

In concluding my comments in this opening section, let me briefly refer to the value of linguistic analogies in social science, since Thompson considers my use of such analogies to be in large part the source of the difficulties he diagnoses. He is aware that I have always rejected the thesis that social life is like a language, in the sense in which such a view was adopted by Lévi-Strauss and others. As he says, however, I do quite often seek to illustrate the recursive qualities of social systems by reference to the syntagmatic and paradigmatic aspects of language use. I feel unrepentant about doing this, so long as one remembers that language use is not an only 'exemplar' of the enactment of social practices, but is incorporated within and expresses aspects of what those practices are. We start to run into problems only if we try to push the comparison beyond helping us understand how the recursive character of social systems should be understood. I would point out, though, that the term 'language' often sounds overly formal for what I want to convey. The term favoured by ethnomethodological authors, 'talk', in some ways provides a more apt parallel.

Marxism, functionalism, evolutionism

No one can work upon core problems in the social sciences without entering seriously into a confrontation with the work of Marx. Although I am not myself a Marxist, and feel at greater distance from some of the main perspectives of Marxist thought than I once did, a continuing encounter with Marx's theories remains important to my outlook. In a very general sense, some of the passages in Marx's earlier writings outlining his conception of human praxis guided me in trying to elaborate my interpretation of the structuration of social life. Marx's aphorism that human beings 'make history, but not in circumstances of their own choosing' states in a nutshell a position I have tried to elaborate in considerable detail. In addition, his analysis of the nature of modern capitalism, especially his account of commodification, also seems to me to retain a certain basic validity. Yet there is much more in Marx that I would reject than I would accept. The materialist conception of history seems to me simply not to work as a generalized picture of human social development; Marx's account neither of the dynamics of capitalism nor of its imminent transcendence by socialism offers more than a partial framework for analysing the character of modernity.

In their contributions to this book, Wright and Jessop take up the question of my relationship to Marxism, Wright devoting virtually the whole of his chapter to this issue. As in the case of other chapters in the book, there are various points they make, and queries they raise, which I cannot undertake to react to here. I shall focus upon the following concerns:

1.   Wright's attempt at a partial defence of functionalism, an approach upon which he feels Marxism is in some large part dependent.

2.   The question of whether or not one can defend evolutionism in social science, something which connects fairly closely to the status of historical materialism.

3.   The problem, raised by both Wright and Jessop, of what are the distinctive features of modern capitalism and its class system.

4.   Jessop's query about why I do not offer any detailed discussions of leading Marxist analyses of the modern state.

1.   The debate about functionalism in social science has gone through two very distinct phases. The first, located mainly in the early 1960s, centered primarily upon the writings of Parsons and Merton. The controversies at that time concerned partly the logic of functionalist interpretations, but also questions of how far functional approaches could cope with issues of change, conflict and power. At that date, some of the leading critics of functionalist approaches were Marxists, or at any rate quite strongly influenced by Marx. The second phase of functionalist controversy has come about over the past decade. Following the publication of G. A. Cohen's book, *Karl Marx's Theory of History: A Defence*, which proposed that Marxism depends upon functionalist notions, this newer debate has concentrated more directly upon Marxist claims and concepts. Authors such as Jon Elster, also writing within a Marxist framework (although a heavily revisionist one), have sought to 'rescue' Marxism from the functionalist embrace into which Cohen locks it. Others, like Wright, while having a circumspect view of functionalist notions, nevertheless hold that some aspects of functionalist thinking can and should be defended, and argue that these are necessary elements of Marxism. That is the perspective Wright argues for in his contribution to this book. My own view is that functionalist arguments are more misleading than helpful in the social sciences, and that there simply is no defensible form of explanation which could be said to be 'functionalist explanation'. I have developed this view in various places, and although Wright says that I have 'completely ignored the most sustained defence of functional explanations in historical materialism' – that is, Cohen's work – I have in fact contributed directly to the controversy which

developed between Cohen, Elster and others.[1] Functional interpretations, I have consistently argued, are only of value in social science insofar as they are utilized to develop counterfactual arguments. It is often helpful for us to ask 'What would happen to item x, or system y, if certain social conditions z are not found?' Such counterfactual questions direct our attention to where explanations are needed; they do not supply them. Moreover, in posing such questions, there is no need to use the term 'function' at all.

Wrights accepts a good deal of this, especially the key theorem of the essential contingency of social reproduction. However, he feels there is one format in which functional interpretation is of basic importance. He gives the following example (surely implausible in substance, whatever one makes of its logic!). The example in question concerns racism. The existence of racism, it might be proposed, can be explained in terms of the fact that it divides the working class, blunting its potential radicalism, thereby having the function of stabilizing the capitalist system of class domination. The fact that racism is 'beneficial' in this way does not as such explain how it comes into being, but accounts for its entrenched character: it would disappear much more readily if it were not for its functional consequences. Such consequences need not be filtered through people's reflexive awareness of them to be effective.

Following Cohen's terminology, Wright argues that the effects produced by racism express a 'dispositional fact' of the capitalist system. But has anything actually been explained here? The answer is 'no'. The dispositional fact that racism is 'beneficial to the bourgeoisie' does not in any way explain or account for its persistence, unless some explanatory underpinning is added to the account. Racism simply happens to have the consequence of being 'beneficial to the bourgeoisie'. The 'happens to' remains to be explained. Basically, there are two ways in which such an explanation could be forthcoming, although in practice these may be mixed in complex fashion. The consequences may come about because they are intended, and therefore deliberately fostered by the actions of some groups; or the consequences may derive from a feedback cycle which no one reflexively monitors. *Identifying what in fact 'happens' constitutes the explanation of the phenomenon in question.*

A somewhat different situation exists where we are considering two or more traits of behaviour, one of which becomes 'selected out' on the basis of the existence of favourable consequences for the survival of a particular trait or form of activity. 'Dispositional facts' are here linked to some kind of specified mechanism of survival value in a given environment of action. Wright provides the example, borrowed from Elster, of the profit-maximizing tendencies of business firms. Firms which do not give sufficient attention to generating profits simply will not survive in the competitive marketplace. This outcome is the same regardless of whether or not those in charge of any particular corporation consciously attempt to profit maximize, or if the business simply generates high levels of profit for reasons which its managers did not know

[1] Anthony Giddens, 'Commentary on the Debate', *Theory and Society*, I (1982).

about. The prevalence of profit maximization is thus explained in terms of its functional consequences within the marketplace.

Can we say that here we have a genuine and useful form of 'functional explanation'? Again the answer is 'no'. The 'must' in the 'explanation' that surviving firms must have adopted profit-maximizing strategies because of their functional characteristics in the competitive marketplace remains a counterfactual if no further grounds for the adoption of profit maximizing are supplied. For it could happen, for instance, that no firm, even in a competitive marketplace, pursues profit maximization. It is only if at least some firms already profit maximize that it follows that other surviving firms in the marketplace 'have to' do so too; the explanation for profit maximization is still lacking. Such an explanation, as everywhere in the social sciences, would take the form of an account of the meshing of intended and unintended consequences of action. Wright's arguments, therefore, do not lead me to alter my view that there is no such animal as 'functionalist explanation'. It is often difficult to avoid slipping into imputed functional interpretations, as a passage Wright quotes from my own writings serves to indicate. The reason for this is that counterfactual thinking, one of the main procedures of all intellectual inquiry, can easily become sloppily transformed into the provision of 'explanations'. But this transformation is logically illicit.

2.   Whether historical materialism stands or falls with functionalism, I am inclined to doubt. It also can be disputed, of course, how far Marxist thought necessarily presumes any version of evolutionism. There are some celebrated statements in Marx's writings in which he asserts that the stages of social development he portrays are simply a unique set of historical processes, not involving generalized mechanisms of change or 'direction'. Other passages in Marx, as for example in the preface to *A Contribution to a Critique of Political Economy*, seem rather clearly to advance a version of evolutionism based upon the idea of the progressive development of the forces of production. In my view, as in the case of functionalism, if Marxism involves a type of evolutionary theory, so much the worse for Marxism. Except as used in a loose sense, as a synonym for 'development', or 'identifiable pattern of change', I do not think evolutionism has any useful part to play in the social sciences.

Wright sets out to question this, basing his account partly upon the thesis that my own approach slips into evolutionism, even while I declare theories of social or cultural evolution to be valueless. In Wright's view, 'the challenge Giddens poses to Marxist theory is not so much anti-evolutionism versus evolutionism, but two substantively different theories of social evolution' (p. 92) – a Marxist one and my own view.

Wright identifies three conditions which justify speaking of a theory of change as 'evolutionary'. Some type of overall 'direction' is implied; at any given stage, the probability that a particular type of social system will persist must be greater than the probability of 'downward progression'; and there must be some mechanism, of some sort, promoting movement up the various levels of the evolutionary hierarchy. If the concept of evolution is formulated in this way, Wright argues, we avoid the more obvious pitfalls of naive forms of social and cultural evolutionism. There is no presumption that evolutionism is unilinear, since stages can be jumped and 'regressions' are possible. Marxist theory, in the guise in which Wright defends it, meets these three criteria. A 'direction' is presumed in Marx's typology of social forms. At any given level in the development of the productive forces, the probability of at least staying at the same level (what Wright calls, following Cohen, 'stickiness downward') is high. A mechanism of change exists – even if it is, in Wright's phrase, 'a weak impulse' – insofar as human beings have a general interest in improving productivity through lessening their daily toil. The typology of social forms I have formulated, Wright says, differs only in content, but not in logical nature, from historical materialism thus conceived. In place of the centrality of the forces of production, I put the notion of time–space distanciation. There is a typology here with some distinct 'direction'; it is 'sticky downward'; and a general mechanism exists since people who have experienced the benefits of living in a framework of expanded time–space distanciation are reluctant subsequently to forgo them.

The issues involved here are mainly empirical rather than logical. I would have no quarrel with the three criteria by means of which Wright defines evolutionism. The first two can be applied to the social world without too much difficulty. The problem concerns the third criterion. In the case of biological evolution, clear mechanisms of change are involved, based upon natural selection and mutation. It simply seems to me false to suppose that something similar exists in the case of human history, and, more specifically, that the forces of production can have this role. The proposition which Wright offers, that people will have an overriding interest in furthering productivity and technological advance, just doesn't conform to the empirical findings of history and anthropology. Hunters and gatherers living in favourable material environments, for example, whose way of life is primarily concerned with the protection of tradition, with ritual, myth and religion (which forms part and parcel of the 'work' they do) have no generalized interest in improving the forces of production.

The scheme of social development which appears in my writings is not based upon some kind of analogue mechanism to the forces of production in Marxist theory. I do not hold, as Wright suggests, that there are 'autonomous evolutionary dynamics' involved. If we look at the period of human history, for instance, at which agrarian civilizations (class-divided societies) came to the fore, we find a variety of influences at work. Military power, the mobilizing role of cultural ideas, experimentations with different forms of state apparatus, together with variations in the forces of production, all play a role.

In sum, I prefer to see my own framework characterized in a way which is mentioned by Wright, but which he is anxious to reject. I 'provide general abstract concepts with which to analyse historical development', but 'no general theory of that development' (p. 102).

3.   Most forms of Marxism give a prime role to classes in interpreting the nature of human history, although the relation of class analysis to interpretation in terms of the expansion of the forces of production remains a rather clouded matter. As a theorem supposed to illuminate large segments of historical change, the thesis that 'all human history hitherto is the history of class struggles' surely cannot be taken seriously. However, I do find important at least certain aspects of Marx's discussions of class, and more particularly his analysis of the class relations of capitalism.

Wright and Jessop raise various questions about my view of the character of modern capitalism and its class system. I cannot respond to all these queries in this context and will limit myself to the issue of the 'class reductionism' of Marxism. Wright and Jessop each address this issue, in slightly different ways. Jessop suggests that there is an inconsistency in my characterization of the schisms or modes of exploitation characteristic of capitalist societies. On the one hand I argue that capitalism is structured in terms of class relations in a more fundamental sense than systems which are merely 'class-divided'. Yet, on the other hand, I distinguish various other basic sources of division, which I argue cannot be reduced to class relationships. While Jessop limits himself to diagnosing the inconsistency, Wright seeks in some part to defend the outlook of Marxism. Although in his discussion it is not easy to work out exactly where his own view lies, Wright seems to hold that class relations somehow undergird, or at a minimum set defined limits to, other types of division.

These are matters about which my views have to some degree shifted across the years, and where in addition I have failed to make them sufficiently clear, so I welcome the chance to elucidate them. In using the term 'class-divided society' to refer to non-modern civilizations, I mean to draw attention to certain of their distinctive features. With some exceptions, the class system of traditional civilizations is founded upon the extraction of rent revenue or corvée labour from a peasantry whose conditions of life in the local community remain substantially distant from the influence of the dominant class. This no longer remains the case with the advent of capitalistic enterprise, in which labour power becomes a commodity. Processes of commodification penetrate many aspects of social activity, and even lead to the commodifying of time and space. In this sense, capitalism is a more thoroughgoing class system than pre-existing types of social order.

At the time when I first set out those ideas, my position was an ambiguous one, because at that point I had not given enough attention to providing a broad institutional characterization of what I was then calling, without qualification, 'capitalist societies'. My approach at that juncture owed too much to Marx and to Weber. Today I still see contemporary (Western) societies as capitalistic. But the capitalist economic order is only one structuring dimension of modernity, even if its influence is very profound. A basic task facing sociology today, as I would see it, is to develop a more cogent account than hitherto of what I have earlier referred to as the multidimensional character of modernity.

However, even 'modernity' is not an all-enveloping totality, with which all aspects of social life start afresh. Some types of institutional ordering and social relationships *pre-exist* the advent of modern institutions, and while being restructured through them are not brought into being by them. *Gender inequality* and *ethnic discrimination* are probably the most deep rooted of these. There seems to be no known society, including otherwise quite egalitarian hunting and gathering cultures, in which men do not in some key spheres hold more power than women. 'Racism', as an outlook based upon erroneous interpretations of biological inheritance, is in some substantial part a modern phenomenon. But ethnic antagonism, prejudice and ethnocentrism are found in all types of social order.

Where do these observations leave us with regard to the question of the primacy of class relationships since the advent of capitalism? I would stick by my previously stated views on this issue, but can set out their basis more clearly than before. I continue to maintain, as I expressed it in *A Contemporary Critique of Historical Materialism* (the relevant passage is quoted in Wright's chapter, p. 88), that there are three main axes of exploitative relationships in modern systems besides that of class: exploitation associated with the use of political power, including military domination; with relationships between ethnic groups; and that associated with gender relationships. Gender divisions and ethnic schisms are more deeply engraved in human social organization, and human psychology, than are the other forms of exploitative domination. Class relationships are associated with one of the main institutional orderings of modernity, *capitalistic institutions*. *Industrialism*, another major institutional clustering of modernity, concerns above all the exploitative relationships between human beings and nature, rather than social relationships as such. Exploitative relationships on the political level here group together *governmental power* and *control of the means of violence*.

Neither gender divisions nor ethnic divisions can be reduced exhaustively to class categories, and are historically and institutionally more deeply engrained than them. Marxist writers these days are much less prone than once was the case to engage in crude forms of class reductionism, particularly in respect of gender, given the critical attacks to which they have been subject by feminist authors. Moreover, there are fewer Marxist writers today who see the labour movement as the only transformative vehicle of any significance in respect of collective protest. But there does seem to be a 'bottom line' according to which, to be a Marxist at all, at some level the thesis of the primacy of class must be sustained. For me, such a position is inherently far too limiting.

4.   Jessop points out that I do not confront Marxist approaches to the state in

any great depth, although I offer various sorts of criticisms against them. This is not the place to rectify that omission, even if I were inclined to do so, but I can at least offer some very brief comments about the ideas of two of the authors to whom Jessop refers, Gramsci and Poulantzas.

I must confess to never having found the works of either of these writers as compelling or illuminating as Jessop does. Both, to be sure, at least to some extent, fought clear of the inclination of many Marxist authors to analyse the state almost wholly in terms of its role as manager of the economic contradictions of capitalism. Gramsci's concern with the various aspects of hegemony, and with the complicated nature of political strategies, led him to avoid such a simplistic viewpoint. Particularly in his later writings, Poulantzas moved to a view of the state similarly emphasizing diverse elements of its make-up. Yet I do not think either author offered much that is useful for analysing major aspects of modern states upon which I want to concentrate attention – especially the institutional form of the nation-state, its territoriality, the character of the nation-state system, and the association of these with surveillance and with military strength.

Gramsci's account of state power certainly provided an important counterweight to 'economistic' interpretations within Marxist thought as a whole. He acknowledged a distinct sphere of the political – concerned, both for state authorities and those who would overthrow them, with power and strategic decision-making. The position of a state within the overall imperialist system is recognized to affect the nature and consequences of political crises, and the forms of hegemonic control which exist at any given point in time. In recognizing the partly independent influence of the 'superstructure', Gramsci broke away from prior Marxist formulations. His various discussions of the balance between coercion and consent were more subtle than those of most previous leading Marxist authors – and most subsequent ones as well, come to that. Yet it was only within the relatively narrow confines of Marxist thinking about the state that Gramsci's work was path-breaking. Moreover, while the concept of 'hegemony' may remain useful – although surely it has been overemployed to the point of abuse – I cannot myself find much in Gramsci that I would regard as particularly helpful today.

Poulantzas was obviously by any token an author of relatively minor stature by the side of Gramsci – whose writings considerably influenced his work. Poulantzas's intervention in debates about the state was nonetheless an important one, and helped emphasize some of the themes to which Gramsci had earlier given attention – particularly the 'relative autonomy' of state power from economic institutions. But during his 'structuralist phase', this insight was burdened with a conceptual apparatus of an awesomely arcane kind. In his later writings, Poulantzas developed interesting discussions of democracy and authoritarianism in contemporary politics. His analyses of 'authoritarian statism' definitely have some continuing relevance – although again I do not feel they were particularly original save within the boundaries of Marxist thought. Of the various strands within Poulantzas's work, his persistent concern with the character of modern law seems to me most interesting and important.

There are two reasons why I have not extensively discussed Gramsci, Poulantzas, and other major Marxist interpreters of the state in my recent work on nation-states and political power. One is that, as I have indicated previously, they do not offer a great deal concerning the main themes upon which I sought to focus. The other is that, although I sometimes draw upon Marxist ideas, I do not feel compelled to give them primacy. In studying state power, as at many other points, it seems to me that a Marxist framework is too restricting to be of particular value.

States, citizenship and war

Marxism involves not just class reductionism, but 'capitalist reductionism' also. That is to say, expansion of capitalism is seen as the fundamental dynamic transforming the modern global order. The lack of attention given in Marxist thought – even if this is by no means confined to Marxism – to the role of nation-states, nationalism and war derives substantially from this emphasis. Jessop accepts this point. But he goes on to raise the question of 'the form of the modern state and its relation to the capitalist economy', asking what general connections I see between these. This is the first problem I shall discuss under the current subheading; I shall discuss questions also raised by Jessop and Held concerning modern states as 'welfare states' in the light of the nature of citizenship rights. Finally, I shall proceed from welfare to warfare, considering the main issue raised by Shaw: how should we analyse the character of militarism and war in the contemporary period?

In answer to Jessop's query (p. 123) about the connections between my earlier and later writings, I do in fact still hold that the 'insulation' of polity from economy is one of the distinguishing characteristics of capitalist states. In my earlier work, however, I tended to see this as an 'internal' dichotomy, between institutional orders 'within' a society. I would now place this analysis, as with other questions concerning modern political systems, more in the context of the relation between nation-states on the one hand and capitalistic economic mechanisms on the other. The 'autonomy' of states does not come about simply because political authorities somehow manage to achieve for themselves some space of action separate from the economic order. Rather, governmental authorities establish bases of power centered upon control of surveillance mechanisms, territorial monopoly, and monopolistic control of the means of violence. The development of the nation-state system and of capitalism represents two intersecting processes, both intrinsically globalizing in character, neither of which can be reductively explained away in terms of the other. A great deal of work still needs to be done, as Jessop rightly points out, to show just how they interrelate, especially on the world level. One of the best indications of this is the large distance which still separates the most sophisticated accounts of the spread of capitalistic mechanisms (such as Wallerstein's world-system theory) from interpretations of the rise of the nation-state system (such as the theories of states as 'realist' actors elaborated in the discipline of international relations).

The concept of citizenship forms one means of helping to analyse the relation between political and economic orders with the emergence of nation-states. There is an inherent tie between the sovereignty of modern states and the development of citizenship rights. Nation-states have sovereign domains, defined by borders, and marked by a degree of administrative concentration and internal pacification unknown among traditional civilizations. Understanding the nature of modern citizenship rights allows us to analyse at least some aspects of modern states as 'welfare states'. I believe – as Held shows in his analysis – that I have said more about these issues in recent work than Jessop tends to acknowledge. However, Held also goes on to elaborate a number of criticisms of my use of the notion of citizenship, and suggests ways in which it should be altered and refocused.

The points Held makes in this regard relate back to my discussion in the preceding section of this response. In analysing citizenship, Held argues, I have been insufficiently critical of the framework within which T. H. Marshall set out his classic discussion. Marshall was concerned to show how the development of citizenship rights blunts the class divisions which Marx saw as characteristic of capitalism. But this is too restrictive, in Held's view. Citizenship cannot be studied as though it were simply a matter of how far it serves to alleviate class inequalities. Other major dimensions of social life, he says, have been closely bound up with struggles to achieve citizenship rights. I agree with this point, although I have perhaps not brought out its significance adequately in my writings on the topic. As Held says, I have tended to overstress the importance of class conflict as a medium of the development of citizenship rights – largely because I have situated my discussion in terms of a critique of the work of Marshall.

However, as Held's own chapter makes clear, to recognize this actually brings the analysis of citizenship more directly into line with emphases elsewhere in my work. I think it is useful to attempt to categorize major types of rights in terms of the analysis I provided in the closing chapter of *The Nation-State and Violence*, and Held seems partly to accept this (p. 173). I did not suggest in that work that this classification covers all aspects of citizenship rights; the point of the discussion was specifically to link such rights to institutional dimensions of modernity. I do not see any great problem in extending this analysis to bring in the other forms of rights to which Held draws attention. He quite often mentions, for instance, rights to do with the position of women in contemporary societies. Connecting these with modernity means for me analysing the phenomenon I have already mentioned previously – how the institutions of modernity intersect with modes of gender inequality, and the struggles which have resulted. Held points out that I have not written in any detail about the nature of social movements, which is true – although no one can write about everything. But while I have not sought, thus far anyway, to provide a full framework for studying social movements, I do think I have set out an outline of such a framework (although I would not claim that it was particularly original). Social movements, in my opinion, are one of the two main systemic forms which the reflexivity characteristic of modernity assumes, the other being organizations (of which the state is itself one). Alain Touraine's idea that social movements operate in 'fields of contestation' with established organizations, each influencing the other in a dialogical process, seems to me a fruitful one.[2] Not all social movements orient themselves directly towards the state, but most are normally brought into a dialogue – or open confrontation – with state authorities, as a result of which acceptance of some of the aims of the movement may be achieved. This in turn influences the character and further ambitions of the movement, such processes of interchange perhaps lasting over many years, with periods of quiescence in between.

Held raises the question of the relation between citizenship rights and the sovereign character of nation-states. It is very clear that some quite fundamental issues concerning government, freedom and responsibility are located here. As is well known, the constitutional rights proclaimed by modern states advance universal values – such as the Declaration of Human Rights built into the American Constitution. But such rights have everywhere been mainly enshrined within the institutions of nation-states, rather than being made an effective part of international law. In his original discussion of citizenship rights, Marshall was mainly concerned with Britain and, as Held says, his account was largely an 'internalist' one. I do not think I can fairly be bracketed with Marshall in this regard. I have tried to see citizenship rights in terms of the creation of sovereignty of states within the nation-state system. What has happened in modern history, as I would see it, is that many types of citizenship rights (such as rights of political participation) have in fact become more or less universalized. That is to say, they have been acknowledged almost everywhere. However, this has come about, not because of a globalizing of these rights themselves, but *because of a universalizing of the nation-state form*. Virtually all modern states, for example, are in some sense 'democratic', and as such accord a range of rights to their citizens. But by this very process, these rights are institutionalized only in sectional fashion, within the confines of discrete states.

How can citizenship rights effectively be translated into the 'human rights' which intrinsically they are? This surely is one of the major problems of our age, although one whose resolution is likely to be protacted and problematic. I am not sure I have much to add to the debates on this issue. As globalization accelerates, it seems likely that there will be pressures towards closing the

[2] Alain Touraine, *The Self-Production of Society* (Chicago: University of Chicago Press, 1977).

'gap' between sectionalized citizenship rights and generalized human rights. But it would be difficult to claim that this process has proceeded very far at the moment. There remains an institutional chasm between the proclaiming of universal or international laws and the contexts of their actual enactment. The example mentioned by Held, the International Tribunal at Nuremburg, is a good case in point. International laws relating to universal rights may have been framed during the course of the Tribunal, but where are the global agencies which can make these count for much in practice? For the immediate future, it seems likely that the promotion of generalized human rights will remain mainly in the hands of nation-states, particularly of course the super-powers. In such circumstances, there is bound to be a continuation of the familiar mixture of moral concern and cynicism which states display in criticizing the lack of effective human rights in some areas of the world, while tolerating their abuse in others, as geopolitical interests dictate.

The development of citizenship rights has been strongly influenced by the impact of war. The advent of universal male suffrage, for instance, was in a number of European countries directly related to the endeavours of govern-ments to generate mass loyalty in times of actual or anticipated warfare. The connection between the ballot and the bullet has been well explored by historians. Many more general parameters of the impact of war upon social and political institutions, however, remain to be explored. As Shaw notes, important work is now beginning to appear in this area, and I hope my book *The Nation-State and Violence* makes some sort of contribution to it. As Shaw also mentions, in that book I stopped short of trying to provide an interpretation of the nature of modern warfare itself. The book lacks, as Shaw puts it, 'a social theory of war and militarism'. Obviously it would be impossible to provide such a theory in the context of this reply, but I can at least indicate what my views about the issue are.

1.   I would disagree somewhat with the interpretation of Clausewitz which Shaw offers, but accept that Clausewitz's work still serves as the necessary backdrop to analysing warfare in the present period. The Clausewitzian thesis that 'war is the continuation of policy by other means' seems to me a basic property of what might be called 'early modern warfare' – that is, warfare up to the period at which the mechanization of weaponry, together with mass conscription and the development of industrialized war economies, initiated 'total war'. The 'absolutism' of war is characteristic, in my view, of the period *prior* to the emergence of total war. The idea that there is no necessary limit to war is precisely what gives some sense to the idea that war is entered into when the limits of diplomacy, or other kinds of constraint, are exhausted. Total war should not be understood as the logical outcome of the absolutism of earlier forms of warfare, but as signalling a *novel* set of circumstances. It took two World Wars to drive this lesson home, and the appearance of nuclear weapons has underscored the point once and for all. When military force becomes so

destructive as to threaten vast swathes of devastation even for the 'victors', diplomacy has to be turned to the means of preventing war, rather than warfare being the end result of failed diplomacy.

This 'reversal' of the relation between diplomacy and war is of key importance in the late twentieth century. One has to presume that direct warfare between the two superpowers is unlikely, although it is a possible eventuality which forms part of the 'risk contour' of modernity for an indefinite period to come. The superpowers have built up an elaborate global network of military alliances and client states. In conjunction with this network, there has developed a pattern of 'orchestrated wars', occurring in areas peripheral to the superpowers themselves. These are wars to which the superpowers, and other industrialized states, may or may not directly send soldiery, but which are essentially 'fought at a distance' and 'kept in bounds' by *de facto* agreements to limit their extent. Orchestrated wars may be very destructive in terms of lives and resources, as the Vietnam War showed. But this destructiveness is kept within bounds, since both sides recognize that they are fighting by proxy, even when their own armed forces are involved. Non-orchestrated wars are probably more dangerous to world peace than those which are more directly tied into the interests of the superpowers. An example is the war between Iran and Iraq, which to some extent cut across the geopolitical interests that divide the superpowers, but carried distinct dangers of escalation, plus more erratic and contingent superpower involvement.

2. Let me now turn to the question of 'militarism'. Militarism is a vague term and is by no means easily defined. If, however, it refers to the traditional warrior values of admiration for war, personal valour and glorious death, almost everywhere in the world militarism is in decline. Even before the period of total war, with the bureaucratization of fighting units, such values were already partially obsolescent. The more warfare moves towards reliance on high technology and electronic control, the less relevant traditional types of militarism become. The technologically advanced armed forces of today possess a great deal of what Mary Kaldor has aptly called 'baroque' weaponry.[3] It is ornate and sophisticated, but most of it, up to and including nuclear weaponry, forms a sort of symbolic display rather than a build-up of fire power destined to be put into effective battlefield use. Samuel Huntington is probably right to say that most modern military leaders are less prone to engage in military adventures, even in respect of orchestrated war, than are politicians.

All this would seem to create the potentiality for a world without war, especially given the fact that the territorial borders of nation-states have mostly been fixed, while processes of globalization undermine some of the principal motivations for which war used to be fought. Yet while this potentiality plainly exists, there is no imminent prospect of a world government which will create on a global scale the processes of internal passification character-

[3] Mary Kaldor, *The Baroque Arsenal* (London: Deutsch, 1982).

istic of most nation-states. In the mean time, the world military build-up continues, as does the routine application of scientific innovation to improving the destructive power of weaponry. The world has to tread a tightrope over potential disaster for many years yet, and no one can say with any confidence how successful this massively dangerous traverse will be.

Nuclear war between the superpowers always remains a possibility; orchestrated wars may flare up into broader conflicts; it may be impossible to prevent the proliferation of nuclear weaponry on the large scale, heightening the dangers already faced; terrorist organizations might acquire nuclear weapons and threaten to use them in pursuit of their aims; processes of technological innovation might create new types of weaponry of immense destructive potential, produced more cheaply and needing less complex technical knowledge than nuclear armaments. All these considerations show how difficult and contingent even the relatively short-term future for humanity is in respect of military power and war.

Capitalism and the modern state

Jessop and Held each raise questions about my treatment of the modern state, although they express their queries in somewhat different ways. Held points out that the emergence of the European states in the post-medieval period was associated with new conceptions of impersonal rule, sovereignty and law – something with which I certainly agree. But how do these factors, Held asks, relate to the development of capitalism? For quite often I speak of modern states as 'capitalist states', and argue that the state in capitalism 'is a state in a class society'. How can such emphases be reconciled with the thesis that modern states involve the mobilizing of autonomous political power? Jessop points to much the same issue, arguing that I nowhere adequately analyse 'how the state is articulated to capitalism'. In fact, he goes on to say, I adopt two different positions in my various comments on this problem. Sometimes I speak of modern states as though they were structured in terms of the framework of capitalistic institutions they administer. This is, in effect, where I speak of modern states as 'capitalist states'. On other occasions I am, in Jessop's words, 'more concerned with the institutional development of societies which happen to be capitalist'. Here the state is not, as such, a 'capitalist state', but 'a state articulated with capitalism' (p. 121).

Two rather separate problems are raised here. One concerns the part played by the expansion of capitalism in relation to the early development of modern states. The other concerns the institutional form of the modern state – particularly the relations between capitalism and democracy. Both are aspects of how economic and political institutions are articulated, but they bring to the fore somewhat contrasting concerns. Of course, each issue raises a host of complex considerations, most of which I cannot even touch upon in this context.

1. Was the early development of capitalism more than contingently connected with the formation of modern states? My answer to this would be 'yes', but that we should be careful to avoid both economic and political reductionism in explaining the nature of the connections.

The early development of the modern state provided an institutional framework within which capitalism could flourish, but was not called into being by it. The modern state was formed as part of a state system in a continent in which no effective imperial centre emerged to replace the Roman Empire. The territorial integrity involved in state sovereignty and the development of impersonal political authority have to be understood as largely separate from the influence of capitalism. These characteristics were formed mainly in the context of monarchical centralization and in relation to conflicting political and military pressures.

Capitalism and the modern state early on had 'elective affinities' and tensions with one another which are still in evidence today. State institutions provided settings which facilitated – and in some ways were necessary conditions for – the expansion of capitalist enterprise. These included the pacification of the social relations – at home and abroad – which capitalistic exchange involves; universal legal codes governing property and persons; the guaranteeing and protection of monetary values; the provision of material means relevant to economic transactions, such as transport, communication and utilities; and, quite often, the direct sponsoring of capitalist enterprise, through state-owned or state-controlled finance or production companies.

On the other hand, the institutional affinities between capitalism and the modern state were, and are, far from complete. Capitalist enterprise is intrinsically universalizing and spreads beyond the borders of states, leading to the creation of power relations which escape the control of governments. The economic exchanges involved in capitalism tend to 'strip away' other aspects of the relationships they engender. In other words, in its 'purer' forms at least, capitalism has no place for moral conceptions, social justice or patriotism. In so far as governments legitimate their rule by reference to such ideals, their objectives and interests may clash with those of business leaders. As unities involved in geopolitical relations with each other, moreover, states have interests that may easily diverge from those of capitalist organizations.

In the contemporary world, the global capitalist economy, and what has now become a world-wide nation-state system, stand in continuing tension with one another. The division of states into ideologically pro-capitalist, state socialist and non-aligned countries, of course, complicates this tension. Notwithstanding current experiments with market liberalization, the state socialist countries continue, at least for the time being, to form a bulwark against capitalistic globalization. The military and administrative 'policing' of the world by the two super-powers to some extent divides along capitalist/anti-capitalist lines, given their respective ideological orientations. But the correspondence is only a rough one because geopolitical considerations are involved, and because both recognize a responsibility to sustain co-operation – even within their mutual antagonism – to avoid nuclear confrontation (see also my remarks on pp. 271–2).

2.   What of the second problem raised previously, the institutional form of the modern state? Are modern states 'capitalist states' and, if so, what should this term be taken to mean? In my view, we can accurately speak of modern political orders (that is, modern Western-style states) as 'capitalist states'. The modern state was pioneered in the West and developed in conjunction with the spread of capitalistic enterprise. Aspects of the capitalist state have since become more or less universal, but other features are specific to it.

What makes a state 'capitalist' is that much of the economic activity that generates the wealth through which government institutions are funded is organized according to market criteria. In other words, goods and services are distributed in terms of the profit–production–investment–profit cycle, rather than in terms of social values of one kind or another. In all capitalist states, there is a 'push and pull' between market-provided and non-market-provided goods and services. No state has ever been, or ever will be, 'purely capitalistic', since there are many barriers – political, economic and ideological – which prevent the subjecting of all aspects of life to market criteria. A capitalist state is dependent upon business leaders for a good deal of its revenue, and recognition of this fact is part of the outlook of all government officials. No government can neglect the accumulation process, which, however, it does not directly control. Divisions between class-based parties tend to centre upon the 'push and pull' of market and non-market provision, since the conditions favouring capitalist accumulation seem on the whole to accentuate inequalities and regional imbalances.

Quite clearly a key question for political thought concerns the connections between capitalism and democracy. Is the insulation of the 'political' from the 'economic' the condition of existence of a democratic polity? Are the freedoms of markets the basis of political freedoms as a whole? To these questions I would answer 'no'. Democracy, citizenship rights and the role of impersonal law are not as such the outcome of capitalism, but derive more from the administrative co-ordination of the modern state. Virtually *all states* in the contemporary world, to repeat what I said in the preceding section, are democratic in the sense that they proclaim values of participation, and accord a range of citizenship rights to their members. The universal appeal of mass democracy today is truly extraordinary if we consider that no state in the world was democratic in this sense prior to the late eighteenth century. It is the 'price' ruling groups pay for the compliance they seek to secure from those subject to their administrative dominance.

Of course, there is a vast difference between the label 'democracy' and actual political freedoms and rights. What role does capitalism play in the very

real political freedoms which the citizenry enjoys in most Western-style states?
The answer, I think, is that a strongly developed capitalistic sector (a)
encourages pluralism and (b) protects large tracts of civil society from direct
governmental control. The benefits and limitations of this are well known, and
are asymmetrical in terms of class divisions. Capitalism, citizenship rights and
personal freedoms are not intrinsically connected over and above the two
points just mentioned. There are other bases of pluralism and of maintaining a
strong civil society. Indeed, one of the most important features of democratic
political theory today, as Held rightly emphasizes, has to be an emphasis upon
the diverse potential institutional 'centres' or 'arenas' of rights and freedoms.

I would again seek to analyse these in terms of the various institutional
clusterings mentioned earlier – those associated quite directly with modernity,
together with those which are more deeply embedded historically and cross-
culturally. In discussing political justice and political freedoms today, we must
move away from the old frameworks of debate. The correlate in political
theory of the transitions in social theory and sociology I mentioned at the
opening of my Reply is the exhaustion of Marxism, liberalism and conserva-
tism alike as traditions of thought – as Held also recognizes. In current times
we must focus attention upon groups previously omitted from political dialogue (such as women or children); upon dimensions of social life also left
largely unanalysed (such as control of information, a basic element of administrative power); and upon novel social contexts (such as the position of individuals, collectivities and states in an increasingly globalized social
environment).

Time–space, ontological security and urbanism

In various parts of my writings I have emphasized that notions of time and
space have to be brought into the core concerns of social theory today. This is
important in a two-fold sense. On a general plane, the framework of structuration theory depends upon grasping the recursive nature of social systems: the
flow of action, which occurs in time–space contexts, instantiates rules and
resources which have no time–space existence (save as memory traces). On a
somewhat more concrete level, deep-lying changes in the co-ordination of
human activities across time–space are characteristic of major periods of social
transition, and of the expansion of modernity in particular.

1.   It is true, as Saunders remarks in his paper, that I came to a concern with
space first of all through grappling with the problem of time. Temporality, it
seemed – and seems – to me, is philosophically enigmatic. Which philosopher
has managed to resolve St Augustine's problem – that time is banal and
familiar as we live it in the course of our day-to-day lives, yet appears
thoroughly impenetrable once we begin to inquire seriously into its nature? I
think it is up to those working in social theory to be alert to the philosophical

dilemmas of temporality – although it would be hopeless to suppose that all these dilemmas could be resolved before we decide how time should be understood in social theory.

In my views on this issue, I have been most influenced by Heidegger. Although in the period of modernity time – like space – is most often thought of as empty extension, in social theory we should accept the force of Heidegger's point that time is constitutive of objects and events. One way of putting this, if it does not sound too paradoxical, is to say that *time does not exist*. Temporality is expressed in the nature of how things are, their persistence and change. (Our nature, as human beings, by contrast, as Heidegger emphasizes, involves a specific understanding of temporality because of our finitude and our awareness of that finitude.)

As Saunders says, in *New Rules of Sociological Method* I did not have a great deal to say about spatiality in an explicit way. But this was not because a concern with space was simply added on later as 'an appendage to the theory [of structuration] rather than an essential component of it' (p. 216). On the contrary, the approach to time I derived from Heidegger already presumes a notion of space, as well as a critique of the equation of space with empty extension. Although we sometimes like to speak of 'empty space', like time space does not exist save as a property of objects and events, expressing their nearness or distance. For me, therefore, time and space refer to the contextualities of social interaction, or if one prefers to express it this way, the intermingling of presences and absences in social life. For many purposes of social analysis, it is useful to think of time–space as conjoined.

I still think it true – as I held when I originally developed the conception of structuration theory – that, in most traditions of thought, time and space have not formed as fundamental a part of social theorizing as they should. Saunders points out that empirical researchers have always been sensitive to the particularities of time and space. But how could this be otherwise? Research has to be done somewhere, and at some time, and can hardly ignore context. However, this has nothing much to do with how far a sophisticated treatment of time and space is built into theoretical thinking about the nature of social life and social systems. Saunders seems to misunderstand my standpoint when he quotes Castells, Urry and Sayer to the effect that there cannot be a coherent overall account of the nature of the spatial. I agree with this, and consider it to be precisely the starting-point of my analysis. I should be entirely happy to endorse the statement which Saunders quotes from Urry: 'it is impossible and incorrect to develop a general science of the spatial . . . this is because space per se has no *general* effects. The significance of spatial relations depends on the particular character of the social objects in question' (p. 231).

2.   Let me now move on to some other issues raised by Saunders, which converge to some degree with those emphasized by Gregory in his contribution. In a way which is more consistent with my own emphases, Gregory

concentrates his discussion upon time as well as space. As he quite rightly says, in interpreting structuration I place a great deal of importance upon the repetitive nature of day-to-day activities, as these are organized in time–space contexts. This is one prime aspect of recursiveness and is closely bound up with the influence of routinization. Gregory poses various questions about routinization, but his main query is: does an emphasis upon the importance of the routine minimize the influence of 'strategic intentionality' and fail to allow adequately for the dislocated or uneven character of social reproduction? Put another way: is an account accentuating the importance of routine a theory which accords undue importance to social stability rather than change? I do not think it is, but this question cannot be responded to on an entirely general level. To address it, we have to analyse some of the differences between different types of society. For the balance between stability and change varies in a basic way between forms of social system, particularly when we compare non-modern with modern societies. All social life, of course – even in the most radical phases of social change, like revolutions – involves continuities. The routines of social activity – for instance, those involved in everyday talk – in all circumstances have a strong 'as usual' quality about them. In all types of society, however, routines are to some extent disjunctive across time and space. Social reproduction is uneven even in the smallest oral cultures. However, in such cultures, and even in class-divided societies, tradition exerts a considerable grip upon what is considered as routine. Tradition should be understood as a mode of routinization by means of which practices are ordered across time and space. Although always open to 'reinterpretation', tradition is marked by the highest degree of stability when it is not understood by its practitioners to *be* tradition, but is simply 'how things are always done'. With the advent of agrarian civilizations, and the influence of writing, 'tradition' becomes understood as one possible form of regularizing time and space. At this point, the traditional becomes open to contestation and active reinterpretation, generating social struggles and clashes.

A characteristic of modernity is not so much that tradition disappears completely as that it comes to be grounded more thoroughly in 'rationally defensible' purposes. In modernity, to repeat what was said earlier, social institutions are always in principle revisable and are in practice subject to that reflexive probing which is in some part constitutive of what modernity is.

The importance of science, technology and the diffusion of innovations, to which Gregory refers, is only one part of this co-ordinating of routinization and reflexivity, albeit a highly important one. Innovations are built into the very character of the routine, in circumstances of modernity, and these are never completely controlled by reflexive monitoring which operates on a discursive level. The modern world is characterized both by a great acceleration in the use of discursive information to seek to control social processes and by the proliferation of divergent trajectories of social development. Modernity simultaneously has a controlled and disjointed character. It is against this generalized backdrop, as I have emphasized previously, that social movements come into being, and act as levers of change.

3. Saunders and Gregory each devote part of their chapters to discussing, and criticizing, the connections I draw between routinization and ontological security. Saunders in particular is sceptical of what I take to be the fragile character of ontological security in the created environment of modern social life. 'Why', he asks, 'should people feel a deep sense of desperation, fatalism, meaninglessness or whatever when they go to work every morning on the same train, but not when in the past they walked to the fields every morning along the same footpath?' (p. 225). Saunders is justified, I think, in pointing to inadequacies in my various discussions of this issue hitherto. It sounds as though I was proposing a romantic view of the past, in which people lived in harmony with one another in the local community and in harmony with nature. I have never wished to advocate such a standpoint, but the comments I have made in various sources upon this issue need further elaboration. I have provided such elaboration in a forthcoming study, and will summarize its content very briefly here.[4]

In all forms of society, I hold, individuals have psychological needs for ontological security. Ontological security is founded psychologically upon the formation of trust relationships, focusing initially upon the parental figures, especially the mother. Erikson says trust in the developing infant is based upon toleration of absence – acceptance that the mother still exists, and cares for the child, even when she is not physically in his or her presence. Trust, to use my terminology, even on a psychological level, is intrinsically a *medium of time–space distanciation*. That is to say, a feeling of security and self-identity is acquired through developing a sense of security in responses of others removed in time and space.

While ontological security rests upon very general psychological needs, its relation to day-to-day routines differs systematically between the non-modern and modern worlds. We can analyse this contrast in terms of an opposition between trust and security, on the one hand, and risk and danger on the other.

In traditional communities, even within class-divided civilizations, the kinship system and the locality provided a fairly systematic grounding for the maintenance of routines. On the other hand, social life in traditional communities was often a fraught and dangerous affair. The sources of danger or risk included above all the threat of epidemic illnesses and plagues, together with environmental disasters such as droughts, floods and earthquakes. In circumstances of modernity, the balance between trust and risk, security and danger, becomes radically altered. Although there are considerable variations in this, by and large day-to-day activities are not structured substantially through kinship relations. The locality no longer has the same significance as a 'boundary' of routinized activities and is enmeshed in a thoroughgoing way in

[4] Anthony Giddens, *The Consequences of Modernity* (Cambridge: Polity Press, 1990).

much more extensive social processes. The acceleration in time–space distanciation characteristic of modernity is itself brought about by trust mechanisms. These are means of transcending time–space through confidence in transactions removed from immediate contexts in which individuals find themselves. Two such types of trust mechanism can be distinguished. One consists of abstract tokens (such as money) making possible exchanges across indefinite spans of time–space. The second consists of 'expert systems' which bracket time and space by means of trust in professional expertise. (An example is the technical knowledge fed into the operation of air travel.) Trust mechanisms of these two types create large arenas of confidence in routinized time–space organization. For example, if I wish to travel from London to Edinburgh, I can do so not only quickly by the standards of previous generations, but safely.

Confidence in such mechanisms, however, is not for the most part psychologically satisfying and is to do with technical effectiveness rather than moral worth. Ontological security in such circumstances has a tenuous nature, and has to be 'actively regrounded' in personal ties with others. In the modern world we have actively to *build trust* by 'opening ourselves out' to others, which helps explain our obsession with 'relationships' between friends, lovers and spouses. The achievement of a continuously validated self is for us a *project*, which has to be worked out and achieved. Risk and danger in the modern world do not for the most part have the forms they used to assume; they derive not from natural hazard but from socially created risk – such as psychological danger or the risk of nuclear war. A 'phenomenology of modernity' has to probe the experience of living in a created environment in which pre-existing ties between trust, security, risk and danger have become substantially transmuted.

It is in these terms that I would now analyse the fragile character of ontological security in conditions of modernity. Many of the routines we follow in day-to-day life in modern societies are materially secure or safe, but psychologically and morally unrewarding.

4. Saunders and Gregory develop a further general objection against my view. I have argued in various books that, for some purposes of analysis at least, the concept of 'locale' is more sensitive and useful than the geographers' more usual notion of 'place'. Saunders and Gregory find this thesis less than compelling. In Gregory's eyes, I talk far too much about locales as settings of interaction, neglecting to give sufficient attention to how the different characteristics of localities are produced. Saunders's criticisms are even sharper. My notion of locale, he says, and the associated concept of region (in the sense in which I employ that term) are unilluminating. 'I can understand', he observes, 'how people may invest meanings in places ... but surely these meanings do not inhere in the spaces we occupy but in the social relations which are realized within them?' I do not in fact think it is true, as Gregory claims, that I

have neglected the production of locales and forms of regionalization. There cannot be a coherent theoretical account of the production of locales in general. We have to examine how different socio-physical properties of environments are brought into being in conjunction with specific forms of social development. The ideas I have tried to provide in this respect may or may not be satisfactory, but do address the issue. Consider the instance of territoriality. In contrasting traditional and modern states, I have argued that we must not treat territory merely as the area which a state occupies, or to which it happens to lay claim. The fact that traditional states have 'frontiers', whereas nation-states 'have borders', expresses distinctive contrasts in their social make-up. In *The Nation–State and Violence* I tried to demonstrate how and why this is so. Another example is my discussion of the created environment. The settings of interaction typical of modern societies, I claim, differ in a fundamental way from the city/countryside relation characteristic of traditional civilizations. The created environment is a manufactured series of settings, in which even the countryside is largely ordered in terms of social influences, rather than being a 'given' world of nature.

In commenting upon Saunders's remarks about location and urban analysis it is important to emphasize that space is not the same as place. We cannot speak about space without talking of the spatial attributes of a substantive phenomenon. In the case of locales, we are speaking of the intersection of the social, spatial and physical. Saunders's discussion, it seems to me, moves between the spatial and the physical without distinguishing these. His argument that space cannot become invested with meaning is a truism once we agree that space as such is contentless.

Saunders asks, if locales and regions 'are more than a backdrop to action, then how exactly do they enter into the reflexive constitution of action?' (p. 230). This question seems to me easily answered, although there are various levels on which a response can focus. Locales are first of all basic to the contextual character of interaction – and thus certainly not irrelevant to structuration theory, as Saunders claims. Language use and the communication of meaning, for example, depend in an essential way upon the regularized monitoring of aspects of physical contexts. This much has been demonstrated both in the writings of ordinary language philosophers and in the more empirical studies of ethnomethodology. Locales do not 'determine' meanings, but features of them are routinely incorporated into how meanings are generated and sustained. On another level, as was discussed in the preceding paragraph, locales and regions have to be understood in terms of their reflexive involvement with social organization and social transformations. The example of the territorial character of states is a case in point. As nations, states enter reflexively into how citizens organize their lives and how governments act. This is the reason, in fact, why it makes some sense to treat modern states as 'actors', as authors in the field of international relations often do.

In arguing that the notion of locale is without much value in social analysis, Saunders takes an example I mention in *The Constitution of Society*, in which I discuss the regionalization of the home as a locale. I point out there that the home is internally regionalized. We do different things in the various rooms, at different parts of the day – there is an interaction between the architecture of the dwelling and social life. Saunders agrees, but asks, so what? Surely this observation is at best a trivial commonplace?

I do not think that is the case at all. Consider in this respect, for example, the work of historians on the emergence of privacy in the post-medieval era. Forms of privacy are clearly connected both to psychological dimensions of personality, and to major aspects of social life, such as the relation between the 'domestic' and the 'public'. This work shows how mutations in privacy shaped, and were shaped by, the changing architectural form of dwellings, whereby certain types of activities are regularly hidden from view. We might take as another illustration the work of historical sociologists on the development of the 'home' as such. The concept of the 'home' is distinctively associated with modernity, and expresses significant alterations in the social layout of dwellings.[5]

5. These observations have a bearing upon the nature of urban sociology. Consistent with the theme that locales are of little interest for social theory, Saunders objects to aspects of my various discussions of urbanism. 'The city' cannot be a coherent object for social analysis, because it is a type of physical/spatial setting. He detects an ambiguity in my view here. I have quite often argued that the study of the city is of basic importance to social theory. Yet I also claim that in the modern era the city has disappeared as a distinct social form with the advent of the 'created environment'. Surely this is inconsistent?

I do not think there is an inconsistency here, in fact. Study of the city is of fundamental importance in social theory because it is pivotal in connecting the analysis of tribal, class-divided and modern societies. The emergence of distinct urban locales is closely associated with the consolidation of class-divided civilizations, separating them both from smaller, non-state systems on the one side and from modern societies on the other. With the development of modern institutions, 'the city' in the traditional sense does disappear, being supplanted by the created environment of modern urbanism. Yet the underlying theoretical standpoint remains the same. Modern urbanism – the built environment as an aspect of the created environment more generally – has to be understood in terms of the interrelation of locales and modes of regionalization with other properties of social systems. The 'city' no longer has clear boundaries which separate it from the 'countryside', and the dynamics of the built environment are transformed; but they become of even greater importance for the overall organization of the system than was the case before.

---

[5] Michael Anderson, *Approaches to the History of the Western Family, 1500–1914* (London: Macmillan, 1980).

Gender and social theory

The fact that there is only one chapter in this book, apart from a few observations in the contribution by Held, which raises issues of gender, and the fact that the contribution in question is written by one of only two female contributors, already say a great deal about the issues which Murgatroyd addresses. I can do nothing other than accept the force of her observation that, like many others working in social theory, I have simply not accorded questions of gender the attention they undeniably deserve. Even up to some ten years ago, in common with so many others, I unthinkingly used the terms 'man' and 'men' to refer to human beings in general. It does not necessarily follow from this that, as Murgatroyd says, I have thereby ignored one half of humanity. Not all aspects of social life are gender-divided, and precisely one of the issues which has to be faced in social theory is how far, and in what ways, the difference that is gender 'makes a difference'. It does not seem to me, for example, that the basic presuppositions of structuration theory vary according to gender, or would have to be revised fundamentally in the light of giving more specific attention to gender relations. Murgatroyd seems to accept this insofar as she attempts to use the theory to illuminate aspects of gender.

Murgatroyd opens her chapter by considering the importance of domestic work, pointing out that orthodox sociology has been forced to undergo considerable rethinking in this area. Prior to the renewed impact of feminism from the early 1970s or so, sociological accounts of work and domesticity usually contrasted places of labour outside the home with 'the family' as a separate and distinct sphere. 'Work' was equated with 'paid employment'. As Murgatroyd shows, this sort of view is fundamentally inadequate. The association between domestic labour, 'housewives' or 'homemakers', and the images of wife and mother, connect on the one side to overall conceptions of masculinity and femininity, and on the other to wider institutional features of the state and division of labour. Although some of these relations seem to be changing fairly rapidly, the connections involved remain quite tight-knit.

Probably few would take issue with these observations today, although detailed exploration of them is difficult and controversial. The more original part of Murgatroyd's discussion concerns those sections of her chapter in which she connects social reproduction to the 'production of people'. Structuration theory, she argues, can be fruitfully applied in this regard. Counterposing economic production to the production of people, she says, is a useful way of supplanting the usual comparison between the public domain of production and the domestic sphere. It is not only material goods which are produced and distributed in any given social system; people are also. Those engaged in the production of people can be defined as individuals who procreate and nurture others in such a way as to 'create' them as human beings.

Much of this activity is concentrated in the domestic sphere. Labour-power, she proposes, is the link between material production and the production of people. 'People-work', she states, 'produces people who embody labour power of various kinds' (p. 157). Labour-power is then fed back into the overall reproduction of social life.

People-producing work, Murgatroyd says, is concentrated within, but not confined to, the domestic sphere. For instance, the medicalizing of health care has subjected pregnancy and childbirth to the overall control of medical professionals. We can also specify direct ties between the production of people and broader aspects of social organization such as class or ethnic divisions. Thus, for instance, we can analyse people-producing work in terms of how far it facilitates or inhibits labour-market opportunities. Whether a married woman decides to look for paid employment will depend upon such factors as what job she might hope to get, the work of her husband, domestic work in which she has to engage, divisions of responsibility in terms of childrearing, and the availability of services to substitute for domestic tasks which she carries out.

While Murgatroyd makes some interesting and important points, I am not sure how far I would follow the particular approach she adopts. Although I was marginally influenced by Bertaux's work – to which she refers in her analysis – I do not find the 'production of people' a very helpful concept. In the first place, it seems to me to stand too close to historical materialism. Her argument is that an account of economic reproduction needs only to be complemented by an account of 'people production' to form a viable interpret-ation of the intersection of gender and other social divisions or relationships. If one has reservations about the degree to which there is a distinctive economic 'infrastructure' underlying other social institutions, this approach loses some of its appeal. Second, it is not very clear exactly what sense is to be given either to 'production' or to 'people' here. Perhaps one might argue that there is a reasonably close similarity between procreation and the manufacture of goods, since in both cases human beings materially make the 'end products'. Even here, though, the comparison seems rather attenuated. For instance, material goods and services are not only produced, but consumed. One cannot very easily see any processes of the 'consumption of people' . . . save perhaps in warfare. The use of the term 'people', which sounds simple, also becomes vague once one starts to examine it more closely. Human organisms are produced physically by the act of procreation, but where 'person' means 'competent human agent', the production of 'people' shades over into social reproduction in a very generalized sense. For human actors routinely and chronically constitute and reconstitute their qualities as agents in recurrent processes of social interaction. Save perhaps for early socialization, it would be difficult to sever off distinctive characteristics of 'people' that can be related to the productive activities of which Murgatroyd speaks.

My approach, therefore, would be rather different from hers. Connecting gender to social theory, and social theory to gender, would seem to raise the following questions. First, are there more or less universal attributes of masculinity and femininity, and if there are, what are their origins? Second, how is gender identity organized and sustained in the day-to-day reproduction of social relationships in different forms of society? Third, given that one accepts that in all known societies, especially in more 'public' contexts, men hold more power than women, how is this to be explained? Fourth, how might we best understand the shifting character of gender relationships with the advent of modernity? I cannot claim that I have much that is novel to offer on these issues, but I do have views about the most relevant or promising approaches to them.

In respect of the first question raised, the answer seems to be a qualified 'yes'. Although comparative research on the problem is difficult, and by no means conclusive, it appears plausible to claim that there exist some very general differences between the psychological make-up of women and men. While we cannot discount biological interpretations, in my view the most apt theoretical framework within which these might potentially be understood is psychoanalysis. To some critics, such a standpoint appears perverse, not only because of reservations they have about the status of Freud's ideas in general, but because of his notorious failure to give much attention to the psychology of women. In her early intervention into the debate about psychoanalysis and feminism, however, Juliet Mitchell was able to show both that Freud's neglect of female psychology can be overestimated and that his work contains an account of gender differences which is both subtle and intellectually powerful.

No doubt Freud's ideas in this area, as in many others, need to be elaborated and modified in order to be made fully effective. The writings of Nancy Chodorow are relevant and stimulating in this respect.[6] In examining gender differences, Chodorow is probably right to place much more emphasis than Freud upon the importance of the mother as compared to the father. Her reworking of the theory of Oedipal transition provides a cogent interpretation not only of feminine psychology, but of its reproduction across the generations. I find helpful Chodorow's reversal of Freud's emphasis in her argument that masculinity rather than femininity is defined by a 'loss', the forfeiting of continuing close attachment to the mother. Chodorow's position seems to me convincing, although I would not want to endorse it in its entirety. Femininity and masculinity are probably more internally mixed and contradictory than Chodorow implies. It also seems likely that divisions between masculinity and femininity do not simply become qualities of men on the one hand and women on the other; rather, they are mixed in some degree within the personalities of the members of the two sexes.

[6] Nancy Chodorow, *The Reproduction of Mothering: Psychoanalysis and the Sociology of Gender* (Berkeley: University of California Press, 1978); *Psychoanalytic Theory and Feminism* (Cambridge: Polity Press, 1989).

If there is anything in these ideas, gender identity rests in some part upon unconscious feelings and imagery. Recognizing this, however, should in no way prevent us from seeing that gender is constructed and reconstructed in the flow of interaction in day-to-day social life. The perspective of structuration theory is directly relevant in this regard, and I would see Connell's work as important in opening up some fruitful lines of thinking here.[7] Gender relations, he emphasizes, are to be understood in terms of the continuity or transformation of practices within what he calls gender 'regimes'. That is to say, in any distinct context or arena within social life, there are ordered ways in which gender differences are transmitted and discursively represented.

He quotes, for example, a study of gender discrimination in a school environment. The research shows that, among both students and staff, there are practices which define and sustain specific conceptions of femininity and masculinity – in sports, curriculum choice, classroom discipline, administrative activities and other spheres. These in some substantial part express, and thereby reproduce, broader institutional patterns in the wider society.

Gender, Connell argues, should not be thought of as a property of individual agents. Criteria of gender identity are embedded in the recurrent practices whereby institutions are structured. It is worth quoting him directly on this:

> 'gender' means practice organised in terms of, or in relation to, the reproductive division of people into male and female . . . [it] is a linking concept. It is about the linking of other fields of social practice to the nodal practices of engendering, childbirth and parenting . . . gender in this connection is a process rather than a thing. Our language, especially its general categories, invites us to reify. But it should be clear that the 'linking concept' is about the making of the links, the process of organising social life in a particular way. If we could use the word 'gender' as a verb (I gender, you gender, she genders . . .) it would be better for our understanding. . . The 'process' here is strictly social, and gender a phenomenon within sociality. It has its own weight and solidity, on a quite different basis from that of biological process, and it is that weight and solidity that sociology attempts to capture in the concept of 'institution'.[8]

On a more concrete level, in respect of the sustaining and reconstituting of gender identity (like Connell) I am particularly impressed with the work of Kessler and McKenna. Their approach is strongly influenced by ethnomethodology, deriving in some part directly from Garfinkel's original discussion of the construction of gender in *Studies in Ethnomethodology*.[9] In that book, in his study of 'Agnes', Garfinkel sought to show that what might be taken to be a 'given' feature of social life – 'being a boy' or 'being a girl' – has constantly to be worked at in all areas of social practice. The very 'naturalness' of gender is

[7] R. W. Connell, *Gender and Power: Society, the Person and Sexual Politics* (Cambridge: Polity Press, 1987).
[8] Ibid., p. 140.
[9] Harold Garfinkel, *Studies in Ethnomethodology* (Cambridge: Polity Press, 1984).

achieved only through complicated, yet routine, management of detailed aspects of bodily gesture, presentation and modes of interaction. Kessler and McKenna develop this position further by looking systematically at the criteria of gender attribution, as these are handled in everyday contexts of activity. Gender identity is created and recreated through the consistent construction of dichotomies – in other words, difference – where no absolute dichotomies exist in biological fact. As they show, examining biological literature on gender, there is not a single physical characteristic, or even combination of physical characteristics, which cleanly and completely separates 'women' from 'men'.

No problems have been more extensively debated in the recent literature than the questions of how far men are universally dominant over women and how such forms of dominance are best to be explained. There is no shortage of accounts which emphasize the overriding importance of genetic factors in explaining universal sexual inequalities. The most prominent current examples are those influenced by sociobiology, but many other variants are to be found. The arguments that have been deployed against biologically inspired standpoints seem to me compelling. In particular, no definite biological mechanism has been identified which could form a basis of differential power between men and women. Moreover, if it is valid to hold that gender identity diverges from clear-cut biological criteria of sexual difference, biological explanations of differential power become hard to sustain.

A more sociological explanation must depend upon indicating how and why gender and power relations tend stably to converge. While there are various forms in which this thesis can be couched, the most persuasive type of interpretation still appears to be that which links divisions of power and inequality to the relative confinement of women (in variable degrees and ways) to domestic contexts, as a result of their central involvement in childbirth and childrearing. This is not a biologically founded phenomenon, in a genetic sense, but rather rests upon the social mediation of biological differences.

A good illustration of the issues involved is provided by considering the connections between gender and war (something not mentioned in Shaw's discussion). Warfare at first sight appears as an unequivocally male activity – and thus could be expected to derive from some sort of genetic variations in levels of aggressiveness between the sexes. But as Elshtain points out in her recent study, there have been notable examples of female warriors, and women have often been vocal in their support for war. On the other hand, many men have been pacifists, and fighting in wars for most male participants has little connection with inbuilt aggressiveness. Values of *esprit de corps* far outweigh those of bloodlust; the whole point of military discipline is to develop modes of behaviour on the battlefield which, far from being biologically built in, have to be more or less forcibly instilled into recruits. Studies of instances in which women have fought routinely in war, such as in the Red Army during the

Second World War, show that in such circumstances the attitudes of female soldiers do not differ markedly from those of males. The conclusion which has to be drawn from this is that, if women in the past have not commonly participated directly in war, this is above all the outcome of the clear separations drawn in virtually all societies between the domestic and public spheres.

When we come to consider how gender relations, and their intersection with other social institutions, have altered over the course of history, I believe that some of my ideas are again of potential relevance. On a general level, for example, it might be possible to link gender divisions to the association of time–space distanciation with power. The connection usually made between inequalities of gender and the division of labour tends to reflect the undue primacy often attributed to allocative resources in influencing social organization and social change. Authoritative resources, however, are at least equally important in generating the reorderings of time and space that I hold to be crucial in major phases of social transformation. Males are ordinarily the 'carriers' of time–space distanciation, their separation from the domestic sphere allowing for specialization in control of writing, information storage and professional expertise. It is possible that some systematic lines of theoretical analysis could be developed on a basis of such a starting-point.

The same may be said of the analysis of the institutional dimensions of modernity. Murgatroyd's chapter concentrates upon gender in modern societies, but, as I pointed out, seems to me to stand too close to an unreconstructed Marxist position. I would propose examining the location and construction of gender differences in institutional contexts spanning each of the dimensions of modernity I previously identified. The development of capitalism has undoubtedly dramatically affected – although in shifting fashion – the differential social positions of men and women. Some aspects of this process are now well known and effectively documented. They include, among other things, the clear-cut separation of 'home' from 'workplace', together with the emergence of labour markets founded upon individual wage contracts. These factors have greatly influenced, but have by no means wholly determined, gender relations within the political sphere. Appropriately developed, in the modes indicated above, the changing nature of citizenship would form one institutional area around which to analyse this type of issue.

This in turn connects to, but is again partly separable from, how gender divisions relate to control of the means of violence. Analysis of the latter sphere would include the study of gender and war, but would also have to incorporate other contexts and types of violence. These institutional dimensions can in some part be distinguished from the influence of industrialism – which of course is a multi-faceted area in and of itself. But by way of illustration one might mention the impact of domestic technology, and mechanization in the home, as significant influences shaping gender relations.

Social science and critical theory

In developing my conception of structuration theory I have frequently emphasized its connections to critique. In his contribution to this volume, Bernstein
concentrates on this issue in order to draw attention to what he diagnoses as
major shortcomings in my account of the nature of critical theory. I should
perhaps say straight away that I regard myself primarily as a sociologist, or
more generally as a social scientist, rather than a philosopher. I do not see it as
a main part of my self-imposed programme to elucidate a detailed view of how
critical theory should be understood. Although I have drawn a great deal of
intellectual nourishment from Habermas's writings, I do not feel myself to be
particularly close to his position, and I would wish to separate my work fairly
definitively – as Bernstein mentions – from the writings of the Frankfurt
School. In what follows I shall try to make more precise the notions of critique
I have in previous writings alluded to only in a fairly casual fashion. But I
cannot pretend that the following remarks are in any way complete.

Engaging in social scientific activity, I believe, raises the possibility, and to
some degree the necessity, of involvement in four levels of critique. These
emerge fairly plainly from Bernstein's own analysis and so I can follow the
sequence of his argument in portraying them.

The first level of critical engagement which social scientists, like any others
concerned with disciplined inquiry, face might be called *intellectual critique*.
This is what Bernstein refers to as a 'minimalist' conception, but I would
simply see it as inherent in the nature of intellectual investigation. There is
nothing particularly problematic about it, either in my eyes or in the view of
Bernstein. Intellectual critique simply refers to the fact, emphasized by Pop-
per among many others, that disciplined inquiry must be seen as carried on by
a community rather than by an individual; any and all theories, concepts and
findings brought forward are open to critical dissection and assessment. I
would take it that this whole book forms an excellent, and I hope constructive,
example of this phenomenon. It is one part of what social science is as critical
theory, but is relatively uncontroversial.

The second level of criticism could be called *practical* critique and raises
more debatable issues, particularly when contrasted to orthodox versions of
the logic of the social sciences. As I mentioned in the opening part of this reply,
I regard the questions raised here as of very great importance. According to
more traditional views of the social sciences, social science generates information about an independently given social world, such information or new
knowledge being cumulative in the same sense as in the natural sciences.
According to this conception, new knowledge can be applied 'technologically'
to bring about practical interventions in social life. This technological view of
social science knowledge, however, blanks out the 'return' side of the double
hermeneutic, the routine incorporation of social science theories, concepts and
findings back into the universe of events they were developed to describe or

explain. While this does not altogether prevent the accumulation of knowledge on the part of the social scientific community, it radically alters its character as compared to natural science.

Because in some respects it is only possible for the social scientist to keep 'one jump ahead' of those whose behaviour he or she is investigating, much of social science appears relatively banal to lay members of society. Yet this seeming banality disguises the tremendous practical impact which social science has had and which is in substantial part constitutive of modernity. Bernstein accepts this point, although it seems to me that he rather trivializes it. He says, for example, that ' "cost–benefit" analysis not only seeps down into our everyday language, but has influenced the ways in which people think about their careers or even their sex lives'. (p. 31). My point is not just that social science concepts and findings 'influence' 'the ways in which we think', but that they become in large part *constitutive of the practices which form institutions of modernity*. This, I take it, is what Foucault was seeking to demonstrate in his analysis of psychiatry and madness. The terminology and empirical claims of modern psychiatry, when they first originated, did not just help us to understand better phenomena which had long existed; they served to constitute new forms of social action and social practice.

Why should one link this reflexivity closely to critique? The answer is that innovations in social science create windows on possible worlds for lay social actors. Social science is virtually always in principle critical not only of the belief-claims, but also of the concepts and frameworks of action, followed by members of society. Such practical criticism is an inherent and inescapable element of engaging in social scientific investigation. This has nothing much to do with 'critical theory' as understood by the Frankfurt School. The investigating social scientist is not, on this level of critique at any rate, setting herself or himself up as a critical evaluator of social practices or as providing guidance for normative standards of action.

The third level of criticism in which social science is inextricably involved is *ideological critique*. At this point we begin to enter the realms with which Bernstein is principally concerned and which have traditionally occupied critical theory as understood by the Frankfurt School. As a way into discussion of this level of critique, let me pursue the reference Bernstein makes to Willis's study *Learning to Labour*. As Bernstein points out, the study of the boys' group which Willis undertook provides information which can be used in quite distinct ways. It could be made use of by the school authorities to tighten up their effective control over pupils; alternatively, it could be utilized by the members of the boys' group themselves to oppose effectively those who stand in authority over them. We have to ask, Bernstein asserts, 'who will use this knowledge, and for what ends?' (p. 32).

Now, this question can actually be taken in two ways, and these separate the levels of practical and ideological critique. It might mean: what happens to Willis's findings as they are reincorporated back into social settings? There is not usually a great deal that an investigator himself or herself can do, or should be expected to do, to *control* this. Concepts and findings will have their own 'fate' within the wider community. That this is so is effectively built into the nature of practical critique. For there is no way of effectively confining the appraisal of ideas and findings solely to some rigorously circumscribed community of observing social scientists. 'Openness to criticism' among social scientists inevitably implies 'openness to utilization' on the part of others.

However, what can be subjected to further analysis on the part of the social scientist is the role of claims to knowledge as aspects of systems of power. This is what I take the critique of ideology to concern. As I have argued elsewhere, ideology should be understood not as false knowledge, juxtaposed to the valid knowledge claimed by science (social or natural), but as the analysis of the conditions under which modes of signification or discourse are incorporated within exploitative systems of domination. Given that social science is reflexively involved in an intimate and pervasive way with what it is about, the critique of ideology necessarily also has to concern social science itself. A further answer to the question: 'who will use this knowledge, and for what ends?' is therefore that we can investigate, actually or counterfactually, how the knowledge generated from a particular research study is incorporated within asymmetrical power relations.

The critique of ideology, it seems to me, is a purely analytic task, part of the basic concerns of social science, since it addresses a continuing and necessary feature of social systems. All systems of power have ideological aspects, and can be studied from the point of view of ideology critique. In the case of social science knowledge itself, the complicating factor is its reflexive involvement with the social world; but this is an empirical, not a logical, source of difficulty. One might then ask: what is the force of 'critique' here? For if the concern is only to diagnose the existence of ideology, in what sense is there a critical engagement with it? The sense in question is the same, in fact, as on level two. That is to say, the diagnosis of ideology is likely to compromise the belief claims of at least some agents involved in a particular set of power relations.

The fourth level of criticism one might designate as *moral critique*. Reaching this level, we disembark upon the terrain which most worries Bernstein in terms of the lapses he sees in my writings. Moral critique concerns assessing the rights and wrongs of contrasting policies or courses of action. On this level, we confront the classical problem of the relation between 'is' and 'ought'. This is not ground upon which I have ventured in any systematic way in my own work. Bernstein quotes some comments I have made on the issue, which actually came from remarks in an interview rather than my published writings. Bernstein finds these comments unsatisfactory and demands that I clarify and expand upon them. This I am happy to try to do, although I am not sure that what I shall say will satisfy him.

I have not basically altered the views I described in response to the questions of the interviewer, although I now find I mixed my metaphors. In the passages Bernstein quotes, I speak variously of setting up two houses, neither of which is a safe house, inquiry and moral critique; and of 'firing critical salvoes into reality' without supposing that all of these represent a fully integrated barrage. What I meant to get at was the following. I do not think it plausible to suppose that one can ground a programme of critical theory, in a way, for example, in which Habermas seeks to do, such that comprehensive rational grounds for moral critique could be provided. I find implausible Habermas's claim that an ideal speech situation is counterfactually implied in any attempt at linguistic communication. On the other hand, I find equally unappealing the idea of immanent critique as suggested by Adorno. One might perhaps argue from a logical point of view that these two viewpoints exhaust all possibilities – that we must accept one, or we are necessarily stuck with the other. Bernstein seems to think so, because he feels that my stance is 'foxlike' and 'dodges some tough issues', rather than facing up to them (p. 27). I do not agree with this assessment, even if I have not attempted to provide an elaborated defence of why I hold to the position I do. I think, in fact, that all of us are, willy-nilly, stuck between the two apparently mutual exclusive alternatives. Who, when defending an 'ought' statement, does not make reference to what is? Moral judgements ordinarily form part of the chains of argument which are thoroughly bound up with factual assertions. I have tried to set out the logic of this viewpoint elsewhere, although even there rather cursorily.[10] I would refer to this position as 'contingent moral rationalism'.

According to this perspective, as practising social scientists we may legitimately make moral criticisms of states of affairs, although we must seek to justify those criticisms when called upon to do so. We cannot ground moral critique in the mode of such justification (or argumentation) itself, and in the sense of finding 'pure foundations' cannot ground it at all. But this does not mean that moral critique derives merely from whims or feelings, or that we are at the mercy of a particular historical conjuncture. Dialogue with any and every moral standpoint is possible, and always involves a fusion of moral and factual dispute. Most of the time, most of us do not find ourselves in circumstances of moral puzzlement when confronted with particular states of affairs, in the way in which philosophical accounts of the difficulty, or the impossibility, of grounding moral evaluations might lead us to suppose.

Let me try to develop these observations further by considering the standpoint adopted by Max Weber. I do not see how it would be possible to maintain the division between 'is' and 'ought' presumed by Weber. According to Weber's thesis, social scientific findings can be applied to specifying the means whereby goals can be attained, and can indicate the likely factual consequences of achieving them. But since, in his view, factual observation and moral judgement are logically completely discrete, the work of the social scientist can in no way have a direct bearing upon the selection of goals themselves. Weber adds to this that goals exist within a hierarchy, which can

[10] Anthony Giddens, *Studies in Social and Political Theory* (London: Hutchinson, 1979), pp. 89–95.

be traced back to some type of ultimate value or values. But this does not seem to be accurate. Whenever we look at any actual debates concerning social issues and related evaluations, we find networks of factual and evaluative judgements, organized through argumentation. Consider, for instance, the following problem. Should we tolerate the existence of large segments of poverty in a modern society, or should we introduce welfare schemes which will redistribute income in such a way that the conditions of life of the poor are radically improved? Debate about such a question, in the context of arguments about the welfare state, would normally be undertaken in terms of economic controversy, which is theoretical and factual as well as evaluative. Those who hold to a theory of a natural rate of unemployment, for example, are likely to take a different view on this issue than would a Keynesian. What if a contributor to this debate who accepted the natural rate theory were to say: in spite of my belief about how the economy works, my overriding priority is to ensure that no one is poor? Such an assertion would not be an end to the debate – the statement of an ultimate value. Discussion could and most probably would continue within networks of theoretical, factual and moral claims. Thus someone who takes such a position might justify it in terms of principles drawn from Christianity. The nature of the network would shift, but no doubt continued dialogue would be possible. I do not want to say, of course, that we could never achieve complete 'closure' between different value claims. But just as in respect of hermeneutics the relativist position flounders, so in respect of moral evaluations there are no value positions situated in discursive networks wholly disconnected from any others.

Moral critique therefore, I would hold, is always justifiable, but rarely if ever in such a way that a universal consensus of participants in any given debate could be attained. It is a separate issue how far social scientists themselves should intervene in practical programmes of reform. To my mind, this question is exactly part of a network of claims that can be debated by social scientists themselves and by others. Such claims depend upon views about such things as whether or not the university should be a place which stands completely apart from the propagation of partisan political views – as Weber advocated. If it is true that moral critique cannot be clearly and absolutely severed from other tasks of social science, it seems difficult to sustain the idea of a complete separation between the academy and politics. My position on this would be that a commitment to the first level of critique, intellectual critique, rests more upon the existence of an indefinite global community of social science than upon any attempt to isolate the academy from practical involvements.

As the term is understood by the Frankfurt School, 'critical theory' does not only concern the issues raised above. The writings of the various figures associated with the Frankfurt Institute took their point of departure from Marxism. 'Critical theory' here means not just assessing the logical nature of critique in social science, but formulating practical programmes of social intervention. How should we conceive of 'critical theory' in this guise from our vantage-point in the late twentieth century? Obviously, such a question cannot be answered simply by means of the considerations mentioned thus far. I would reply to it in the terms I attempted to outline in the closing chapter of *The Nation-State and Violence*. Political theory today must break free from the 'class reductionism' and the 'capitalism reductionism' of Marxist theory and practice. It must confront the multi-dimensional character of modernity, recognizing that involvements or ideals pursued along one dimension may stand in some tension with those relevant to another. For instance, the interests of male workers in maintaining high levels of employment may not be fully compatible with programmes providing for greater sexual equality within the labour force. A set of economic innovations might benefit workers in a particular industry, but run counter to ecological concerns. Critical theory today remains closely connected to the activities of social movements, but we cannot suppose that the labour movement has a special, privileged place here. The view that there is a single revolutionary subject, incorporating the overall interests of everyone, in the manner in which Marx claimed for the proletariat, has to be abandoned once and for all. This leaves us in a far more messy situation than anyone strongly influenced by Marxism would find tolerable. The late-twentieth-century world faces a truly formidable array of problems, some of which were barely foreseen at all in the nineteenth century or even in the early twentieth century. At the same time, the limitations of the traditions of social and political thought we have inherited from that period become more and more apparent. Social science can, and must, rework its schemes of analysis – one reason why the current debates over the nature of modernity are so important. It also seems to me necessary to engage in new forms of counterfactual thinking to provide a stimulus to social transformation. For instance, how should we conceive of a possible social order which is democratic in respect of control of the means of violence? This is not an issue in which pre-existing forms of normative political theory provide us with much help. From an intellectual point of view, the tasks which confront us here are exciting as well as challenging. From a practical standpoint they are sobering because of the sheer immensity – and in some part, seeming intractability – of the problems which humanity today faces.

Structuration theory and empirical research

Over the past few years, particularly since the publication of *The Constitution of Society*, people in a diversity of fields have made use of concepts drawn from structuration theory in pursuing empirical inquiries. Areas in question include the study of stratification, organizations, educational systems, processes of urbanism, state forms, traditional communities, gender and ethnic divisions, mass media, legal systems, and others besides. I have been pleased, although also rather surprised, by the number and proliferation of such endeavours. On the other hand, on the whole I do not feel overly sympathetic towards the ways in which most authors have employed my concepts in their work. Most often, this is because they have tried to import the concepts I developed *en bloc* into their research, seemingly imagining that this will somehow lead to major methodological innovations. I have never believed this to be a sound approach, which is one of the main reasons why in *The Constitution of Society* I emphasized that the theory should be utilized only in a selective way in empirical work and should be seen more as a sensitizing device than as providing detailed guidelines for research procedure.

While many have attempted to employ my perspective in a direct way in empirical study, others have taken a more negative stance. In other words, they have argued that structuration theory provides few or no useful pointers to the conduct of empirical work. An example is a lengthy review by Thrift.[11] Writing about the chapter in *The Constitution of Society* in which I relate structuration theory to problems of empirical investigation, Thrift says that he finds this discussion 'deeply disappointing'. He sees my attitude as altogether too qualified, arguing that the theory 'should have a considerable amount to say ... about the conduct and methods of research'. The disappointment comes from my not having delivered goods which it seemed to Thrift that the enterprise I have undertaken could reasonably be expected to convey.

Gregson's contribution to this volume contains some parallels to Thrift's view, although the conclusions she draws are different. Concentrating her attention on the same chapter in *The Constitution of Society* referred to by Thrift, she finds the connections I draw between structuration theory and the empirical research unconvincing. They lack, she says, 'the degree of specification required for empirical work' (p. 240). It is all very well to be told that all social research involves an ethnographic moment, that lay members of society are skilful and knowledgeable, or that one must have a sensitivity to how action is co-ordinated across time and space; but these are too far removed from the groundwork of empirical research to be of any value in guiding it. The various examples of research work which I refer to in the chapter in question were all carried out without any need for the concepts which, as it were, I have foisted upon them. Picking up my emphasis upon ontology rather than epistemology, Gregson concludes that the concepts connected with structuration make up a 'second-order theory', concerned 'with conceptualizing the general constituents of human society' and distinct from 'first-order theory', which generates concepts that apply directly to specific empirical settings.

I agree with some aspects of what Gregson has to say, but not with others. In my view, we should recognize what might be called the *relative autonomy* of theory and research. Theoretical thinking needs in substantial part to proceed in its own terms and cannot be expected to be linked at every point to empirical considerations. The more encompassing or generalized a set of theoretical

[11] Nigel Thrift, 'Bear and Mouse or Bear and Tree? Anthony Giddens's Reconstitution of Social Theory', *Sociology*, 19 (1985).

notions is, the more this is the case. Empirical work, on the other hand, cannot proceed in the absence of abstract concepts or theoretical notions, but these are necessarily drawn upon selectively and cannot be ever-present. The category 'empirical work' is very large, moreover, and covers numerous different sorts of inquiries. Some types of research have local, descriptive objectives, while others attempt more to explore explanatory hypotheses. Research responds to contextualized inquiries, and one of the main errors of those who formulated canons of research under the aegis of logical empiricism was to regard the only 'authentic' work as that which sets up specific hypotheses, derived from theory, and proceeds to seek to test them. The 'how?' and 'why?' questions which social research answers are too variegated to be subsumed within so neat a scheme.

Similarly, 'theory' covers a multiplicity of endeavours. The main tenets of structuration theory, as Gregson rightly points out, are intended to apply over the whole range of human social activity, in any and every context of action. Other concepts I have coined or worked with, such as 'the commodification of space' or 'surveillance mechanisms', have somewhat more substance, in the sense in which they direct attention to specific processes or aspects of concrete social systems. However, I would not myself draw a distinction between 'first-order' and 'second-order' concepts. Theory is also contextual. Some concepts and theoretical schemes are more abstract than others, and those involved in the general suppositions of structuration theory do indeed operate at a high level of abstraction. But even the most abstract concepts interlace, or can be connected with, more specific ones. This is as true of the notions of structuration theory as of any other generalized standpoint in the social sciences.

One might if one likes make a rough distinction between 'theory', as a generic category, and 'theories', where the latter term refers to explanatory generalizations. Structuration theory clearly belongs to the first of these types rather than the second. As I have pointed out in *The Constitution of Society*, the significance of 'theories', as compared to 'theory', can easily be exaggerated. Some writers are prone to pour scorn upon the tendencies of the social sciences to produce abstract conceptual schemes at the expense of explanatory generalizations – theory, rather than theories – but I do not think such complaints for the most part are justified. No doubt many arid conceptual webs are spun, but so also are many vapid or uninteresting generalizations proposed. 'Theory', in my view, is at least as important in the social science as theories; I would not accord one logical priority over the other.

I do not agree with Gregson's contention that structuration theory is largely irrelevant to empirical research. Being abstract and generalized, and being 'theory' as contrasted to a set of 'theories', it is necessarily at some distance from particular research projects. I would still maintain today the position I set out in the chapter previously referred to in *The Constitution of Society*, which I would see as more relevant to the conduct of empirical research than Gregson allows. Structuration theory is not intended as a method of research, or even as a methodological approach. The concepts I have developed do not allow one to say: 'henceforth, the only viable type of research in the social sciences is qualitative field study'. I have an eclectic approach to method, which again rests upon the premise that research enquiries are contextually oriented. For some purposes, detailed ethnographic work is appropriate, while for others archival research, or the sophisticated statistical analysis of secondary materials, might be more suitable. But I do think the framework of structuration theory both provides concepts relevant to empirical research and also warns against the pitfalls of some types of research procedure or interpretations of research results.

The objective of my discussion in *The Constitution of Society* was to demonstrate these points, and I need only briefly recapitulate them here. In some part my remarks concerned the logic of research; to some degree they were directed towards illustrating how the concepts of structuration theory 'look' when examined in relation to concrete research tasks. For instance, it is a logical feature of social research, following from the double hermeneutic, that all research endeavours have an ethnographic or 'anthropological' aspect to them. Since this is a logical point, by definition it does not disclose anything directly which is an option for a researcher; it sets out what all social investigation, without exception, involves. Yet it would be wrong to say that it is without direct relevance to the conduct and interpretation of research. Thus someone who believes she or he is dealing only with 'hard facts' – say in the shape of a mathematical analysis of quantitative variables – might both misconstrue what those 'facts' are and other conclusions to be drawn from them, if the point is ignored. Cicourel demonstrated this effectively enough some while ago in his discussion of the use of official statistics in social research.

In my discussion I looked at several pieces of research, of a heterogeneous character. The point, as I believe I made clear, was not to demonstrate what research 'inspired by structuration theory' would be like; it was, as I put it at the time, to work out 'the logical implications of studying a "subject-matter" of which the researcher is already a part' and to elucidate 'the substantive connotations of the core notions of action and structure'.[12] Looking at an investigation of a directly ethnographic kind – Willis's study – I sought to show that some of the main virtues of the research derive from the fact that the researcher was sensitive to some of the key emphases formally elaborated in structuration theory. I also wanted to show (something Willis was also very conscious of) that small-scale, detailed ethnographic work can show us a great deal about institutional reproduction. In relating the empirical observations to such reproduction, moreover, no functionalist assertions of any kind are required. The other examples I used were designed to show how structural constraint, contradiction and institutional change could be examined in research contexts involving quite different empirical procedures from that

[12] *CS*, pp. 376–8.

adopted by Willis. I sought to demonstrate that the analysis of structural constraint presumes an empirically grounded interpretation of motivation; that, *per contra*, the empirical study of contradiction cannot just proceed on the level of motivated action, but presumes the study of structural constraint; and that the effective empirical analysis of institutional change means grasping the relations between reflexively monitored transformations and unintended consequences of action.

Structuration theory is a broad perspective upon the study of action, structure and institutions. Its relation to empirical research is much the same as that of competing perspectives or schools of thought. Robert K. Merton's codification of functionalism, as set out in his book *Social Theory and Social Structure*, for example, offers an overall orientation to social analysis, but scarcely provides recipes for empirical research. As Bernstein shows, many of the presuppositions of structuration theory stand in direct contrast to the framework which Merton established, and which served as an overall orientation for a whole generation of sociologists. I should be happy indeed were my writings to have anything approaching the influence exerted by those of Merton. The main point in this context, however, is that the status of the two endeavours is approximately the same. Merton tried to establish close ties between the more abstract principles he endeavoured to set up and other theoretical and empirical work upon which he became engaged. The same also applies in my case, as I indicated in the opening paragraphs of this reply. There may be no 'structurationist programme' of research, but I can certainly sketch what I would take to be some principal empirical concerns upon which social research should be focused.

Let me first of all, however, connect some of the general emphases of structuration theory with empirical work by 'reversing the coin' from the style of presentation I adopted in the chapter in question in *The Constitution of Society*. In that chapter, as mentioned, I analysed certain aspects of concrete research projects in order to provide an empirical illumination of some of the basic elements of structuration theory. It might be helpful here if I briefly proceed in the opposite fashion, indicating how social research might proceed when consciously informed by the structurationist outlook.

Let us suppose we wished to study marriage relationships, and the break-up of marriage, in a number of communities of varying socio-economic levels. Our main interest is in the nature of marital relationships and in the origins and consequences of marital separation. Information is obtained from various sources: fieldwork study in two or three of the communities in question, in-depth interviews and the use of local archival materials. How might some of the notions of structuration theory be used as sensitizing devices in the pursuit of such a research inquiry?

The prime underlying orientation, both of the planning of the investigation and the interpretation of its results, would be towards examining the complexities of action/structure relations. This is a mixed process of *observation* and *decoding*. As an operational principle of research, what structuration theory suggests is not that we should seek to categorize or classify the rules and resources involved in a given area of social conduct, but rather that we should place the emphasis squarely upon the constitution and reconstitution of social practices. Investigating 'structure' in the structurationist sense is more than simply looking for patterns in how the behaviour of some individuals connects with that of others. It means delving into the subtle interplay between the intractability of social institutions and the options they offer for agents who have knowledge, but bounded discursive awareness, of how those institutions work.

We would ground the research, therefore, in an attempt to examine stasis and change in the reproduction of institutionalized practices. The 'marriage relationship' is a set of expectations held by partners about each other, sanctioned within the overarching framework of the legal system. These expectations 'enter into' the relationship, but they are only constituted in and through the regular habits, strategies of behaviour and so forth which partners follow, inside and outside the relationship itself. Consider, for instance, the question of how far the marital relationship itself is strongly emphasized in social interaction, or alternatively is fairly well submerged in other kin ties and obligations. This is best studied through showing how regularized day-to-day, or more periodic, activities serve consistently to remake – or perhaps help unmake – wider kin ties. Thus one instance of this, in matrilocal marriage, might be the practice which women have of popping in to see their mothers on a regular and routine basis. Where such a practice exists, it expresses informal conventions which are reconstituted in its very enactment. The practice may be relatively 'untheorized' by those concerned, since it is simply accepted as what is 'done' in the area. Alternatively, a greater range of skilful, strategic thinking may be involved where the practice for one reason or another has come under pressure. Thus if husbands now expect wives to spend more time in the home, caring for and improving it – or if they expect wives to take on paid employment – various more calculative and 'thought-through' modes of sustaining daughter–mother intimacy might have to be devised.

'Structure' here is embedded in practice (or, in actuality, in a diverse, fragmentary and sometimes contradictory series of practices) in which it is recursively implicated. Study of the 'everyday' or the 'day-to-day' forms a basic part of the analysis here, many seemingly trivial or mundane features of what people do being the actual 'groundwork' of larger-scale institutions. It is in the durability of institutions that we look to discern the structural properties of systems of relationships in which people's activities are engaged. In empirical terms, this immediately means an 'opening out' across time and space. In other words, it necessitates a historical or developmental perspective and a sensitivity to variations of location. In the case of the hypothetical research project, this would involve far more than just a gross comparison of communities in terms of variations according to geographical situation or class composition. It would mean – ideally at least – a thoroughgoing study of the contextualities of institutionalized patterns of interaction. For instance, the pattern of daughters popping in to see mothers might be temporally sedimented as tradition and spatially organized via locales in which a considerable degree of gender segregation is maintained – through a combination of matrilocality and a male 'pub and club' pattern.

Localized forms of practice can be 'mapped' institutionally within wider social systems in terms of what I have sometimes called 'structural sets' (or simply 'structures' in the plural). Studying structural sets is best understood as examining the articulation of institutions across time and space. Structural sets are formed through the mutual convertibility of rules and resources in one domain of action into those pertaining to another. In the case of the putative research project, a number of such articulations could be diagnosed and analysed. For instance, marriage relationships, gender and labour markets are connected through certain general conditions of mutual convertibility which 'lead into' the situated practices in which agents are involved. As discussed previously, gender cannot be seen as simply a number of characteristics possessed by individuals, but rather has to be understood as structured via rules and resources specifying connotations of sexual difference. Gender divisions represent differential 'convertible currency' in labour markets, since the institutionalized practices which prevail in the economic domain mostly favour men rather than women. Labour market characteristics articulate with the domain of family life, which in turn helps restructure gender. Insofar as these connections span the wider societal system, they provide for similarities of behaviour and experience which in some part transcend regional and class differences. Structural sets are implicated in what in *The Constitution of Society* I called circuits of reproduction: feedback systems by means of which structural sets and structural principles are grounded and regrounded in institutionalized practices 'stretching' across time–space regions. Studying concretely just how the interconnections between marriage relationships: gender: labour markets: marriage relationships are 'played out' means seeking to identify how these 'conversions' between institutional areas are reproduced in actual conduct.

Conditions of change are built into reproduction circuits, especially in the context of modern societies, in which they are in some part reflexively organized. Suppose we wish to investigate why there are increasing levels of separation and divorce in the communities in the research study. How might we analyse this? Many factors can of course influence processes of social change. But in empirical work, as in theoretical reflection, it is crucial to try to identify how unintended consequences interlace with the forms of knowledge which, both on practical and discursive levels, actors bring to bear upon the contexts of their behaviour. In the research with which we are concerned, this task could be approached on various levels. Like so many other areas in modern societies, the institutional milieux of marriage and divorce have become highly mobilized reflexively – via, for example, the regular revision of divorce laws and other legal provisions, which are understood by everyone to have to 'correspond' in a general way to alterations in conditions of social life. These alterations are monitored sociologically, this knowledge filtering down to the day-to-day modes of behaviour which people follow in marriage and other aspects of their personal lives. What results are shifting forms of awareness involved in the practices that actually express marriage relationships, and in the objectives which individuals seek to realize in or through those relationships. Difficult as such a task may be, it would be incumbent upon the research to capture these interconnections empirically.

Let me generalize from these observations. What would a structurationist programme of research for modern social science look like? First, it would concentrate upon the orderings of institutions across time and space, rather than taking as its object the study of 'human societies'. The term 'society' may well be so engrained in sociological discourse as to be ineradicable, and I do not feel it necessary to avoid using it. However, where we speak of 'a' society, we have to be fully aware that this is not a 'pure social form', but a politically and territorially constituted system. It is one mode of 'bracketing' time and space among others, that bracketing process itself being the primary object of study in social science.

Second, a structurationist programme would analyse social systems in terms of shifting modes of institutional articulation. Every social system, no matter how small or ephemeral, or large scale and more permanent, gains its systemic qualities only through regularities of social reproduction. The ways in which such regularities – which consist of social practices – are organized in and through the behaviour of contextually located actors have to be subjected to empirical investigation. Modes of institutional articulation – across time and space – are the 'building-blocks' of time–space distanciation.

Third, such a programme would be continuously sensitive to the reflexive intrusions of knowledge into the conditions of social reproduction. This has nothing intrinsically to do with contrasts between the small scale and large scale, or between 'micro' and 'macro' analysis. We can see this from the fact that world-wide connections are today reflexively monitored – as, for example, in the case of investment decisions taken by the leaders of the giant corporations.

Fourth, a structurationist programme would be oriented to the impact of its own research upon the social practices and forms of social organization it analyses. This is an aspect of reflexivity which involved us in the various levels of critique noted earlier. The problems it raises are formidably complex, but are quite central to the 'self-understanding' of the social sciences in the current era.

To my mind, however, the empirical implications of structuration theory have to be pursued primarily through the introduction of considerations – concerned with particular types of social system and their transformation –

which are not part of the theory itself. These are bound up with the themes I set out at the beginning, and this is an appropriate point at which to close the circle in ending my commentary upon the contributions to this book. The chief focus of contemporary social science – although it is a very broad one – has to be upon analysing the shattering impact of modernity, against the backdrop of the limited usefulness of the traditions of thought which we have inherited in the social sciences. Such study demands serious theoretical reappraisals, combined with the pursuance of a diversity of empirical inquiries. Do we now live in a world which has lurched away from earlier trends of social and cultural development expressed in modernity? Or do we now live in a period shaped by the radicalizing of modernity: the first time at which modernity has become globalized (which is my view)? How should we best examine the increasing intrusion of distant events into the intimacies of personal life? What are the social textures emerging from altered modes of the co-ordination of time and space, as this affects overlapping types of social system? How should we conceive of, and further elaborate, the critique of ideology and moral critique in the face of the massive transformations of our time? Momentous questions, certainly, but I cannot see how anyone working in the social sciences today – whether engaged in carrying out empirical research 'on the ground', or pursuing more theoretical reflection – can avoid them.

Select bibliography

The following bibliography is a selection of Giddens's writings and of the secondary literature. We make no attempt to provide a comprehensive list. The only articles which appear in section 1 are those which have not been included in Giddens's collections of essays.

1 Works by Giddens

1964
'Notes on the Concept of Play and Leisure', in *The Sociological Review*, 12, 73–89
1966
'A Typology of Suicide', in *Archives européennes de sociologie*, 7, 276–95
1970
'Durkheim as a Review Critic', in *The Sociological Review*, 18, 171–96
'Recent Works on the History of Social Thought', in *Archives européennes de sociologie*, 11, 130–42
'Recent Works on the Position and Prospects of Contemporary Sociology', in *Archives européennes de sociologie*, 11, 143–54
1971
Capitalism and Modern Social Theory: An Analysis of the Writings of Marx, Durkheim and Max Weber (Cambridge: Cambridge University Press)
(ed.), *The Sociology of Suicide: A Selection of Readings* (London: Cass)
1972
Politics and Sociology in the Thought of Max Weber (London: Macmillan)
(ed.) *Emile Durkheim: Selected Writings* (Cambridge: Cambridge University Press)
1972
The Class Structure of the Advanced Societies (London: Hutchinson; New York: Harper & Row)
1974
(ed.), *Positivism and Sociology* (London: Heinemann)
(ed. with P. Stanworth), *Elites and Power in British Society* (Cambridge: Cambridge University Press)
1975
(with P. Stanworth), 'The Modern Corporate Economy: Interlocking Directorships in Britain 1960–1970', in *The Sociological Review*, 23, 5–28
1976
New Rules of Sociological Method: A Positive Critique of Interpretative Sociologies (London: Hutchinson; New York: Basic Books)
Excerpts from 1975 Address to the American Sociological Association in San Francisco, in *Phenomenological Sociology Newsletter*, no. 4, 5–8
1977
Studies in Social and Political Theory (London: Hutchinson; New York: Basic Books)
1978
Durkheim (Glasgow: Fontana)
'Elites and Privilege', in P. Abrams (ed.), *U.K. Society* (London: Weidenfeld & Nicolson)

1979
Central Problems in Social Theory: Action, Structure and Contradiction in Social Analysis
     (London: Macmillan; Berkeley: University of California Press)
'An Anatomy of the British Ruling Class', in *New Society*, 50, 8–10
1981
A Contemporary Critique of Historical Materialism, vol. 1, *Power, Property and the State*
     (London: Macmillan; Berkeley: University of California Press)
The Class Structure of the Advanced Societies, 2nd edn (London: Hutchinson; New York:
     Harper & Row)
'Agency, Institution and Time–Space Analysis', in K. Knorr-Cetina and A. Cicourel
     (eds.), *Advances in Social Theory and Methodology: Toward an Integration of Micro- and
     Macro-Sociologies* (London: Routledge), pp. 161–74
'Modernism and Postmodernism', in *New German Critique*, no. 22, 15–18
1982
Sociology: A Brief but Critical Introduction (London: Macmillan; Berkeley: University of
     California Press)
'On the Relation of Sociology and Philosophy', in P. Secord (ed.), *Explaining Human
     Behavior: Consciousness, Human Action and Social Structure* (London: Sage), pp. 175–89
'Mediator of Meaning', in *Times Literary Supplement*, no. 4118, 240
Profiles and Critiques in Social Theory (London: Macmillan; Berkeley: University of
     California Press)
'Historial Materialism Today: An Interview with A. Giddens', in *Theory, Culture and
     Society*, vol. 1, no. 2, 63–77
'A Reply to my Critics', in *Theory, Culture and Society*, vol. 1, no. 2, 107–13
'Commentary on the Debate', in *Theory and Society*, 1, 527–39
(ed. with D. Held), *Classes, Power and Conflict: Classical and Contemporary Debates*
     (London: Macmillan; Berkeley: University of California Press)
(ed. with G. Mackenzie), *Social Class and the Division of Labour: Essays in Honour of Ilja
     Neustadt* (Cambridge: Cambridge University Press)
1983
'Comments on the Theory of Structuration', in *Journal of the Theory of Social Behaviour*, 13,
     75–80
1984
The Constitution of Society: Outline of the Theory of Structuration (Cambridge: Polity Press;
     Berkeley: University of California Press)
1985
The Nation-State and Violence, vol. 2 of *A Contemporary Critique of Historical Materialism*
     (Cambridge: Polity Press; Berkeley: University of California Press)
'Marx's Correct Views on Everything (With Apologies to L. Kolowkowski)', in *Theory
     and Society*, 14, 167–74
Review essay: 'Liberalism and Sociology', in *Contemporary Sociology*, 14, 320–2
'Jürgen Habermas', in: Q. Skinner (ed.), *The Return of Grand Theory in the Human Sciences*
     (Cambridge: Cambridge University Press), pp. 121–39
Introduction to M. Weber, *The Protestant Ethic and the Spirit of Capitalism* (London: Allen
     & Unwin)
'Time, Space and Regionalization', in D. Gregory and J. Urry (eds.), *Social Relations and
     Spatial Structures* (London: Macmillan), pp. 265–95
1987
Social Theory and Modern Sociology (Cambridge: Polity Press; Stanford: Stanford Uni-
     versity Press)
(ed. with J. Turner), *Social Theory Today* (Cambridge: Polity Press)
1989
Sociology (Cambridge: Polity Press)
The Consequences of Modernity (Cambridge: Polity Press; Stanford University Press)

2 Works on Giddens

Archer, M. 'Morphogenesis versus Structuration: On Combining Structure and Action', *British Journal of Sociology*, 33 (1982), 455–83

Ashley, D. 'Historical Materialism and Social Evolution', *Theory, Culture and Society*, 1 (1982), 89–92

Badham, R. 'The Sociology of Industrial and Post-Industrial Societies', *Current Sociology*, 32 (1984), 1–14

Berger, J. 'Handlung und Struktur in der soziologischen Theorie', *Das Argument*, Jg. 19 (1977), 56–66

  Review of Giddens, *A Contemporary Critique of Historical Materialism* vol. 1 (1981), in *Kölner Zeitsschrift für Soziologie und Sozialpsychologie*, Jg. 36 (1984), 175–7

Bertilsson, M. 'The Theory of Structuration: Prospects and Problems', *Acta Sociologica*, Jg. 27 (1984), 339–53

Betts, K. 'The Conditions of Action, Power and the Problem of Interests', *Sociological Review*, 34 (1986), 39–64

Callinicos, A. 'Anthony Giddens: A Contemporary Critique', *Theory and Society*, (1985), 133–66

Carlstein, T. 'The Sociology of Structuration in Time and Space: A Time–Geographic Assessment of Giddens's Theory', *Swedish Geographical Yearbook* (1981), 41–57

Cohen, I. 'Breaking New Ground in the Analysis of Capitalism', *Contemporary Sociology*, 12 (1983), 363–5

  'The Status of Structuration Theory: A Reply to McLennan', *Theory, Culture and Society*, 3 (1986), 123–34

  'Structuration Theory and Social *Praxis*' in A. Giddens and J. Turner (eds.), *Social Theory Today* (Cambridge: Polity Press, 1987), pp. 273–308

  Structuration Theory (London: Macmillan, 1989)

Collins, R. 'Society as Time-Traveller', *Contemporary Sociology*, 12 (1983), 365–7

Dallmayr. W. 'The Theory of Structuration: A Critique', in A. Giddens, *Profiles and Critiques in Social Theory* (London: Macmillan), pp. 18–25

Eraly, A. 'L'Action et la structure chez Anthony Giddens', *Revue de l'Institut de Sociologie*, Université de Bruxelles (jg. 1984), 299–308

Gane, M. 'Anthony Giddens and the Crisis of Social Theory', *Economy and Society*, 11 (1983), 368–98

Gregory, D. 'Space, Time and Politics in Social Theory: An Interview with Anthony Giddens', *Society and Space*, 2 (1984), 123–32

Gross, D. 'Time–Space Relations in Giddens' Social Theory', *Theory, Culture and Society*, 1 (1982), 83–8

Held, D. Review article on Giddens, *A Contemporary Critique of Historical Materialism*, vol. 1 (1981), *Theory, Culture and Society*, 1 (1982), 98–102

Hirst, P. 'The Social Theory of Anthony Giddens: A New Syncretism?' *Theory, Culture and Society*, 1 (1982), 78–82

Holmwood, J. M. and Stewart, A. 'The Role of Contradictions in Modern Theories of Social Stratification', *Sociology* 17 (1983), 234–54

Horne, J. Review article on Giddens, *Profiles and Critiques in Social Theory* (1982) *Sociological Review*, 31 (1983), 769–72

Joas, H. 'Giddens' Theorie der Strukturbildung: Einführende Bemerkungen zu einer soziologischen Transformation der Praxisphilosophie', *Zeitschrift für Soziologie*, Jg. 15 (1986), 237–45

Kiessling, B. *Kritik der Giddenschen Sozialtheorie* (Frankfurt: Lang, 1988)

  Die 'Theorie der Strukturierung', *Zeitschrift für Soziologie*, Jg. 17 (1988), 286–95

Layder, D. *Structure, Interaction and Social Theory* (London: Routledge, 1981)

'Power, Structure and Agency', *Journal for the Theory of Social Behavior*, 15 (1985), 131–49

McLennan, G. 'Critical or Positive Theory? A Comment on the Status of Anthony Giddens' Social Theory', *Theory, Culture and Society*, 2 (1984), 123–9

Munters, Q. J. et al. 'Anthony Giddens: Een Kennismaking met de Structuratiethorie' (Wageningen: Landbouwhogeschool)

Parkin, F. 'Reply to Giddens', *Theory and Society*, 9 (1980), 891–4

Pred. A. 'Power, Everyday Practice and the Discipline of Human Geography', *Space and Time in Geography: Essays Dedicated to T. Hägerstrand* (Lund), pp. 31–55

'Structuration and Place: On the Becoming of Sense of Place and Structure of Feeling', *Journal for the Theory of Social Behavior*, 13 (1983), 45–68

Reichert, D. 'Möglichkeiten und Aufgarben einer kritischen Sozialwissenchaft: Ein Interview mit Anthony Giddens', *Geographica Helvetica*, no. 3 (1988), 141–7

Shotter, J. '"Duality of Structure" and "Intentionality" in an Ecological Psychology', *Journal for the Theory of Social Behavior*, 13 (1983), 19–43

Sica, A. 'Locating the 17th Book of Giddens', *Contemporary Sociology*, 15 (1986), 344–6

Smith, C. W. 'A Case Study of Structuration: The Pure-Bred Beef Business', *Journal for the Theory of Social Behavior*, 13 (1983), 3–18

(ed.). 'Special Topic Paper: The Duality of Social Structure, Structuration, and the Intentionality of Human Action', *Journal for the Theory of Social Behavior*, vol. 13, no. 1 (1983)

Smith, D. '"Put not your Trust in Princes" – A Commentary upon Anthony Giddens and the Absolute State', *Theory, Culture and Society*, 1 (1982), 93–9

Smith, J. W. and Turner, B. S. 'Constructing Social Theory and Constituting Society', *Theory, Culture and Society*, 3 (1986), 125–33

Spaargaren, G. Poel, H. v. d. and Munters, Q. J. 'Het Oeuvre van Anthony Giddens: Centrale Thema's en Hoofdlijnen', *Sociologische Gids*, Jg. 33 (1986), 302–30

Thompson, J. B. 'Rethinking History: For and Against Marx', *Philosophy of the Social Sciences*, 14 (1984), 543–51

Thrift, N. 'On the Determination of Social Action in Space and Time', *Society and Space*, 1 (1983), 23–57

Turner, J. H 'The Theory of Structuration', *American Journal of Sociology*, 91 (1986), 969–77

Urry, J. Review of Giddens, *New Rules of Sociological Method* (1976), *The Sociological Review*, 25 (1977), 911–15

'Duality of Structure: Some Critical Issues', *Theory, Culture and Society*, 1 (1982), 100–6

Willmott, H. C. 'Unconscious Sources of Motivation in the Theory of the Subject: An Exploration and Critique of Giddens' Dualistic Models of Action and Personality', *Journal for the Theory of Social Behavior*, 16 (1986), 105–21

Wright, E. O. 'Giddens's Critique of Marxism', *New Left Review*, no. 138 (1983), 11–35

Review essay: 'Is Marxism Really Functionalist, Class Reductionist, and Teleological?', *American Journal of Sociology*, 89 (1983), 452–9

Index

Abrams, P., 186
absence, presence and, 7, 62, 185–214, 276
absolutism, 109–10, 137
abstraction, levels of, 66–71 Figure 3, 237, 243–6, 295
abstractions, contentless, 133, 231–2
action: non-randomness of, 37–45, 48–50; range of options in, 73–5, 258–9; *see also* unintended consequences; stratification model of, 59, figure 1, 71–4, 240, 245; structure and constraint, 3–4, 71–6, 106; web model (Hägerstrand), 193–6
action theory, 39–40, 239
Adorno, T. W., 291
Albert, Michael, 99n
Althusser, Louis, 3, 56, 79, 86, 104, 242
Anderson, B., 131, 201
Anglo-American philosophy, 19, 23, 26
anomie, 222, 225
anthroponomy, and the production of people, 154–5
anti-urbanism, and spatial fetishism, 223–32
Arendt, H., 16
Austin, J. L., 7, 63
authoritarianism, 266
autonomy, citizenship and, 162–84, 267–70, 272–5

Bauman, Zygmunt, 4, 5–7, 34–55; G.'s response to, 7, 253–9
Bell, David, 167n
Bendix, Richard, 167n
Benveniste, E., 7
Bernstein, Basil, 257
Bernstein, Richard, 4, 5, 19–33; G.'s response to 5, 288–93, 297
Bertaux, Daniel, 154–5, 283
biology, evolutionary, 92–3, 94, 263
Borges, J. L., 35
Bourdieu, P., 60n, 74n, 200, 201
Bourdon, R., 241, 242
Bringing the State Back In (Evans et al.), 131
Britain, 130, 164, 217–18, 269
Bromley, Simon, 103n, 115n

Callinicos, A., 211, 213
Cameron, Gordon, 227n
capitalism, 11, 83, 85, 90, 136–7, 224, 251, 252; commodification in, 67, 260, 264; 'disorganized', 201–2, 212; distinctive features of modern, 264–5; historical geography of, 186–7; labour contract, 177–8; legitimation crisis, 197, 201–3; and

the modern state, 272–5; nation-states and surveillance, 103–28, 259–67; organization of, 104–6, 182; pacific or militaristic, 139; private, 145–6; uneven development, 198, 202
Capitalism and Modern Social Theory (Giddens), 11
capitalist states, 13, 121–5, 180–2, 274
Carneades, 37
Castells, M., 8, 200, 203, 204, 213, 228, 229, 276
Central Problems in Social Theory (Giddens), 3, 61–2, 149, 186, 217, 242
change, social, 14, 91–4, 100, 201–4, 251
child psychology, 156, 157
childbirth, management of, 158
Chodorow, Nancy, 284
Cicourel, A. V., 296
citizenship: and autonomy, 162–84, 267–70, 272–5; class and, 163–6; and gender issues, 287; roots of modern, 170–2; states and war, 267–72
citizenship rights, 16–17, 122n, 123, 124, 172–6, 178–80, 233n, 268–70; Marshall versus Giddens, 166–70; war and, 139, 270
city: eradication as social form, 221, 228–9, 281; as power-container, 220, 225
civil rights, 163–4, 164–5, 168, 171
class: and citizenship rights, 16–17, 122n, 163–6, 171–2; definition of concept, 86–7, 99; primacy of, 12, 89–90, 102, 122, 264–5; and the production of people, 159–61
class differentiation, and spatial separation, 217
class societies: and class-divided societies, 67, 83, 86, 135, 220, 264; and created environment, 221–3
Class Structure of the Advanced Societies, The (Giddens), 11, 67–8, 133, 152, 215
class struggle, 14, 141
Clausewitz, Karl von, 15, 132, 142–4, 270
Cohen, G. A., *Karl Marx's Theory of History: A Defence*, 79n, 80, 87, 94, 260–1
commodification, 67, 104n, 148, 205, 212, 260, 264; of knowledge, 199; of labour, 104n, 201; of land, 201, 222; of time and space, 191–2, 210–11, 221, 264
communism, 14, 111, 141
Comte, Auguste, 1
Connell, R. W., 285
consciousness: discursive, 25–6, 59, 198, 239; practical, 25–6, 59, 239
consensus, 5, 35, 172, 292